This compelling book argues that American patriotism is a civil religion of blood sacrifice, which periodically kills its children to keep the group together. The flag is the sacred object of this religion; its sacrificial imperative is a secret which the group keeps from itself to survive. Expanding Durkheim's theory of the totem taboo as the organizing principle of enduring groups, Carolyn Marvin and David Ingle uncover the system of sacrifice and regeneration which constitutes American nationalism, show why historical instances of these rituals succeed or fail in unifying the nation, and explain how mass media are essential to the process. American culture is depicted as ritually structured by a fertile center and sacrificial borders of death. Violence plays a key part in its identity. In essence, nationalism is neither quaint historical residue nor atavistic extremism, but a living tradition which defines American life.

CAROLYN MARVIN is an Associate Professor of Communication at the Annenberg School for Communication, University of Pennsylvania. A winner of the Franklyn Haiman Award for Outstanding Scholarship in Freedom of Expression, her previous publications include *When Old Technologies Were New* (Oxford, 1988).

DAVID W. INGLE has served in the US Army in special operations and in the US Navy as an antisubmarine warfare specialist. He is now a doctoral student in clinical psychology at Widener University, Pennsylvania.

Blood sacrifice and the nation

Cambridge Cultural Social Studies

Series editors: JEFFREY C. ALEXANDER, *Department of Sociology, University of California, Los Angeles, and* STEVEN SEIDMAN, *Department of Sociology, University at Albany, State University of New York.*

Blood sacrifice and the nation

Totem rituals and the American flag

Carolyn Marvin
The Annenberg School for Communication, University of Pennsylvania

AND
David W. Ingle

CAMBRIDGE
UNIVERSITY PRESS

PUBLISHED BY THE PRESS SYNDICATE OF THE UNIVERSITY OF CAMBRIDGE
The Pitt Building, Trumpington Street, Cambridge CB2 1RP, United Kingdom

CAMBRIDGE UNIVERSITY PRESS
The Edinburgh Building, Cambridge CB2 2RU, United Kingdom
40 West 20th Street, New York, NY 10011–4211, USA
10 Stamford Road, Oakleigh, Melbourne 3166, Australia

© Carolyn Marvin 1999

First published 1999

Printed in the United Kingdom at the University Press, Cambridge

Typeset in Times 10/12.5 pt   [SE]

A catalogue record for this book is available from the British Library

Library of Congress Cataloguing in Publication data

Marvin, Carolyn.
    Blood sacrifice and the nation : Totem rituals and the American
flag / Carolyn Marvin and David W. Ingle.
        p.   cm.
    Includes bibliographical references and index.
    ISBN 0 521 62345 6 (hbk) – ISBN 0 521 62609 9 (pbk)
    1. Flags – Social aspects – United States.   2. Political culture –
United States.   3. Nationalism – United States.   4. Totemism – United
States.   5. Sacrifice – United States.   I. Ingle, David W.
    II. Title.
    JC346.M27   1998
    306.2′0973–dc21   97–25640 CIP

ISBN 0 521 62345 6 hardback
ISBN 0 521 62609 9 paperback

Contents

Illustrations

List of graphs

Acknowledgments

The anthropologist Evans-Pritchard observed strikingly different levels of religious belief among members of the Azande tribe. In so doing he challenged our modern predisposition to think of so-called primitives as religiously uniform. Writing this book has provided David W. Ingle and myself with not so dissimilar encounters with members of our own American tribe, among whom there are also strikingly different levels of belief in the religious power of nationalism. In general, we had only to announce the subject of this book to elicit suspicions that we were either unabashed patriots, fundamentalist believers in what Harold Bloom has called our unacknowledged civil religion, or flag-destroying iconoclasts. That we were in the presence of religious taboo was often signaled by awkward silences and jokes as both non-believers and the faithful tried to figure our take on that delicate topic, the deep, unspeakable meaning of the American flag.

Very special thanks are due to Kathleen Hall Jamieson, Dean of the Annenberg School for Communication, who provided both a critical leave semester and the financial support to secure many of the illustrations found in this book. In countless personal and professional ways, her support has made this a far better project. Indeed it was a suggestion of hers that first made me think in terms of analyzing our understanding of the flag. To Jeff Alexander and Elihu Katz who generously believed in the project in different ways, I owe a profound debt of gratitude. Also to Martin Marty and especially James W. Carey, both of whom encouraged me in ways that made a real difference and offered helpful critiques at a strategic point. Larry Gross, Sam and Sandy Sugarman, Conrad and Jean Marvin, Jeff Marvin, Janet Marvin, John Massi, Joshua Meyrowitz, Pamela Sankar, Stewart Hoover, Phebe Shinn, Debra Williams, Deborah Porter, Janice Fisher, Scot Guenter, Nadine Strossen, Raymond S. Rodgers, Sarah P. Ingle, Joe Turow, Susan Williamson, Charles Wright, the Marine officers and recruits we met during a wonderfully interesting stay at Parris Island, South Carolina, George Cahill of the National Flag Foundation and Whitney Smith, director of the Flag Resource Center, all contributed to this project in a variety of different ways. Flag entrepreneurs Randy Beard, Bill Spangler, Brian O'Connor, Joe Rojee, and Jay Critchley made time for much appreciated interviews. Cambridge editor Catherine Max was endlessly gracious and helpful. I am profoundly grateful for her support, and for that of Jenny Oates, the most generous and capable of copy editors. With fellow flagburners Jeffrey Gerson, Steve Smith, and Dred Scott Tyler, I share a special bond. Long may they wave. I fondly thank all my students who joined in the excitement of this project, who made discussions of nationalism both immensely challenging and fun, and who kept looking at me when I first tried to talk about it with a tolerant indulgence that suggested I was out of my mind but it was an interesting pathology.

David Perlmutter, Nancy Morris, Chris Smith, Oren Meyers, Brigette Rouson, Brittin Skelton, Chris Smith, Rona Buchalter, Jessica Fishman, and Michele Strano offered much appreciated assistance during the course of these intellectual wanderings. I especially thank Ramona Lyons, Marc Ostfield, Bonnie Datt, Dave Park, Peter Ginsberg and Heather Steingraber, each of whom contributed in very special ways. Chris Koepke offered useful statistical consultation. Tim Blake constructed an elegant computer coding program that enabled us to record endless flag images for evaluation, and David Graper and his staff provided excellent computer support. Special, special thanks to Andrea Wagner, who labored long and hard over the index, and to Amy Sarch, Barbie Zelizer, Laura Grindstaff, and Sharon Black for assistance above and beyond the call of duty.

Without the major intellectual contribution to this project by David Ingle, its shape and content simply would have been different – less rich, and less complete. In long and intense conversations over the course of the entire study that made this project part of a shared bond, it is fair to say we have hashed out all the ideas developed here between us. Dave's assistance with the analysis of sports, war, the military, and not only these, has been significant and original. Both of us worked on the coding categories for the appendix which offers an operational manifestation of the totem myth, but he designed the system that permitted us to code and analyze thirty-six years of images in *Life* magazine, and did all the original coding. That coding played a crucial role in helping think out additional crucial aspects of the totem theory employed in the analysis.

This is our project. We have watched the flag wave and the totem system operate since 1989, when this project began with a classroom exercise. From the standpoint of flag study, we were lucky that during the period of the formulation and writing of these ideas, the United States engaged in several calendrical rites of renewal and one crisis of the gods. That is, the country waged war, participated in the Olympics, and conducted two presidential campaigns unusually full of totemic doubt, all major occasions of patriotic practice for our observation.

Carolyn Marvin
Philadephia, Pennsylvania

1

Introduction

> The power of religion depends, in the last resort, upon the credibility of the banners it puts in the hands of men as they stand before death, or more accurately, as they walk, inevitably, toward it.   Peter Berger[1]

What binds the nation together? How vulnerable to ethnic and religious antagonisms is our sense of nationhood? What is the source of the malaise we have felt for so much of the post-World War II period? Above all, what moves citizens to put group interests ahead of their own, even to surrendering their lives? No strictly economic explanation, no great-man theory of history, no imminent group threat fully accounts for why members of enduring groups such as nations consent to sacrifice their immediate well-being and that of their children to the group. Whatever does, tells us a great deal about what makes nation-states enduring and viable. This book argues that violent blood sacrifice makes enduring groups cohere, even though such a claim challenges our most deeply held notions of civilized behavior.

The sacrificial system that binds American citizens has a sacred flag at its center. Patriotic rituals revere it as the embodiment of a bloodthirsty totem god who organizes killing energy. This totem god is the foundation of a mythic, religiously constructed American identity. Our notion of the totem comes from Durkheim, for whom it was the emblem of the group's agreement to be a group. Durkheim was less clear about how this agreement is forged. Though he regarded totemism as a form of social organization suited to traditional societies, he hinted broadly about its traces in post-traditional ones. We intend to show totem dynamics vigorously at work in the contemporary United States. We lay out the practices and beliefs that furnish the system without which the nation is in danger of dissolution. Their focus is the magical and primitive use of the flag, the totem object of American civil religion.

If there were any doubt about the importance of the flag in American life, the deeply emotional debate about whether flagburning should be legal is a useful reminder.[2] Such controversy constitutes a kind of renewable resource for the imaginative life of the nation. Disagreement about what the flag means among those for whom it is the supreme symbol of political legitimacy is part and parcel of jostling for place among groups in a pluralistic society. More important than the fact that the flag is an object of struggle and veneration is what makes it worth struggling over, and how it enacts transformation and authority. That process is the subject of this book.

How does the flag operate in American life? Religiously, in a word. → Durkheim's model is foundational but incomplete, for it fails to explain how the totem binds collective sentiment. In American civil religion, the flag is the ritual instrument of group cohesion. It transforms the bodies of insiders and outsiders who meet at a border of violence. This is the kernel of the totem myth, endlessly re-enacted in patriotic life and ritual, and always most powerfully in the presence of the flag. Though the structure of totem myth is as familiar to Americans as anything can be, it remains largely unacknowledged. Though it governs our political culture, we do not recognize it. When it threatens to surface, it is vigorously denied. What it conceals is that blood sacrifice preserves the nation. Nor is the sacrifice that counts that of our enemy. The totem secret, the collective group taboo, is the knowledge that society depends on the death of its own members *at the hands of the group*.

The totem myth is concealed by the conviction that individualism is the defining myth of America, a way of thinking that seems far removed from any group idea. Individualism is better understood as a highly visible piece of the more encompassing myth it disguises. Laid bare, it is an episode of the totem narrative that tells how a sacrificial hero is selected to die for the group. Not only individualism conceals the totem myth. So does our inability to recognize the religiosity of our political culture. Observers from Joseph Campbell to René Girard see little spirituality in Western life. Campbell has gone so far as to say that contemporary culture has no myth, though he more often claims that our myths are simply debased. From this perspective, violence and disorder are thought to characterize societies without good integrating myths.

For Anthony Giddens, George Mosse, or Ernst Cassirer, on the other hand, myths emerge primarily at moments of great disorder. Whether myths are the cause or consequence of social order and disorder, good myths are often regarded as a property of virtuous nations, and immoral nations are thought to have bad myths. In fact, myth is a constitutive element of every enduring group's self-representation. Assigning virtue or vice depends more on the observer's position than on any feature of the myth itself. Mythic American nationalism has been used at different moments for purposes of vastly different moral weight and consequence. We explore how American national identity is created and maintained, not whether it is good to do it or whether we should do it differently.

Nationalism and sectarianism are alternative systems for organizing enduring groups. Both are religions of blood sacrifice. The resemblances between them have been ignored by theorists of sectarianism unwilling to see in it the worldly violence that energizes nationalism, and by theorists of nationalism who see sectarian violence as a threat to stable states. In the wake of events following the collapse of the Soviet Union, it has become more difficult to deny the religious character of nationalism and its essential connection to violence. Nevertheless, Western commentators continue to assert that nationalisms seething in Russia, Central Europe, and Asia reflect ancient *ethnic* hatreds, a contemporary term with primitive overtones. In fact, deadly, sacrifice-based challenge to totem authority is a feature of our own society as much as any society now in turmoil. The difference is that our totem rituals have so far mostly worked to keep internal and external totem challengers under control. We examine why.

The claim that Americans are devotees of a powerful civil religion is deeply suspect. Americans generally see their nation as a secular culture possessed of few myths, or with weak myths everywhere, but none central and organizing. We see American nationalism as a ritual system organized around a core myth of violently sacrificed divinity manifest in the highest patriotic ceremony and the most accessible popular culture. Though it uses a Christian vocabulary, its themes are common to many belief systems. Our failure to acknowledge the religiosity of this system obeys the ancient command never to speak the true name of God. It is said that so-called primitive societies fail to recognize distinctions between their religion and their culture. This is the first of many resemblances between ourselves and cultures we consider to be different from us by virtue of a special condition of savagery or villainy or both. A feature of our modernity is projecting on other cultures impulses we believe we do not possess and deeds for which we claim no capacity. By remaining displaced observers of our most important acts, we define ourselves as a nation.

Following Weber, analysts traditionally define the nation-state as the legitimized exercise of force over territorial boundaries within which a population has been pacified. The nation-state protects the nation, more vaguely defined as the commonality of sentiment shared by members of a language group, ethnicity, or living space. All observers acknowledge the imprecision of such a definition. Nor does it explain why these properties constitute a "nation." We say the nation is the shared memory of blood sacrifice, periodically renewed. Those who share such memories often, but not always, share language, living space, or ethnicity. What they always share and cultivate is the memory of blood sacrifice. In totem myth, the felt or sentimental nation is the memory of the last sacrifice that counts for living believers. Though the sovereign nation, or nation-state, is an agreement about killing rules that compels citizens to sacrifice themselves for the group, the felt nation makes them want to. Neither the nation or the nation-state can exist without such memory myths, or not for long. Their maintenance is an ongoing sacred labor shared by rulers and those who grant them authority.

How does violence cause the group to cohere?

[handwritten margin note: constructing the social from the body]

Blood sacrifice is a primitive notion. We define as primitive those processes that construct the social from the body. Since every society constructs itself from the bodies of its members, every society is primitive. The term nevertheless has a pejorative meaning from which so-called civilized societies strive to distance themselves. What is the distinction between our society and those that seem different enough to be labeled primitive? The crucial comparison may be the relative prevalence of practices in which the body is immediately present and its relation to social action directly observed, and those of disembodied, or textual practices in which the body is not only removed, but denied by active effacement. Relative to the textualized, body-denying social organization of industrialized nation-states, small-scale, face-to-face societies are less textual and more bodily in their social organization.

[handwritten margin note: modern textualized nation-states; propriety associated with body invisibility]

Textually organized societies can never eliminate the body from the social order despite their efforts to move it beyond the range of awareness. Propriety in textualized societies is associated with bodily invisibility. The more textually organized a society, the greater its failure to recognize its own ritual capacity, the more secular its self-perception, and the shriller its deprecation of its own religious elements. Nevertheless, *bodily* sacrifice is the totem core of American nationalism, as it may be of all religion. At the behest of the group, the lifeblood of community members must be shed. Group solidarity, or sentiment, flows from the value of this sacrifice. The totem god of society, which turns out to be society itself, cannot do without its worshippers any more than its worshippers can do without the god of society. It must possess and consume, it must *eat* its worshippers to live. This is the totem secret and its greatest taboo.

Tribal members are forbidden to kill one another in the presence of the totem. There is an important exception to this rule. Public discourse treats it as a last resort, something the community dreads doing. In fact, it is no exception, but the sacrificial heart of the totem system. The creation of sentiments strong enough to hold the group together periodically requires the willing deaths of a significant portion of its members. The lifeblood of these members is shed by means of a ritual in which designated victims become outsiders and cross the boundary of the living group into death. The most powerful enactment of this ritual is war. This totem sacrifice is the hidden foundation of the system that leads us to define the nation as the memory of the last sacrifice.

How do we know?

A hologram contains the information to reproduce a whole image in every one of its pieces. Flag practice and nationalism are like that, each piece a holographic element of a group myth. To start from any point quickly leads to the entire structure. American culture is holographically saturated with the flag. It is a pervasive presence in mass media, in advertising, in manufactured and home-made artifacts of every description, on the street, and in the institutions of daily life. Since flag practice and imagery are everywhere, the difficulty is not sampling it, but constructing the complete myth to which every instance of patriotic practice is a contribution. The whole history of the nation offers evidence. The most persuasive comes from living memory, which demonstrates the power of the totem in our own present rather than some ideal or benighted American past. The cult of the flag is no quaint historical residue, but a living source of American myth.

Totem myth suits the military conscript systems of industrialized nations that sacrifice large numbers of citizens in wars of attrition. For any leadership to survive such a brutal strategy, soldiers and their families must be committed to the cause. The rise of the religiously regarded flag coincides with the introduction of this ritual of mass sacrifice in the United States. The triumph of nationalism achieved by the bloodletting of the Civil War helped restructure the American economy from a local to a national base. It also helped assimilate waves of immigrants in the late nineteenth century. In a reorganized continental community struggling to forge a national identity, the bloody flag emerged as a talisman with transforming proper- *mass media* ties. Its sacralization required, and requires still, the enthusiastic assistance of mass media.

Though new modes of production and dissemination have shifted the reproductive scale of American media, media have never altered their basic religious function with respect to the flag. This is to re-present it in multiple arenas along with the totem system it governs. By furnishing the stock of images and metaphors that filter and remodel totem myths, media play a key role in structuring our sense of ourselves as a nation. They convey assent to patriotic symbols for a national audience. No American living a reasonably conventional life can avoid the flag, either in person or as a member of the audience for its endless media multiplications. Since rituals of blood sacrifice alone establish the flag's magical potency, media neither create nor dilute its sacred character. Their task is to re-present and disseminate what blood sacrifice creates. They keep totem symbols vibrant, effective, and ever present.

Domains of flag practice

Totem myth and ritual are played out in fields of activity we call *domains*. Each inhabits distinctive physical and social spaces, addresses characteristic groups and deploys unique communicative strategies. First is the *totem domain,* from which all others are derived and to which they ultimately refer. This is the ritual space occupied by the totem class. The President and members of the armed forces are its principal members. They live in communities segregated from the rest of society and organized around disciplinary ordeals. They are charged with the holy task of guarding the flag and offering the sacrifice that keeps it alive. Powerful prohibitions govern totem class members, who are ritually transformed by touching death.

The steadfast loyalty of citizens in the *popular* domain sustains and recreates the totem through fertility and connection rather than sacrifice and death. In this domain citizens not only touch the flag but remake it endlessly. In the strict sense they defile it, but dismembering and rearrangement in this context symbolically enact the revitalization of the community. The vernacular flag is not distanced from ordinary life. It acts as an immanent rather than transcendent divinity. It is a popular instrument of magical action, regenerating totem leaders in seasonal rituals of popular election. Popular flags also ritually separate warriors from society as they go into battle and re-attach them when they return.

Groups in the *affiliative* domain believe they represent the community as it ought to be. They envy the totem even when they oppose it. They practice exclusive membership, relations of passionate alliance or rebellion toward the totem, and shared ordeals. Varying in their embattledness with the totem, they include groups such as the Boy Scouts, the Ku Klux Klan, religious denominations, militia groups, Hell's Angels, and labor unions. Affiliative groups celebrate team sacrifice and deeds of valor. Cultivating quasi-totem pomp, they seek to bend the totem to their will. They are regularly disappointed by the administered state, which always falls short of their ideals. Denied the privileges of totem power, they doubt their status and must endlessly prove themselves. Affiliative struggle is fundamental to the totem system and the most dangerous threat to its unity.

Relations among the totem class, affiliative groups, and citizens who constitute the popular domain structure the nation. Each domain may join or mate with any other. The combination of any two domains implies the subordination of the third. The continuing quest of each domain to join another at the expense of the third is the engine that drives political life. To consolidate its legitimacy, the totem domain seeks to unite with the popular. Popular and totem groups have historically joined forces against Communist cells, the Ku Klux Klan, sectarian groups and street gangs, affiliative groups all. Affiliative groups compete with the totem for a popular following with which to mate. Affiliative and popular groups together may try to topple the totem. This was the dashed dream of the Confederate States of America in the Civil War. Affiliative groups may also ally with the totem against a popular insurgence or against other affiliative challengers. Even in their suspect state, affiliative groups are central to the totem system, for the achievement of totem legitimacy requires a consensual tilt in a shifting affiliative hierarchy whose cooperation is both necessary and unstable. We will examine these patterns in American political culture.

The choice of a subject as emotionally freighted as nationalism requires a discussion of our own relationship to it. Although we admire the richness and complexity of nationalism and the energies that fuel its transforming power, the moral evaluation of patriotic practice remains the responsibility of the citizens whose creation it is. Our task is not to to say what patriotism ought to be, but to understand nationalism as a system for generating feelings of profound sociability and belonging through the primitive construction of the social out of the flesh and blood of group members. The participants in that system are free to embrace, modify, or reject it, for nations and citizens always have options. Though we undertake to illustrate the pervasiveness of nationalism in American life, we regard even its most fervent devotees as persons possessed of whole lives with multiple interests. Still, we see the totem god hovering close by, ready to be called forth in group crises and in the periodic rituals that keep its memory alive. But totem gods are not indestructible. Nor is national unity a foregone conclusion. The nation could die, as many have. If it does, others will spring up. What is indestructible is a pattern of enduring group behavior rather than any particular expression of it. By showing how violence is an essential social resource, just as denying it constitutes an important group-making tool, we aim to illuminate the dynamics of patriotic nationalism.

Our analysis is not intended to take aim from the safety of the text at those who put their bodies on the line for the nation, or at any who subscribe to alternative faiths. We seek to understand nationalism in the United States, an important case that resembles others, since enduring groups model one another in mobilizing and disciplining group members for sacrifice. This means that the sacrificial system of nationalism can be challenged effectively only by those who embrace with still greater commitment alternative sacrificial systems to replace it. The location of killing force is a variable in this scheme. Structure is the constant element. The principles of group connectedness that underlie American nationalism thus have relevance for other countries and causes for which people willingly offer their lives. By giving meaning to violence, a chief energizing component of group life despite the most emphatic denials of its centrality, patriotic practice affects all who identify themselves as citizens of any nation. We dedicate this book, therefore, to sacrificial warriors, whose fate it is to be cast out from every border.

2

That old flag magic

Symbolism is a primitive but effective way of communicating ideas.
West Virginia State Board of Education v. Barnette (1943)[1]

This is a book about religion, specifically, the religion of American patriotism. Though nationalism does not qualify as religion in the familiar sense, it shares with sectarian religions the worship of killing authority, which we claim is central to religious practice and belief. Nationalism and sectarian religion share something else related to killing. Wherever religion has been fervently embraced, it follows in the minds of believers that it is entitled to glory in missions of conquest that reflect God's will. Jesus's disciples felt it; a Weberian Protestant ethic suggests it. Islam did this for centuries for its believers before European nation-states accomplished it for Christianity. In an era of Western ascendancy, the triumph of Christianity clearly meant the triumph of the states of Christianity, among them the most powerful of modern states, the United States. Though religions have survived and flourished in persecution and powerlessness, supplicants nevertheless take manifestations of power as blessed evidence of the truth of faith. Still, in the religiously plural society of the United States, sectarian faith is optional for citizens, as everyone knows. Americans have rarely bled, sacrificed or died for Christianity or any other sectarian faith. Americans have often bled, sacrificed and died for their country. This fact is an important clue to its religious power.

Though denominations are permitted to exist in the United States, they are not permitted to kill, for their beliefs are not officially true. What is really true in any society is what is worth killing for, and what citizens may be compelled to sacrifice their lives for. To understand what truth is for the United States as a nation, we must inquire into the national doctrine and practice of sacrifice and death. Questions about sacrifice and death are profoundly religious. It is their presence that makes nationalism the most powerful religion in American culture. For despite a sturdy American tradition of separating *sectarian* faith from the state, *national* faith is inextricably wedded to governance, which is ultimately the question of who shall live and die. Only nationalism motivates the sacrificial devotion of citizens, without which there can be no effective governance. In relation to *that* faith, sectarian religion is best understood as a jealous competitor.

To argue that nationalism is the most powerful American religion is not new. A long line of American thinkers has argued that civic life has, or ought to have, the structure of a civil religion.[2] Conceiving the nation as an object of civic worship troubles indigenous political and cultural categories nonetheless. Conventional wisdom holds that religion as an ideal order rejects violence. By contrast, nation-states unapologetically reserve to themselves the privilege of killing. Even where observers concede the necessity of ultimate force as a matter of group survival, those who long to live in peace may deny that political beliefs and practices can justly be compared to the beliefs and practices of traditional sectarian groups. They are reluctant to confer the virtuous title religion on a group that kills. This reluctance lies at the heart of what makes nationalism the most powerful American religion. Indeed, the refusal of Americans to acknowledge the indissolubility of religion and nationalism rests on a motivated misunderstanding of the genuinely religious character of American patriotism and the violent character of genuine religion. What the motive for this misunderstanding is will emerge in the course of the discussion.

Sectarian groups in the United States exist officially as denominations, churches that have surrendered all claim to monopoly status.[3] Those who argue that sectarian religion is antithetical to killing obediently comply with the first commandment of religious nationalism. This is that groups subordinate to the nation-group, such as sectarian groups, may not kill. The first principle of every religious system is that only the deity may kill. The state, which does kill, allows whoever accepts these terms to exist, to pursue their own beliefs and call themselves what they like in the process. In the broadest sense, the purpose of religion is to organize killing energy. This is how it accomplishes its social function of defining and maintaining the group. By this standard, nationalism is unquestionably the most powerful religion in the United States.

Taking a leaf from René Girard, we argue that collective victimage constructs American national identity. This mechanism expresses itself through a primitive belief in the transformative power of the *totem,* a term the sociologist Emile Durkheim made famous. The Durkheimian totem is "the sign by which each clan distinguishes itself from the others . . . It is at once the symbol of the god and of the society."[4] Such a totem is central to the formation of American national identity. While the term *civil religion* has been applied to some features of patriotic piety, its full structure has never been convincingly articulated. Conventionally understood, civil religion remains a pale imitation of the sectarian model to which it refers. We will show that the totem system of American patriotism is a symbolically coherent, deeply primitive, powerfully religious enterprise organized around a violent identity-crystallizing mechanism. We propose that the totem is the violently sacrificed body symbolized by the flag. The flag ritually transformed is the god of society renewed.

Because violence is considered immoral at best and barbaric at worst, its role in nation-state cohesion has been minimized and denied. In totem terms, it is taboo. The nature and function of violence was imported into the discussion of nation-states by Max Weber. It has been customary ever since to distinguish between state and nation, and to define the state as the body that claims a monopoly on the legitimate use of violence, and the nation as an image based in sentiment, conceived as benign attachment.[5] We say the *sentimental* formation of the nation creates the group idea and depends fundamentally on violence. The state exists merely to implement the social compact thus sentimentally forged. Once formed, the nation must be re-formed again and again in violent sacrifice expressed through a religion of patriotism structuring official and much popular culture and organized around the flag. This civil religion determines who may kill and what for, how boundaries are formed, and what national identity is. That faith is deeply held and constantly re-created in the stories, images, rites and legal codes of national culture. We call this set of beliefs and practices about sacrificial violence the *totem myth*. In our scheme, civil religion and nationalism are synonymous terms for the sacralized agreement that creates killing authority and specifies the relationship of group members to sacrificial death.[6]

The idea that violent blood sacrifice creates nation-state unity is at odds with arguments that stable modern nations enforce social norms not chiefly by force but other means. These include social pressure implemented by surveillance, a view especially identified with Anthony Giddens, and the notion that national identity is fostered by collective textual imagination, a view associated with Benedict Anderson.[7] In such analyses violence is presented as primitive and morally suspect, a failure of social structure rather than an elemental component of it. Two such analysts, Balibar and Wallerstein, treat violence in this way as a property of defective groups. They contend that aggression is a "fictive essence" provoked by nationalists and racists to create and secure group identity.[8]

Nationalist and racist communities do manifest group-structuring violent impulses, but so do all enduring groups. Though Balibar and Wallerstein classify aggression as residual "animality" (read, primitivism), they do not so label practitioners of violence who present themselves as resisters of aggression. By arguing that some groups designated as oppressed properly use physical force to resist others designated as oppressers, Balibar and Wallerstein enact the pattern at the heart of all group-forming. They utilize a purification ritual to separate members of their own group, whose deployment of violence they label as moral, from primitives who exercise violence immorally. They observe the *totem secret*, or taboo, by insisting that the death of our own does not originate with ourselves. All group-sustaining violence likewise poses as a reluctant response to violence that originates beyond group borders, that is, with others.

We use the term *taboo* to describe the tension between the violent mechanism that sustains enduring groups and the reluctance of group members to acknowledge their responsibility for enacting it. To protect themselves from recognizing the source of group unity, citizens render totem violence and its symbols sacred, that is, unknowable. While totem violence is regularly enacted in rituals of unifying blood sacrifice such as war, this knowledge must be separated from devotees, as sacred things are, whenever it threatens to surface explicitly. It is denounced as primitive, an attribute of groups that are not like us because they are eager to use violence. The totem taboo is thus constituted by the inadmissible equation of violence, the sacred, and the primitive. We will treat *violence* as a structural rather than contingent social force, *religion* or the sacred as unassailable social truth, and *totemism*, standing in for the primitive, as the fundamental representation of society to itself through killing rituals performed on the bodies of its supplicants. We argue that our own society is as primitive as any, and that all enduring groups are primitive in this way.

Are we primitive?

I have so many images for it – this state of being a citizen, of being civilized. I see it as a net that holds me in place, keeps me from falling. I see it as a fabric – a network of individual threads, intertwined, pulled tight – that keeps me warm, that I can wrap around both me and others. I see it as property, a house, a structure, a made thing, walls to keep out the cold, a door to keep out the unwanted, a roof to protect me from the night and its terrible undifferentiated darkness.

But I see it, too, as a weight. I see it as a barrier, an obstacle between me and something I don't know or understand. I see it as a mediator, a filter that allows only certain kinds of experiences through. And I am attracted to the moments when it disappears, even if briefly, especially if briefly: when the fabric tears, the net breaks, the house burns.

Bill Buford, *Among the Thugs*[9]

The missionaries go forth to Christianize the savages – as if the savages weren't dangerous enough already.   Edward Abbey[10]

As no discussion of violence can begin without Weber, no discussion of the primitive should begin without Durkheim. By suggesting that the worship of society is submerged in the idea of the holy, and the holy is manifest in the totem, Durkheim long ago re-framed a narrow, anthropological debate about relations in primitive societies as a discussion about the representation of society to itself. What his contemporaries took to be a limited mechanism of primitive organization, Durkheim took to be the palpable sacred symbol of the social. By arguing that religion constitutes the foundation of society, and the totem is its concrete expression, Durkheim posed a dilemma of identity for citizens of the modern nation-state. Is it the so-called primitive alone who deeply embraces society-guaranteeing norms and forms, or are primitives more modern than we imagine? Are patriots who revere the nation really primitives after all? Though Durkheim observed totem residues in contemporary practices, he felt them to be of slight social consequence. Though he described the totem principle of the primitive clan as its "flag," he hesitated to embrace the reverse logic that a flag implies the existence of totem principles.[11]

Critics of the primitive – modern distinction often take pains to demonstrate the sophistication of so-called primitive people. Fewer efforts are made to show primitive processes at work in contemporary society. At most, suggestive examples of Tylorean survivals are tossed out to provide amusing lessons in humility administered by the theorist. Potent in its inferiorizing stigma, the primitive remains the category of the Other. It merely has been vacated of authorizable examples by commentators eager to exhibit their moral enlightenment. Perhaps the notion of the primitive cannot be rehabilitated for any analytical purpose, but for us it is neither a moral category nor any material condition. It refers to a domain of experience, namely, constructing the social from the body, and specifically, from blood.

From the beginning, persons born into the group as physical bodies must be fashioned into group-sustaining social bodies. The fundamental primitive process that transforms individual bodies into social ones is sacrifice. Ever-present in traditional and industrial societies, sacrifice is always primitive. An American, in this context, is one who bows down to a violent authority. That is, he offers himself to the group in the guise of the state's

2.1 Abraham Lincoln as American primitive in parsed flag costume. 1863 political cartoon.

killing authority. Group members who "work hard and follow the rules," to use a recent description that has found favor by referencing sacrifice (though obliquely, as is customary in taboo discussion), observe thereby their ritual duties. When submission results in death, this body becomes more than American, it becomes a totem god of Americans, the apotheosized sacrificial body.

How sacrifice organizes belonging is reflected in the words of a Marine sergeant who surrendered to authorities as an illegal alien, a man without a country. He had concealed his out-group status through eleven years of military service.

Should I have to make the ultimate sacrifice one day, I would willingly die defending America, said Sergeant Lightfoot, wearing pressed khakis, service ribbons and a forage cap. My only regret would be that I would not die as an American.[12]

Robed in sacrificial vestments and bearing a record of devotion and piety, Lightfoot asks for a blessing, the metamorphosis of his individual body into a social one. According to his commanding officer (in totem terms, his religious superior), Lightfoot was "deserving of special consideration because he has demonstrated his commitment to America by his willingness to defend it with his life." The irrefutable sign of national faith, which we call patriotism, is making one's body an offering, a sacrifice. To die for others is the ultimate expression of faith in social existence.

The flag and civil religion

I repeat, government is impossible without a religion: that is, without a body of common assumptions.   George Bernard Shaw[13]

Whether civil religion is an appropriate label for American civic piety is an old debate. We discern three major perspectives. One denies the existence of civil religion.[14] Another defines civil religion as the sum of social impulses held in common by a political community. This commonality consists in an ethic of civic good will joined to belief in an ontological transcendance with no particular attributes.[15] A third view argues that religion, civil or otherwise, is what culture is. This is our approach, framed within a totem structure.

Civil religion does not exist

In this view, religion is a system based in a cult of divine beings.[16] American civic piety and patriotism are judged to be irreligious because they make scant appeal to a supernatural metaphysics. The point of contention between those who think civil religion describes patriotic practice and those who do not concerns the definition of the sacred. We say the doctrines and ceremonies of nationalism clearly reference the sacred. In later chapters we argue that the divine beings invoked in national rituals are the dead totem fathers embodied in the flag. Nor is this is the only religious test patriotism satisfies. George Kelly, an opponent of the civil religion thesis, proposes that religion is:

(1) a justification and consolation for the most wrenching human tragedies, especially mortality;
(2) a guide to one's dignity of place and meaning in the cosmos, especially in view of personal inadequacy and the need of expiation; and
(3) a primary bond of social cohesion expressed in rituals or ceremonies that connect human beings to each other and the sacred.[17]

Whatever one thinks of the answers nationalism provides, these are precisely the questions it addresses.

John Wilson argues that genuine religions exhibit six features that are not found in American civic piety. These are:

(1) cultic aspects, including provision for frequent ceremony or ritual;
(2) recognized leadership offices invested with effective authority;
(3) explicitly defined individual participation that establishes grounds for membership;
(4) doctrines of correct belief; and
(5) a coherence among these categories that makes the concept of religion applicable.[18]

In fact, this list turns out to be a close description of the totem system we will present. Still, Kelly argues that the visible symbols "we would naturally attach to the common practice of a civil devotion have been more and more emptied of substance, commitment, and participation." It is hard to imagine that he could be thinking of the flag, imbued with symbolic substance as it is, and commanding commitment and participation.[19] "Whatever else civil religion is," he continues, "with its penchant for communicative symbols and collective ceremony, it is not an indicator of the self-sacrifice of individuals."[20] On the contrary, self-sacrifice is the central theme of an American civil religion of patriotism organized around the flag.

According to critics of the civil religion thesis, patriotism fails to command the fervor that identifies true religious feeling.[21] Statistics suggest otherwise. Fifty-eight per cent of respondents in a 1979 Gallup poll agreed that religion is "very important," a substantially higher percentage than in all other Western industrialized countries surveyed.[22] To a 1981 Gallup poll question, "Are you affiliated with a church or religious organization?" 57 per cent of American respondents answered yes.[23] For comparison, a *New York Times* poll during Ronald Reagan's first presidential term found that 52 per cent of surveyed respondents considered themselves "very patriotic," while 38 per cent considered themselves "somewhat patriotic." Less than 1 per cent considered themselves unpatriotic, 3 per cent weren't sure, and 7 per cent considered themselves "not very patriotic."[24] As for the fickleness of public enthusiasm for the flag and its rituals, rhythmicity of fervor is part of the history of every religion. Nor is ritual attentiveness a full measure of devotional fervor. No sectarian faith is captured in a single set of observances. There are distinctive varieties "from the garlic-and-babushka style of the vestigial Catholic ghetto to the social sophistication of liberation-minded priests and nuns; Protestantism allows for everything from tent revivals to incense-shrouded rituals."[25] Civil religion is no different. Many "fair-weather patriots . . . need a war or a holiday to make them stand up for the country," as one journalist put it. "Waving the flag on the Fourth of July is like going to church on Easter."[26]

Scholars have searched for a civil religion of patriotism more in discourse than in gesture, and in relatively limited discursive forms such as presidential pronouncements and inaugural speeches. By thus narrowing the field of investigation, they observe the totem taboo and see scant reason to credit the religious character of American civic piety. Roderick Hart, for example, frames his skepticism this way.

As a "religion," [American civic piety] does not take verifiable action. It does not give alms to the poor. It does not even hold bingo games. Rather, it is a religion which exists within and because of discourse. Since it does nothing it is doomed to tag-along status existentially.[27]

We will discover how American patriotic piety enacts and recalls powerful cultural transformations, how it holds bingo games in its own way and gives hope, if not alms, to the culturally dispossessed. Presidential pronouncements offer too narrow a slice of culture for evaluating a civil religion of patriotism. Even a broader range of discourse, such as press descriptions of Fourth of July festivities or televised depictions of the Persian Gulf war, is not sufficient. Patriotic expression is rooted in gesture, especially the gestural magic of the flag. We must inquire about a civil religion not only of language but of gesture, especially the supreme gesture of blood sacrifice.

Homogenization of faith

A second perspective argues for civil religion as a social contract between sectarian faiths and the state. Civic rituals foster tolerance toward sectarian faiths, which offer programmatic support in return. Civil religion expresses consensus about the obligations of social life, a practical ethic of brotherly love, and a notion of transcendental reality on which morality is based. This view is captured in President Eisenhower's comment that religion is a good idea no matter what beliefs it embraces. A Durkheimian twist would be Lyndon Johnson's inaugural pronouncement that we are a nation of believers who believe in ourselves.[28] This view misses the antagonistic relationship between civil religion and sectarian faith. It also fails to identify the fertility and sacrifice rituals that elicit and affirm civic devotion at the expense of other belief systems. We argue that sectarian faiths are better described as jealous competitors of civil religion than as allies of the state. Engaged in a constant stand-off with the state and one another, they cooperate because they must.[29] If, as Peter Berger claims, civil religion guarantees sectarian pluralism, this is because the state reserves to itself the authority to kill and denies it to competing religious systems.[30] It has vanquished its rivals but permits them to exist under watchful control.

Substance of culture

Where civil religion has failed to pass muster as a theology, a third approach revises the definition of religion to invest patriotism with sacred impulses. Clifford Geertz famously defines religion as: "(1) a system of symbols which acts to (2) establish powerful, persuasive and long-lasting moods and motivations in men by (3) formulating conceptions of a general order of existence and (4) clothing these conceptions with such an aura of factuality that (5) the motivations seem uniquely realistic."[31] This definition demands less in doctrinal requirements and addresses a larger congregation of worshippers than do traditional definitions. In this view the essence of religious thought is not that it concerns the divine or expresses the ineffable. It may take these forms or others to explain enduring features of existence, the world, and duties owed the social body. It enlarges the net for catching religious content by collapsing it back into social structure. Its adherents favor a Durkheimian view of society as sacred.[32] Michael Novak's claim that presidential auras and sports events are expressions of civil religion is a variant of this view.[33] So is Will Herberg's observation that Americans are tolerant of differences in sectarian doctrine and practice, but unashamedly intolerant about the true common religion of the United States, the 'American Way of Life.'[34] This unacknowledged faith has symbols and rituals, holidays and liturgy, saints and sancta. "It is a faith that every American, to the degree that he is an American, knows and understands."[35]

Why have theorists failed to offer a compelling account of American civil religion? They have certainly failed to identify the sacred object at its center. Both champions and detractors of civil religion have considered the flag only in passing. Martin Marty, a critic, denies the flag even the most obvious role: "In the operative aspects of its national life, in the university, the marketplace, or the legislature – America remains secular, with no single transcendent symbol to live by."[36] The transcendent utility of the flag that occupies a prominent wall of the New York Stock Exchange, that stands beside the speaker's chair in every state legislature, that adorns a pole in front of every public school and sits on the stage at every university commencement speech, that stands beside the altar in American churches, that marches with the Ku Klux Klan and civil rights activists, that adorns spacecraft, that signifies war and peace – the transcendent utility of this flag eludes him.

Theorists of civil religion have also failed to present a symbolically unified set of doctrines and practices. Catherine Albanese makes an effort. Her "constitutive" categories of American civil religion include national saints and arenas of sacred space and time.[37] Sacred spaces include battlefields and shrines such as Mount Vernon, Gettysburg, and Arlington National Cemetery. Ritual time includes the Fourth of July, Washington's birthday, Memorial Day, and Armistice Day. Fourth of July fireworks and patriotic liturgies of public address are classified as ritual practices. National saints include the founding fathers, and Lincoln, Franklin Roosevelt, and John F. Kennedy. Among venerated objects, Albanese singles out original copies of the Declaration of Independence and the Constitution, but she offers no structure for articulating ritual, object, and symbol to one another, and the flag merits barely a mention in her scheme.[38]

Is this absence of a symbolically coherent framework within which to locate nationalism a theoretical failure, or the way things are? Contemporary symbol systems are frequently characterized as incoherent. Even for Mary Douglas, who argues that many of our ideas about the Otherness of so-called primitives are misconceived, such disjointedness is an identifying feature of modernity. Compared to the unified symbols that order the lives of those in traditional societies, she observes, "our experience is fragmented. Our rituals create a lot of little sub-worlds, unrelated. Their rituals create one single, symbolically consistent universe."[39] Could there be more coherence to the symbols and practices of nationalism, our pervasive modern religion, than we realize? Among national systems such as Nazism there is an impressive coherence of symbolic channels. However, Nazis are also considered primitives, or Other, despite their modern location. Do other national systems differ from Nazism in degree or in kind?

Totemism

Discussions about whether civil religion is a true variety of religious species echo earlier debates about the authenticity of totemism, also contrasted to "true" religion in its time. To Robertson-Smith and Sir James Frazer totemic systems were false primitive religions distinguished by barbaric sacraments. They simply ignored the sacrificial character of the more familiar religious traditions to which they compared totemism. Levi-Strauss holds that totemism is an analytic illusion, an etic conceit projecting modes of thought at work in our own psychology.[40] He echoes Rousseau, who observed that no philosophers had ever described the state of nature: "They spoke about savage man and they described civil man."[41] Of course, if civil religion is the practice of setting apart the social compact as holy, a totemism that projects ourselves may offer important clues about how this is done.

Freud also wrote about totemism, analogizing primitive and modern beliefs. He describes the totem as the common ancestor of the clan, its guardian and helper.[42] He notes that clansmen are under a sacred obligation to refrain from killing the totem, to avoid eating its flesh, and not to profit from it directly. The sacrificial relation of devotees to the totem is the basis of all social obligation. Clansmen must treat one another as blood relatives because each is descended from the totem.[43] These relations closely parallel American flag practice and doctrine. Sacrifice for the flag establishes a blood kinship that may be stronger than the familial bond. In totem doctrine all Americans share a sacrificial obligation to these blood kinsmen. The flag must not be used in commercial undertakings for profit and must not be physically damaged or dismembered in any way. Embodying the totem god, the flag not only symbolizes sacrifice; it demands and receives it as well.

For Durkheim, the group becomes a group by agreeing not to disagree about the group principle. But what is the group idea? And how does sentiment accomplish it? Durkheim does not answer directly. We propose that collective victimage is the source of group sentiment and its essential mechanism. Recall that the raw material of society is bodies. Organizing and disposing of them is its fundamental task. The social is quite literally constructed from the body, and from specific bodies dedicated and used up for the purpose. The underlying cost of all society is the violent death of some of its members. Our deepest secret, the collective group taboo, is the knowledge that society depends on the death of these sacrificial victims *at the hands of the group itself.* This is the totem principle made plain.

Anthropologists traditionally have attended to three clusters of totem attributes: the predilection of kinship groups to identify themselves with plants and animals (though Durkheim noted that totem groups have embraced symbols as various as "a *flag* [emphasis added], a coat of arms, a saint, or an animal species" and even stars and rain);[44] rules governing social relations between and within totem groups, and between totem objects; and rituals and taboos directed at securing totem blessings for the group.[45] As to why groups distinguish themselves with representations at all, Franz Boas theorized that group markers have utility wherever genealogical links between any two persons are remote enough that group members cannot immediately identify one another as kinsmen.[46] Where group markers substitute for personal knowledge of kinship links, it seems clear they must be able to inspire loyalties as strong as those of kinship. There is evidence that they do. At their totemically most devout, Americans describe themselves as "born under the flag." The claim of totem descent expresses a powerful kinship to those who have merged with the flag in sacrifice. Sacrifice is the source of this sentiment.

A 1924 study by Ralph Linton is a unique effort to explore totemism in modern societies. Linton studied the segmentation of the American Expeditionary Force during World War I into "well-defined and often mutually jealous groups, each with its individual complex of ideas and observances."[47] Within the AEF, the Rainbow Division sought to meld units from different states whose regimental colors were "as varied as . . . the rainbow." Among the totem attributes Linton observed in the Rainbow Division were:

(1) segmentation into groups conscious of their identity;
(2) adoption of the name of an animal, thing, or natural phenomenon for group identification;
(3) the self-referential use of this name with non-members;
(4) the use of an emblem by group members to adorn themselves and their weapons and vehicles, with a corresponding taboo on its use by other groups;
(5) respect for the "patron" and its representations; and
(6) a vague belief in the protective role of the totem emblem and its value as an augury.[48]

Such attributes would be totemic among "uncivilized" people, Linton concluded. But he did not classify the Rainbow Division as totemic since its members lacked marriage regulations and belief in blood descent from the totem.[49] Both claims are debatable. Patriotic rhetoric and gesture claim descent from the totem based on blood relations among symbolic fathers and brothers established by sacrifice in war. Exogamy regulations offer a more complex picture than Linton recognized, but this is because the military is a *component* of the American totem system, not its whole expression. In American totemism, exogamy rules organize popular elections, the chief ritual of group mating, and provide a mechanism for reconciling internal group differences so the tribe can turn its attention to collective survival. Arguably, one function of exogamy is to set up emotional bonds among rival groups to check violence that might escalate into mutual destruction. This is a central function of election ritual.

In the large, differentiated tribe of the United States where knowledge of kinship links for all group members is impossible, the flag identifies group members and ritually sanctifies group sacrifice and regeneration. It goes without saying that only persons ever do any of the things we attribute to group action. To speak of the flag or totem as doing or acting is to reify individual actions that make up group processes. When we ascribe agency to a totem flag, we use the rhetoric of ritual analysis to specify connections among the elements of American civil religion. When we say the flag governs death by regulating blood sacrifice in war, or that the flag is renewed through a two-party mating system of exogamous electoral clans, we know individuals acting in groups are the actors in every case. Since our analysis is of symbolic rather than institutional connections, this vocabulary helps make those symbolic connections explicit.

Exogamous totem fertility is the subject of a later chapter, but we advance a preliminary account here. Two major clan groups bearing animal identities are descended from the flag, the tribal ancestor, for whom the emblem of a totem eagle is occasionally substituted. During seasonal festivals called elections, representatives of the elephant and donkey clans form an exogamous mating pair that produces a reincarnated savior king, an embodied totem president who bears a sacrificial charge. The ritual would be improper if the members of the mating pair were from the same electoral clan, or party. A second mating pair consists of the victorious candidate and voters who vow fidelity to him during the general election, a tribal wedding ceremony. In this ceremony, tribal members pledge themselves to one or the other of the electoral pair in return for the savior king's promise that he will sacrifice himself at the behest of the group. In a properly conducted ritual some citizens must leave their own clan to mate exogamously in the ritual of voting with the candidate of the other clan. This is how the seasonal totem is regenerated from mating pairs selected from opposing clans. The successful mating partner emerges as winner.

The function of totem-governed electoral politics is to move social conflict away from internal divisions of blood and heritage expressed by ethnicity or sectarian faith, and towards rule-governed conflict in which political parties with shifting and cross-fertilized memberships negotiate for power and peace. In addition to political parties that engage in ritual mating with candidates to regenerate the embodied totem at seasonal intervals, there exist groups of affinity by blood, either through kinship or common ordeal. These affiliative groups are also the subject of a later chapter. They constitute both a reserve source of leadership if the totem fails and the gravest of threats to nation-state cohesion. Affiliative groups may collect under one or another political party banner. Catholics, African–Americans, or coal miners – affiliative groups all – may express a traditional devotion to the Democratic party, but the party itself has no exclusive membership rules. Its ritual efficacy would be called into question if it did.

The cross-fertilized membership of the two great non-exclusive electoral clans deflects potentially murderous struggle. It reorganizes the identities of contending groups by focusing away from irreconcilable differences associated with exclusive affiliation by blood and subordinating these differences to blood ties of totem sacrifice. Campaigning in South Africa during its first free elections, President F. W. de Klerk, the leader of the National Party that built apartheid and participated in its demise, spoke to voters as follows:

We are a new party. We are the party now with support from all South Africans. We're no longer a white party. I'm white, but my heart pumps the same red blood as the red blood in the heart of every South African.[50]

De Klerk rejects racially based blood ties for national ones. Such fertilization deflects internal friction while integrating the contributions of antagonists in an orderly fashion. In the American totem system, devotees are likewise asked to renounce blood ties to ethnicity and clan for politics and party, which substitute blood kinship to the nation.

Nationalism

Imagine there's no country
It isn't hard to do
Nothing to kill or die for
And no religion too.   John Lennon

That we are unique is the assertion that defines us. Other groups may resemble one another, we reason, but ours is unlike all others. In this vein, journalist Leslie Gelb argues that most states founded on principles of ethnic, religious, cultural or linguistic exclusivity have been no better, meaning no different, than the empires they replaced. But the United States, he writes, is a unique "vessel for representative government and protection of individual rights, not a vehicle for race and religion." America "has mostly lived up to these aspirations and acted mostly as a peace-loving nation."[51] Just so does nation-state dogma deny its exclusionary, death-dealing history. This is not because nationalism is demonic, but because this is the character of nationalism.

To construct the essence of the nation as inclusive and peace-loving is to claim for religious motives a history with other legitimate interpretations. It is to classify one's own group as morally special, chosen, in a word. It is to deny that group identity rests on killing. Every enduring group expresses this exceptionalism. Some theorists are more aware than others of the killing principles that organize national groups. Bruce Kapferer's comparison of Australian Anzac nationalism with the Sinhalese Buddhism of Sri Lanka is one example.[52] Lynn Hunt's work on the French Revolution treats similar themes of religious nationalism in the ritual sacrifice of Louis XVI.[53] Timothy Crippen argues that "the new gods of national identity and integrity" are as sacred as those of traditional religion.[54] "The twentieth century was marked not by the strength of classes and not even by a struggle of ideas," writes John Lukacs. "It was marked by the struggle of nations."[55]

Among the handful of theorists who have examined the religious character of American nationalism is Carlton Hayes, who argued that Western nationalism adapted many features of traditional Christianity, in the shadow of which it first appeared, and to which it has lent a nationalist edge ever since. Citizens are born into the nation-state, Hayes observed, as supplicants once were born into the Church. They have no choice but to be citizens, just as medieval Christians were compelled to embrace the faith of their birth. Like their medieval counterparts, crusaders for nationalism are buried in gravesites marked with the ensign of their service. The pomp and circumstance of funerals for national potentates and heroes rivals that of medieval bishops. Hayes recognized that nationalism is a collective faith of works. "So long as public rites and ceremonies are decently observed," he writes, "the hearts of the individual worshippers need not be too closely searched," though whoever jests publicly "at the expense of the national cult is eligible for mad-house or penitentiary."[56] Hayes sees what most observers do not. The symbol of national faith and the central object of its worship is the flag.

Curious liturgical forms have been devised for "saluting" the flag, for "dipping" the flag, for "lowering" the flag, and for "hoisting" the flag. Men bare their heads when the flag passes by; and in praise of the flag poets write odes and children sing hymns. In America young people are ranged in serried rows and required to recite daily, with hierophantic voice and ritualistic gesture, the mystical formula: "I pledge allegiance to our flag and to the country for which it stands, one nation, indivisible, with liberty and justice for all." Everywhere, in all solemn feasts and fasts of nationalism the flag is in evidence, and with it that other sacred thing, the national anthem.[57]

An analysis of the flag is not a complete account of American civil religion any more than an analysis of the cross is a complete account of Christianity. Still, it is essential. As "the species of thing which serves to designate the clan collectively," the flag signifies the sacrificial gesture that seals and sanctifies the social compact.[58] It is not *like* religion; it *is* religion. Nor is it casually religious, with a whiff of the sacred here and there, modeling denominational religion but fragmented and weakened by modernity.

The social geographer Wilbur Zelinsky suggests the flag has a visual power and presence comparable to the medieval crucifix.[59] The flag, like the crucifix, derives meaning from a coherent system of signs and practices in which bodily sacrifice is central. In another context, Harold Bloom asserts that believers in the pro-life movement equate the flag with the sacrificed, or aborted, fetus. He calls the flag and fetus "our Cross and our Divine Child."[60] Neither Hayes, who details flag practices, nor Zelinsky, who likens the flag to the cross, nor Bloom, who equates the cross and the flag, elaborates these claims. Hayes does say that nationalism has a god "who is either the patron or the personification of one's patrie, one's fatherland, one's national state."[61] We argue that the flag is the god of nationalism, and its mission is to organize death. Though Zelinsky argues that nationalism takes over where conventional faiths have failed and left the field, he never speculates on the nature of the failure. We suggest it lies in the historical transfer of killing authority from church to state. So complete has been this transfer that Benedict Anderson may claim without challenge that "nation-ness is the most universally legitimate value in the political life of our time."[62]

For many theorists writing before the breakup of the Soviet Union, nationalism has been portrayed as having no essentially violent character. Benedict Anderson, Liah Greenfeld, and Ernest Gellner all argue that national identity is communicatively constructed.[63] Anderson and Gellner trace the rise of nationalism to the historical growth of populations skilled in reading written vernaculars and to popular leaders who wrested authority from dynastic communities governed by religious elites wielding interpretive monopolies over sacred texts. For Liah Greenfeld, nationalism is the core idea around which contemporary human communities are organized, the constitutive element of modernity. Its medium is not force but language. She rejects "the politically activist, xenophobic variety of national patriotism."[64] Though Greenfeld adopts Max Scheler's concept of *ressentiment* from Weber's claim that the nation is based in sentiments of prestige manifest in the face of challenge by other groups, she does not acknowledge the identity-crystallizing role of challenge put to its ultimate test, which is violence. Other thinkers do, but generally as a demonstration of social failure. Tom Nairn considers nationalism "the pathology of modern developmental history."[65]

Anderson characterizes the nation-state as an imaginary model of space and time populated by persons unknown to oneself, and collectively bounded by a horizon conforming to the reach of a written vernacular. National "realities" are disseminated in novels and newspapers, media proper to the nation-state idea. For Ernest Gellner, schools transmit the national idea. In both instances, citizens imagine other community members through mediated, especially written, modes. Anderson, Gellner, and Greenfeld all fail to account for the deeply felt emotional legitimacy of the nation, though Gellner says more than he knows in observing that a man must have a nationality "as he must have a nose and two ears."[66] Here is tacit recognition that the most basic of modern identities is built on the primitive actuality of the body. Similarly, Anderson writes that "official nationalisms," a concept roughly analogous to our notion of the totem, "can best be understood as a means . . . for stretching the short, tight, skin of the nation over the gigantic body of the empire."[67] That metaphor, offered in the context of an argument that printed texts transmit nationalist sensibility in capitalist economies, argues inadvertently for a primitive social body. Elsewhere acknowledging death as a prominent theme of nationalism and religion, Anderson misses the connection between them, which is that nations exercise the killing power sectarian religions once claimed for themselves and still claim when they are powerful enough, or when they are able to ally directly with nationalism.

In assigning power to text, Anderson assumes that text-based language is the foundation of national identity. On the contrary. The spoken vernacular, body-sourced and face-to-face, connects language to the nation understood as a community of bodies. By focusing on colonial administrators who direct the formation of national consciousness by exercising textual skill and power, Anderson entirely ignores the role of blood sacrifice. Though he wonders how nationalism inspires profound loyalty and sacrifice, he never shows how it springs from shared textual experience.[68] Nor can he, since nationalism is a community of blood and not text. Not by accident, ceremonies of nationalism are about death and not literature, though literature may remodel blood sacrifice. When armies assemble as fighting forces, their members are deployed in loyal, close-knit groups. Effective armies are not faceless bureaucracies in which soldiers apprehend their comrades at the distance of the written word, but countless small bodies of men and women tightly bound in mutual comradeship. A textual community does not fight. An army is not a textual community, but an organization of hunting groups melded under a totem and always in danger of slipping away from it.

Language and ritual

Few things more directly threaten the strict separation of church and state, a purifying ritual to which many citizens are devoutly committed, than a sacred flag. If the flag is not plainly a divine being or the agent of one, there is no threat to this separation according to a folk notion of religion that requires belief in the supernatural. Here is the harshest charge against any claim that the flag is the sacred object of a civil religion of patriotism: the natives reject the analyst's interpretation. On the other hand, the natives may not be reliable observers of their own behavior if they have religious reasons to ignore it. Even by the strict requirements of folk religion, the supernatural character of the flag in the American civil religion of patriotism is plainly manifest on ceremonial occasions. At other times such characterizations are conscientiously shunted aside in accordance with the taboo provisions under which it operates. We must account for both affirmations and denials of its sanctity.

The answer lies partly in the different ritual tasks of language and gesture. We accept Roy Rappaport's argument that the most basic group understandings would soon be cast into confusion if they depended on language alone.[69] The symbolic power of language lies in its capacity not to be tied to concrete referents. Language can lie and its meaning can drift. By comparison, ritual gesture is uniquely suited to constitute the foundation of social order. Ritual gesture always and undeniably demonstrates public assent to group symbols, whatever the private beliefs of performers. Not private belief, but willingness to execute public obligations is necessary for group survival. However, though nation-states are constituted in the sacrificial public gesture that creates them, ritual language still plays a distinctive and esssential role. First, utterance can be performative in an illocutionary sense.[70] Language also elaborates totem myth for devotees. Finally, it protects the sacred character of the totem by refusing to speak the name of God, and even when language denies the sacred character of the totem, it subversively affirms it. This claim requires further development.

What is sacred is powerful and, therefore, dangerous. It must be set apart. Deification is one way of accomplishing this, but overt efforts to deify the flag as sacred place it in competition with sectarian faiths, and cause the state to speak the forbidden name of God. Denying the sanctity of the flag honors the ancient command not to speak God's name. Indeed, those who suggest the flag is sacred in any but the most ritually guarded contexts call down on themselves the wrath of the community. They reveal the delicate compromise between *gestures* that present the flag as sacred and *language* that protects it from challenge by deying its religious meaning. Consider the history of forced flag salutes. Despite persecution, Jehovah's Witnesses in the 1930s and 1940s refused to participate in compulsory classroom recitations of the Pledge of Allegiance. Their resistance led to *Minersville* v. *Gobitis* (1940) in which the Supreme Court explicitly denied the Pledge's religious character but also ruled that school children could not refuse to say it.

By placing fealty to the flag above refuseable religious oaths, the court suggested that the magic of flag prayer was greater than any competing supplication, and that failure to perform the rites of flag worship would imperil the community. Not even children could be released from this obligation. The court's decision made plain the holy nature of the flag in effect, while denying it in words. Such a split between word and gesture was nonetheless perilous and threatened to reveal the taboo. Close on the heels of *Gobitis*, a second decision, *Barnette* v. *West Virginia Board of Education* (1943), granted the Witnesses' right to refuse the oath.[71] By thus striking down compulsory flag worship for schoolchildren, the court avoided explicitly acknowledging the religious functions of patriotism and restored the taboo on speaking God's name. Though the new decision tacitly acknowledged that a compulsory Pledge was a religious oath, the court never conceded that the Witnesses had recognized this fact because of their identity as fundamentalists, a euphemism for religious primitives who are inescapably modern. The fundamental elements of this history are repeated in the more contemporary decision by the Girl Scouts of America to revise the oath its own members take in the presence of the flag. "On my honor, I will try to do my duty to God and my country," the official oath read until 1993, when the organization voted to make "to God" optional, a gesture toward sectarian pluralism. What they did not consider optional, for it was not even discussed, was "my country." Thus they honored the real taboo.

Attributes of the totem flag

The totem is the guardian and ancestor of the clan, the god embodied, and its emblem. In the United States the totem emblem is the flag. We will detail its dynamics in subsequent chapters. Here is a preliminary account of elemental totem properties derived from Durkheim and re-cast in American terms.

The signifying totem

The totem is the transcendent group idea endlessly manifest in the group's materialized expressions of itself. According to Durkheim, its emblem occupies a "considerable place" in tribal cultures.[72] In the Australian tribes observed by Spencer and Gillen and analyzed by Durkheim, it appears on every sort of object. It marks important places, arms, war canoes, funeral implements, utensils, walls, poles, and clothing. Americans do not place the flag, the totem emblem, on canoes, but it does adorn their official airplanes, battleships, spacecraft, and limousines. It occupies a "considerable place" in American culture, and is likewise associated with key tribal figures and artifacts that give the tribe its materially extended form. It flies from the frame houses of small-town America, it stands at the front of the classroom, it is placed next to the President. It marks political celebrations, war, and sports. All things so marked may stand for the whole society.

In the current era of secure patriotism, it is possible to acquire an entire wardrobe of flag clothing, to outfit an entire household in flag-patterned bed and table linens, to set the table with flag dishes, to buy the kids' flag toys, and to deploy flag motifs in furniture, rugs, and draperies. For upscale consumers, Bloomingdale's June, 1991, catalog featured a whimsical flag mailbox ($45. 00), flag beach towel ($14. 99), flag birdhouse ($29. 94), knit wool flag pillow ($85. 00), flag serving tray ($25. 00), and flag clock ($49. 95).[73] Horchow's *American Spirit* catalog for July, 1991, featured stars-and-stripes sneakers, a patriotic silk blue- and white-striped silk top covered with sequins in the shape of an American flag, and matching shorts, for $360. Matching costume jewelry cost a further $200. Also featured were flag motifs on table mats, party fans, napkin rings, hand-painted wooden apples, dolls, quilts, and other early-American-style artifacts. The cover of the catalog displayed a pie with a raised design of eagle and stars next to a crumpled flag napkin.[74]

Particularly important to mark are the bodies of devotees whose sacrifice is the ultimate offering to the totem. Tribal societies mark with tattoos since scarification with group symbols, says Durkheim, is "within the capacity of even the least advanced societies." Even in technologically advanced societies, scarification remains a minor ordeal of totem initiation. Patriotic tattoos are common among American warriors and groups with totem aspirations. During the Gulf War, the press reported an upsurge in requests for flags and eagles at tattoo parlors:

Soldiers enter Rocket Rick's Tattooing saying, "I'm going to fight; I want the flag," said Rick Hincher, owner of the tattoo parlor next to Fort Benning in Columbus, Ga.[75]

The taboo totem

Durkheim says, "If a belief is unanimously shared by a people, then . . . it is forbidden to touch it, that is to say, to deny it or to contest it. Now the prohibition of criticism is an interdiction like the others and proves the presence of something sacred."[76] Rules of avoidance surround the totem and the flag that embodies it. These are principally against touch, the original and most important taboo, but also against wearing, consuming, and killing the totem. They are reflected in the opinion of Chief Justice Rehnquist that the government has a duty to insulate the supreme national symbol from harm, and that the flag must be set apart, as the sacred is, from what is merely debatable.

The flag is not simply another "idea" or "point of view" competing for recognition in the marketplace of ideas. Millions and millions of Americans regard it with an almost mystical reverence regardless of what sort of social, political, or philosophical beliefs they may have. I cannot agree that the First Amendment invalidates the Act of Congress, and the laws of 48 of the 50 states, which make criminal the public burning of the flag.[77]

In civilian and military protocols the flag must not touch the ground, it must hang in proper alignment, it must not be lower than other flags, it must appear in the place of honor on the right, it must not be used as a receptacle or covering. Crisis triggers obligatory ritual exceptions. The flag is the only proper casket covering in funerals with military honors. In war, the group ritually kills the very tribe members who otherwise enjoy protected status. In this protected status, group members are taboo like the flag, and for the same reason. They embody the group in their persons. The flag signifies the special condition of sacrifice, of lifting the killing taboo for the sake of the group.

The flag is not one of an equivalent set of patriotic nominatives, roughly equal to the Constitution, the Declaration of Independence, the Statue of Liberty, Uncle Sam, George Washington, Benjamin Franklin, the liberty pole, Thanksgiving, and so on. As Catherine Albanese notes, no public outrage accompanies burning an effigy of George Washington or Abraham Lincoln. Generations of tourists to the Statue of Liberty have not been religiously discouraged from adorning it with discarded chewing gum. Even igniting copies of the Constitution probably would not produce the level of outrage that accompanies flagburning, though flags exist in hundreds of thousands of "copies," just as the Constitution does. The desecratory taboo applies to the flag alone, for only the flag signifies the sacrificed body.

The definition of the holy as what is set apart, whole and complete, one and physically perfect, explains why there is horror in burning or cutting the flag, and danger in its being dismembered and rendered partial. A worn and tattered flag is ritually perilous and must be ceremonially burned so that nothing at all is left. The flag is treated both as a live being and as the sacred embodiment of a dead one. Horror at burning the flag is a ritual response to the prohibition against killing the totem. Only ritually designated persons such as veterans, who have touched death in the service of the flag and are themselves set apart, may ceremonially violate the flagburning taboo. Totem–mimetic apprentices such as the Boy Scouts may also perform this ceremony using procedures that protect against desecratory danger. Countervailing body magic may also protect the totem's power:

> We can imagine no more appropriate response to burning a flag than waving one's own, no better way to counter a flag-burner's message than by saluting the flag that burns, no surer means of preserving the dignity even of the flag that burned than by – as one witness here did – according its remains a respectful burial.

The true totem is unknowable, unspeakable, untouchable, and unviewable. Precautionary rituals shield us from knowing that we kill our own, while transferring the force of this taboo to the flag, which assumes its sacred character. The transmissibility of taboo is a property of contagious magic. The flag transfers its power to important persons and things, which in turn become taboo. Things include designated objects and communal acts. Persons include the President and other members of the totem class. A commentator on the 1992 vice-presidential debate said Senator Albert Gore was "more presidential [than his opponent]. He stayed aloof from . . . the fighting."[78] To be presidential is to be totemic. To be totemic is to be set apart. Once a president is elected, his freedom of movement and that of others to touch him are severely restricted. A ruler "must not only be guarded, he must also be guarded against," writes Frazer.[79] Because of his magical power, contact originating with him may bless and protect the touched believer. It also may kill the believer, whom the President has the power to send to death. Likewise, contact originating with citizen–subjects is fraught with danger for the savior–king. A taboo zone must be established around the embodied totem to insulate the profane and sacred from one another.

The funeral of Dwight D. Eisenhower illustrates the creation of such a space. A contemporary *Life* magazine cover photo gazes down from the ceiling of the Capitol rotunda on the former President, lying in state. In the cover image, empty unpeopled space surrounds the flag-shielded casket. Around the border of the Rotunda are crowded the tiny heads of the mourners. None ventures into the carefully guarded space around the casket. It may not be crossed except in stylized, ritual fashion by uniformed totem priests whose every gesture dramatizes the sacred nature of the dreadful zone of totem death. The dead President's power is visually expressed in the taboo space around him. Taboos exist, says Freud, because people desire to do what is forbidden. It is forbidden to touch the totem and appropriate its power, which is the power to kill its own. If clansmen were permitted to exercise that power, the community would quickly destroy itself. When totem violations are not redressed by acts of atonement and purification, there will be grave consequences. According to Freud:

If the totem is imperiled, it must be avenged in the most energetic fashion by the whole clan, as though it were a question of averting some danger that threatened the whole community or some guilt that was pressing on it.

It is equally clear why it is that the violation of certain taboo prohibitions constitutes a social danger which must be punished or atoned for by all the members of the community if they are not all to suffer injury . . . It lies in the risk of imitation, which would quickly lead to the dissolution of the community. If the violation were not avenged by the other members they would become aware that they wanted to act in the same way as the transgressor.[80]

Expiation for totem violation always involves the renunciation of something desirable, even life itself.

Unable to speak the name of God directly, a taboo-observing society avoids direct discussion of totem power by euphemizing it. When recruits arrive at Marine boot camp for initiation into the sacred mysteries, the life and death secrets of the body, the sign that greets them is, "Parris Island: The Place Where It All Begins." The unreferenced "it" appears repeatedly in discussions of totem sacrifice. "I was shooting down the street and thinking, 'We're going to fight to the last man, and we'll be out of ammunition. And that will be it,'" explained an Army Ranger who survived a firefight in Somalia that killed eighteen Rangers and forced a pullout of American troops in 1993.[81]

In a 1943 War Department report on harnessing "the powerful potential

2.2 Zone of taboo magic surrounds dead totem. President Dwight
Eisenhower lies in state beneath Capitol Rotunda.

combative spirit latent in our national character" for all-out war, the euphemistic "it" avoids direct discussion of the killing mission.

Certain factors are extremely important . . . Perhaps first is the attitude toward death and military service. Never should it be lost sight of that the soldier is in the service of society . . . and that this life has meaning almost wholly as it contributes to the good of all. For better or for worse he is now in it – the struggle to achieve a better life and to forestall calamity. *This is it.* [original emphasis] One life more or less is unimportant. The good soldier is thence adjusted, ready for anything he may be called upon to face. This frame of mind, characteristic of high morale, is the first essential for relegating fear to a secondary role – the business at hand is the thing.[82]

Consider also a mythicizing media account of the President. During a week when the Bush administration attempted to project the image of totem power, the press was invited to witness a light-hearted presidential stroll among blooming cherry trees, and an early morning totem visit with school children.

At 8 a.m., Mr. Bush read aloud from "Harry, the Dirty Dog," to about two dozen first graders sitting on the floor in the Diplomatic Reception Room of the White House. He told them how his own dog, Ranger, had killed a rat. The children told him about pets who were sick, dying or dead. Then the President of the United States went to the Oval Office for his daily intelligence briefing.[83]

Death is the hidden subject of the conversation between the children and the totem President. Indirectly, the children bring their concerns about death within the family circle to the man who holds its power in his hand, who receives the life and death secrets of intelligence reports. Indirectly, the President describes his own death-dealing agency in dispatching villainous outsiders who are not pets (not only non-human, but not even permitted animal guests in the human group) who cannot be loved and accepted within the family circle. The President's pet has the power to protect the children by dispatching dangerous outsiders.

The totem taboo is manifest in other ways. Reviewing a late-night striptease series on Home Box Office, television critic Walter Goodman described a segment of a Miss New World contest, "whose operators say the young women are judged by their facial expressions, personality and 'most especially' their smiles."[84] He continued, "The camera is particularly attracted to a woman who paints her body into an American flag to music. Personally, I kept my eye on the smile." Even for the cosmopolitan critic of popular spectacle there is pressure to make a bow, however humorously, toward the sanctity of the symbol.

Less subtle was the reaction of television executives to counter-culture celebrity Abbie Hoffman's violation of the totem taboo by wearing a flag shirt on the *Merv Griffin Show* in 1970. Hoffman recalled:

I came out, wearing a suede jacket with long fringes. After introductions all around I said it was hot under the lights and would anybody mind if I took off my jacket?
   "Go ahead," said mild-mannered Merv. When I removed my jacket Virginia almost clawed off her new face lift in horror. Even Arthur (Fish'n Chips) Treacher managed to look genuinely appalled. Merve tried to pretend he didn't notice I had just unfurled Old Glory.[85]

   Hoffman describes ritual responses to violation of the totem taboo. The shirt desecrates the totem flag by cutting up and partitioning it. Worse, the flag is brought into forbidden contact with a sacrificially unwilling body, one opposed to the Vietnam War. Gazing on the forbidden is a severe violation and may cause viewers to mutilate themselves, an act Hoffman metaphorically attributes to guest Virginia Graham. Merv Griffin is effectively struck blind, and thus exempted from the obligatory horror of acknowledgment. Network executives were unwilling to expose their audiences to the ritual peril of taboo violation. Hoffman continues:

The next night we all gathered at our apartment, ready for anything, we thought. Right before the program was to begin a disembodied voice told us that there would be an important announcement preceding the telecast of the previously recorded Merv Griffin show. Then the screen filled with the image of a very grave-looking man as the voiceover announced, "Ladies and gentlemen, vice-president of CBS, Robert D. Wood." He looked as if he were about to tell us there had been an earthquake in California and all of Los Angeles was floating out to sea. Instead he gave us this caution:
   An incident occurred during the taping of the following program that had presented CBS network officials with a dilemma involving not only poor taste and the risk of offending the viewers but also certain very serious legal problems. It seemed one of the guests had seen fit to come on the show wearing a shirt made from an American flag [not true; it was a shirt with a flag motif]. Therefore, to avoid possible litigation the network executives have decided to "mask out" all visible portions of the offending shirt by electronic means. We hope our viewers will understand.[86]

   The Hare Krishna sect incorporates the totem taboo in its fundraising practices. Taking advantage of the rule by which properly socialized group members may never take without giving, airport-patrolling Krishnas boldly thrust flowers into the hands of travelers to set up pressure for return donations. Airport visitors often reach into their wallets for token offerings when the Krishnas refuse to take the flowers back, declaring them gifts. Other travelers throw their flowers on the ground to cancel the obligation to exchange money for the "gift" of the flower. According to an observer of these interactions:

You know what the Krishnas are doing in some cities to counteract that strategy? They're now pinning small American flags on the lapels of passersby because they know that Americans won't throw their flag on the ground.[87]

The numinous totem

Not only death identifies the flag as sacred. Special emotional states are manifest in its presence. Rudolf Otto describes the encounter with the holy as a shudder accompanied by feelings of "peculiar" dread.[88] It is commonly described by bodily sensations of blood running cold or flesh creeping. For Otto, this shudder is a pre-linguistic, pre-rational reaction to a heightened state of arousal or fear. The numinous emotion tells the worshipper he is in the presence of the utterly meaningful. Freud borrows an electrical metaphor from Wundt to describe these feelings:

Persons or things which are regarded as taboo may be compared to objects charged with electricity; they are the seat of a tremendous power which is transmissible by contact, and may be liberated with destructive effect if the organisms which provoke its discharge are too weak to resist it.[89]

The totem is always radiating its holy quality and communicating its power. Reports of goosebumps at the sight of the flag tell us of the awe in which its admirers hold it.[90] Vera Sautter, a 65-year-old resident of Lincoln, Nebraska, explained during the Gulf War, "My heart goes pitty-pat and I get tears in my eyes when the flag goes by. It means that much to me."[91] Her neighbors, patrons of Don Johnson's flag shop, were described as "people who look for the union label, buy American cars no matter what the consumer guides say and get a chill when they hear the first strains of the *Star-Spangled Banner*." Such speechlessness in the presence of the deeply felt suggests a gestural dimension of bodily expression separate from language and associated with religious phenomena.

Athletes often speak about the emotional poignancy of the moment of flag-raising. At Barcelona in 1992, American Jennifer Capriati won an Olympic gold medal in tennis. The press faithfully reported the elements of a properly conducted ritual in which "the 16–year-old Capriati mounted the medal stand, put her hand over her heart and watched the American flag being raised." An accompanying picture offered evidence of additional piety. Wearing a flag-patterned Olympic jacket, a gold medal around her neck and a renewing bunch of flowers in her hand, she brushed away tears.[92] "It was so emotional," Capriati said of her feelings as the national anthem sounded. "I had the chills the whole time. I just can't believe it."[93]

David Jacobsen described his transformation by the flag after years of imprisonment during the 1980s as an American hostage in Lebanon:

"When I got off the plane [from the ordeal of his capture in Lebanon] and saw the flag, I cried. To this day, whenever the *Star-Spangled Banner* is played, I get a tear in my eye."[94]

Those touched by the flag may be forever changed. No stronger testimony exists than that of Confederate General William C. Wickham, who could not discard his feelings for the Union flag. After the war he wrote:

I never saw the United States flag, even when approaching me in a battle, that I did not feel arising those emotions of regard for it that it had been wont to inspire. I have, in like manner, said that one of the most painful sights I had ever seen was on the night of the first battle of Manassas, when I saw an officer trailing the flag in the dust before a regiment of the line.[95]

To have the wholly opposite reaction, to be nauseated and sickened by the flag, as doubters may be, is not so different from being religiously chilled by it. The flag's transformative power is the same; so is the response. Only the valence of the response is different. In each case the flag alters those in its presence. Its aura transforms them.

The protective totem

The totem cannot lose. Not that it never does in the bitter reality of warfare, or that it should not in narrative moral reconstructions of history. It cannot so long as it governs the group. This is its logic and function. The patriotic statement that Americans are an unconquerable people, common at times of totem peril, is a deadly serious statement of totem faith.[96] The totem wards off evil and protects from harm. During the nineteenth century, the flag was often depicted as a mythic protector in children's fiction. Scot Guenter has described a children's story from St. Nicholas in which:

The flag mysteriously saves a boy named Joe trapped in a burning house on the Fourth of July – the flagpole bends over to him when he finds himself cut off on the second story; he takes hold of the banner, pulls himself out of the blazes, and shimmies down to safety.[97]

The flag historian George Henry Preble offers a number of nineteenth-century stories about totem flag protection. Following a bitterly contested presidential election in Mexico, an insurgent mob approached the embassy residence of the Honorable Joel R. Poinsett, US Minister to Mexico, in search of Spaniards seeking shelter there. Shots were fired. Poinsett directed that an American flag be unfurled on the balcony. According to the story, the shouting ceased, the soldiers dropped the muzzles of their guns, and the crowd retreated as Poinsett stood beneath the flag and declared its protection for all in his household.[98] Following the German invasion of Norway in 1938, journalists described the evacuation of Ambassador Daisy Harriman and an assistant in cars with flags draped over the roofs "to warn Nazi pilots." This language suggested the thin cloth flags posed a serious menace to fighter bombers.[99]

If the totem does not deliver, if its magic is not effective, if outsiders overrun and penetrate its borders, if its army is defeated, if it ceases to resist and quits attacking, if the enemy surrounds and absorbs it, its boundaries will disappear; it will cease to exist. Group members must willingly exchange themselves for the totem. If the totem fails, only sacrifice renews its power. The graver the violation, the riskier the restorative sacrifice. Failure of the protective totem is thus a moment of great anxiety. Before the United States entered World War II, the bloody campaign of German U-boats against American merchant mariners occasioned such concern. Bound for Sierra Leone in 1940, with American flags painted on its sides, the freighter *Lehigh* was torpedoed and sunk. *Life*'s headline read, "The American Flag Goes Down Before a U-Boat Torpedo in the South Atlantic."[100] The magical demise of the ship was described: "For a while, the Lehigh settled placidly. But once the U. S. colors dipped below water, she began to sink fast."[101]

The communicating totem

To protect supplicants from overwhelming totem power there are pre-scribed modes for communicating with the totem. Collective rites of communication through bodily disciplines of not-touching indicate rever-ence and abject devotion and visibly preserve supplicants from contagious totem power. The Pledge of Allegiance is a collective prayer of submission, the *Star-Spangled Banner* a collective hymn of thanksgiving for totem pro-tection. Proper performance requires supplicants to assume ritual postures, hand on heart and attentive visual focus on the flag. Correct devotional behavior is the surest path to totem blessing. A New Jersey high school prin-cipal was remembered by a grateful parent for showing this path to his son:

"My boy wouldn't stand for the national anthem," the man said. "You tore the newspaper out of his hand, made him get up. Now he's a college graduate, owns his own home, good job. Thanks, Coach."[102]

The blessings of correct totem communication were described by President Warren Harding at the 1923 National Flag Conference to for-mulate a civilian flag code. Harding told the delegates that every salutation to the flag "makes my consecration to my country and the flag a little more secure." He urged delegates to codify proper behavior for the anthem as well:

Don't you think we ought to insist upon America being able to sing "The Star-Spangled Banner"? . . . I have noted audiences singing our national air – that is not the way to put it – I have noted them trying to sing our national air and outside of about 2 per cent, nearly all were mumbling their words, pretending to sing. Somehow I would like to see the spirit of American patriotism and devotion enabled to express itself in song. Mr. Chairman, if that is not unseemly, I hope you will include it in your code as one of the manifestations of reverence to the flag.[103]

The importance of getting the spell right was suggested by an E. R. Squibb & Sons advertisement in *Life* magazine during World War II:

You stand in the audience, eyes uplifted, singing at the top of your lungs. All around you, friends and neighbors.

Suddenly you falter. The others falter also. The burst of song that had begun to swell into a wave of patriotic fervor dies down to an uncertain murmur.

You no longer feel quite so patriotic. You feel abashed.

May we be forgiven if we offer a simple wartime suggestion? It's this: Shut yourself up in your room for five minutes and commit to memory all the words of, at least, the first verse of "The Star Spangled Banner."

And these from the fourth stanza:

"Then conquer we must, for our cause it is just,

And this be our motto: 'In God is our trust.'"

These are words immortal. Learn them. Sing them. Let the whole world know you believe in them.[104]

The anthem is an opening ritual for all national team sports events. During televised performances, shots of the living, rippling flag are typically interspersed with shots of members of the totem class, usually the color guard, in solemn salute. Other shots display players and fans in reverent postures. Their heads are bowed, their eyes are shut in prayer, their hands or hats cover their hearts.[105]

The most complete communication with the flag involves sacrificial union, a state of merging with the totem that verges on consubstantiality. This is the most intimate of all communication with the flag, since it requires crossing the magic barrier between the supplicant and the totem. According to Mary Douglas, group members agree:

To breed a host of imaginary powers, all dangerous, to watch over their agreed morality and to punish defectors. But having tacitly colluded to set up their awesome cosmos . . . delusion is necessary. For unless the sacred beings are credited with autonomous existence, their coercive power is weakened and with it the fragile social agreement which gave them being.[106]

In any contest between the holy flag and the profane supplicant, the flag must prevail or totem power would be in doubt. The supplicant who breaches the taboo barrier must be destroyed, while the totem triumphs and is regenerated. The supplicant nourishes and preserves the totem. Ritually reconstituted as sacred, he becomes the totem.

Presidential flag talk underscores this solemn duty. After conferring his blessing on the opening session of the 1923 flag conference, President Harding observed:

> I can understand how the flag owes considerably more to the service men of the Republic than it does to the ordinary citizen, but I cannot understand why the soldier or the sailor or the service man in national defense owes any more to the flag than anybody else in the United States of America, and so everything we do to bring the flag into proper consideration by the citizenship of the Republic is entirely commendable and deserves to be cordially praised.[107]

With totem indirection, the President acknowledges that human sacrifice feeds the totem. He suggests that all citizens owe the totem their lives. It is the responsibility of the President "to bear the awful authority of deciding to send your sons and daughters in harm's way," as George Bush once put it, to say when citizens must satisfy the totem appetite.[108] President Harding continued:

> One word more, and I will return to the tasks of the Executive. We have an obligation quite apart from the consideration of the colors: we have a great obligation to maintain in America unimpaired the things for which the American flag stands . . . that is the task of good citizenship and in its performance there will be coming a reward to all of us and we shall be assured of our contribution to a greater and better Republic.[109]

Coming down from "the tasks of the executive," a totemically insulated zone of implied ordeal, he urges the people to preserve the totem unimpaired and undamaged. He invokes the taboo that protects it from transforming contact, that is, from lack of respect. Respect is the category of taboo acceptance. The President assures the faithful that observing the taboo means a better and greater republic – a more cohesive and secure social body.

3

Theorizing the flagbody

It's like stepping on your family to burn the flag. Who'd want to do that?
Citizen comment[1]

The flag represents a living country and is itself considered a living thing.
36 U. S. C. 176(j)

In an era when Americans are less sure than they once were about what it means to have a national identity, Congress has several times proposed a constitutional amendment to protect the flag from desecration and several times rejected it. The first effort was mounted in the wake of two Supreme Court decisions that legalized flagburning.[2] Even the Court, splitting five to four in both cases, seemed unsure what American identity requires. Reviewing the defeat of the flag amendment, National Public Radio noted that during five hours of House debate there had been flag hats, flag pantyhose and flag bathing suits, but no Bill of Rights bathing suits.[3] Nor, observed NPR, does the Bill of Rights fly in the ballpark.

Why doesn't the Bill of Rights wave over the ballpark? What does flag clothing signify? Are standards and constitutions different? NPR suggested that the flag is more "accessible" than the Bill of Rights as its microphones wandered off to ask passersby what the Bill of Rights was, how many amendments were in it, whether anyone could name them or fill in the blanks if parts were read to them. A familiar vignette of civic ineptitude, this exercise demonstrated how uncertain a grasp of the particulars and significance of the Bill of Rights many citizens possess. Few such problems attach to the flag. Americans recognize it easily. They offer confident accounts of its meaning. They believe the flag has a generally agreed upon significance and they know what it is.

Like other signs, the flag makes sense within a system of differences.

Understanding what the flag is within this system requires understanding what it isn't. Its semiotic topography can be mapped by observing symbolic practice in public discourse about flag desecration. On this basis we argue that what the flag is not is a text. In the debate we examine, the particular text it is not is the Bill of Rights, the revealed text of American civil religion. What the flag is, at the level of ritual gesture, is a body. Since bodies are common to all of us, they are useful for representing socially important things.[4] Nor is the flag just any body, but the special body sanctified by sacrifice. The *flagbody* that is not-the-text is a key element in American flag symbolism. Embedded in the snippet of media culture with which this chapter begins, it points to an entire patriotic order. There is more. While the *sacred* sacrificial body is symbolically exchangeable with the flag, the *profane* body is not. Not only is the sacred flagbody not-the-text and not profane. There is a *waving* sacred flagbody and a *wrapped* sacred flagbody, as different from one another as sacrifice is different from regeneration, which may not be very different at all.

When is a body not a text? (When it flies in the ball park)

Text and *body* are ancient antagonists and antithetical poles in a discourse that has swirled around them for centuries.[5] Text is the weapon of those whose cultural power derives from educational and other textualizing credentials that exempt them from expending their bodies in pursuit of social resources. Those who are skilled at producing and using texts are most entitled to preserve their bodies and shield them from physical effort and danger. By contrast, the body is the emblem of those without textual credentials, whose bodies are available to be used up by society, and whose power and participation derive from whatever value their bodies have for cultural muscle-work. The most dramatic expression of this muscle-work is war. Among other things, the power of the textual class is the power to dispose of the bodies and lives of the non-textual class. *Text* and *body* represent competing concentrations of economic and social power, characteristically different concepts and artifacts, and distinctive logics and value frameworks. From this perspective, the flag desecration debate is a piece of the symbolic struggle between partisans of the body and the text to set the cultural terms for allocating social resources such as honor, prestige, and authority.

The flag is an artifact based in oral culture. As a category, *oral* is best thought of not as aural information exclusively, though the term has traditionally meant this. It is best understood as a mode of the immediately present, non-textual body displayed in several sensory channels at once.[6]

Conventional definitions of orality overlook the essential co-presence of visual modes. Broadly understood, orality encompasses speech, bodily gesture, and displays of bodily ornament, including cosmetic marking, masks, costumes, and other visual representations of the body.[7] Every extension, part or representation of the body stands for it metonymically. A piece of hair cut off at death becomes a sign of its owner. So does a dagger wielded by bodies to fight for land and handed down as witness to bloody struggle. A national or tribal flag stands in this way for the bodies that constitute a community. A flag has the status of an emblem or escutcheon that represents the body and is magically invested with its powers and vulnerabilities.[8] In Congressional hearings about flagburning legislation in 1927 a soldier testified:

> I was in the service for two years, and I learned a few lessons about the flag in the service. I learned some things that I had not realized before. I learned, for instance, that the flag is not an ornament to be waved, but that it is a living creature.[9]

The living flag is non-textual. A patriot wrote:

> Flying against the sky at the top of a tall pole, whipped by a brisk wind, even a badly designed flag is beautiful. Reproduced in full colour in a book or in a poster, however, even the most sensitively designed flag is dull. The magic seems to be in the very *cloth* of it, the way the material catches and lets go of the breeze.[10]

For having flown in a particular lived battle or touched the casket of the remembered deceased, an individual flag may become an oral memory artifact. Such valuing is always body-based. "You are the only person who deserves to be caretaker of this flag, a flag I love because it represents all that is noble in just one dead soldier," wrote a veteran to presidential candidate Ross Perot.

Written language conceals and denies the body in order to exercise control over it or, more accurately, to give bodies that control texts power over bodies that do not. By comparison to the dramatic and performing body, text is circumspect and constative. If the body is concrete, text is abstract. If the body is particular, text is universalizing. The dialogue between texts and bodies creates honor, purity, authority, and other forms of cultural power.[11] In a modern world the text is the heavy favorite, if never the exclusive winner in this competition. Briefly put, texts master and discipline bodies. Thus, children's bodies are disciplined in school by teachers who represent the authority of the text, but these lessons are imparted in a way that will permit children to discipline untextualized others in their turn. In legislative skirmishes about the flag, champions of the embodied flag, or *flagbody*, jockey for cultural advantage with defenders of the

disembodied text. For now, Congress has placed a higher value on the Bill
of Rights that signifies the cherished text than on the flag that signifies the
cherished body.

Translated into the terms of class analysis, the class that so far has won
the flag debate dictates culture to the class whose real bodies are offered to
the sacrifice of the country, and whose symbolic bodies are cast aside whenever the flag is burned. Flagburning is the symbolic equivalent of desecrat-
ing the bodies of citizens who are sacrificed to the flag. Whether the text
class will permit the profaning of symbols sacred to the class whose bodies
are at risk is the question in the flagburning debate. From the solemn induction of recruits setting off for boot camp to the consecrated remembrance
of those who have fallen, patriotic ritual presents the flag as a symbol of
bodily sacrifice. If all members of a single military unit die in combat, their
regimental colors are retired, for the flag dies when the group does. When
Ernest Ivy Thomas, an original Iwo Jima flagraiser, was killed in action, a
reporter wrote: "I knew Thomas, and this is not an easy story to write. But
one thing helps. From where I sit, I can see the flag over Suribachi."[12] The
sacrificed body is resurrected in the flag.

During the Gulf War, American POWs gazed out from Iraqi broadcasts
with damaged bodies and beaten and bruised faces. On their return, all were
thin, some limped, others walked with crutches. The most visible damage
was suffered by Staff Sergeant Daniel J. Stamaris, Jr., wheeled from the
plane on a flag-draped litter. The wounded soldier and the flag mutually
elaborated one another's sacrificial significance. "As the military band
played the national anthem on the chilly tarmac, he raised himself slightly
from his stretcher and offered a smart salute."[13] This primary association
of the flag with the bloodletting rite that preserves the community makes
American soldiers privileged stewards of the symbol. They hoard the symbolic capital of the flag from those who have not been initiated into the
bodily suffering of war. Non-initiates are said to be unfit to appropriate the
symbolic currency of the flag asserted by those who have become the
suffering body it signifies. Embodying what the flag signifies, initiates claim
the privilege of issuing, by uttering with their bodies, the meaning of the
sign.

A meeting of blood and ink

The flag desecration debate that was ended by the Gulf War played out the
conflict of texts and bodies on the stage of public culture. We will track this
conflict in two television programs that were shown at the height of the
debate. Both originated from network affiliates in Philadelphia. Faithfully

observing media conventions for presenting conflict, both were organized as adversarial encounters. Both programs involved discussions among parties representing different positions in the flagburning debate. One program included the principal author of this book, invited because of controversy surrounding her actions in burning a flag in a college free speech class shortly before the passage of the Flag Protection Act in September, 1989.[14]

That program was shown shortly after the defeat of the proposed flag amendment in the House of Representatives.[15] Additional panelists were a law school professor and civil rights attorney named David Kairys, and Francis Rafferty, a city councilman known for his confrontational style. At the time of the debate, Rafferty had acquired local notoriety for shoving, on camera, the gay co-ordinator of the city's AIDS programs, to whom he was politically opposed. The altercation delighted many in his tough Irish constituency in one of the poorest blue-collar sections in the city. The opening salvo went to Rafferty. He was asked what flagburning "did" to him, as a veteran. It was as though his very person were injured by seeing the flag burned and spat on in footage introducing the program.

MODERATOR: Councilman Rafferty, you are an Army veteran, we just saw several American flags being burned. We even saw one man spit on the flag. What did it do to you to see that?

RAFFERTY: Well, you know it bothers me to see 'em burn, of course. . . . You know they really pick their shots where they burn a flag. I'd like to seen 'em burn a flag outside my office; I'd like to seen 'em burn a flag in South Philly; I'd like to seen 'em burn a flag in front of a Gold Star mother, and let's see how far they get.

For Rafferty flagburning was an assault on the sacrificed body that called for physical retaliation against the body of the flagburner. He focused on what the flag means to a Gold Star mother who has lost a son in combat. "They think it's nothing," he said of flagburners who dishonor the artifactual equivalent of the body that makes the ultimate sacrifice. The true meaning of the flag is known by observing what Gold Star mothers do with it.

When a Gold Star mother . . . gets that flag, you have to watch them. You have to watch what they do with that flag; they cradle that flag like they do a baby, and to them it's a symbol of that son, and when you burn that flag, you're taking another shot at her son, a son whom she'll never see again. It's more than just a flag, it's that baby, that's what it is.

Babies are pure bodies. The strongest of all physical and social bonds are said to exist between mothers and children. Rafferty equated the flag not only with the body, but with the most intimate of all bodies, the child that is made from the mother's bodily sacrifice in childbirth.

Asked to respond, David Kairys shifted the discussion from mother and infant as flagbody equivalents to a disembodied notion of the flag. He tried to strip flagburning of the embodied significance Rafferty had given it by recasting flagburning as one of a number of textually equivalent expressive forms. For Rafferty flags were virtual bodies, and holy bodies at that. For Kairys flags were virtual texts. He compared flagburning to:

when the Islamic world was upset because Salman Rushdie wrote a book that really insulted their religion, we kind of looked at them and mocked them, like, why would they be upset by a book, don't they understand free speech?

Pursuing his point, Kairys offered a textual analogue in the person of Elijah Lovejoy, editor of a nineteenth-century abolitionist newspaper in an Illinois community that favored slavery. In 1837 Lovejoy was murdered by a mob bent on ending his abolitionist editorializing. Kairys compared Lovejoy's beleaguered dissent to the hypothetical South Philadelphia flagburner's. Lovejoy was as much a martyr to the flag as any war veteran, Kairys argued. By this logical sleight of hand he transformed the unpopular and dishonorable flagburner. He equated him first with the unpopular but retrospectively honorable abolitionist, and then with the popular and honorable veteran. Lovejoy's body had been sacrificed for the textual right to express sentiments at least as unpopular in their day as flagburning.

The moderator introduced a different sort of text, pornographic magazines with images and writing associated with dishonorable bodies. At some newsstands, he noted, the body depicted on the cover was concealed so only the title, the textual identity of the magazine, was visible. Such texts were restricted through their association with profane bodies. Rafferty picked this up. The Supreme Court, he said, had ruled that shameful-body texts, or pornography, are subject to community standards. The same "line finally has to be drawn" at flagburning, also associated with profane bodies. Rafferty's line divided his own fighting-ready body from textual elites who countenanced flagburning.

The smarter we get in this country, the less respectful we get . . . She's a professor. As far as I'm concerned she prostituted her position as a teacher.

Rafferty thus equated flagburning, especially by a woman, with prostitution, the most profane activity with which a woman can dishonor her body. Flagburning was one of a category of body behaviors, including pornography, that pollute the body of the community.

For the textual partisan, text is a virtual weapon. Divorced from the body, its effects cannot be physical. The partisan of the body has a different perspective. Body symbols have actual force. The flagburning prostitute who abuses the totem body must therefore answer to the body of the community. In Rafferty's view student witnesses to my flagburning were prevented from a proper bodily response by their need to acquire credentials in the textual world that makes the rules.

She got all those kids out there. They're her kids, they're her students. There ain't too many of them going to take her on . . . They're going to try and get in there and get outta there with the best marks that they possibly can.

In a world of textual power exercised through grades and schoolbooks, students depending on me for textual credentials were not in a position to do the right thing.

I know what I woulda done; I know what I'd'a told my son to do, okay? Now people don't die for something, and . . . Let her use a flag just because she wants to get a point?

Compared to the suffering of real bodies, the abstraction of the textual world is absurd. And I was the bad body, the whore. Rafferty addressed me directly with an insult that left no doubt about my connection to the shameful body:

Why don't you burn your bra? Why don't you burn something that's close to you instead of a flag?"

Pressed by the moderator on whether I had a right to *say* I wanted to burn a flag, Rafferty conceded I did but sensed a trap. "I'm not going to get into a word game with a lawyer and a professor," textual occupations both.

I'm just going to tell you emotionally how I feel about something. Now I can imagine the five of us sitting in the Academy of Music and a beautiful play is going on, an opera or something being sung, and I jump up and say, 'Asshole!' [This body-language was bleeped by the producers.] . . . I'd get thrown out of there, and rightly so I'd get thrown out of there.

Rafferty believed that if he had uttered the name of a profane body part at an occasion defined and dignified by its textual associations (opera must be faithful to its score and libretto; dramas must be faithful to their scripts), its high-brow aficionados would not hesitate to shield their pursuits from linguistic defilement. The body language Rafferty chose for his example specified a taboo bodily orifice. For Rafferty *asshole* was an unsanctifiable, shameful-body word that could never be genteelly associated with text-identified forms such as opera and theater. This quality of honorable-body gentility, honorable partly for being decorously concealed by the text, was the measure of expression worthy of protection in a sensible society.

The discussion moved to the speech/action distinction. This is the jurisprudential notion that greater legal protection is extended to offensive speech than to action that offends. Kairys challenged Rafferty's effort to define speech as language, and action as non-linguistic body behavior. To place flagburning more securely in the category of protected speech, Kairys marshaled an example of expressive conduct from a working-class context despite its obvious textual attributes. He felt sure Rafferty

wouldn't want to ban the right to walk up and down the street with placards, to protest whatever one wants to protest, to carry a picket sign.

As Rafferty was on the verge of protesting that this was not action, but speech, Kairys countered, "That's total conduct, that's not talking."

At a loss to manage this confusion of previously distinct categories, Rafferty regrouped by citing the frustration of those he claimed to represent. He predicted they would express their frustration in bodily terms.

They [Kairys and Marvin] deal with different people than I do. Of course, I'm with the middle class guy, the blue collar guy, and I'm telling you, I hear it every day, man, "I'm up to here, I'm up to here, I'm up to here." And that's all you ever hear and I'm telling you something, man, we're going to make the sixties look like a picnic in the next ten years.

Rafferty complained bitterly about textually credentialed elites who ran the country at the expense of those whose bodies were sacrifice during any war and cast off when their usefulness was past.

The majority does not run this country, the minority runs this country, and that's the intellectuals, that's you professors, that's the liberal wing of this country. You run this country and you run it the way you see fit. There probably ain't fifty guys in Congress who ever served in the services left.

Bitter about planned cuts in veterans' benefits, he added:

You know you're taking a shot at the very people who gave their lives for this country, their lives and limbs, and now, put 'em aside. They served. You know, when we need 'em again, we'll . . . holler, "Go get 'em, guys, anchors aweigh!' and they'll all start joining, the same kids again, and all die again, and we'll just forget about 'em again.

The discussion moved to other things – whether flagburning debates divert the electorate and its leaders from the real business of governing, whether conservatism is consistent with flagburning laws, whether anything is sacred. Though I sought to avoid body–text dichotomies in my own remarks, when Rafferty accused me of burning the flag for publicity, I proffered a textual model as my strongest line of defense:

What I did was legal [sanctioned by authoritative texts] and what I did was in defense of the Bill of Rights. I think Tom Foley said it very well this week when he said, all countries have flags, but only one country has a Bill of Rights.

What is peculiar about this statement is that it reverses the direction of actual cause. The Bill of Rights shields flagburning and not the other way around. Invented in a beleaguered moment, this reversal did convey my underlying textual devotion to the Bill of Rights and my view of it as more imperiled than flagbodies, a proposition elaborated in House Speaker Tom Foley's statement that flags are multiple and fungible, while the Bill of Rights is singular.

In his closing statement, Rafferty repeated his alienation from textual allegiances and his embrace of a body-based perspective:

I'm not going to pretend to be a philosopher or a lawyer or a student of the law, I'll just give you my gut feeling.

Throughout the broadcast Rafferty assumed the defense of the sacred sacrificial body at the heart of the community's identity. Kairys and I rose to defend the sacred text we placed at the heart of the social compact. Rafferty fought to elevate the sacrificial body over text, which represented the interests of a more advantaged class than his constituents. Because of the ability of the textually skilled professional class to set the terms of debate, he had trouble with some of the arguments and found it impossible to reject textual supremacy across the board. He himself believed the text was in some way purer than the shameful body. He argued that high-culture text forms like opera and theater should not be defiled by profaning bodies and could not parry the argument that carrying placards is expressive conduct, since picketing seemed to him more like the honored speech of text than the dishonorable speech of the profane body.

Confronted by a class that values text and displays contempt for the body by tolerating profane flagburning, Rafferty defended the flagbody but accepted other invidious distinctions between texts and bodies, indeed, adopted them eagerly. He was most in a quandary over profane body language. He argued that the epithet *asshole* was properly banned from polite company that regards textual attainment as the epitome of culture. Since *asshole* was valued expression among his own supporters in some contexts, a fact he granted in an off-camera exchange but was uncomfortable defending in company where standards of language were prescribed by notions of schooled text, he was uncertain of its ultimate status. (Though *asshole* is hardly exclusive to the body class, the social style adopted by textual class members may conceal this fact more successfully in public, for example, from Rafferty.)In addition, while lawyers and professors speak on media occasions in ways that signal deference to dictionaries and other artifacts of textually disciplined language, Rafferty's language was colloquial and vernacular and more distanced from textually standardized usage. His was language learned in interaction with bodies outside the institutions of textual socialization we call schools.

For Rafferty, there was the good and sacred body of the flag and the bad and profane body of prostitution, bra-burning, and inappropriate street talk in the hallowed halls of the Academy of Music. His adversaries had the advantage in this contest because their adherence to the superiority of the text over the body in virtually every case was firm. They might dismiss bad-body talk as trivial or repudiate it as bad taste. They did not take the magic of the sacred body seriously enough to revere it, or to fear its contamination or symbolic destruction, or to fend off attacks on it symbolized by flagburning. What they did fear was assaults on the magic of the text, which they believed the Bill of Rights possessed.

Equal invisibility under the letter of the law

The other program was shown on Flag Day, 1990, a week before the flag amendment defeat. This program featured a moderator and two guests: Republican Congressman John Hall Buchanan, Jr., of Alabama, appearing on behalf of the public interest group People for the American Way, and Eugene Smith, Commander of the Sixth District of the American Legion and an African–American. Both men were veterans.[16] Beginning, as in the first program, with a direct link to body sacrifice, the moderator inquired of the American Legion commander:

I ask you, sir, as a veteran of World War II, and China, India, and Burma, who got shot at and who risked your life countless numbers of times, when you see that flag burning, does that offend you personally?

Smith replied, "Personally, it offends me because it means that the sacrifices that many like myself have gone through [have] gone down the drain." If we are truly free, the moderator parried, aren't we free to negate the symbols of freedom? The district commander spoke in reponse of "abusing" freedom, choosing a term of bodily harm.

The congressman recalled joining the Navy. He would "never forget the first time I stood in the uniform of our country and saluted the flag." This memory depicted bodily submission to the sacrificial flag.[17] But then he invoked the familiar text-based hierarchy: "I think the way you salute, truly honor the flag, is to salute the Constitution and the Bill of Rights." The congressman offered criteria for distinguishing unacceptable textual violations from acceptable violations of the body without noticing that they contradicted each other.

It would be unprecedented if the Congress passes an amendment weakening First Amendment protections. It has never happened in two hundred years. It is unprecedented. I think it's unnecessary because once in a while somebody burns a flag as a kind of protest and it must be a very effective kind of protest because it's caused such a hullabaloo.

Whereas a violation of rights guaranteed by the text of the Bill of Rights would be unacceptable even once to the Congressman, he classified occasional violations of the flagbody as the cause merely of hullabaloo, not catastrophe, and not even threatening since they were infrequent. (Enforcing a textual *guarantee* of rights depends, it should be noted, on the state's willingness to use violent bodies concealed behind the text to do it.)If the body is inviolable, this is because the text is more so.

If 99 per cent of the people say that they're going to cut off the commander's head 'cause they don't like the look on his face, and they all agree on it, they still can't cut off his head or otherwise limit his constitutional [textually established] rights, or yours or mine.

Legal text constrains murderous bad-bodies that exercise force in defiance of its dictates. Only bodies commanded by those who command the text are authorized to kill; others are not. To those who believe the flag signifies the body, as the commander does, whoever "kills" the flagbody by burning it murders the community body. Smith argued from body logic for limits on expression.

I can't go down to City Hall and make an obscene act at City Hall because I don't like the way the city administration is operating and not be arrested. I can't do that. Philosophically, I can be against what they're saying, but when I go and make this thing a physical thing, the moment I become violent and physical . . . Burning the flag is violent and physical as much as anything else.

To act against the flag is to act against a virtual body. Flagburning as bodily speech was as unacceptable to the district commander as obscenity, and for the same reason. By comparison, "philosophical" speech was body-distanced and abstract, the very model of acceptable textual speech. To the district commander pornography and flagburning were not speech because they were not text.

The most interesting body issue was raised by a caller who charged that no self-respecting African–American could subscribe to the idea that the flag symbolizes sacrifice in the cause of freedom. The caller argued that freedoms for working men and women had been wrested from the government, not bestowed by it benignly, not least in the case of African-Americans who had served disproportionately in Vietnam in comparison to their numbers in the population. The commander rejected the idea that race, as bodily an issue as there is, had anything to do with flag desecration, though both the white moderator and white congressman felt otherwise. It was this body issue that made flagburning acceptable to the congressman, who otherwise professed to be offended by it:

> Growing up in the bad old days, and I mean bad old days of discrimination and white supremacy and prejudice, I was really impressed through my life with the deep patriotism of the people in the black community but I have to tell you, if I had been a young black American instead of a young white American, I might have been tempted to burn the flag in protest or worse, because my rights had been trampled and those of my people had been trampled, generation after generation, and nobody was doing anything about it in a country that was supposed to be free.

Why did this body argument appeal to the congressman who was otherwise attached to textual values and arguments? In fact, the congressman's example does not grant the importance of the body. It denies it. Race is fundamentally a matter of ascribing significance to body features. It is the text, which is to say the law, that homogenizes bodies and makes them equal and so conceals them. The Congressman was comfortable with an argument that promoted textual (legal) values over bodily (racial) ones. It paralleled Kairys' textual example of Elijah Lovejoy, who offered his body to the idea that differences among persons as a matter of skin color were inferior to textually defined claims of equality.

Even the Supreme Court, as text-bearing an institution as we have by virtue of embodying the dispositive force of the Constitution and Bill of Rights, reproduced the cultural split between the bodily and textual dimensions of flag meaning. "Pregnant with expressive content," Justice Brennan wrote in *Texas* v. *Johnson*, "the flag as readily signifies this Nation as does the combination of letters found in 'America'."[18] Dissenting, Justice Rehnquist argued that "flag burning is the equivalent of an inarticulate grunt or roar that, it seems fair to say, is most likely to be indulged in not to express any particular idea, but to antagonize others."[19] Rehnquist equates flagburning with the profane animal-body, its grunts and roars implicitly contrasted to honorable speech with textualizeable content, the threshold for "ideas."

Shortly after the second flagburning decision, members of the Revolutionary Communist Youth Brigade spread an American flag on a Los Angeles sidewalk. Chanting "Viva La Revolution!" they trampled it and set it afire. Next, they "produced a bloody head from a butchered pig, plopped it on the sidewalk where the flag had been, stuck a tiny flag between the nostrils, and set it afire."[20]

Here the body that cannot be symbolically exchanged with the flag is the defiled pig, traditional Western animal of uncleanliness and baseness of state.[21] The bloody pig stands in sharp contrast to the sacrificed flagbody it mimics. What is sacred is untouchable and unique. To re-present it dishonorably is heresy.

Consider two more examples of the profane body that cannot be exchanged with the flag. After comedienne Roseanne Barr audibly mangled her own ballpark performance of the *Star-Spangled Banner*, the national anthem to the flag, she followed up with profane body gestures – grabbing her crotch and spitting – before an audience of 30,000 at a baseball doubleheader between the San Diego Padres and Cincinnati Reds.[22] Public response was visceral.[23] "I almost upchucked my dinner; it was like burning the flag," fulminated opera star Robert Merrill, former semi-pro pitcher and performer of the anthem for nine presidents.[24]

"Bacchanal at the Beach," a newspaper story in the *Philadelphia Inquirer*, detailed misdeeds by vacation renters in the resort town of Avalon, New Jersey. Residents named seven incidents, not just "minor summertime annoyances," but major offenses. Every one featured profane body behavior, and flagburning was one of them.

- The party with live music so loud people 22 blocks away complained.
- The two men who climbed atop their roof in midday to urinate into a trash can on the ground below.
- The woman and five men who engaged in group sex on their far-from-secluded dock.
- The raucous middle-of-the-night games – soccer, baseball, horseshoes – played right outside neighbors' windows.
- *The group that burned the flag on their front lawn one afternoon* [italics added].
- The man who emerged onto his deck at 4 a.m., naked, yelling to the neighbors to wake up.
- The all-night party that culminated in an alleged gang rape.[25]

Wrapping the body in the flag

Symbolic meanings never exist independently of subjects who use them, but symbolic practice creates a stock of symbols that social subjects may reproduce or modify. In an appealing metaphor, Mark Poster asserts that communicative patterns are "wrapped" in language.[26] We propose that bodies are often wrapped in the flag. More than a suggestive metaphor, this is a systematic practice in fashion, sport, and civic life. Here the sacrificial male body is not usually at issue. The body that is literally and publicly wrapped in the flag is the regenerative female body from which the bountiful American way of life flows. The regenerative flag may be explicitly sexual. The *New York Times*, for example, urged upscale readers readying the flag for the Fourth of July to wash it by hand and "treat it [like lingerie,]" or intimate body clothing, unless it was too worn or dirty, in which case it must be burned "in private."[27] Since commerce is a primary arena of regenerative activity (but requiring the significant sacrifice of money and labor), contemporary representations of the female flagbody are mostly commercial. Neither the explicitly sexual nor the commercial exhausts the stock of regenerative flagbody representations, however.

We have said that regeneration and sacrifice are two sides of the same ritual coin. Besides its sacrificial warrior sons, for example, Greek mythology contains a number of sacrificial maidens who offer themselves to insure victory in war. In these myths, the dressing ritual is central to the funerary rite.[28] The funerary dress is the maidenly peplos, which consists of a large, rectangular piece of fabric folded vertically and hung from the shoulders with a broad overfold. Procedures for folding, draping, and wearing it are presented in great detail. The wrapped female flagbody of American myth is suggestive of the Greek sacrificial peplos. It is the female equivalent of the waving flag the sacrificial soldier carries in our own myth, and that wraps his regenerative casket.

As female flagbodies may be sacrificial, male flagbodies may likewise be regenerative. Flag-wrapped male bodies included the American golfer Payne Stewart, photographed winning the 1990 British Open in a New Glory flag shirt ($57.50) advertised by Sak's Fifth Avenue on Flag Day in the *New York Times*.[29] During its first year of existence no less than 14,000 stars-and-stripes safe-sex condoms were distributed by Old Glory Condom Corporation.[30] Advertising slogans like "Never Flown at Half Mast" connected the flag-wrapped, erect male body part to regeneration rather than sacrifice, the somber message of a flag at half-staff. In a different way, flag-draped caskets convey the unmanned state of the soldier in death. To be unmanned is to be female. Even if female bodies are the most visually regenerative, the sacrificed soldier is ultimately regenerative as well. The body committed to the earth is the seed of future generations. The buried soldier is symbolically (and not actually) regenerative as the male organ wrapped in a condom is symbolically (and not actually) regenerative. The most impressive of regenerative national-civic symbols, the Washington Monument, stands in the capital as a memorial to the Father of His Country, ringed since 1959 by a magic circle of American flags. The arrangement could be construed as a symbolic expression of male and female union to make a nation.[31]

In later chapters, we argue that the totem idea requires both a transcendent deity manifest in a taboo, sacred flagbody, and an immanent deity embodied in an accessible, fertile one. Typologically, the first is male and the second female. Arguments about which of these representations is ritually correct – the regenerative flag comprised by the people, or the sacrificial flag distanced from them – merely rehearse complementary alternatives. Though commercial use of the flagbody first became a subject of desecratory concern during the forging of a high culture of patriotism after the Civil War, custom has long integrated flagwrapping into what passes for American folk culture, which is shopping.[32] Thus the desecration debate provided an occasion for the fashion industry to wrap women in the accessible, regenerative flag.

A $625 hand-knitted wool "Betsy" stole by Ralph Lauren, a flag replica, draped the otherwise nude body of television star Sherilyn Fenn on the July, 1990, cover of *New York* magazine.[33] During the year of the debate, flag bathing suits, shorts, tube tops, socks, bedroom slippers, sheets, scarves, and evening gowns were much in evidence. Ralph Lauren's $300 stars-and-stripes sweater sold out, and three different flag bathing suits at $72 a suit moved briskly.[34] Bloomingdale's Winter, 1990, catalogue featured a reversible wool flag jacket with white stars on a field of navy blue on one side, and red and white stripes on the other, for $279. 98. The most expensive flag couturier was Perry Ellis, with a $2,000 cashmere flag stole.[35] American Express pursued its advertising campaign of famous cardmembers with a photograph of Texas Congresswoman Barbara Jordan clutching a large American flag against her august, which is to say, maternal person.

Porn consumers were treated in the summer of 1990 to posters for the film *Laze*, featuring industry star Victoria Paris nude from the waist up and strategically covering her nipples with small American flags. If anyone objected, there was no press notice. But several months later, the Veterans of Foreign Wars protested indignantly when pop idol Madonna wrapped a bedsheet-sized flag around herself and used it to play peekaboo with erotic lingerie and combat boots in an MTV video campaign, "Rock to Vote."[36] Flanked by two Marine-style male dancers of ambiguous sexual orientation, Madonna promised to give spankings for not voting. Madonna may have been more objectionable to VFW members than Victoria Paris for publicly and defiantly linking the profane and politically divisive message of sexual desire to the flag. Madonna associated the flag with sex, but this was sex for pleasure, unsanctioned by the sacrifice of childbirth and the family, the condition of harmonious community-building fertility.

Cultural propriety distances recreational rather than procreationally dutiful sex from the flag. Refusing this convention may be risque and daring. *Spy* magazine fabricated this pornographic fantasy of the female flagbody by flagburning opponents Senator Joseph Biden and President Bush in which:

The small butane flame licked at her unfurled edge, flickering like a snake's tongue, winking like a lecher, teasing her like the cruelest Rio playboy making cynical sport of a dewey-rich spring-break virgin from Kansas City. Or Dubuque.

And then – at first a barely perceptible flash – it caught. Its petrochemical passion took hold of her being and she was powerless, yielding as it made its way up her lean stripes and toward her deep-blue rectangle. An acrid smell pierced the air. Shamed, she yearned to cry out – and yet, inanimate, she could not. And no law could save her.[37]

Betsy Ross

As every schoolchild knows, the mother of the country is Betsy Ross. In the iconography of American civil religion, she is visited by George Washington, who "calls on the humble seamstress . . . in her tiny home and asks her if she will make the nation's flag, to his design. And Betsy promptly brings forth – from her lap! – the flag, the nation itself."[38]

We come full circle to the Gold Star mother, a modern-day Betsy Ross cradling the flag, her dead son, through whose sacrifice the nation is born again. Like Betsy Ross, the Gold Star mother is emblematic of the sanctifying drama of the American holy family – mother of the country, father of the country, and holy sacrificed child.

During the 1990 election campaign, the Republican candidate for State Senator from the 4th District in Philadelphia distributed a campaign flier that depicted Betsy Ross sewing her flag and weeping over the Democratic candidate. "It makes me want to cry," said Betsy Ross.[39] Accompanying photos depicted the Iwo Jima Marine Memorial, white crosses at the graves of soldiers at Normandy, and a group of protesters torching American flags. The Democratic candidate ran on a pro-choice, gay rights platform. If Betsy Ross is the mother of the American holy family, an exemplar of the heterosexual cycle of regenerative women and sacrificial men, a candidate who threatened those nuclear boundaries would certainly make her weep. Burning the flag, and being pro-choice and in favor of rights for gay men and lesbians, is very much like stepping on your family.

In the holy family of American civil religion Betsy Ross is the legendary first flagmaker. When asked to name the best-known figure from American history after presidents, generals, and statesmen, its citizens pick Betsy Ross.[40] The Betsy Ross House in Philadelphia is a small, two-story rowhouse in the oldest part of the city. Each year thousands of tourists, mostly school children and families, come to see where the flag was born. There is not much to see in the Betsy Ross House that is actually Betsy's. What is thought to have been the parlor where Betsy sewed the flag takes up most of the first floor. A few relics are here, including a thimble found by workmen renovating the house, period scissors and reading glasses. Most surprising is Betsy herself. Or rather a mannequin dressed in period clothes to represent her. With her 1970s fashion model cheekbones and heavy-lidded, seductive gaze, Betsy Ross is slim and glamorous. She is not seated in the straight-backed fashion of primly posed women in paintings from the early national period. She drops one shoulder, her neck curves, her head leans forward to inspect what her arms, each at a different height, hold out gracefully before her. Originally, perhaps she held beach clothes. At the Betsy Ross House, the flag is draped across her arms. What arrests one at the Betsy Ross House Museum is this model of the late twentieth-century female consumer positioned amidst an array of humble period artifacts.

Unlike the museum, the souvenir shop at the Betsy Ross House has nothing shoddy or tentative about it. What Americans do well and comfortably in any situation is shop, and there is much to buy. Here citizens participate in constructing their national identity by purchasing colorful and varied items, including children's books about flag history that constitute a significant patriotic genre because of their socializing impact. Although most scholars doubt the Betsy Ross story, a popular tradition of the body has kept it alive. The Betsy myth is an oral tradition that celebrates the sacrificial maternal body. It models the Annunciation and birth of Christ. It stipulates how women create the nation. Since giving birth is a sacrificial act, and children are the nation, women create the nation in mythic logic by sacrificing their own bodies. In fact, mothers sacrifice twice in this scheme, first bearing children, and then offering them for war. The Betsy Ross myth codes this by portraying Betsy as creating the flag out of her own lap. The nation-child is made from her sacrificial body. The child becomes the sacrificed, or messianic nation-body, the sign of which is the flag.

Whether Betsy Ross sewed the first Stars and Stripes has been a subject of controversy since her grandson George Canby made this claim in 1870. The dispute sets a textual tradition of historical documentation against an oral tradition of popular mythicizing. The enduring popularity of the Betsy myth is a sore point for those who believe the "patriotism that never falters, even at the cannon's mouth" depends on the patriot's fidelity to fact.

This sentiment from the *True Story of the American Flag* in 1908 reflects just this preference for high text over profane, misspeaking bodies:

Statements of such a character, when allowed to go unrefuted, do harm to the history of any people, inasmuch as they encourage others to build "air castles" and purchase old portraits to be palmed off on others as *our* "grandfather" who "fit" in the Revolution, or *our* "grandmother" who carried supplies to the troops at Valley Forge.[41]

Alternatively, such elaborations might be understood as a mythic assimilation of the citizen to the totem, a popular strategy for participating in totem magic. If, by sympathetic and contagious magic transmitted through the bodies of one's own ancestors – the grandfather that fought, the grandmother that carried supplies – one becomes a living blood model of nation-creators, totem identification is complete. The sympathetic remodeling of history in the tale of "our" grandmother is supplemented by the contagious magic of the relic, icon, or other magic emblem of totem forebears.

Skeptical historians miss the significance of this natal legend sown in the fertile post-bellum soil of a country seeking new identifying narratives after the Civil War. The Betsy Ross myth is a memorable creation story passed along as oral tradition. Through Betsy, a living Revolutionary witness, her family to the third generation (which recorded the story), secured an imaginatively intimate connection to the era in which she lived. Her presumed role in the creation of her country transforms her descendants. Betsy emblematizes the Revolutionary generation of "Republican mothers."[42] The nineteenth-century children of these custodians of civic morality implemented the division of gender labor between public and domestic spheres. The Betsy myth sanctifies female occupations such as needlework and child rearing as forms of totem creation, as enthusiastically as it champions public-spirited totem sacrifice for males.

The Betsy myth entered a textual tradition when men began to record it, beginning with Betsy's grandson, George Canby. He claimed to have heard the story of the flag directly from her lips as a child. According to Oliver Parry:

In 1857, when Clarissa Sydney Wilson, the oldest Claypole daughter of Elizabeth Claypole [Betsy Ross] and her successor in business, was retiring from the business and moving from Philadelphia to Fort Madison, Iowa, she gave the subject some thought and requested her nephew, William J. Canby, to transcribe the story at her dictation and as she had often heard her mother tell it, probably even then having in mind a desire to simply perpetuate the story for its interest to the descendants of the maker of the first of our now glorious flag.[43]

These documents include affidavits of oral testimony published by Oliver Randolph Parry in 1870 and 1871 from eight of Betsy's female descendants. Parry presented them in a paper to the Bucks County Historical Society in Doylestown, Pennsylvania, along with a piece of the original pine flooring from the store of the house where Betsy was presumed to have lived and made the first flag. In another affidavit, journalist Charles M. Wallington claimed to have saved this flooring when the original was taken up in 1881. From this relic of the true floor, Wallington made a table top which he covered with a flag.[44] Another male descendant, Betsy's great-great grandson, Edwin Satterthwaite Parry, published the highly romantic *Betsy Ross: Quaker Rebel* in 1930. Invoking the contagious and sympathetic magic of kinship, he proclaimed himself a "Lineal descendant of Betsy Ross" on the title page.[45]

The case against Betsy as the creator of the first American flag is most strongly made by the absence of any mention of her in connection with the flag in Congressional records, Washington's diary or any other Revolutionary documents. There is no proof Washington knew or met her. Given the interest of the young nation in recording so many other aspects of its creation, any significant contact between Betsy and the contractors for the first national standard should have been written down. Betsy herself left no letters or writings. Her world was an oral one. "One's friends, for the most part, lived near at hand, and communication with others was confined largely to visits or to brief messages carried by mutual acquaintances."[46] Betsy was said to have told the story of the first flag "on many occasions to her daughters, nieces, grand-daughters and others. The younger women who helped her in making flags naturally heard it most frequently." But none published it.

As presented by Parry, other details of the story have the ring of oral tradition. Betsy Ross was born in 1752 on a mythically propitious day for a maker of the embodied totem: a holy day, the first day of the week, the first day of the month, the first day of the new year, in the natal city of the nation. She possessed the virtues of a blessed mother, being "bright and winning" and "beautiful as a young woman."[47] Her first husband, John Ross, nephew of a signer of the Declaration, was assistant rector of Christ Church, where George Washington worshipped. Betsy was said to be a folk healer making formulas and compounds for her neighbors.[48] Such body-based, hands-on healing skills express female magic. Betsy was a fine needlewoman and a good housekeeper, a doer of charitable deeds, in every way suitable for the sinless role of flagmother.[49] Her daughter claimed that Washington was often in Betsy's home for friendship and business, and that Betsy had embroidered ruffles for his shirt bosom and cuffs.[50] She is thus placed in intimate relation to Washington's body through needlework, the same bodily endeavor that brings forth the flag. In Parry's account, the father of his country is a man of history and planning who knows his fate and seizes it, while Betsy is unaware of the role she will play.[51] In the traditional portrayal of pregnancy for women, her destiny must be revealed to her, in this case, by the patriarch of the country whose mother she will be.

According to the affidavits, Betsy Ross was visited in 1776 by George Washington, her husband's uncle, Colonel Ross, and Robert Morris, a Quaker financier and shipowner. In most accounts, Washington showed Betsy a design and asked her to create the first national flag. She replied that she did not know if she could do it, but she would try. She then offered her own innovation to the flag proposed by these men of the world. Until she showed them, they did not know a five-pointed star was easier to cut from fabric than a six-pointed one. Washington's visit, an Annunciation scene, is the central event of the myth, the symbolic occasion for regenerative coupling between the mother and father of the country. Edwin Parry claimed it was the focus of Betsy's own memory of the origins of the flag. In a well-known illustration by Charles H. Weisgerber, *Birth of Our Nation's Flag*, exhibited at the Columbian Exposition in 1893, the Annunciation and birth are condensed into a single image. Betsy holds the flag on her lap for presentation to the viewer. Washington stands beside her, accompanied by the wise men George Ross and Robert Morris.

Within the framework of the flag Annunciation, Betsy's statement that she does not know if she can do as Washington asks signifies her symbolic virginity. She has never made a flag before. Just as Joseph does not figure in the Christian Annunciation, Betsy's husband does not figure in the flag Annunciation. A military accident that killed John Ross left the flag's creator without a husband and in a state of childlessness. Betsy's promise to do what is asked of her displays obedience to her ritual duty. Astonishing the great Washington by showing him the utility of a five-pointed star leaves the intellectual creation of the flag to him, but its embodiment and execution are hers. This unity of male form and female substance – Washington's design and Betsy's bringing it to fruition – is the creative paradigm of the sacred.

Frances Yates long ago identified the classic mnemonic structure of oral memory.[52] What is to be recalled is figured in striking and dramatic images situated in architectural places. No image could be more striking than Betsy with the colorful flag on her lap. Memorialized as a national shrine, the Betsy Ross House makes an admirable memory place. Weisgerber, painter of the three wise men, Betsy Ross, and the flag, spearheaded the movement to acquire it for the nation by collecting subscription dimes from thousands of school children.[53] The Betsy myth is an oral mnemonic for a national memory tradition, especially for school children to whom a mother's word is authoritative.

Despite expert skepticism, ordinary citizens embrace the Betsy myth. When one flag scholar challenged its authenticity on a popular television show, he received a flood of indignant letters. One offered as rebuttal a clipping from a pre-World War I scrapbook:

A private in the Revolutionary War when he was told there was no American flag said, "O gee, ain't that fierce? I'll tell the captain."

When the captain heard it he said, "O gee, ain't that fierce? I'll tell General Washington."

When General Washington heard it he said, "O gee, ain't that fierce? I'll tell Betsy Ross."

When Betsy Ross heard it she said, "O gee, ain't that fierce? You hold the baby and I'll make one right away."[54]

This is the logic of the Betsy myth. What the group knows is what its members tell each other, and everything depends on the creative center where the women are. The flag comes from Betsy's body. It is "the baby." The only sacrifice that counts is blood sacrifice. By its means, men defend the totem borders, and women produce the totem center. A tale of female blood sacrifice for the flag is family lore at Annin & Co., the largest and oldest flag manufacturer in the United States. Like the Betsy Ross story, this creation story unfolds in the world of flagmaking as a business endeavor, an expression of the regenerative commerce that reproduces the body of society.

One early visitor to the showroom was a distinguished-looking woman who stunned young [Louis Annin] Ames by stabbing herself in the hand with a diamond brooch. As blood dripped from the wound, she calmly anounced, "I want you to make me a flag this exact shade of red." The customer . . . was Jefferson Davis's widow.[55]

The Confederacy is an important Other in American history. The lifeblood of the post-war Confederate nation was ritually constituted, among other things, in the sacrificial remembrances of grieving women. Whatever the historical facts of this mythic flag creation at the oldest, most famous American flag manufacturer, this tale emblematizes group creation in a totem flag sanctified by female blood sacrifice when men are no longer able to offer themselves.

The Bill of Rights does not fly in the ball park, a world beyond texts, a world of striving sacrificial bodies. In the waving flag, the sacrificed American body reigns supreme. Where the flag is a wrapping for regenerative bodies, the bountiful American way of life is on display. Both flags are variations on a body-referenced symbolism that finds expression in the flagburning debate. In times of social tension, images of the body protect and redefine moral and social boundaries. Defenders of flag desecration laws advance a model of the sacrificial citizen body. Those who argue that flagburning should be legal, even if it shows poor "taste," a concession to body-referenced standards, use models of textual magic to offer a contrasting view of the nation's symbolic foundations.

4

The totem myth:
sacrifice and transformation

We owe God a death.   Shakespeare, *Henry IV*

The flag symbolizes the sacrificed body of the *citizen*. This label has meaning
only in reference to the group that defines it, the *nation*. Blood sacrifice links
the citizen to the nation. It is a ritual in the most profound sense, for it creates
the nation from the flesh of its citizens. The flag is the sign and agent of the
nation formed in blood sacrifice. Still, raising a piece of cloth and calling it
a flag will not declare territory and form groups, at least not territory that
will be respected, or groups that will endure and fight to produce borders.
The power of a flag must be sacrificially established. The point was made by
Vladimir Zhirinovsky, whose challenge to Boris Yeltsin in Russia's first
parliamentary elections caught the attention of the West. Opposing the division of Russia into republics, Zhirinovsky complained that the countries
created by these new flags were abstract symbols only. "They don't understand that you have to pay with blood for this process."[1]

If myth without violence has no power, as Zhirinovsky proposes, violence without myth has no order. Myth and violence fuse in blood sacrifice.
Through a system of group-forming rituals, a myth of blood sacrifice organizes the meaning of violent events after the fact. This retrospective creation–sacrifice story is the *totem myth*. Myth transforms disordered violence
into ordered violence that engenders the group. Key elements include the
transformative violence that creates a border, the flag that signifies this
transformation, and the border so engendered. Group-forming episodes
include the sacrificial crisis that sets in motion a quest for boundaries, the
ritual journey to death's border, the crossing where insiders and outsiders
exchange identities, and the resolution of the crisis. The success of these
episodes depends on a willing sacrifice who keeps the secret that the totem
eats its own to live.

Endlessly re-enacted, the totem myth confers a quality of radiance on all the players in its drama, including the flag, which thus acquires a distinctive aura for celebrants. It becomes potent, "saturated with being," in Mircea Eliade's phrase.[2] The transformed flag sets in motion further actings-out of the totem myth. These confer more radiance on the flag, which creates more occasions for mythic transformation. These may be commemorative or mission-oriented. From time to time they are messianic, for the memory of the nation exhausts itself and must be restored.

What holds society together – blood sacrifice

Our way of ruling is to kill each other, and what shall be the rule if we are not allowed to kill?

                    Representatives of the Swazi nation to Great Britain, 1889[3]

History is what hurts.   Fredric Jameson[4]

Violence is the generative heart of the totem myth, its fuel. Group members yearn for it, though all suggestions of its appeal to morally motivated persons are vehemently denied.[5] Robert Ardrey compares it to a layer of molten magma buried beneath all human topography, forever seeking expression. "To deny its incidence in all human groups – male, female, old, young, the immature – is the most flagrant of discriminatory attitudes." Violence is discriminatory. It sorts group members by transforming them. It classifies Us and Them. Since it carries risks as well as rewards for those it defines, it must be monitored. This is one of the chief functions of patriotism. To group members violence signifies the primitive, the Other at the border. Healthy modern societies are thought to be cohesive without violence, and it is assumed to have no useful role in their maintenance. By contrast, primitive societies are said to practice violence shamelessly. In popular mythology blood sacrifice is a feature of primitive societies, but not our own. We argue that blood sacrifice is our defining feature.

When practitioners of violence surface in spite of everything, they are mythologized as loners and outliers, border-dwellers, primitives visibly different from normal citizens who are strangers to violence. "Civilized" societies overwhelmed by disordering violence (Nazi Germany, Cambodia, Rwanda, and the Balkans come to mind) are described as barbaric and savage. "A civilized country does not resolve conflicts in a manner that causes so much human suffering, death, and destruction," a Swedish diplomat admonished Russians bombing the breakaway province of Chechnya.[6] What we call primitive is that violence from which we seek to distance ourselves.[7] Defined by violence, classified as primitive, the Other is not us.

Zhirinovsky and accomplices were described as "persistent spear carriers of xenophobia, anti-Semitism and, in some cases, outright Nazism" as if these were not thoroughly modern ideologies.[8] While denouncing the borders erected by Nazis and anti-Semites, this speaker does not hesitate to label barbarians and raise the gates against them. Calling others primitive, the labelers purify themselves.

Efforts to portray ourselves as peacemakers break down. Media violence is only the most obvious example. A *New York Times* reader blamed the 1992 Los Angeles riots, an unprecedented episode of civil unrest, on media violence. "All this creates the belief that violence is normal," he wrote.[9] Nothing could be more normal, statistically speaking. In 1991 deaths from firearms in the United States rivaled deaths from motor vehicles. In that year there were 43,536 vehicle-related fatalities and 38,317 deaths from firearms.[10] Since 1980 more than 1,500,000 abortions have been performed each year in the United States. Indeterminate levels of euthanasia take place in medical facilities.[11] In 1991 the United States was also the most criminally violent of industrialized nations. More than two million people were beaten, knifed, shot or otherwise assaulted annually within its borders, about 23,000 of them fatally. Second-place Scotland boasted less than one-fourth the US rate of criminal violence.[12] Even when gun murders are excluded from US figures but included for other countries, "Our stabbing, choking and strangling rate alone puts us in first place in the murder sweepstakes."[13]

Many analysts claim that media violence exaggerates societal violence. George Gerbner, for example, argues that media displays of violence are disproportional to the violence that individual citizens are likely to experience.[14] In relation to violence, however, citizens live not as individuals but within territorial zones defended by legal violence explicitly forbidden to them. Since individuals are not expected to defend themselves against violence, the more relevant measure is the total incidence of violence within specific perimeters patrolled by local police, state police, and national armed forces rather than any particular individual's chance of encountering it. In urban areas, where most Americans live, media *under-represent* violence that occurs within the territorial perimeters of law enforcement. Listening to a police scanner on any day in a big city will easily confirm this. Other incidents escape the attention of law enforcement altogether. This is not to say that media violence is not pervasive. "American television dotes on death, the violent kind," writes a commentator reflecting a widely held view.[15]

The point is that violence is present at every level in the community. It is a ritual preoccupation of popular media for a reason. Analysts argue that it sells, and this accounts for its popularity. But why does it sell? It sells because it presents the central issue that engages enduring groups. Violence is both the greatest threat to their survival and essential to their existence. Violence, defined as the level of physicality necessary to control someone else's behavior, is surely not essential for creating every group.[16] But we are concerned with enduring groups whose members will shed blood in their defense. To join an enduring group is to commit to a system of organized violence. This lesson is difficult and repugnant. Our refusal to recognize the contribution of violence to the creation and maintenance of enduring groups is the totem taboo at work.

The totem myth

Only the dead have seen the end of war.   Plato

Social theorists are interested in borders. For Peter Stallybrass and Allon White, "cultural identity is inseparable from limits, it is always a boundary phenomenon and its order is always constructed around the figures of its territorial edge."[17] The image of society, says Mary Douglas, "has form; it has external boundaries, margins, internal structure. Its outlines contain power to reward conformity and repulse attack. There is energy in its margins and unstructured areas."[18] This energy is violence. Violence is contagious, devouring everything in its path. Only resistance, a border, restrains it. Borders without energy are impotent. Energy without borders is dangerous. Patriotism is a religion of the borders organized around a myth about the violence that begets them. This religion is as necessary to the American nation–state as its standing armies, its police and its administrative apparatus. Something like it is necessary to all groups that strive to be enduring. "The dream of a united Europe . . . is dead," wrote Anthony Lewis about the failure of hopes for a politically United Europe as the Bosnian civil war dragged on. "It died when the European Community refused to act against Serbian aggression – when it would not lift a finger to stop mass racial murder on its own continent. The Community survives, but it is a soulless creature."[19]

The borders that a group will defend with blood ritually produce and reproduce the nation.[20] The nation it produces is the shared memory of sacrifice, it is whatever is the last sacrifice that counts for group members. When the remembered boundaries of a nation are tested in new wars, new memories of sacrifice reconstitute it. The nation re-enacted by new blood sacrifice may be physically coterminous with the old one or present entirely different boundaries. The totem myth is a tale about the relationship of violence to borders. A schematic version goes like this:

Members of the totem group travel to the limits of what is familiar and known. They reach the border, an area of confusion where identities are exchanged between insiders and outsiders, and cross over. The crossing is violent and bloody – sacrificial in a word. This dramatic encounter with death marks the exact border of the community. The act of crossing establishes a clear contrast between who is inside and who is outside the community. Border crossers become outsiders dead to the community. The flag marks the point of their crossing. It is the sign of those who have crossed, of devotees transformed. The community celebrates and reveres its insiders turned outsiders, taking steps lest they come back and punish those who did not cross over. From within the boundaries, the community fears and worships these outsiders it consumes to preserve its life. Some wrestlers with death return, carrying tales of the transformed. These undead feel guilty for not crossing over. The community is joyful, whether at the death of sacrificial outsiders or the return of insiders, it is hard to say. The community welcomes these returning border-crossers back to the fertile center by removing the mark of death they carry. Thus the group reconsolidates itself.

As a narrative of group identity, totem myth is a staple of official and popular culture. It structures our understanding of war and peace and of ourselves as a group. It appears in all media. Its variations are endless. Though no single expression contains all its elements, a classic version appears in a 1943 *Life* news feature describing "Bill the Wisconsin boy," fallen in the Battle of Buna in World War II.[21] In this story the chaos of war becomes the cosmos of a transforming totem journey. Wisconsin, explains this version of the tale, "was where his folks belonged – and his girl." Bill comes from the regenerative female center protected by the totem. "He never considered himself a warrior, exactly." Bill and his buddies travel to New Guinea, a place beyond every familiar border. It takes them a while to recognize the liminality of their new existence. "Their job was to become hunters; to learn the ways of the emerald-green jungle, to become one with the giant trees and palms, the tangled undergrowth, the thick kunai grass higher than a man's head, the bottomless marshes, the mud that oozed up from foxholes and trenches." They have left the clear borders and distinctions of civilization and returned to a primitive state of "vicious Indian warfare." There are, of course, no Indians in Buna, neither native American nor Asian subcontinental. The metaphor is mythic American primitive.

The totem quest for Bill and his buddies is to move outward to a border where they will become outsiders or dead men, who are identical in totem myth. Theirs is an ordeal of ambiguity, a liminal journey. "Bill and his buddies crept and crawled, listened and stalked through what seemed to them a nightmare." The enemy was difficult to identify, "wily as a cat, quiet as a ghost, tenacious, not afraid to die," animal-like, inhuman, conversant with death, the ultimate outsider. All around Bill "were jungle sounds that he had to learn to recognize – animals maybe – or maybe a lurking Jap. And suddenly a twig would snap and Bill would fire – quicker than he could think whether it was friend or foe." Bill has entered a domain where borders and definitions are up for grabs. Animals are non-human; Japs are animals. Animal and human sacrifice are the same; friend and foe are indistinguishable. Both may be dead men. Bill begins to change, to age from his ordeal, to resemble death the outsider. Each morning, "his beard a little longer, his cheeks a little more sunken, he and his buddies would creep on, foot by foot, pushing the Japs toward the invisible sea."

In early December Bill and his buddies learn that others before them have pushed down to the sea, a border. Following these progenitors through hell, Bill approaches the banks of the symbolic river of death. Transformed by the mythic unimaginable "it," he will lie and be resurrected.

The shore down to which he fought his way was a charnel house where the stench of Jap bodies rotting in the tropical sun seemed like the breath of hell. He charged through, emerging onto the smooth white beach, chasing a bunch of Japs, hot and tired and blazing mad. And it was right there that he got it.

He felt a terrible blow on his heart that whirled him around. It knocked him flat on the beach, face down, with his helmet on.

Dying in his warrior's armor, the sign of his death-toucher's status, Bill is at this moment a fully transformed totem sacrifice.

Now comes the resurrection, the metamorphosis into a sleeping child ready to be reborn, to whom the lullabye of "Taps" will be sung at the totem center where Bill's sacrifice and others will be invested with restorative significance.

He lay there while the tide came in, creeping up with soft white waves to cover him – once – twice – maybe three times. He lay with his arms half buried in the clean Papuan sand, his legs drawn up a little, as if in sleep. It was the first rest he had had in a long time. But he would never go back to his girl in the farmlands of Wisconsin.

Sacrifice releases regenerative power. The dead warrior becomes the regenerated child identified by his fetal posture and womb-like covering of water. In fact, he has two roles. Especially if he lies unburied or unsung, he is the restless, dangerous ghost-father pulling future sacrifices, on whom the community's life depends, across the border. In the funeral ritual he will be reassimilated and transformed from a father owed for sacrifice who will need future blood tributes, into a child embodying the renewed life of the community, on whom its future also depends.

The border encloses and defines the generative center. Together they make a nation that may be clearly manifest only in crisis. Croatian journalist and novelist Slavenka Drakulic spoke of her own awareness of patriotism, the ideology of membership in a sacrificial group, before and after armed attacks by Serbians.

> I never asked myself if I was a patriot. I didn't need to, because I was sure I was. I remember as a child sitting on the balcony of our apartment in Split and watching the busy street below, the roofs and distant sea. I felt that all that – the city, the landscape, even clouds – was mine, that it belonged to me and that I was an inseparable part of it. And there was the sweet taste of my language, of words as I said them aloud . . . But, as it happened, I suddenly found myself in a war that defined patriotism for me as well as for everyone around me. And the measure was clear enough. It was readiness to sacrifice oneself in the name of patriotism: *dulce et decorum est pro patria mori.*[22]

The unaware patriot, the child, is initially undifferentiated from a regenerative maternal center. Challenge awakens a need for definition and borders. To establish a border that defines the center, this passage suggests, some citizens must separate and die. Death creates a border. This is why it is honorable and sweet to die for one's country.

The semiotics of the physical flag elaborate a drama of male sacrifice and female regeneration. In its male aspects the flag on its pole sits at the outermost point of its staff. This is a border, the point of crossover from human to divine, from profane to sacred, from center to periphery. The flag soldiers carry into battle signifies their willingness to go to the border and die. This flag functions like the Christian cross that also stands at the border between life and death and also signifies sacrificial willingness, and recalls the origins of European nation–states within the sacrificial system of Christianity. The myth of the sacrificed Christ who dies for all men makes every sacrificed soldier a remodeled Christ dying to redeem his countrymen. Every soldier becomes a redemptive sacred figure to subsequent generations of celebrants.

The flag that marks the border is also rooted in the regenerative center of the cosmos. It is attached to an *axis mundi*, a flagstaff, a tree of life like the cross. The victorious flag raised on its male staff is joined to the female earth. Like the traditional quincunx, an ancient figure, the flag marks boundary and center, male and female elements of the cosmos.[23] Just as every insider is a sacrificial outsider in the making, just as every outsider may be no different from us than insiders are, the flag is also doubly coded. It is center and border, now one, now the other. What keeps killing organized is a clear border. Borders allocate killing authority. Moments of greatest uncertainty about killing authority are marked by the greatest show of flags, when groups are in doubt about their identity. Flags massed at the border focus attention on competing claims for killing authority and

4.1 Totem flag marks border that transforms willing sacrifices. Korean War.

indicate that sacrifice to re-impose authority is imminent. When these claims are resolved, flags migrate to the center.

The totem secret

No beast [was] offered to the gods which was not too holy to be slain and eaten without a religious purpose, and without the consent and active participation of the whole clan.   Robertson Smith[24]

We depart from Durkheim's theory of the totem at three points. First, we assert that archaicness and modernity have no bearing on whether social systems are totemic. Durkheim regards totemism as archaic, though he sees totem residues in modern life. Second, we argue that violence unifies enduring groups. For Durkheim groups are held together by sentiments of solidarity. He does not say how these sentiments are forged, but only that it is taboo to challenge the group's agreement to be a group. We say killing agreements hold the group together. A strong group is one with a widely shared consensus about who may kill and be killed. Organizing, not eradicating violence is the task of group survival. This would have seemed odd to Durkheim, who denied any essential role to violence in traditional societies.

Durkheim reverses the usual equation of violence with the primitive, suggesting that only more advanced cults spill the blood of sacrificial victims and only occasionally. Though he asserts that sacrifice creates society, violent sacrifice is no more than a special case to which he devotes scant attention. We say the knowledge that only the totem may kill its own is what is taboo for group members. When the totem goes to war, its grievance is not that its members have been killed or are in danger, *but that a power besides itself has killed or threatens to kill them.* For the group to cohere, acts of totem violence against its own must be rendered unknowable. What is thus set apart is the essence of the sacred. The violent specificity of the totem secret is missing entirely from the Durkheimian scheme. It constitutes our third point of departure.

Violence surrounds us. Without boundaries to contain it, it is everywhere undifferentiated. There is no end to it, no place it cannot come. Slavenka Drakulic describes the horror of unorganized violence, "that wipes out all personal differences and feeds on hatred for the 'other.' That feeds on differences of all kinds. That asks for more sacrifice and more blood, that makes the war go on."[25] For killing to stop, some must submit to others. Whoever is able to seize and enforce sole killing authority is the totem. Organized killing power must be asymmetrical. Devotees must bow down to it. It is set apart and has the power to set apart others for sacrifice. Organized violence is focused violence. The totem re-directs killing from the regenerative center of the group to its borders. Violence is no longer everywhere the same. The difference between where violence is and is not is a border. It is what police call "the thin blue line . . . between society and chaos" in describing themselves both as totem agents and border dwellers.[26] Killing creates death, which has this quality: more than anything else, it demarcates insiders and outsiders. In the system of cultural distinctions that constitutes a group, life and death are ultimate distinctions visited on bodies, the raw material of groups. A dead man is not a member of the group. Violence removes members from the group by causing their death. Thus it is forbidden to them. Violence is the condition of border dwellers, both those who suffer killing authority and those who are ritually authorized to implement it. War offers the most dramatic chance for groups to exercise the assymetrical killing power that brings violence to an end. Consider this Gulf War example of symmetrical claims to killing power:

"You know that singer, Sinead O'Connor, says they're murderers and we're murderers," said [Reuben] Parmer, a 32–year-old electrician from nearby Jonesboro [Georgia], referring to the iconoclastic musician. "But I don't think that's so . . . I believe you've got to draw the line somewhere, and this is the place we should draw it."[27]

The totem stands ready to kill any group member who kills another. But naked retribution by the totem against its own would show that violence exists within the group. The totem therefore creates a sacrificial class to absorb the anger group members feel toward one another and sends it to the border. Sacrificial designates go willingly, becoming murderers so we can kill them more easily. The totem sends them to die but it is not their visible executioner. Violating the totem killing prerogative, the *enemy* executes the members of the sacrificial class. To re-establish its imperiled killing prerogative, the totem must send more group members to die. Death is pushed to the border. Life at the center is purged of murderousness. The totem kills its own to expel violence and create a state of difference, an asymmetrical killing power that projects violence outward.

The regenerative center is the true killer of its children. If this knowledge is exposed, the killing agreement will be in doubt. The totem will be unable to project violence outward, threatening chaos within. Those who have been to the border know the secret. "We knew that we were considered to be expendable," recalled a participant in the D-Day invasion of June 6, 1944. "That was the price of doing it . . . I didn't tell my mother I wasn't coming home, but I knew I wasn't coming home."[28] Because they have touched death, sacrificial designates cannot return to the center without special rituals of reinstatement. These insiders turned outsiders must cast off the knowledge of who sent them to die. They forswear revenge and refuse to tell what they know. If they agree, they are reincorporated. They do not disturb the joyous unity of the group that has killed its children.

Death is not the only difference that sorts groups. Body features, clothes, cuisines, kinship, and beliefs distinguish them. So do language, custom, territory, and morals. Differences that sustain groups are constructed as matters of life and death in a classificatory crisis. Detached from death, differences are negotiable. They are more or less great, more or less important, more or less clear. Death is the definitive boundary. It distinguishes who submits from who does not.[29] We recast René Girard's account of how violence escalates as follows. Disputants reject a killing arrangement that has kept borders in place. If competing claims for territory, respect, or privilege begin a dispute, these will quickly be re-focused on killing power. Each side claims the right to use force against whomever stakes a claim to what it desires. The real object of struggle is the right to kill the challenger. Both sides desire it. Neither will submit. To use Jesse Jackson's term for those who foment ethnic conflict, they are "matchmakers of hatred."[30]

Matchmakers exist in a state of lawlessness in which the possession of legitimate killing power is up for grabs. At such times group members may be unable to discriminate borders confidently. In the months before the assassination of Prime Minister Yitzhak Rabin, placards featuring the Israeli leader wearing Arab headdress or an SS uniform began to appear at domestic political rallies. Draping Rabin in the garments of the historic enemies of the Jewish nation reflected uncertainty about borders. It posed the defining question of all groups: Are we Us, or are we Them? The group whose killing authority we do not question is the group to which we belong.

The willing sacrifice

What makes the flag on the mast to wave? Courage!

Cowardly Lion, *Wizard of Oz*

I regret that I have but one life to give for my country.   Nathan Hale

A group-defining rule is that insiders under totem protection may not be killed. During a sacrificial crisis this rule is ritually inverted.[31] This is how the group signals itself that it faces a crisis. The dynamics of sacrifice, or insider death, are as follows. Insiders consent to leave the group, which colludes in their execution. "Uncle Sam wants you!" goes the famous recruiting slogan in which Uncle Sam stands for the nation calling its sons to death, ritually transforming them. The selection of the sacrificial hero, the insider who agrees to become an outsider, is a key episode in the totem myth, since a willing sacrifice keeps the totem secret. In American patriotic myth, individualism produces the sacrificial hero. The myth of individualism helps enforce the totem secret by denying the presence and interest of the group, but *individuals* receive this label only in relation to a group from which they have separated. Parables of individualism explain how the group is advantaged by its fearless nonconformists. To defy convention, as individualists do, is to step across the border. Separation is a sacrificial move. A sign of submission, it designates the holy. The lonely hero volunteers to bear sacrificial burdens for the group. The flag he carries signifies his willingness to be expelled from the group, to cross the border. Guilt is a condition of resistance to being pulled across the border, a recognition by insiders that they are called and do not wish to leave the group. Since the dead are all the same, violence makes all the living guilty. They are reluctant to cross the border. They are responsible for expelling those who do.

During the presidential contest between George Bush, a veteran of the most popular American war of the twentieth century, and Bill Clinton, a Vietnam draft dodger, campaign talk focused on whether the good sons were those who were willing to sacrifice in Vietnam or those who were not. The discussion did not address whether the fathers were good fathers to send the sons to a bad war. Only the willingness of the sons to die could be publicly examined. The taboo discussion was the fathers' willingness to sacrifice them. Clinton's claim that his behavior was ordinary among his contemporaries is the guilty logic of the fertile center. What death-touchers do is always extraordinary. As Eliade says of Abraham, who was commanded to sacrifice Isaac,

He does not understand why the sacrifice is demanded of him; nevertheless he performs it because it was the lord who demanded it. By this act, which is apparently absurd, Abraham initiates a new religious experience, faith.[32]

In the words of a disgruntled veteran Vietnam was a "folly." But ritual duty trumps even a bad cause.

Those who joined the service made the choice and sacrificed for our country. Draft resisters who went into jail or exile likewise made the choice and sacrificed for their convictions. But those privileged children who faked a "calling" to exempted professions, or got daddy's doctor or lawyer to pull strings, or defrauded the draft board and ducked the choice, spurned all sacrifice and put Honor last on their list of priorities.[33]

Boys become men by touching death. Those who refuse belong to the regenerative class of children. The willing sacrifice is unnatural, a social exception. This makes him god as well as man. In a speech to Israelis within hours of Yitzhak Rabin's assassination, acting Prime Minister Shimon Peres described the normally dour Israeli leader in the language of willing sacrifice. He depicted the prime minister's final day as exceptional, even magical:

It was a happy day in his life, probably the happiest day in his life. We spent the whole evening together; never did I see him more happy, more excited, more complete with himself.[34]

A willing sacrifice is happy in his fate. The messianic sacrifice of the insider-turned-outsider is a sacred mystery, unimaginable and unknowable because it involves leaving the group, which is death. Sergeant Edward Swanson of Houston, disappointed by the lack of opportunities for glory in the Gulf War, measured himself against the sacrifice symbolized by the flag: "I thought it would be a chance to find out my true colors. I am glad there were so few casualties, but I would have liked a little more resistance."[35] Resistance is a border. The young men are willing. They want to know what it is to go to the border and touch death. Observing young soldiers leaving for the Gulf, an Army infantryman who had lost half a leg in Vietnam modeled those who modeled him: "You're seeing yourself in their faces, and you know the horrors of what's about to happen to them."[36] They will be transformed by touching death.

The post-World War II Western film classic *Shane* (1953) explores the fate of the willing sacrifice.[37] A stranger rides in from nowhere. In a gun duel he dispatches a villain who has killed totem insiders, settlers who represent the fertile center and an end to the border-crossing drifter's life that Shane embodies. In a final speech he tells the young boy who idolizes him why he cannot stay. "There's no living with a killing, there's no going back," he says, a wandering spirit transformed by death-touching. Generally interpreted as a film about the end of frontier or border life, *Shane* is an allegory about the end of World War II, about those who are lost and cannot return. Border life is the life of the sacrificial class. The boy notices Shane's wound, the mark of the insider turned outsider, the mark of death. "Right, wrong, it's a brand, a brand sticks with you." The dead are not right or wrong, but all the same. Shane reassures the boy that he is beyond any notion of death mattering. He is willing. The totem-father-to-be gives his ghostly charge to the young sacrifice-in-training who still lives at the regenerative center. "You go home to your mother and father and grow up strong and straight, and Joey, take care of them, both of them." Joey's body will model the flag held high, the sign of willing sacrifice.

They Were Expendable (1945), directed by John Ford, disguises the totem secret in its ritualized account of the American surrender of Bataan in World War II.[38] As Bataan falls, MacArthur and his generals, totem sacrificers, are dispatched to safety. MacArthur's men hold him in religious awe. In the closing scene enlisted men abandoned by their own army march along the surf of Bataan, a border. All hope of rescue is gone. They gaze devotedly after the plane that carries their departing officers. As the plane flies toward sunset, men's voices sing the *Battle Hymn of the Republic*, and MacArthur's messianic pledge, "I will return," flashes across the screen. It is not likely to be these officers who will meet God the soonest, as this Valhallian scene suggests. The true sacrificial offering is these enlisted men. The totem secret is kept. The ending is ritually proper.

What René Girard calls the peril to distinctions or classifying differences, precipitates the search for a sacrificial scapegoat that will be thrust outside in a violence-expelling, border-defining gesture. Totem violation stirs devotees to identify their substance with the totem and offer it to repair the breached taboo. Believers willingly exchange themselves for the totem. Drawing off totem peril, or death, with spells of imitative and contagious magic, they embody it. A story about how totem challenge may inspire perfect sacrifice explains how the peril to classifying differences originates and is resolved:

Craig Mills was in 12th grade at Washington High School in the northeast when the Iran hostage crisis began.

It seemed to this boy, who loved John Wayne, who was always pushing himself to excel at everything he did, that other countries were always trying to humiliate his country.

They burned the flag. They burned the president in effigy.

"We both just wanted to bomb the hell out of Iran," said Mills' longtime friend Saul Ravitch. "That was where it sort of crystallized, him going into the Marines."[39]

To desecrate the totem is to claim its killing power, to set in motion a contest of escalating menace. As each side mimics the other, the killing rules that separate them are imperiled. Sacrifice alone will show who possesses authentic killing power. If no sacrifice consents to cross the border and resolve the peril to distinctions, the totem may die. In this story the willing sacrifice is the boy who loved John Wayne, the mythic, heroic outsider. The boy who was always "pushing himself to excel at everything he did" is willing and perfect, a hero in the making. He has already practiced separating from the group in preparation for border crossing.

Ritual displays of willing sacrifice are standard in media accounts of totem deaths. Two Philadelphia firefighters killed on the job were portrayed as eagerly engaged in border missions:

John J. Redmond and Vencent Acey always wanted to be the first in, and they never wavered, fire officials said. When they strode onto the fire scene, they gave what was needed to put out the blaze, and their bravery helped keep losses down.[40]

Sacrifice preserves the group. Like flags that remain upright and rally soldiers, firefighters face death and do not flinch. A member of the Heavy Rescue unit, Acey was a death-touching outsider, "a Green Beret of firefighting." His spiritual preparation was unceasing:

"He was dedicated to the training. He was always studying, reading. He was preparing himself for promotions. It was a way of life for Vence," [Acey's commander] said. "It wasn't a job."[41]

He added, "When something like this happens, it reminds us of our own mortality. All we can do is serve." Only our deaths avenge those who have given everything. "You break down society into givers and takers," explained a veteran firefighter, "and the Fire Department are all givers."[42] The Fire Marshal's Office described the totem journey: "They love what they do and go the distance." A willing sacrifice reflected:

"I know it sounds strange, but I look forward to each fire," said Firefighter Bill Johnson, a 17–year-veteran. He added that the moment in training class when the instructor issued his warning was "also the moment when I knew this was the job for me," adding, "and I never looked back."[43]

Intimates of the victim are ritually bound to certify his willingness to die. Standing in for both victim and society, the family by blood or ordeal testifies that the victim bears no grudge in death. No blood vegeance will be sought on his behalf. No blame attaches to the group. When the deaths of eighteen Army Rangers in Somalia threatened to expose the totem secret, the *New York Times* interviewed their families. A victim's brother was reassuring:

"Ever since childhood, he wanted to do it," Mr. Pilla said. "He was always playing Army in the woods as a little kid. He was interested then in strategies and tactics. He liked to push himself as far as he could go."[44]

The story foreshadows the journey of the willing sacrifice to the border of death, as far as he can go. Corporal Jamie Smith's father said his son "wanted that special feeling inside him that he did something others didn't do."[45] A retired soldier, the father knew that whole categories of human beings are systematically reserved for sacrifice. "Was it worth it?" he asked himself, inquiring whether the ritual had worked properly. His answer was totemic. "It's not really a soldier's position to decide whether or not it's worth it." Sacrificial willingness assuages the guilt of the community that sends soldiers to die by denying its killing agency. Jamie's father felt "sadness – absolutely," he said. "But I am not bitter. It was my son's deci-sion. I could not have stopped him."[46] The son was willing. The father is blameless. The ritual is complete.

In a sacrificial crisis the totem compels reluctant insiders to become out-siders. Shoah survivor Elie Weisel describes the moment when his father was beaten at Auschwitz. That violent desecration created a sacrificial crisis for the son. This transcript is from a televised interview.

BILL MOYERS: And can you remember what you were thinking as you saw your father beaten?

ELIE WEISEL: It pains me to this day because of [my failure to] "honor thy father". I remember I felt like running to that man, that couple who beat him up, and throw myself either at his feet for mercy, or beat him up. But I didn't do it.

BM: Why?

EW: I was afraid . . . of being beaten or killed . . . I felt fear, and I felt guilt. To this day I feel guilt . . . My father all of a sudden felt he had to go to the toilet, and there was a couple and he went to the couple, and said, "Can I go to the toilet." And all of us, hundreds and hundreds of people were there, lined up. And the couple measured him up with this look and gave him simply a slap in the face, only one, and my father fell to the ground. It lasted a second. My father got up and came back. And during that second, I staged my own trial. I accused myself, I defended myself, and I pronounced the verdict on myself.

BM: Guilty?

EW: Guilty.

BM: Of?

EW: Of not behaving as a son should have.[47]

The father embodies the totem. Violence against him breaches the totem taboo. The command to re-establish boundary protection precipitates sacrificial crisis. It presents the morally equal alternatives of self-sacrifice and killing the outsider who desecrates the totem. Failing to obey the totem imperative, Wiesel refuses to die. He cannot kill the desecrator without sacrificing himself, which he is unwilling to do. Thus his totem fails, and he becomes an outsider in spite of himself. He is forever guilty.

Creating enemies

> It was my will that the whole youth of Paris should arrive at the front covered with blood which would guarantee their fidelity. I wished to put a river of blood between them and the enemy.
>
> Danton to the future Louis XVIII[48]

Girard claims the hostility of every group member threatens to dissolve the group. The real source of aggrieved feelings is a brother. By focusing group violence on the *savior* and the *scapegoat*, our translation of Girard's notions of surrogate and ritual victims, the group discharges these impulses. Though we set out to kill the scapegoat, the enemy beyond the border, only the savior's death makes the ritual work. "It's always the good people that this happens to," a firefighter lamented for a lost comrade. "It's true what they say – only the good die young."[49] A minister eulogized a pilot killed by terrorists in Dhahran by comparing him to "another young man in his thirties who touched many lives and died young." The guilt we feel about the killing we cannot admit to reconsolidates the group. The surrogate victim, the savior, is the son we expel into death. The ritual victim, the scapegoat, makes our anger and killing acceptable and disguises its real target. Our rage at the scapegoat provides a pretext to kill the savior. With the death of enough sons, the group finds relief from internecine tensions. These will build again, for the savior son becomes in death the demanding totem father who calls for more blood and more sons. The group will need more willing sacrifices on whom to vent its anger. New victims will be expelled along with the burden of group violence they carry. If not, the group will perish, a casualty of internal disunity. "We can crane our necks and peer across the oceans for as long as we please in search of a threat to America," observes commentator Bob Herbert, "but the gravest threat, without a doubt is the epidemic of murderous violence here at home."[50]

The manufacture of enemies takes place with or without a credible external threat. Ethnic combat in Rwanda and Yugoslavia occurred among people who had co-existed peaceably for years: "Until Yugoslavia broke apart, Croats and Muslims reportedly lived easily with Serbs here . . . They were work mates, husbands and wives, and students at the single high school."[51] In a study of four wars and a near war, historian Donald Kagan asserts how small a role "considerations of practical utility and material gain, and even ambition for power itself, play in bringing on wars and how often some aspect of honor is decisive."[52] Honor is totem code for ritually satisfying or group-ordering death. In the quest for a foe upon whom to lavish our hostility we may choose among all the dangers in the world. Some are more useful than others for disguising our motives. For example, the invasion of Pearl Harbor provided Americans with one of the most unifying enemies in their history since a large number of dramatic deaths unauthorized by the totem created an urgent need for ritually re-ordering disordered death. Does this mean group threats are never objective? Perceptions of the enemy are rarely objective in any condition, and more is always at stake for group identity than the simple existence of a threatening foe. Still, the more credible the threat, the more completely our motives are concealed, the more blood we can demand, the more unifying the ritual.

The totem secret demands that we must pose as unwilling killers. Our side must not shoot first. Whoever does is no sacrifice but an outlaw, a violator of totem rules. It is not we who want the blood of our sons. The enemy causes the sacrifice. Violence exists because of the Other at the border and not because of us. Even the claim that insider lives are sacrificed to repel the enemy is counterfactual. "Is this worth dying for?" the *New York Times* asked on the eve of the Gulf War.[53] Dead men do not repel enemy outsiders. Only live ones do. What accounts for the patriotic misspeaking that some men die to make others *free*, the totem code word for group membership? The demand for insider death is the irrational terrifying heart of the sacrificial crisis, its dark secret. We offer our children to repel violence at the borders where outsiders and vengeful dead fathers are.

As dangerous and frightening as the enemy, the dead ancestors demand that the sons march to avenge their deaths. Exhorting the graduates of West Point to their border calling, General Douglas MacArthur declared, "The long grey line has never failed us. Were you to do so, a million ghosts in olive drab, in brown khaki, in blue and grey, would rise from their white crosses, thundering those magic words: Duty, honor, country."[54] This ghostly spell is totem myth condensed, a mnemonic for soldier sacrifice. Duty is the ritual journey to the border. Honor is transformation in sacrificial death. Country is the border that death defines. Ancestors and enemies are outsiders. Because we kill them, both demand blood. Because of them, death comes to our group and so defines us.

Effective sacrifice requires that the scapegoat who offers the pretext for killing our own must resemble the real target of vengeance, the members of our own community. This resemblance must not be so close that we start to kill those from whom we seek to divert violence. In 1943 *Life* published an account of Japanese popular theater to explain the psychology of the enemy to American readers. The traits attributed to these ritual victims resemble American soldiers in every respect. The Japanese are depicted as loyal, brave, willing to fight to the death, regarding death in the service of their own totem as honorable, and possessed of a popular culture filled with heroic violence.

Their behavior is so different from our own that Americans are apt to dismiss them simply as being funny. But they are more than just funny. Their military behavior in this war has revealed a cold-blooded ruthlessness, not only toward their enemy but also toward themselves, that has shocked us. Their blind loyalty to their superiors seems to be matched only by their stubborn fanaticism in the face of death. The legend has grown that they will commit mass suicide rather than be taken prisoner.

Such unfunny conduct in battle is really part and parcel of the over-all character of the Japanese people and not just a sudden manifestation of inordinate courage

4.2 World War II totem chieftain General George C. Marshall flanked by flags and totem ancestor, General John J. Pershing.

by their soldiers. For centuries these people have been indoctrinated to regard death as an honorable estate – a final ceremony which achieves glorious results here and hereafter . . . Japanese culture is packed with this age-old concept of violent death, and nowhere is it exhibited in more gory detail than in the traditional Japanese theater. To an American who understands Japan's ideals and philosophy as revealed on its native stage, the action of Jap soldiers on Guadalcanal or Attu becomes considerably more comprehensible.[55]

Beneath a rhetoric of disclaimer, the Japanese stand accused of being like Americans. This is what makes their deaths ritually useful. We have observed that violence is precipitated by attaching life and death to attributes that groups are seen to share equally. Equality claims also make it possible more easily to transfer our angry impulses from group members to a suitable scapegoat, a ritual victim.

The best guarantor of the totem secret is the enemy. It does no good for a soldier to go up to the border and not cross over. In the liminal fog of battle the outsider is an enemy brother who pulls the insider over. Because of him the group may deny the totem secret while acting according to its dictates. "We Americans will not forget that when we speak together, when we act together, when we pray together, the enemy trembles and the walls come tumbling down," a returning prisoner of war declared.[56] Together we place our own in harm's way. It was said that green troops did well under General George S. Patton because they feared Patton behind them more than the Germans in front of them.[57] What willing sacrifices love about their enemies and their fathers is that both make them men; their enemies by pulling them across the border, their fathers by pushing them.

Insiders and outsiders meet at the border, a liminal zone where identities are confused, and one side becomes the other in an instant. Scapegoats and saviors may discover they are all sacrificial outsiders, all dead men-to-be. "The problem is you can't tell the bad guys from the good guys," Corporal Jamie Smith wrote from Somalia just before his death in a firefight.[58] An Iwo Jima veteran recalled fighting there. "It was like standing in the cauldron of hell, performing an act of total self-destruction, killing your brother."[59] Soldiers know the totem secret. When they return they must be stripped of it and ritually reincorporated.

The secret is always at risk

If any question why we died,
Tell them, because our fathers lied.   Rudyard Kipling

When external threats recede, the sacrifice of excess males on the battlefield may become the slaughter of excess males in the streets of the city. New strangers must be invented to create boundary-defining sacrifice. "It is when social space can no longer be defined and guarded that terror appears at the door," Robert Ardrey writes.[60] "I think they should stop worrying about Bosnia," said a Chicago postal worker in the summer of 1994. "If they want to send the troops somewhere, they should send them to the South Side of Chicago."[61] All killing puts the totem secret at risk, but some conditions are more perilous than others. The secret is especially at risk in the absence of unanimous victimage. The cry raised against Lyndon Johnson during the Vietnam War, "Hey, Hey, LBJ! How many kids did you kill today?" was generally taken to refer to Vietnamese children but did not exclude the children of America. When protesters at a Gulf War Welcome Home parade carried signs reading, "Killing people doesn't make me proud," onlookers shouted, "Shoot them!"[62] As Boris Yeltsin struggled to keep the Russian confederation together with an unpopular military action against the breakaway province of Chechnya, Moscow's largest daily visually portrayed the totem secret:

Editors superimposed a photograph of a grinning Defense Minister Pavel S. Grachev over another of dead Russian soldiers laid out on the snow. The doctored photo makes it look as if the general's right foot is treading on one corpse.[63]

During the vice-presidential campaign of 1976, candidate Bob Dole famously remarked, "I figured it up the other day. If we added up the killed and wounded in the Democrat wars in this century, it'd be about 1. 6 million Americans, enough to fill the city of Detroit."[64] His opponent Walter Mondale replied, "I think Senator Dole has richly earned his reputation as a hatchet man tonight." Instead of charging the murder of America's children to its enemies, Dole charged it to American citizens. He did not articulate the greatest taboo, that the entire group wishes for the death of its own. But blaming one political party threatened the secret enough for Mondale to shift the category of executioner away from the collective responsibility Dole hinted at, and back to Dole the "hatchet man."

The risk to the secret increases when the totem displays pleasure in killing. During the 1989 invasion of Panama the secret briefly threatened to show itself this way:

During a news conference following the invasion of Panama, President Bush was deeply embarrassed when pictures of coffins arriving at Dover Air Force Base were broadcast live, on a split screen, while Mr. Bush could be seen laughing with reporters.[65]

Finally, the secret is especially at risk when our side shoots first. In 1995 the State of Texas executed Jesse Dewayne Jacobs on a legal technicality for a murder both prosecution and defense agreed he did not commit. Such an occurrence threatens our sense of ourselves as reluctant executioners. We must be able to differentiate our group from primitives, who are said to practice violence shamelessly. The *New York Times* editorialized:

A state that calls itself civilized yet elects to use the death penalty must do all it can to prevent the execution of the innocent. *Otherwise its people cannot for long live with themselves.*[66] [italics added]

Those who die by the totem's hand must be clearly marked off to preserve a clear boundary between insiders and outsiders. If there is no boundary members could become unrestrained killers, primitives, to one another and place the group at risk.

The most controversial election commercial in American history threatened the totem secret on all three counts. Seeking to stoke fears that 1964 Republican presidential candidate Barry Goldwater would wield nuclear weapons recklessly, the Democrats aired a commercial of a young girl in a blooming meadow picking daisy petals, a regenerative vision of the fertile center. She counts haphazardly and not always accurately from one to ten, that is, childishly, toward the future. The camera zooms in on her right eye as she looks up, alarmed, at the count of "nine." An adult male voice begins counting backward with harsh precision in an easily recognized countdown to a missile firing. At zero there is an audible explosion and the image of a mushroom cloud. The buried sound of the explosion is the bed for President Johnson's voice:

These are the stakes. To make a world in which all of God's children can live. Or to go into the dark. We must either love each other, or we must die.[67]

The commercial addresses our greatest fear, the death of the group. The totem instructs us that hostility can only be repaired by sacrifice. This is the totem secret, thinly veiled. But exactly who needs to love each other? In the context of the nuclear threat, surely the reference is to the Soviets and Americans. But the countdown is in English! The conclusion that our side has launched death and destruction is inescapable; the victims, our own young. The Soviets are nowhere to be seen. If Barry Goldwater wants to kill our own, he must be thrust to the border and denied the presidency. The commercial outraged Republicans. President Johnson quickly ordered it withdrawn. How did it threaten the secret? It implied that President Barry Goldwater would relish killing, the victimage it proposed was not unanimous, and our side appeared to shoot first.

The totem leader

Upon the King! Let us our lives, our souls, our debts, our careful wives,
our children and our sins lay on the King!   Shakespeare, *Henry V*

Grandfather, you were the pillar of fire in front of the camp and now we
are left in the camp alone in the dark; and we are so cold and so sad.
                    Noa Ben Artzi Philosof, at the funeral of Yitzhak Rabin[68]

For Durkheim the totem is no illusion. Devotees, he felt, would not embrace with their lives empty symbols lacking transformative power. We agree that the devotee does not deceive himself. The power he feels is truthful and real. It is society. But how can devotees believe society is real unless they see it act? They must have proof of its existence, a visible body. When Jesus allowed his disciples to place their hands in his wounds, the Word of God was shown to be incarnate in the son beyond all doubt. The President is the national totem incarnate. His is the one office that can never be empty, even for a moment. Since he embodies the group, special fears accompany his death. An attack on him is an attack on us. What affects him affects us. He is flesh of our flesh, as metaphors of kinship and bodies attest. On hearing that Rabin had been assassinated, a citizen testified that his pain "was as searing as an ulcer."[69] "When he was shot, we felt we lost a part of ourselves," said a student.[70] "It's like there's a big hole in me," said an El Al airline steward.[71] "Farewell, Daddy," read a placard held by a visitor to Rabin's grave."[72]

The group idea is vulnerable to exhaustion and collapse. When a leader's expression of it no longer unifies the group, it must be detached from him and revivified. Following Rabin's assassination, the acting prime minister reminded Israelis, "The nation also knows that the bullet that murdered you cannot and will not kill the ideas you advocated."[73] The discarded savior becomes the scapegoat. The group unifies around his expulsion and projects the group idea on a new leader. "New Deal, New Society, New Contract, New Covenant," recalled a citizen about the succession of American presidents and group ideas. "Same dragon, different head."[74] Though he may be killed or assassinated, in democratic countries the leader typically dies a political death, banished from the fertile center.

The test of the savior king is his ability to define the group by defending the blood border. If he fails, he loses everything. So may the group that is tied to him. During the grimmest days of World War II, Winston Churchill's totem promise to England was, "I have nothing to offer but blood, sweat, toil and tears." These are offerings of the body, fleshly proofs of willing sacrifice. By embodying the group idea, the leader proves it exists.

By offering his body, he proves it matters. Group members can only discover if their fantasy of group existence is real by enacting it together. When it falls short of expectations, we blame the leader for our failures, for the exhaustion of our will to live in common. Larger than life, he is publicly sacrificed to our reconstituted resolve to be a group. Society *is* the embodied power to dispose of group members. By deflecting antagonism and guilt onto him, we deny we sacrifice each other to keep the group alive. Since he offers himself willingly, we need not recognize we have killed him. In a 1979 essay journalist James Fallows describes that process:

Jimmy Carter tells us that he is a good man. Like Marshal Pétain after the fall of France, he has offered his person to the nation. This is not an inconsiderable gift; his performance in office shows us why it's not enough.

Such talk is prelude to sacrifice.

Like every member of the totem class, the president is a border dweller. He faces inside and outside. He is killer and killed, savior and scapegoat. Mediating between life and death, neither wholly one or the other, he dwells in liminality. He is removed from contact with ordinary persons. Harry Truman called the White House the big white jail. For William Howard Taft it was the loneliest place in the world.[75] The president's own killing role is definitive but concealed. In the typically veiled context of a staff firing, Franklin Roosevelt once remarked that a president has to be something of a butcher.[76] Ordering American bombers to kill Libyans, the protagonist of the romantic film comedy *An American President* (1995) insists, "You've just seen me do the least presidential thing I do," though issuing the killing command defines presidential power.[77] "He has no enforcer," a dissatisfied Democrat explained about President Clinton following mid-term election losses. "If you cross him, absolutely nothing happens to you."[78] A totem who cannot kill cannot define the group. Halfway through his presidential term, a voter faulted Clinton for being "wishy-washy. But if he is able to define himself again, if he makes some heads roll . . . I might vote for him again."[79]

The president must be in a fit state to create sacrificial victims. The traditional proof is his own transformative journey to the border to look death in the face. Service in World War II provided this experience for eight presidents beginning with Dwight Eisenhower, Supreme Commander of Allied forces in World War II. As the body memory of World War II receded, Bill Clinton was the first postwar president to lack wartime service. He had not been "tempered," or magically transformed by war. Worse, he had refused the totem call. In his official role as steward of the nation's sacrifice at D-Day anniversary ceremonies, Clinton called his generational cohort "the children of your sacrifice." Positioning himself as a child who had been too young to sacrifice in the good war, he passed over his unwillingness to serve in the bad one. He was the uninitiated son. War had not made him a man, a death-toucher. His image as totem sacrificer remained insecure. Charged with accommodating every point of view, he seemed to have no borders. Media priests described him as without a foreign policy vision. They meant he seemed unable to kill.

What makes sacrifice ritually successful?

Substantial group attention, treasure and energy is directed to blood sacrifice in war. No other ritual so transforms the group. What makes any event good material for group-unifying sacrifice depends on the following factors.

Blood must touch every member of the group

Merely as an idea, sacrifice has no permanent value. Real stakes are measured in bodies. The value of a sacrificial episode depends on how many bodies touch blood directly and how many other bodies are linked by personal ties of blood and affection to them. Enough bodies must suffer and die so many families will feel the pain of sacrifice that constitutes the stuff of social kinship. When all bleed, everyone is kin. The two most ritually successful wars in American history were World War II and the Civil War, in which the largest number of Americans perished. In World War II virtually everyone was connected to the war through the body of a loved one, since 82 per cent of American males between 20 and 25 were drafted or enlisted. In the Civil War nearly one in every ten able-bodied male adults was killed or injured on the Union side. In the South the number was one in every four, blacks included.[80] Consider these figures for American casualties from the Civil War forward:

Civil War (1861–65):[81]

Union forces:	2,213,365
Confederate forces:	1,082,119
Total forces:	3,295,484
Confederate lost:	258,000
Union lost:	364,511[82]
Union wounded:	281,881
Union casualties:	646,392

Confederate and Union dead: 623,026
Confederate and Union wounded: 471,427
Total casualties: 1,094,453

World War I (1917–18):
1915 US Population: 100,546,000[83]

Served: 4,743,826
Wounded: 204,002
Lost: 116,708
Total casualties: 320,710[84]

World War II (1941–45):
1941 US Population: 133,669,000[85]

Served: 16,112,566
Wounded: 671,801
Lost: 407,318
Total casualties: 1,079,119[86]
MIA/POW: 139,709

Korean War (1950–53)
1950 US Population: 152,271,000[87]

Served: 5,720,000[88]
Wounded: 103,284
Lost: 54,487
Total casualties: 157,771[89]
MIA/POW: 10,218

Vietnam War (1959–75)
1965 US Population: 194,303,000[90]

Served: 8,744,000[91]
Wounded: 153,303
Lost: 58,151
Total casualties: 211,454[92]
MIA/POW: 932

Gulf War (1990–91):
1990 US Population: 249,900,000[93]

Served: 541,425[94]
Lost: 148[95]
Wounded: 467
Total casualties: 843[96]
POW: 21

Sacrificing our own is the supreme ritual of war. If enemy deaths were the most ritually compelling, the Gulf War would have been an enduring unifier of Americans. After twenty-six days of fighting, Iraqi casualties were estimated at between 10,000 to 40,000, with perhaps 60,000 wounded.[97] Though the deaths of only 147 Americans testified to impressive American military superiority, its weak sacrificial impact on the totem group caused the Gulf War to fade quickly as a unifying event. Wars whose unifying effects endure must be costly. Casualties in World War I constituted about 0. 3 per cent of the total population. World War II casualties were 0. 8 per cent of the total population. Korean and Vietnam casualties constituted about 0. 001 per cent of the total population each. The number of Congressional Medals of Honor conferred for each war also follows the argument. Nearly half the roughly 3,400 Medals, the nation's highest recognition for sacrifice, were awarded for acts of Civil War valor. World War I produced 96 Medal winners; World War II, 439; Korea, 131, and Vietnam, 238.[98] Not winning or losing, but serious bloodletting is the important factor in ritual success. This explains the power of Nazi and Confederate flags to attract committed followers long after the decisive defeat of their armies. These flags are attached to "nations" that have met other sacrificial requirements, especially significant bloodletting. For the majority of Americans these flags manifest a high degree of profane magic because they denote ritual enemies credited with instigating the greatest blood sacrifices in American history. They have a potency not even achieved by the Soviet flag during the Cold War, which exacted no significant sacrifice of American blood.

The large number of Civil War dead also accounts for the enduring historical memories of combatants, family members, and descendants of the identity-producing sacrifices of both the Confederacy and the Union. While Union victory determined once and for all that the United States was a single nation whose identity had been forged in the blood of its own, the memory of devastating Confederate losses long kept a sense of separate community alive in the South, a separateness gradually weakened by the loss of living memory of Confederate sacrifice and by twentieth-century war losses of Southerners on behalf of the whole country. Though competing histories of bloodletting continue to vie for Southern loyalty and identity, it is fair to say that blood sacrifice to the nation as a whole has become the primary sacrificial identity of Southerners.

The sacrificial victim must be willing

Having already dealt at length with willing sacrifice, we add only a few points here. Preserving the totem secret requires cooperation from both sacrificed and sacrificers. Insiders must offer themselves willingly, or appear to. To protect the totem secret we say that soldiers "gave" their lives for their country. While unwilling sacrifices may be reconstructed in death as having been willing, the most useful sacrifices declare in advance of leaving that they face death willingly. Unpopular and divisive, without an enemy convincing to a large portion of the citizenry, the Vietnam War was a failed ritual sacrifice. With a body count comparable to the Korean War but drawn out over two long decades, victimage seemed neither massive nor unanimous. Formal declaration of war provides an important ritual opportunity for groups to communicate to themselves their willingness to sacrifice their own. The Vietnam War was never officially declared, and this was another element in its ritual failure.

The special case of group identity forged from unwilling sacrifice, as in the Jewish Shoah or the European enslavement of Africans, is worth considering. Within the United States neither Jews nor African–Americans are totem groups. They are affiliative groups whose members share a sacrificial history. Though we shall discuss affiliative groups in a later chapter, suffice it to say that unity through shared victimage alone is less powerful than belonging to a group that claims the totem power to kill its own. Modern Israel is the totemic Jewish nation, no longer the incomplete sacrifice of a totemic Other, but able to redeem the unwilling sacrifice of its members by killing its willing own in the face of totem challenge. Once a group is willing to kill its own to secure its identity (a process euphemistically called "resistance" to keep the totem secret), it can appropriate past instances of unwilling sacrifice in the search for sacrificial justifications to re-establish the killing authority of its own totem. African–Americans in the United States have debated whether to sacrifice their own in order to usurp totem power, the message of groups such as the Black Panthers and the Nation of Islam. A different approach was taken by Martin Luther King, Jr., whose non-violent civil rights movement offered sacrificial bodies on behalf of the totem group without trying to seize its power. His message was that instead of defeating the totem, African–Americans must pursue membership in the dominant society by making their sacrifices assimilable.

Victimage must be unanimous

The point is Girard's.[99] War must be popular. The entire group colludes in the secret. A credible enemy is the most reliable producer of unanimous victimage. "I don't want them to be sacrificed needlessly," a citizen told journalists inquiring about his support for American troops in Bosnia.[100] His remark implied approval of other sacrifice. The more credible the enemy, the more enthusiastically the group sends the surrogate victim to die amidst general lamentation for the loss of its young, the more group members believe they are not the cause. Daniel Jonah Goldhagen has argued that German sacrifice of the Jews in World War II was "unanimous" in totem terms, though unwilling.[101] Thus the war failed to produce German unity. Other responses than constructing surrogate and ritual victims are possible. A group may disavow its own killing rules and submit to those of the threatening group. Protesters are often regarded as bad group members who do exactly this. Since enduring groups are constituted by the agreement that only they are entitled to kill their own, "objective" threats are those in which outsiders seek to exercise totem killing power. When this prerogative is challenged, the group must re-establish it or defer to the killing rules of the challenger and thus join his group.

Still, why do mothers surrender their children to the murderous group will? Given the pretext of a convincing scapegoat they may be surprisingly willing. The mother of the assassin of Israel's prime minister found irresistible the demand that group members must distance themselves from the violator of the totem taboo. A good group member, she disowned her son. "He's put himself beyond the bounds of this house. Today he's not mine anymore. Gali's not mine," Geula Amir wept. The assassination of Rabin provided only short-lived unity since his victimage was not popularly willed, however much it may have expressed the wishes of some group members. Without unanimous victimage, the totem secret could not be disguised. A Jew had killed a Jew. "With all the anger that people had toward each other, I can't believe that we have come to this," worried an Israeli mother. "Some people are saying that we'll . . . be all right. But others are very worried about the future."[102]

> *At the launching of the undertaking there is genuine uncertainty*
> *about the fate of the group*

In the best rituals, devotees feel group survival is at stake. The *need* for ritual is never in doubt. The more uncertain its outcome, however, the greater the ritual magic that will be deployed and the more transformative will be the result. Ritual uncertainty is greatest when both sides in a dispute make credible claims to enforce killing power. An American participant in the Normandy invasion recalled, "The moment of the invasion was a great and solemn moment; it was a prayerful time. Because one didn't know! And everything was at stake, everything."[103] "When I think of the beaches of Normandy choked with the flower of American and British youth," Churchill told Eisenhower, "and when in my mind's eye I see the tides running red with their blood, I have my doubts. I have my doubts."[104]

Wars and presidential elections are the most important national rituals. Both require uncertainty for maximum efficacy. In the best elections there is a choice, as the rhetoric goes. Ritual uncertainty drives the debate about whether television networks, sources of totem revelation for devotees, should broadcast voting results from the eastern and central United States before polls close in the west. Observers fear that reducing uncertainty about election outcomes dampens voter participation and diminishes ritual success. The issue is not that someone won't win, but that congregants won't perform their ritual duty and vote. A dramatic case of ritual uncertainty was the 1960 presidential election in which Mayor Richard Daley and Senator Lyndon Johnson engineered vote tallies in Illinois and Texas to manufacture the margin necessary to elect John Kennedy. The losing candidate, Richard Nixon, chose not to contest the election result. By submitting to the appearance of a genuinely uncertain election, the only ritually successful kind, he declined to create an opportunistic group crisis to disrupt the contrived group crisis of presidential election.

> *Outcomes must be definite. Borders must be re-consecrated. Time must begin again*

The greater the ritual uncertainty, the more satisfying the resolution when it comes. Dramatic structures frame outcomes best. Elections, for example, proceed through well-marked stages. What these are and how long they last are well-known to the group. An exception is the ever-lengthening unofficial campaign before and after presidential primaries, a development that has been criticized as ritually flawed. The importance of clear-cut ritual structures was suggested by sportswriter Robert Lipsyte, lamenting "the unfinished decade, the 1960s," that lasted thirty years. It began when boxer Muhammad Ali inconclusively beat Sonny Liston for the American heavyweight title in an emotionally charged fight.

That inconclusiveness became a signature of those times. We still don't know the outcome of the Vietnam War (will Coke or Pepsi win?). And the War on Poverty, the Civil Rights movement, the drive for gender equity – all were highly promoted contests that we have slowly come to realize are continuing struggles without a final result.[105]

Only another ritual can repair a failed one

Successful rituals require blood stakes, unanimous victimage, and willing sacrifice. The anticipated outcome must be thrillingly uncertain. The result, when it comes, must be clear. Most rituals satisfy these conditions only partially, if at all. Their success will be correspondingly qualified. But even incomplete and faulty rituals may bring the group to a new, if rarely enduring, sense of itself as a corporate body. When a talented New Jersey high school senior was killed in a car crash, her friends sacrificed their own work to complete the science contest entry she had nearly finished and won a posthumous prize. A school official recalled how her blood sacrifice unified the group:

Day after day the pain was so intense . . . Everybody was hugging, touching. We kept pulling together rather than separating apart. I really feel we have a connection through this that will keep us together for the rest of our lives.[106]

But here is a description of an old photograph, a mediation of a ritual event, that gets closer to the process by which blood sacrifice unifies groups:

A large group of men and women were standing near a tree. Hanging from that tree was a bloodied corpse. Smiling men, women and children stood at the base of that tree, pointing up at the dead black man as if directing the camera's eye toward the corpse.

These white people beamed. There were great smiles on their faces, as if they took great pride that this bloody black corpse hung from that tree. They had done it, you see. They had killed the man. And they were glad.[107]

Failed rituals produce disunity. The greater the failure, the larger the division. Since all rituals eventually fail to elicit renewing sacrifice from devotees, what counts is the duration for which they succeed, and the intensity of the sacrificial commitment. Successful rituals engender new rituals, and only another ritual can address a failed ritual. This could be another war, a new presidential election, or some other event.

What the flag means to school children

What the flag means to its citizens may be glimpsed in a sample of school children's essays for a Flag Day contest sponsored by the Betsy Ross House in Philadelphia in 1989. The sacrificial semiotics of the flag are fully displayed. Thirty-nine teenagers considered "What the Flag Means to Me." Their principal themes are that the flag represents sacrifice and freedom, the totem word that signifies the human and makes it coterminous with

4.3 School children worship the totem on the eve of World War II.

one's own group. For these budding citizens the American flag is intimately engaged with bodily gestures. Our choice to limit them is a matter of space.

What does the flag mean to me? . . . Wherever I go and see the American flag, I feel free, and proud to live in America.

Red stands for the blood that is shed during the wars. The blue is for the sky that looks down upon the people during the fighting and corruption that takes place. The white symbolizes all of the courage the people have.
    The flag also stands for freedom and peace.

When you see the flag waving high in the breezy sky, hear the echos [sic] of the soldiers' voices, in the *Star-Spangled Banner*, and put your hand on your heart, think, and be proud that you are an American.

A nation's flag is a stirring sight as it flies in the wind. The flag's vibrant colors and striking designs stand for the country's land, its people, its government, and its ideals. A nation's flag can stir people to joy, to courage, and to sacrifice. Many people have died to save their countries from dishonor and disgrace.

The Flag means truth, honor, Justice, and most of all freedom. The Flag is a symbol of the good in all people. It means freedom of religion, freedom of choice, freedom of speech, and freedom of expression. The Flag is a rememberence [sic] of all the people who died for these freedoms.

It symbolizes the courage of the people who founded the nation and the people that made it what it is today. It symbolizes the pride that I have for my country, the hardships, and the joys of the country. Most of all it symbolizes our country's freedom.

In the early days the flag symbolized the tight bond of the thirteen colonies . . . and how if they could peacefully pull together they could make the United States a better place for all.

The flag means liberty and freedom. It's amazing how the old red, white and blue could withstand such a fierce battle as it did . . To think of all the gruesome fighting that went on, and to see the glorious flag shining in all its beauty and splendor to remind us that anything is possible if we try.

In my eyes, red stands for the blood that was shed for the unselfish sake of our country, white stands for the clouds that each brave Soldier's soul passed while fighting and dying for our country, blue stands for the oceans where many hard battles were fought, and where many men died trying to protect the pride and freedom of our country.

The red, white, and blue United States flag symbolizes freedom and courage. Freedom for the great liberties we have, and courage for the courage of our forefathers to fight for what they believed in.

The American Flag is important to me because to me it means freedom. When we went to war to fight for Independence we won. The flag is like a reward that will always remind us of our Victory. I think the reason we salute the flag is to show respect for those who died fighting for our Independence.

The flag is a symbol of freedom, bravery, honor. Many men have died to keep our country a free nation and the flag is the symbol of that. The American Flag is the most ultimate symbol of democracy in the world today . . . I would proudly defend my country if it was needed. The flag has stood during wars against Great Britian [sic], Germany, Japan, etc. and was a light in our darkest hour.

It is a symbol of what our fore-fathers fought for and what they acheived, so that our generation will not have to fight . . . It is a wonderful feeling when you can stand and sing the "National Anthem" while watching it blow in the wind at a baseball game.

As I look at our national flag, I see . . . all those [who] worked so hard to make this country the land of the free and the home of the brave, these United States of America.

The flag is a symbol of liberty, but it is the people of the United States who keep liberty's torch burning throughout eternity . . . Red was for the blood that was shed for freedom at Valley Forge. White was taken from the bandages which helped pave the way for freedom. Blue was from the sky which showed how free this country is.

Our American flag stands for freedom . . . The flag has been a standing point and support system for all men who have fought in the war. It represented their reason for fighting. It was a blessed reminder.

The thing that I love most about this country, and the flag, is that it represents *FREEDOM*.

When I was a small child, I was glad that my birthday fell on a holiday. Now that I'm older and I know what the holiday represents, I can relate to those who died for their country and the flag . . . I now know that our flag may have been the only thing that kept people going during early wars . . . In my opinion there wouldn't be a United States if not for the flag. The flag is what pulled our country together in its time of need . . . I also feel gratitude towards our flag. To me, it's the single most important part of the United States of America.

To me the flag means freedom and the courage to fight for what we believe in. Without these two things the United States would not be the great country it is today. The flag also stands for the blood that was shed by all those brave men and women who fought for our country's freedom.

The United States flag stands for liberty. Liberty is what the whole world should have . . . Our flag stands for freedom, liberty, and the American way. The flag also stands for the ability to fight for the freedom.

As it waves in the air, even through the violence and disasters, through wars and death, and even through times when our country has failed, it proves "whose broad stripes and bright stars" will always be there.

The flag of the United States means to me a symbol of freedom, our loyalty to our country. When I see the US flag I see patriotism, veterans who put their lives on the line to save our flag. The flag reminds me of back in colonial times when the flag was being made, and the people then who fought for it.

5

Death touchers and border crossers

In some societies whole categories of human beings are systematically reserved for sacrificial purposes in order to protect some other categories.
René Girard[1]

To attract the peoples' devotion the totem must be real and tangible. It must be seen to act. Ritual is its medium of action, sacrifice its most sacred transformation. Sacrifice is also an act of group violence, creation, and memory. Those who oversee blood sacrifice to the totem are the president, the military, law enforcement, and other state agents. They constitute the totem class, a special segment of the totem group, which is the whole nation. Each totem class member enacts the group idea and makes it real by modeling killing authority, or death. Yet how do we know the totem when we see it?

A strong totem forces recognition on its challengers. Consider the experience of an American journalist cycling through rural Vietnam in early 1995. Three young men wearing long-sleeved brown shirts and caps with gold stars pinned to them flagged him down and seized his passport. Not recognizing their totem authority, the journalist snatched back his passport, an artifact of his own totem allegiance. The man holding it "instantly turned angry, pointing to the star on his hat as if to say, 'Don't you know who I am?' and aimed an imaginary gun at me."[2] This is the totem revealed. The gold star he bears is an element from the flag of the Republic of Vietnam. The gun signifies the killing power his group confers on him. His totem body incarnate is taboo. A taboo that others must respect defines a group. Whoever violates our taboos has the power to destroy us.

Changes of totem state are ritually implemented transformations in the service of group life and death. Totem rituals include presidential elections, declarations of war, induction into the military, promoting soldiers from enlisted to officer corps or regular to elite units, and decorating soldiers for valor. They include military and state funerals in which fallen members of the totem class become totem ancestors, that is, the flag itself. They include boot camp initiations that convey totem tradition to the young and reaffirm it in the eyes of the mature. The most potent initiations feature dramatic gestures in the name of the flag at points of totem danger, especially war. There are three categories of totem ritual. Routine rituals are priestly ceremonies of remembrance and *commemoration*. They may be regular or occasional, contrived or opportunistic. *Apostolic* rituals are mission-oriented. They ensure proper totem succession. Both apostolic and commemorative rituals remodel and recall *messianic sacrifice,* the third category of totem ritual. Messianic sacrifice *retrospectively* re-creates the bond between the totem and its devotees. By reclassifying past apostolic deeds as group transforming, it celebrates a long line of murders.

Sacrifice to the totem god, the nation, implies the existence of a religious community of devotees who execute the sacrificial mission. This community is the military, though it strains conventional wisdom to think of soldiers as a religious class. This is because the totem taboo makes all who kill, even with official sanction, subject to powerful social ambivalence that flows from suspending the totem taboo for ritual sacrifice, a necessary and dangerous enterprise. Military and sectarian groups do possess similar attributes. Their members are sacrificial. Touching death, they are transformed. The totem group teaches how to touch death through a living oral tradition of body knowledge about group-making and boundary maintenance. In this tradition the flag signifies the totem god and his sons, the dead fathers who guard the borders of the group. The work of the flag is transforming bodies, places, occasions, and things. To understand the religious power that flows to and from those who kill and die for the flag, we examine the military.

Military as sacred community

The boundaries of an empire are the graves of its soldiers.   Napoleon

Victor Turner observes that few post-traditional rituals oblige all citizens. Though citizens do choose whether to participate in many social arenas, Turner overlooks the compelling obligations of law. Citizens must at all times obey the law, the concrete expression of totem killing rules. In time of totem danger, the armed forces may also oblige all citizens. The military is the prototype totem group, a model for integrating citizens from all backgrounds into a body with uniform experiences and duties. The commander-in-chief and his agents, including soldiers, comprise the totem class. At the president's word young men kill and die. Death magic may be directed outward toward the enemy or inward toward totem class members ritually prepared for sacrifice, whichever produces carnage enough for the totem to feast on.

"The soldier, above all other men, is required to practice the greatest act of religious training – sacrifice," General Douglas MacArthur told graduating West Pointers in 1962.[3] The military historian John Keegan adds:

Even a pacificist should admire the military virtures – should admire, and indeed have those virtues themselves: self-abnegation and willingness, if necessary, to sacrifice their lives for what they believe . . . That is the ultimate military virtue, that I will lay down my life if called upon to do so . . . That's what ultimately makes soldiers different. But I won't choose whether I will or not lay down my life; I have already promised that I will. It is forsworn; it is given away; I would say a soldier has mortgaged his life. He's said, "Here's my life and I can only have it back again when the end of my service comes and I salute for the last time . . ." I think a pacifist is the same except his willingness to sacrifice his life never goes.[4]

Totem class members model and train for death. In units training for war, commanding officers may direct a certain number of men to step out of formation across an imaginary border to signify how many will die before hostilities cease to rehearse totem acolytes in the sacrifice that is expected of them. Sacrificial lambs know their fate. "You put your life on the line to save your country. That's what war's about," explained an Iwo Jima survivor.[5]

Borders are thresholds of contagious magic separating zones of purity and impurity, order and chaos. Touching both what the group is and isn't, borders are perilous zones of transformation, shifting and unstable. Transformative violence creates definitive borders. Uncontained, it also threatens to set in motion an irresistible, border-destroying chain of retribution. In order not to destroy the group, violence must be thrust outside it. It is no accident, Robertson Smith observes, that where human sacrifice is practiced, it takes place outside the city.[6] The totem group designates the armed forces to enforce and patrol the border. Though the sacrificial blood of soldiers is pure and sacrifice is regarded as a purifying ordeal, border-dwelling soldiers become impure and contagious by shedding blood. They pose a pollution threat to the regenerative center, which fears to mate with violence. "These civilians . . . think we are jar heads who should stay away from their daughters," observed a 21–year-old corporal.[7]

The community expels the sacrificial, border-creating class through whose deaths it purifies itself. Since violence is contagious, death-touching soldiers must be set apart. Living separately, dressing differently, they observe an ascetic vocation. Proximity to death is a measure of their holiness. All their attention is focused on death and all their most honorable tasks relate to it. According to Bernard E. Trainor:

Within the armed forces the distinction between a combat veteran and one who has not seen combat is significant. It is a gulf that exists until one bridges it in a test by fire. Those who have not crossed it tend to discount its importance. For those who have, there is a vague feeling of unfulfillment.[8]

We will have more to say about the guilt of those who touch death but do not make the ultimate sacrifice.

Liminality is van Gennep's term for the fluidity and indefiniteness of ritual borders. Liminality is always a comparison to degrees of relatively greater structuredness. Though military units are socially liminal with respect to civilian society, structure within them is exceptionally clear and unambiguous compared to structure within civilian society. This is because disorder within the military, whose members are tasked to kill, could quickly destroy it. On all other counts, the soldier's life is highly uncertain compared to the stability of life at the fertile center. "We are the first to fight, the first to die, the first to be called upon to serve our beloved country and the first to be forgotten," a Vietnam veteran wrote, describing the border position of soldiers in the hierarchy of totem sacrifice.[9]

Victor Turner has constructed a series of Levi-Straussian oppositions counterposing liminality and status in the ceremonial life of a Central African tribe.[10] Liminal attributes constitute the left item of each pair in the following list. On the right side are status distinctions that articulate social structure. We extrapolate Turner's liminal categories to war and warriors in American society. War, an ordeal of ritual liminality, contrasts with the settled structure of civilian life. It contrasts with what war is not and what it may transform.

Transition/state
War is a transition that leads the group to a state of victory or loss.

Totality/partiality
War is a total experience. Soldiers must stay until the killing mission is completed.

Homogeneity/heterogeneity
Every soldier wears the same uniform.

Communitas/structure
In battle, distinctions of rank collapse in the common effort to save the group.

Equality/inequality
The risk of death is borne by every soldier. Death brings tragedy and glory equally to all.

Anonymity/systems of nomenclature
Armies at war are treated as organisms and not as assemblies of distinct individuals with unique histories and personalities.

Absence of property/property
The government issues soldiers what they need. Resources and deprivations are shared equally.

Absence of status/status
Men at war discard civilian statuses; they have only military status.

Nakedness or uniform clothing/distinctions of clothing
Soldiers wear the same uniform. In battle even officers shed markers of rank.

Sexual continence/sexuality
Sexual activity on the job is strictly forbidden.

Minimization of sex distinctions/maximization of sex distinctions
Male and female soldiers wear similar uniforms.

Humility/just pride of position
The fundamental commitment of soldiers is to the mission, a team rather than individual effort.

Disregard for personal appearance/care for personal appearance
In the field personal vanity must be sacrificed to the task.

No distinctions of wealth/distinctions of wealth
The institution provides what is needed.

Unselfishness/selfishness
The greatest honor accrues to those who sacrifice themselves to protect their buddies.

Sacredness/secularity
Soldiers at war are set apart from civilians.

Sacred instruction/technical knowledge
Technical knowledge is sacred instruction in wartime.

Silence/speech
Those who take orders must not question them.

Suspension of kinship rights and obligations/kinship rights and obligations
Soldiers are required to leave their families and other obligations to take up war.

Continuous reference to mystical powers/intermittent reference to mystical powers
Devotion to war in the name of the totem is the constant message.

Foolishness/sagacity
Heroism in arms requires high disregard for personal safety.

Simplicity/complexity
Soldiers' tasks are clear and well-defined: to accomplish the mission.

Acceptance of pain and suffering/avoidance of pain and suffering
This acceptance defines the sacrificial class.

Heteronymy/degrees of autonomy
Group integrity surpasses every individual concern.

If, as Turner suggests, Ndembu ceremonial culture resembles Christian monasticism, the latter resembles military culture. Like the pilgrim, the soldier travels to strange lands. He lives in a community whose members serve by suffering. Soldiers live ascetically, forsaking sex, comfort, rest, and adequate food. They are paid little. Alienation from the fertile center is a theme of military hardship. As priests do, men under arms eat food, wear clothing, use implements, and live in housing provided by the institution. A mark of the military priest's devotion is the ring worn by West Point graduates on the third finger of the left hand, much as nuns in some orders wear wedding rings to show they are brides of Christ.

Pollution taboos and purification rituals attract the blessing of higher powers on the undertakings of soldiers. Mary Douglas observes of Old Testament Israelites that "the army could not win without the blessing and to keep the blessing in the camp they had to be specially holy."[11] Little has changed for modern soldiers. To prepare for the ordeal of suspending the totem taboo, soldiers must undergo purifying ordeals. Tasks must be completed. The soldier and his camp must be scrupulously clean and well-ordered. Ritual states of wholeness, purity, and humility require pristine uniforms and perfectly executed gestures.[12] Soldiers under orders are required to display simplicity of manner and restraint in speech. They offer vows of total obedience to a chain of totem command that ends with the president. The god wants only perfect sacrificial offerings, faultless victims whose spilled blood imparts life to the community.[13] That this system has no relation to conventional morality merely underscores its magical power.

Border-crossers model and train for death. Initiation into death-touching begins with boot camp, which separates recruits from their families, especially mothers whose control many are leaving for the first time. In boot camp civilians are transformed from "maggots" and "nasty things," Marine Corps jargon for the profane, unholy, and grotesque, into initiated members of the totem class.[14] Other hierarchies sort additional levels of insider- and outsiderness. Relative to recruits and regular troops, elite units are most remote from the regenerative center. Farthest out are spies without uniforms moving among enemy outsiders, whom they resemble exactly. They are "spooks," the equivalent of ghosts who have crossed the border and been transformed. Unlike uniformed captives who may not be shot according to international law, there are no rules for spies, who exist in complete liminality. Even in death, they have no names and become merely pieces of the flag enshrined. For each spy killed in service a star is inscribed on the wall of the CIA's Hall of Honor above the legend, "In Honor of Those Members of the Central Intelligence Agency Who Gave Their Lives in the Service of Their Country."

Other elite units wear uniforms but perform covertly at the boundaries of geography and legality. They include Navy Seals, Army Special Forces, and Army Rangers. Their uniforms differ from those of regular troops. Their living quarters are set apart. Their culture is different. Their non-conformity is held to make them excellent innovators and border changelings, but unpredictable commanders of large military groups. By tradition, Green Berets are denied generalships because they are rule-breakers, i.e., border-crossers within military structure. Another group at the edge are Secret Service agents who define and guard the taboo space around the embodied totem. Their border attributes are on display in presidential motorcades where agents selected to be visible jog in formation around the moving limousine that holds the president. Since presidential limousines are designed to withstand assault by tank or bomb, these agents add no genuine protective dimension. Their presence says, we are death, the totem border. If you seek to penetrate it we will kill you, even at the cost of our lives. A former presidential escort explained their demeanor: "They don't smile; they're dead meat." They are defined by their willingness to sacrifice for the totem, as the following story suggests:

The assassination of President John F. Kennedy put the [Secret Service] in a nervous funk that did not fully lift until President Ronald Reagan survived an assassination attempt in 1981, in part because a Secret Service agent took a bullet meant for him.[15]

When American troops went to Somalia in 1993, the first American to die was an outsider: Sergeant Lawrence Freedman perished in a land mine explosion on an undisclosed mission. A member of Special Forces and a professional spook, Freedman was said to have "died the soldier's death he always preferred." The press constructed him as a willing sacrifice unwilling to speak of his experiences beyond the border. A willing sacrifice is a friend of death, the ultimate border-dweller. Freedman's sister mused, "We've all come to the conclusion that, just as he hit the mine, he probably got that twinkle in his eye and that ridiculous grin on his face, and said: 'Ohhhhh, s – !'"[16]

The image of a smiling death's head uttering spells suggests that Freedman himself is death. A gathering of mystery mourners dressed as outsiders displaying no emotion, an attribute of ghosts, repeated this symbolism. At a Fort Bragg memorial service, "men in biker regalia and Special Forces Association jackets stood stoically," ghost outsiders to a man. Embodying death, they do not look back at the living. "Some of them looked like they could rip your throat out," a reporter said. "They're the kind of guys who you're afraid to look into their eyes, because you know there'd be nothing there."[17]

Uncommunicative about his life beyond the borders, Freedman himself was a ghost outsider. He had been in Delta Force, the secret commando group sent to liberate American hostages in Teheran. It was believed he worked for the CIA. He disappeared on assignment for weeks at a time. Divorced from a first wife, separated from a second, he was estranged from the totem center. "His life was a secret from us," said his father, who asked a Pentagon official at the funeral what his son had been doing in Somalia. "The man went right on to the next sentence. He just ignored the question." Freedman never told his family how he earned two Bronze stars and more than twenty medals. "The record will not reflect the many operations he participated in . . . in isolated places, far from familiar voices," the deputy commander of Army Special Operations said at his funeral at Arlington National Cemetery. Freedman "was not the kind of soldier who told war stories." To those inside the boundaries, outsiders cannot speak of their experiences.

Freedom, free will, and robots

'Cause I'm proud to be an American
Where at least I know I'm free
And I'd like to thank the man
Who died who gave that right to me.   Lee Greenwood

Asked what the flag meant to him, a flag factory worker offered, "It means freedom."[18] He might have been any number of people with whom we have spoken over the course of this study. "It means freedom, and my buddies who died," an Iwo Jima survivor told us.[19] "I'm proud to be an American, where at least I know I'm free," says the country and western song. It continues: "The flag still stands for freedom, and they can't take that away." Those who belong to the flag are free and in a condition of maximum difference from those not so blessed. The unblessed are unfree, in the condition of robots and animals. Christianity, another totem religion, says men alone are endowed with free will that makes them human and accountable to God, the only power entitled to take away their humanity, that is, their lives. Only the nation, likewise, may sacrifice its own. Submission to the killing rules of our group, which we call devotion to freedom, distinguishes the patriot from the possessor of doubtful patriotism, and therefore, doubtful humanity. To belong to the totem community is to be human. Not by accident, the word most often chosen by African–Americans to describe their aspirations is *freedom*. "Freedom is so close," exhorted Jesse Jackson, invoking the long history of the struggle for civil rights and for admission of African–Americans to the status of being human, "we can touch it and taste it."[20] In the United States, to be free is to be fully human. A human being is a touching, tasting body.

Death secures freedom. To die for the group is to give one's flesh and bone to reconstituting it. Dying is the primitive process that creates the social body. Of course, not death literally secures freedom, but what living soldiers did before they died. A favorite theme of General George Patton's speeches was: "Nobody ever won a war by giving up his life. He won a war by making some other poor bastard give up his life."[21] The slip of the tongue in claims that "they died for freedom," is pervasive enough to suggest its importance. It tells us that the group must sacrifice its own to create enduring existence, which is freedom. Another sacrificially created, totem-worshiping group makes the point: "For God so loved the world that he gave his only begotten son, that whosoever believeth in him shall not perish, but shall have everlasting life."

When the first African–American soldier, a dogcatcher, was inducted into the Army in World War II, he remarked that Japs were "just like those mongrels I been catching."[22] This inside-the-boundary statement signaled his new position relative to Japs and animals beyond the boundary, where he once had been. Among the groups to which soldiers do not traditionally belong are animals, homosexuals, directionless kids and – until recently – women. Another important boundary is between robots and freedom. What distinguishes the Corps in its own eyes is that Marines take initiative, exercise judgment, and think for themselves. Marines, a branch of the Navy, characterize members of other services as robots or automatons. Army soldiers describe Marines and sailors as robotic, and the Navy distinguishes its personnel from the automatons of the Marines, the Army, and the Air Force. According to an informant, the Department of Defense sometimes described the differences between American and Soviet forces during the Cold War as differences between robots and free men.

Popular ambivalence toward the totem class is often expressed by casting soldiers and policemen as automatons, robots, and soulless conformists. Such charges thrust them to the border of the human group. When a police demonstration-turned-riot in New York occasioned public criticism, the president of the Patrolmen's Benevolent Association complained of being judged by inhuman standards in a letter to the *New York Times*:

> With respect to the police, it's how dare the robots display emotionalism in public?
> Police officers . . . whether on duty or off, are supposed to be conditioned – programmed – to exercise superhuman restraint.[23]

During the 1992 Winter Olympics, robot stories compared the old Soviet teams to the de-flagged Unified team of *perestroika*. Under their own flag, Soviets had seemed soulless automatons to American commentators. Without it, they became human beings. "The Soviets are known for playing without emotion," explained a CBS commentator. "They seem a lot more human without the regime behind them."[24] The shift assigned powerful agency to the Soviet flag. "In the New World order, where enemies become rivals, the grudge matches of the past have given way to a sense of pity for the competitors without a country," explained Harry Smith during a medals ceremony as two Unified flags were hoisted.[25]

Military tradition and the body

> My first wish would be that my Military family, and the whole Army, should consider themselves as a band of brothers, willing and ready to die for each other.   George Washington[26]

One of the truly impressive artifacts of modern warfare is a full-scale battle formation at sea, a vast death-dealing organization of men and ritual implements that reproduces totem geography. At the totem center of these formations are flagships, aircraft carriers named for presidents and surrounded by a protective border of ships and planes. Such group-forming occupies the focus of military ritual, training, and culture. The core of military experience in group-forming is imparted in a thriving oral tradition whose medium is the body of every soldier, but it is also an aspect of military ritual, costume, edifice, and emblem. It can be discerned in the soundscape of cadence, inspection and review, and throughout the visual organization and daily routine of military life. Its lessons are iterated and reiterated up and down the chain of command, in training and in war stories. Soldiers are most familiar to us in images that show them conforming their bodies to the group discipline of military postures and gestures such as marching or standing at attention. This body work is prologue to the lesson of supreme sacrifice, of submission to the totem group. This lesson is prepared for, imprinted on, and enacted by the body, the currency of group behavior and memory in rituals that ensure totem succession.

Chief among these is boot camp, an initiation rite shared by many adult males in American culture and some women. Its most famous site is the Marine Corps Recruit Training Depot at Parris Island, South Carolina. In aspect and location Parris Island is far removed from civilian life. "Whatever you find elsewhere, you can find on Parris Island in the extreme," an officer wrote us. "Parris Island itself is extreme, and trains young men and women to face the extremes of life."[27] The Island fascinates and repels civilians. This ambivalent estimation is something of which its inhabitants are intensely aware. They are well-versed in media lore about the military in general and Parris Island in particular. The most disliked media theme is the berserk outsider: the ex-Marine killer gone amok on civilians, though he might have been booted out of the Marines or belonged to other services as well, and despite the fact that ex-soldiers and ex-Marines are mostly law-abiding.

A recruit population trimmed down by an unpopular war in Vietnam has also been reduced by scandals involving recruit injury and death. Over the past two decades threats to bring Parris Island and its traditions to an end have spawned a "new" Corps in which corporal punishment has become illegal, and even harsh language is officially curtailed. What has not changed is the notion of how groups are formed and why this matters. Various justifications are given for why these changes do not violate the tradition of "forming" in which recruits are physically, psychologically, and socially stripped of identities they bring to the Corps and re-made into bonded groups able to maintain their integrity and accomplish tasks under combat pressure.[28] Recent revelations suggest the survival of "blood stripes," a secret ceremonial among elite units in which medals are pinned to the bare flesh of willing initiates. Preserving the secrecy of these traditions benefits the unit, since the totem class must respond with punishment whenever official rule violations of this kind are made public. Short of war, the group learns through such ordeals which of its members can take pain and who can be counted on to put group loyalty ahead of personal interest. Both are critical qualities for fighting groups. Such ordeals also rehearse the totem model in which the group sacrifices its own and group members participate as willing sacrifices.

The most popular reason for disavowing the overt physical punishment and humiliation that formed generations of platoons is that the Corps now attracts a better educated and socialized recruit. This claim rides shotgun with before-and-after accounts of transforming the "nasty things." Street gangs, broken families, drugs, and poor academic performance are the narrative ingredients that make for a poor and immature offering to the armed forces. Such tales celebrate the Corps' transformations of unformed recruits despite their presumed better class. In the litanies of obstacles to initiation arrayed for us on a visit to the Island to observe the ordeal for which it is famous, this not obviously parallel point was often added: "Some of these recruits have never even worn shoes." The charge of shoelessness seemed inapplicable to the recruits we saw and at odds with the requirement that recruits must have a high school diploma. Still, it was repeated with conviction as a border transformation story suitable for visitors. When we finally asked an officer if it could be true, he assured us many recruits had worn only running shoes in their previous lives, acquiring leather shoes for the first time as recruits. Government-issue boots are rigidly constructed cheap leather. Breaking them in may be painful, especially for those accustomed to sneakers. As a statement about the initiation of the unformed barbarians who come to Parris Island, the story may revitalize a traditional description from a period when many recruits could not afford shoes. It also suggests the importance of the term 'boot camp' in reference to marching, the most visible group activity. Virtually everything in Marine lore and training is about defining the group.

To become totem class members, recruits at boot camp must be fundamentally re-embodied. First, the look of their bodies is dramatically transformed. Their heads are shaved, they are forced to give up clothes and personal possessions, to alter their natural body movements and change their most familiar bodily routines. They are disoriented and fatigued in relation to old habits and identities. Their experience of time is re-organized. In the custom of religious communities time is measured in reference to group tasks: Training Day One, Training Day Two, etc. Soldiers learn to speak more freely than civilians about bodies and their secrets. As a group they cultivate the border language of body magic that civilians regard as profanity. A familiar feature of military culture is discussing how to damage opponents' bodies and prevail in ordeals of bodily injury and suffering. Other oral traditions of military life make use of specific attributes of male bodies. Marching songs and cadence, roared group cheers, and shouted commands at distinctive pitches and rhythms display the potential and force of the male voice and create group identity around it. Marching to drums is a great war dance. Drums musically represent artillery and rifles. From calling cadence to performing inspection, the entire exchange of auditory responses is a group hunting song.

At boot camp drill instructors embody the line of totem succession. For recruits, they are the most immediate totem ancestor. They embody totem authority. They are keenly aware of their mythic role as totem caricatures, reminding themselves and visitors that they must "portray that image of a drill instructor twenty-four hours a day." For this purpose, much depends on the instructor's voice and head. His voice acquires a distinctive frog pitch from constantly shouted correction, punishment, and encouragement. His characteristically angled campaign exaggerates the size of his head and the aggressive tilt of his jaw. An alert and aggressive posture called "military bearing" completes his image. Recruits not only submit to their drill instructors, they learn leadership, aggression, testing, and self-control by imitating them. DIs are models and instigators of group-forming, re-forming recruits into group members or banishing them to protect the group.

Besides training in physical skills and courage, bonding with one's buddies is the essential boot-camp experience. The goal is that groups should be "tight," a metaphor of a perimeter without gaps. This task requires taking individuals from different backgrounds who are unknown to each other and have no reason to trust each other and turning them into bonded units by having them suffer and triumph, achieve and fail together. Bodily lessons in group integrity begin with moving in synch with others while marching and cleaning, answering shouted commands and questions together, competing together, and shooting together. Greater and greater group challenges are offered and met together. To set the stage for a new group identity with its own history and shared commitments, old group identities are destroyed.[29] Recruits are goaded to create units hostile to outside invaders and insiders who fail to act as group members. Members must leave when the group commands it, and groups must expel whoever fails to follow such commands willingly. Platoons become microcosmic totem groups, their members at once victims and sacrificers.

Group-forming requires eliciting and even instigating intra-group conflict that directs hostilities inward rather than outward. Since lifting the killing taboo requires simultaneously inhibiting those who break it from turning on the group, potential rebellion is controlled by linking the identities of sacrificial insiders to the existence of outside killers. The calling to touch death becomes a ritual quest for identity. As the group assumes an organismic character, members act out consolidation by expelling or absorbing weak and uncooperative group members. Eliciting anger from slow-to-bond members may force them to acknowledge and act on their attachment to the group. Group members "bust ass" to test group commitment, threaten one another with expulsion and play out patterns of affiliative struggle that must not be allowed to dissolve the unit and can be used to make it stronger.

A popular theme of training stories is compelling uncooperative group members to act out the state of the group or their relation to it. Such members might be forced to sit facing a wall, or facing away from it and toward their buddies lined up and sitting as a group. A drill sergeant may try to integrate a separating member by assigning his punishment to others. So confronted, separating members may accept their punishment rather than allow a sacrificial substitution, making a contribution to group welfare at last. One instructor dealt harshly with a non-member who breached the invisible perimeter surrounding a drill instructor and his platoon. As the instructor addressed his men, the hapless outsider walked between them. Issuing a tongue lashing and corporal punishment on the spot, the instructor modeled the severe penalty that must be dealt to whoever tries to divide the group, which must always be defended.

Another training story concerns defining group perimeters through urination, a body-produced taboo barrier to outsiders. This drill sergeant's account explores how group identity and fraternal loyalty are transmitted through bodies at the level of primary groups:

Anytime you put [people] together in a stressful environment I think you bond somehow because you're all in the same boat. I've got guys that I grew up with, you know, in the city. I lived in an all-Italian neighborhood, and you know how it is in that community. But I've got guys I went to kindergarten with I knew for eighteen years before I left for the Marine Corps. I thought I was tight with them, but I've been tighter with Marines . . . I went to the Med twice, for two and a half years I was with the same guys, got pissed off with them, I was a lance corporal, got pissed off, got the shit details with them. We all starved together, we all partied together, we all lived together. They, we went on ship and lived again together, lived in the barracks together, went back on ship and lived again together – and there's something forms, you all understand each other. I could put a thousand dollars on my bed, leave for three hours, and it would still be there when I got back, and if someone else tried to touch it that wasn't in that platoon . . . It becomes your family, like, you mess with my brother, you know, and they would kill. That's why, like, when I grew up, when my brother and I went out it was like, if anyone got beat up and I saw it, I better come home beat up too, you know, 'cause my father says, "You never watch your brother, don't let me ever catch you watching your brother, and there's no such thing as a fair fight. If your brother's getting his butt licked, get in there. That's your family, you know, and the same thing recruits learn, they're all together, that's why they won't let no one ever mess with – it's almost like outta respect, 'cause I tell them, "You don't cut through anybody's platoon, you're damn sure not going to cut through my platoon." But then you gotta be careful because . . . by third phase [a late training period designation], like, all right hey, calm down, hey, get, you know, you tell 'em, like, hey, don't do nothin' stupid, hey, you want to get off this island in two days? You're outta here in two weeks, don't do nothing stupid, you know . . . I've had first phase [an early training period designation] recruits come into my barracks when we're checking out? I'll be in my last week of training, these guys were on the bus, you might as well say, and they were just check-ing out, but we need all the recruits to go somewhere to check out and pay bills. We'll have forming or Training Day 3 recruits come in to be fire watch or gear watch. My recruits'll just terrorize 'em and uh, I've had recruits . . . a Training Day 3 recruit will be in the head, and it's funny, you know, he'll be in the head going to the bathroom and when you find them in one of the troughs, I'll say, "Hey, so what-ever is the number, hey, why is there a Training Day 3 recruit going to the bathroom in your head?" No one in there, fifty-eight recruits will surround this guy. They know not to touch him. They're like, "AHHHHHHHH! WAKE UP!" It's like, he'll run! And it's funny, it just terrorizes 'em, and I know 'cause it happened to me, I got put on fire watch and that's why. It happened to me, so I do it, you know, and they'll come out, all the recruits come outta the head [mimics their cockiness] and they know that you let them have a little fun. Hey, now it's back to normal, they know they [have to] get their [military] bearing, don't lose your bearing, you know? They know they got their fun and the guy comes out [mimics fear], when you have fifty-eight guys, they're scared, they think they're going to beat the crap out of them. They know they're playing a game like I play with them. Yeah, like, I tear 'em, I stress the muscle. It's funny, you know, it's all in good fun, that's Parris Island, you know . . .[30]

The lessons of group bonding were vividly articulated by the writer William Manchester in a memoir of his experience as a World War II infantryman in the Pacific. Wounded at Okinawa, he violated medical orders to return to his comrades and almost certain death at Sugar Loaf on Oroku Peninsula.

It was an act of love. Those men on the line were my family, my home. They were closer to me than I can say, closer than any friends had been or ever would be. They had never let me down, and I couldn't do it to them. I had to be with them, rather than let them die and me live with the knowledge that I might have saved them. Men, I now knew, do not fight for flag or country, for the Marine Corps or glory or any other abstraction. They fight for one another. Any man in combat who lacks com-rades who will die for him, or for whom he is willing to die, is not a man at all. He is truly damned.[31]

Perhaps there are two totem secrets, one sacrificial and one regenerative. It may be that men who love each other so threaten the regenerative order of the center that they must die. The willing sacrifice of the sons who love one another would then be the revenge of the center on the border, just as the revenge of the totem ghosts at the border on the center is also the blood sacrifice of its sons. In totem crisis the world turns upside down. The center that loves its children sends them to die, while killers at the border cherish one another. Both secrets put the group at risk by blurring the necessary distinction between center and border that maintains the integrity of the group.

Women: outsiders inside the group

In totem myth men defend culture while women maintain and consolidate it. The male principle is differentiation and exclusion, the female principle is connection and reintegration. The border is an area of separation for ritual sacrifice, the center an arena of joining and augmentation. Totem myth instructs devotees in the cultural topography of groups, the unit of social survival. It rehearses a traditional division of sexual labor in which men's bodies are sacrificed for fighting, and women's bodies are sacrificed to the nurture of children. Neither task is exclusive to one gender, since men are necessary to the regenerative process and women's work is famously sacrificial. Totem myth nevertheless organizes the tensions between them by arranging specialized roles. Thus priestly border defenders strive to tear themselves from connecting mothers or lovers in order to serve the fathers. Here is an incomplete totem myth, a Honda motorcycle advertisement rendered as a totem journey promising escape from women at the fertile center. Text and image depict a biker, America's symbol of the outsider, speeding down the highway:

Mile after mile of red rock canyon unfolded in front of my handlebars. But no matter how hard I tried, I couldn't get her last words out of my head. As I came over the ridge, I kicked it into fifth and suddenly I couldn't hear a word she said.[32]

This version of the totem journey to the border is an adolescent fantasy. It describes the appeal of the border to the uninitiated. Women, the totem center, are what border travelers seek to escape. The journey in question is not the one across the border that makes men of boys. It lacks comrades and death.

The non-male bodies of women offer a point of invidious comparison and group-defining for male soldiers. At Parris Island, the drill sergeant who proudly trotted out the urination story above as a successful group

5.1 Columbia and States as regenerative female center of nation in Civil War lithograph. Totem fathers occupy

ritual did so about the time a female midshipman at Annapolis was handcuffed to a urinal by male midshipmen in an incident that ended the career of a Navy rear admiral.[33] While urination rituals are common enough in male initiation, they appear to be forbidden for females. Are women members of the tribe and subject to its usual customs, or outsiders? The threat, wrote columnist Anna Quindlen, was to "'cohesiveness,' what we civilians might call male bonding. In other words, they may have to fight or serve beside those with whom they lack proper kinship."[34]

Though sexist talk in the Marine Corps is officially frowned on, the most enthusiastic and deeply felt descriptions offered by drill instructors and officers at Parris Island described male group-forming. Such accounts were always hastily amended, mid-conversation and with embarrassment, to include women. Recent efforts by women to move into male military preserves have been met with deep hostility. The starkest evidence is provided by systematic incidents of sexual rape and harassment of women recruits in Army boot camp. When Shannon Faulker sued for admission to the Citadel, an all-male public military college, a journalist wrote, "To change, its champions say, would be to die."[35] An alumnus declared, "We know how to train young men how to be men. We don't know how to train young women to be men."[36] At Parris Island, pressure from the "Mothers of America" was cited as an obstacle to proper Marine training. We heard that boot camp most transforms the young man who has been overprotected by his mother. "First we make him a man," we heard, "and then we make him a Marine." To separate from the regenerative center is to die symbolically and become a man. This transformative anecdote was offered by an officer: "The same guy who would belch at the Burger King three months ago is now [at graduation] leading that mother around by the arm." A symbolic infant with no bodily control has become one who controls the mother.

Soldiers are ultimately defined by their combat roles in a community where killing and blood sacrifice are the highest duties. In hearings before the House Armed Services Committee, chairman Les Aspin described combat arms as the "essence" of each service, to which "the whole promotion system and prestige in the service is oriented."[37] Failure to touch death constitutes a major impediment to the advancement of women through the ranks. Granting this, military brass remained opposed to placing women in front-line units. "Combat is about killing people," said Air Force Chief of Staff, General Merrill A. McPeak. His concern was not that women would die.

Even though logic tells us that women can do that as well as men, I have a very traditional attitude about wives and mothers and daughters being ordered to kill people.[38]

In response Representative Patricia Schroeder "audibly sighed," object-
ing that, "There just doesn't seem to be the respect, even among the top
leaders."[39] The connection was clear. Respect comes from killing. Though
thousands of combat positions were opened to them in 1994, women are
barred from all ground combat with a "high probability of direct physical
contact with the personnel of a hostile force."[40] They remain excluded from
armor, infantry, and field artillery, the forces most likely to take casualties
from hand-to-hand combat. "What this basically says is that people who
will make up the future leadership of the Army will be all guys," commented a senior officer.

Objections to women as battlefield killers taps the same issue that makes
abortion controversial in the larger society. In both cases women claim the
killing power that is reserved for and must be ritually delegated by the
totem. Recanting her pro-choice position, the defendant in *Roe* v. *Wade*,
the Supreme Court's landmark abortion decision, described this power as
"the right [of women] to slaughter their own children."[41] To justify killing
power requires sacrificial purification. Those who desire power must
demonstrate that they deserve it by touching death themselves. To justify
their exercise of killing power over others, women must present themselves
as sacrificial victims. Thus there has been increased attention to the plight
of women as victims of rape, domestic violence, and crimes related to
sexual discrimination and harassment. Structurally, such appeals parallel,
even if they do not reproduce, those of white males whose war sacrifices
were until recently celebrated as justification for their own superior social
status and power. Mythic attention to the victimization of groups in search
of killling power does not suggest that such victimization is imaginary, or
that the sacrifices of others are less important by comparison. What is of
interest is the chain of mythic logic that accompanies every claim to power.

Rites of appeasement

Soldiers train to cross borders and touch death in war. The dead stay
beyond the border forever. Some who do not die never get back, or remain
unsure if they have returned. These are the damned. These unassimilated
soldiers wrestle with visions of totem fathers and brothers who demand
more blood. They are socially and spiritually lost, dead to the group. They
feel painfully at odds with civilians who have not shared their experiences,
who are not haunted by ghosts they cannot abandon. The encounter
between society and those who cannot return from sacrificial expulsion is
mutually uneasy. A homeless veteran remembered no public outpouring for
the soldiers of Korea. He recalled "the butchery of Pork Chop Hill, con-

sidering those who died there 'very lucky.' Each night, he sees men he killed standing at the foot of his bed, staring."[42] The dead demand more sacrifice, more blood. They must be pacified and kept at bay. According to Freud, the purpose of religion is to expiate the guilt of descendants by explaining the death of ancestors. In totem rituals survivors and descendants declare the debt to totem ancestors paid by the latest sacrificial offering, and themselves undeserving beneficiaries. Where beneficiaries are undeserving, more blood will be needed. If God does not take Isaac from Abraham today, he will tomorrow, since we owe him a death.

The dead must be acknowledged. They must receive offerings. Surveying the ranks of headstones at Arlington National Cemetery, a young visitor explained, "If I had the time, I'd read every one of the stones and lay something on them to let them know we were here."[43] She has absorbed the meaning of the ceremony, but not the compulsion to perform it. Those who have seen the dead display a different piety. Memorial Day provides the ritual occasion to elicit once more the guilt that inspires sacrificial memory. A Korean war veteran pondered his survival:

November 4, 1950. That's when [Walter] Bray's platoon was wiped out in Korea. A bullet shattered his right ankle. The Chinese stole his boots. For much of the three-week march into thirty-three months of imprisonment, other American prisoners carried or supported him. "I didn't even know these guys," says Mr. Bray, suddenly donning his sunglasses. "Many of them died in the camp, buried, unmarked on those barren hillsides or dumped in the river. But I didn't. Why?"[44]

Rites to appease the dead bring them to life by remodeling them. Bray re-creates their sacrifice and ceremonially offers himself on their behalf.

Part of his answer involves telling and retelling the story of their sacrifices. He speaks in schools . . . He marches in hometown parades because those distant buddies can't. And with [Jack] Hadley, he walks, then limps, miles of cemeteries every May [placing flags on the graves].[45]

Bray's buddy Jack Hadley has talked to the dead every Memorial Day for twenty years:

"This may sound stupid these days," he says, clearing his throat and stopping by the next grave. "But I stand by each of these stones, and I talk to the guy, you know, silent-like and I say, uh, 'Listen, thanks for your sacrifice, pal. Your people still think of you.' I hope someday someone will remember me like that. Isn't that what a Memorial Day is supposed to be?"[46]

Among those who demand blood, the most immediate ancestor may be the most demanding, since he is most compelling avatar of the creation–sacrifice that gives rise to us all. William Manchester describes the

5.2 Totem class marks ultimate group border by propitiating angry dead who might return.

unspoken charge of his father, a veteran of the Argonne, dying at the onset of World War II from the "wounds of 1918, which had never really healed," marking him as a ghost outsider. In the last moments between father and son, "His eyes said: *Avenge me!*"[47] Of his own citation for extraordinary valor, Manchester writes, "Those shining words didn't really apply to me. Indeed, at times it seemed to me that they applied to no one except the dead."[48] In this felt rejection is the unceasing conviction that not enough blood has been shed. Only more dead will answer the father's charge. An officer who sacrificed an arm and leg in Vietnam wrote of returning Gulf soldiers:

They have paid another installment on a great debt that will never be erased as long as there is tyranny in the world. Just like the generations of 1941 and 1950 and 1965, they kept up the payments for us all. And, like their predecessors, they paid in time, in effort, and they paid in blood.[49]

If the debt cannot be paid, enough blood will never be shed.

"A Fallen Soldier's Tribute to the Flag" in the *San Francisco Examiner* memorialized Staff Sergeant Michael R. Conner, the first Bay casualty in the Gulf War. Sergeant Conner had written a Christmas poem from the desert, a traditional place of visions.[50] It relates a visit by spirits angry about flagburning, then in the news. Flagburning desecrated the totem their blood had nourished, the totem they have, in short, become. The poem is an entry in the mythic genre of human visitors who reveal mysteries beyond the grave.[51] Western tribal literature includes the descent of Dionysius to bring back Semele, of Orpheus to bring back Eurydice, of Heracles to bring back the three-headed Cerberus, and of Jesus, the sacrificial son, into Hades. Displayed in three full newspaper columns, the text of the poem was printed over a gray-toned, ghostly American flag:

> I had a dream near 3 a.m.
> That crashed into my night
> A multitude of warriors
> Standing in full sight
>
> On their anguished faces
> Were grim and hateful glares;
> They wore Marine Corps blouses
> Yet all they did was stare
>
> I saw wounds of Belleau Wood,
> I saw the scars of Guam,
> The dead were there of Heartbreak Ridge
> And a company from 'Nam

Then, one spoke out and asked me
A question loud and strong:
"Can they burn the flag we died for?
How can it NOT be wrong?"

I did not have an answer
To ease their angry pain
I could only give excuses
For a country gone insane . . .

I saw the flag on Iwo
Just before I died
I saw that lead pole lifted
Where the flag was safely tied

I know it's just a symbol
That flies above our graves,
But let it be a symbol
Of what these men and I had gave

With that, the dream was over,
And I awoke with fear and shame.
To think a FOOL can trample
The flag that bears OUR names . . .[52]

The ghosts' wounds and their initial uncommunicativeness identify them as dead. The notion that the dead may be dishonored suggests they care how they are treated. They vouchsafe a vision to the poet at the moment of his own imagined death. The flag is a sacrificial emblem "of what these men and I had gave." In traditional solar myth the revelation to the human traveler occurs when the sun dips below the earth at night. The voyager wakes to tell his dream to living men in sunlight. Tylor writes:

Visits from or to the dead are matters of personal experience and personal testimony. When in dream or vision the seer beholds the spirits of the departed, they give him tidings from the other world, or he may even rise and travel thither himself, and return to tell the living what he has seen among the dead. It is sometimes as if the traveller's material body went to visit a distant land, and sometimes all we are told is that the man's self went, but whether in body or in spirit is a mere detail of which the story keeps no record. Mostly, however, it is the seer's soul which goes forth, leaving his body behind in ecstasy, sleep, coma, or death.[53]

The body images the soul. Border-crossers bear stigmata that mark them for death. In Westerns and war films an incidental wound often signals a sacrificial character's vulnerability in advance of the fight that kills him. To be wounded is to model dying; the Achillean opening in one's armor contagiously permits more death to enter. If wounds suggest the transformative effect of border-crossing, scars tell where the warrior has been when he returns to the land of the living. To cross the border is to be marked.

Wounds signify religious transformation, that is, death-touching. First blood is a familiar sign of adult initiation. In males it is proof of sacrificial willingness; in females, of ability to give life. First blood in boot camp is drawn in boxing, the first combat training with bodily contact. Recruits enter a priesthood of men with shared border experiences who display the totem mark in the bearing of their bodies and on their persons. Medals, emblematic wounds, are valued signs of transformative death-touching. "Their history is on their chest," declared the director general of naval history discussing the suicide of Chief of Naval Operations Admiral Jeremy Boorda after he had worn combat decorations to which he was not entitled. Medals convey the sacrificial history of the body that bears them. "They are the sacramentals of the military profession," wrote a retired Marine Corps general.[54] To claim false sacrifice is one of the most dishonorable sins. "I can't imagine how he could face the other service chiefs," remarked a journalist who had been preparing to break the Boorda story.[55] Boorda had shot himself in the chest, where the contested medals had been, as reporters prepared to confront him. In the end, he sacrificed for his medals after all. He made, in fact, the ultimate sacrifice.

Ritually unresolved sacrifice

One of the fierce struggles of World War II was the Battle of the Bulge, Hitler's last desperate gamble on the Western front. The Fifth and Sixth Panzer Armies inflicted 19,000 casualties on American forces and took 15,000 prisoners. The death, injury, and capture of 10,000 Wehrmacht troops finally dashed German hopes during a month-long battle of attrition. Wounded, sick, and exhausted soldiers fought on both sides. On the Allied side every salvageable man was sent back to the front. A medical officer described these sacrificial victims as personifications of death.

It's very hard to forget the expressions on their faces. They have a kind of hollow, lifeless, slack-jawed expression, and they almost don't see you as you go by. And after a while you learn not to greet them because their minds are elsewhere. It's almost as though they're going to a hopeless doom.[56]

War surpasses civilian comprehension. "You just can't understand it until you've walked through this valley of death," wrote a field officer in Vietnam.[57]

The totem story is not over when the killing is. Departing soldiers are marked for death; returning soldiers are marked by it. The killing taboo must be reimposed both on those who have touched death and those who have sent them to die. Failure to reassimilate endangers the group, since unassimilated soldiers may expose the totem secret. Failure also imperils soldiers, who, in order to conceal the totem secret, are labeled enemies so long as they remain outside the group. The community regards ambivalently the soldiers they gave up for dead, who were sent to die but did not. Soldiers likewise mistrust the community that sent them to die.

How to re-connect border-crossers to the community without exposing the totem secret? The character of Colonel Kirby, played by John Wayne in *The Green Berets* (1968), describes the dilemma of returning border-crossers. Holding his rifle, Kirby explains:

> It's a funny thing. A fella takes one of these into battle. If, by the grace of God, he comes out in one piece, he carries a strange sense of guilt all the rest of his life.[58]

Whoever breaks the killing taboo may be re-claimed, but only by renouncing his violation and crossing the border under proper ritual conditions. His guilt is "funny" and "strange" in the religious, liminal sense. Soldiers who refuse to surrender their identities as death-touchers remain outsiders. If society fails to reclaim these death-touchers in their midst, chaos follows. To remove the mark of the journey requires a mating ceremony between soldiers and the community to which they return.

Ghost outsiders

Though the largest number of American war dead in recent history was killed in Vietnam, these soldiers were not laid to rest for a long time. The ritual purpose of war is to re-define borders and renew the totem. Vietnam was a war without a clear beginning, a clear outcome, or a clear enemy. It ended in border confusion. Because it was a failed ritual, its soldiers were not easily released from death-touching and re-attached to the social body. Returning veterans were not communally celebrated nor dead ones communally grieved. Without rituals of reabsorption, the sacrifice remained incomplete. A Vietnam veteran recalled, "Once a young co-ed sat me down with some of her fellow students and asked with an earnest smile, 'Just how many babies did you kill?'"[59] Another described a college class in which a professor ordered him to explain how it felt to "murder innocent peasants in Southeast Asia."[60] If the community was ambivalent about reassimilating killers in order to conceal its own murderousness, some veterans were reluctant to shed their death-touching status. Some of these disaffected vets adopted the outlaw persona of bikers to symbolize their estrangement from society.

Even when the totem secret is exposed, insiders may resist it. A 1990 episode of the television series *L. A. Law* dramatized this issue. The episode featured two protagonists. One, a Vietnam veteran, had burned a flag in a cemetery on Memorial Day to protest cuts in veterans' benefits. Burning the flag is the gestural equivalent of exposing the totem secret. This is part of its felt horror. The flagburner was assaulted by the son of a Vietnam soldier who knew his own father as a memory, a bodiless ghost. Confronting his antagonist and border-dwelling double with the totem secret, the veteran cries, "You're just a victim of the same lies, the same delusions that killed your old man . . . The United States of America killed your father!!" The veteran's attorney equates his client with the defendant:

None of you were in Vietnam. And there isn't the slightest chance that you . . . or *I* . . . could ever know the frustration . . . the *rage* that Bob Westin must know, having risked his life for a country that would only ignore him upon his return.

Likewise, you will never know the emptiness of Dan Ramel . . . or the rage *he* must know . . . having lost his father to a war that the people of this country willingly forget. They are both victims of the Vietnam war. And no jury anywhere could ever make them whole.[61]

An unassimilated veteran is an outsider. A young man uninitiated by a father whom the totem has sacrificed is also an outsider with no clear sense of borders. Both are damned.

During the Gulf War the living and dead of Vietnam were said to be in need of restitution. Living vets were depicted as jealous of the attention showered on Gulf soldiers, or as patient, wounded, and unseen – functional ghosts watching a new generation at the feast. Unassimilated veterans joined their resentment to the felt anger of dead soldiers in a lost cause. Ticketed for illegal peddling, the source of his livelihood, a disabled veteran in a camouflage cap decorated with an American flag observed his social location: "It's like years ago when you went out on patrol and the sergeant said, "You're the point man. The point man was the guy to get it. Today, we're the point men."[62]

Vietnam veterans say they didn't get any flagwaving. The complaint tells us the ritual importance of flags as transformative agents of re-integration. The triumphant flagwaving reassimilation of Gulf soldiers was widely seen as offering passage back across the border to everyone outside it. "You all not only helped liberate Kuwait," President George Bush declared at his first meeting with returning Gulf soldiers, "you helped this country liberate itself from old ghosts and doubts."[63] When it looked as though assimilation might finally be theirs, some outsiders claimed the death marks they bore could not be erased. This veteran rejected all efforts to sever living comrades from dead ones:

Including Vietnam vets in the public flagwaving doesn't clear the stale air from the mental flag-draped coffin they've been living in. It doesn't breathe new life into the 58,135 who came home in real hermetically sealed containers or the 2,394 who never came back.[64]

Though politicians and citizens might believe the wounds of Vietnam were mending, "Vietnam should not be left to fester, but it also should not be closed. It should remain a boil on the nation's butt, that hurts when policymakers sit down to plan another war." Death-touchers and the sacrificed were a curse on the country that had given them up for dead, to whom they believed they were as good as dead.

The press treated welcome home ceremonies for Gulf soldiers as fertility rites. "Along blocks lined with streams of flowing yellow ribbons and lampposts decked with yellow bows, some spectators yelled out their thanks" at one parade for returning troops and veterans. Dignitaries were everywhere:

Veterans from many wars marched, including marines in sharp blue dress uniforms and those from the Gulf in their tan desert fatigues. Color guards held their flags stiffly aloft in the mild breeze, which also carried the strains of brass bands and bagpipes.[65]

For those who remembered the bitterness of Vietnam such ritual sights "chased away those disconcerting memories." But guilt was not far beneath the surface in a story about an armory where parade participants were separated from homeless men living there. A security guard and a partition divided returning Gulf vets and the homeless vets of Vietnam, totem insiders and outsiders. There was a border incident:

At one point in the homecoming, a hand with a tiny American flag peeked through the partition that bisected the armory. The wall separated the desert veterans from veterans of another struggle – the 150 homeless men who call the armory home . . . Many of the shelter's residents slept, curled up in blankets atop spartan cots. Others milled about or shot a game of pool, out of view of the dignitaries and families.
"A lot of these guys had been in Vietnam," one of the homeless men said of the others in the shelter. "See the kind of welcome they're getting now."[66]

Had Vietnam been a popular war, a man with Bill Clinton's draft history might never have won the presidency in 1992. His victory was testimony to how honorable the Vietnam War had not been, and how little Vietnam veterans mattered in public life.

Outsiders at the wall

On the ten-year-anniversary of the Vietnam Veterans Memorial, *Life* magazine followed a group of vets under care for post-traumatic disorders on a pilgrimage to the "Wall." An opening anecdote described one man in a state of flashback and nightmare, a dream state inhabited by ghosts. The substance of his dream was, "I never get to the other side."[67] This vet, Bill Mohr, was described as without attachments to the living world.

His wife has left him. His parents are dead. He is unsteady, if not unstable. "I believe something happened," he says. "But I can't figure it out."

An earlier *Life* article described the condition of outsider vets as "a disorder of men who . . . dispatched the enemy without blinking – a disorder of the good soldier." Those who do not blink are death-touchers without human reflexes. They have no seeing eyes. They are not living men.[68] The night before the visit, Mohr's comrades in twilight existence wandered wakefully, "appearing and disappearing like ghosts." Therapy consists in facing the Wall, which *Life* equated with the totem border and its sacrificial ordeal.

"Why am I afraid of facing the wall?" asks Frank Ham, who earned three Purple Hearts . . . No one answers Ham. He says, "Because once you face the wall, you've got to deal with it." The "it," of course, is not really the wall but what it has come to stand for, namely death, heroism, memory, fear, guilt, gratitude, and waste.

The malady of the vets is described as a constant border struggle, an interminably liminal existence, a living death. Because Vietnam was a war without borders, these vets are lost. They cannot separate themselves from the ghosts of Vietnam. They were expelled but cannot return. The wall is depicted in death terms as "an enormous, embracing, black granite tombstone."[69] It is recalled as the site of a suicide, a mythic fate of unassimilated veterans.

Perhaps the best known Vietnam veteran to commit suicide was Lewis Puller, Jr., who wrote a Pulitzer-prize autobiography about coming to terms with the sacrifice of both legs and parts of both hands in an unpopular war.[70] A member of the group that brought the Vietnam Veterans Memorial to fruition, and a tireless lobbyist for veterans, he was also the son of the most decorated Marine in history, General Chesty Puller, a Korean War hero. Measured against his father, the son's sacrifice, suffered within weeks of his arrival in Vietnam, must have seemed misspent and futile. Reflecting on Puller's death, a veteran articulated the dilemma of incomplete sacrifice:

For men with blood on their hands, men stained by the butchery of combat, the real fight for survival starts when the guns grow silent. For us, suicide is a chronic afterthought, a dark idea that follows dark memories. Most of us resist the incessant impulse to destroy ourselves, but many of our comrades, too many, do not. They lose the war long after the fighting has stopped.[71]

At a memorial service, Jan Scruggs, the originator of the Vietnam War Memorial, read a passage from Puller's autobiography that suggested the pull of the dead on unassimilated veterans:

In what became an often-repeated rite of homage, I returned to the memorial with a single red rose and, seeing my reflection in its polished stone, came to understand how inextricably linked the memorial and I were by the bloodshed of my brothers.[72]

In suicide Puller remodeled sacrificial death at the border. He saw himself as a ghost, an insubstantial image reflected in stone. Like the Wall, he was death.

Dissipation of the totem

Memorial Day, an early summer holiday of ceremony, parades, recollections, and decorating graves with flags, originally commemorated the dead of the Civil War. President George Bush called it one of our "most solemn observances. On this sacred day, we honor those who died fighting for freedom."[73] A World War II veteran of New Guinea, the Solomons, and the Philippines recalled how, thirty years before, he had marched in Memorial Day parades that lasted for hours:

"Oh, it was inspiring," he said in a faint echo of the voice that roared orders into the whine of enemy dive bombers. "It was glorious. The flags, the bands, everybody in uniform with ribbons and medals, the legionnaires with their caps, the spectators cheering you on. There was that feeling of being appreciated for what we did when we went away."[74]

The ritual elements of Memorial Day include a blessing by the embodied totem, who lays a wreath at the Tomb of the Unknown Soldier. Curtains of flags decorate Robert E. Lee's mansion, backdrop to the Tomb of the Unknown. At the local level there are community parades, sacrificial feasts of regeneration, and media remodeling. This small town was typical:

Each year Bergen County [New Jersey] appropriates $27,000 to buy 46,000 little American flags. Before the public holiday hoopla, scores of veterans privately take armloads of flags. They walk along endless rows of tombstones in every cemetery. At each grave marked as a veteran's they stick a fresh flag into the ground. Which is how Decoration Day was named back in 1868.

But these modern veterans do more. "We honor that one comrade with one flag," said [veteran Walter Bray]. "But each flag also honors all the guys without graves. We must think of them."[75]

On the first Memorial Day after the Gulf War, many American cities and towns held big parades for their new veterans. Though the good feeling of that war had dissipated a year later, it would have been unthinkable for Memorial Day to go entirely unobserved. Testimony that the ritual duty had been performed was offered by the *New York Times,*

Throughout the day, the nation's war dead were honored in public and private ceremonies. There were stirring speeches and flag waving, patriotic songs and salutes, and neighborhood parades in which veterans marched with prideful strides and children, too young to learn any lessons from war, were delighted by the rumbles of drums and the blare of bugles.[76]

But in New York interest in the holiday was so slight "as veterans of the so-called great wars have died or have grown too old to march," that the traditional Broadway parade to the Soldiers' and Sailors' Monument at Riverside Park was canceled for the first time in seventy-three years. The *Times* remodeled the ritual elements of Memorial Day for readers while describing its demise:

In suburbs and hamlets across the land, Americans will still remember the nation's war dead tomorrow and on Monday with thundering parades, band concerts, fireworks displays and other events draped with the battle flags of Guadalcanal and Normandy, of Inchon and Chu Lai.
But just a year after the gigantic emotional outpouring of millions of people in the Desert Storm Parade up the Broadway Canyon of Heroes, the organizers of an event that has been the city's symbolic centerpiece on Memorial Day since 1919 have decided to forgo a parade that might have drawn only a handful of veterans, many of whom would have hobbled with age or infirmity along an all-but-deserted route.[77]

The sacrifice had lost its renewing power. Memorial Day veterans offered death without life. The press chronicled the change. "Who are all those old men, somebody's grandfathers?" a headline read.

This May holiday has become lighthearted, parade-happy and full of cold drinks. And then along come these dour old-timers with their colored jackets and ties and their old-fashioned peaked caps bearing unrecognizeable medals and indecipherable abbreviations. The stronger men in the old uniforms carry tall flags, and a sprinkling of sidewalk spectators remove their hats or cover their hearts. But not many, because that stuff is out nowadays.[78]

Laying the traditional wreath at the Tomb of the Unknown Soldier, Vice-President Dan Quayle declared, "A society that has nothing worth dying for has nothing worth living for." He reiterated the regenerative function of sacrifice and the totem principle that the group may kill for ultimate social truth. The fact that the vice president, an unheroic political figure of undistinguished military record, was an acceptable stand-in for the embodied totem as wreath-layer at the holiest shrine to the sacrificed dead of the nation, was also a message about the declining power of the holiday.

Televised for a national audience, the 1992 National Memorial Day concert in Washington, DC, focused on the totem service and suffering of African–Americans and women. These were groups whose sacrificial claims had only recently been acknowledged in many cases, among other outstanding and incompletely honored claims on the body politic. What women and African–Americans were not was the largest group of surrogate victims in any American war. By some accounts that group consisted of white males, whose cultural and social power had long been justified in sacrificial terms, though even this label melded many different ethnicities with varied histories of striving for totem recognition. To some traditionalists, the choice to single out the contributions of any besides the totem group to all wars was less an expansion of the domain of sacrificial remembrance than an affiliative division of credit that signaled a lessening of dedication to the nation's most compelling memories of totem sacrifice and the ritual duties of commemoration. Said one veteran, "People now seem preoccupied with everything in the world but those who made the supreme sacrifice."[79] It was perhaps a warning that new sacrifice would be needed.

The failure of the Gulf War to renew the country's interest in Memorial Day meant its offering had been too small to create new group memories of sacrifice.

Over the years our parade got smaller and smaller. The spectators became fewer and fewer, and participation by vets fell off. Guys were getting old. Some moved away, retired to the Sun Belt. The younger ones were not too interested. You couldn't seem to get them out.[80]

We are condemned to repeat what we forget. The dead ancestors must not be neglected. If they do not receive the offerings of remembrance due them, sooner or later they will exact them in blood.

6

Strategic tinkering: totem memory and succession

Ritual is *the* basic social act.   Roy Rappaport[1]

Senator, you're no John Kennedy.   Sen. Lloyd Bentsen

Ritual enacts totem order. This order is no abstract system lacking practical effect. If the United States is not engulfed in civil war, this is because it has a strong, functioning ritual process in place. A bare-bones definition of ritual is memory-inducing behavior that has the effect of preserving what is indispensable to the group. What is indispensable for the totem group is periodic bloodshed to re-create borders. This bloodshed repeats the fundamental act of group creation we call *creation–sacrifice*. In a well-functioning totem order, new blood sacrifice is experienced as a reinvigoration of founding values. The group is refreshed; time starts over. Between creation–sacrifice and its commemoration there is a reciprocal relationship. Creation–sacrifice invests each commemoration with significance. Commemorative repetition revivifies creation–sacrifice. Replicating the act of perfect creation ritually constructs cosmos, the divine order, out of undifferentiated chaos.[2] By ritually dressing new disorders in the garments of primal bloodletting, group life is sustained.

The mechanism of ritual remodeling is *re-presentation*. More than simple reflection or likeness, re-presentation offers the thing itself in magically revivified form. A New York state assemblyman could say of the flag during a legislative debate about flagburning: "This is not just a symbol or icon. It is the *embodiment* of everything that America stands for [italics added]."[3] His remark is significant within the totem system. The flag offers proof of the holy body that believers require. It is the skin of the dead ancestor held high. Flagraising resurrects the sacrificed body in the presence of witnesses. This tangible proof of totem power to defeat death makes it emotionally compelling. The group goes forward in the name of the sacrificed body it resurrects. This is the Durkheimian totem. The cohesion it ritually effects is remarkable to group members. Its power is *magical.*

Magic is an effect that demonstrably exceeds the natural limitations of human bodies. Sir James Frazer long ago classified all magic as *contagious* or *sympathetic.*[4] Each is a distinctive mode of transferring power. *Contagious* magic crosses boundaries. It alters by contiguity, contact, and connection between a magical agent and a supplicant. Substance flows into substance, magically violating and breaching form. This is the magic of investiture in which the acolyte is transformed by the touch of the priest whose body is the medium of a sacred power. The ultimate expression of contagious magic is transfiguration by death, the final transformer of bodily boundaries. The power of *sympathetic* magic resides in mimesis. Form is communicated through replication, which Malinowski calls analogous action. This is the magic that enables children in Halloween costumes to appropriate a fearful power by modeling it. Supplicants do not receive sympathetic magic so much as perform it. They speak its gestures and put on its forms. Both contagious and sympathetic magic are regenerative. They communicate power by making more. Both inhabit blood sacrifice. To shed another body's blood or have one's own blood shed engages contagious magic by reforming bodily and, therefore, social boundaries. To remodel killing and dying is to amplify their power sympathetically by re-creating what has gone before. Sympathetic magic is the mode of mass media.

Rituals create and control experience by re-enacting the creation of the world. At the fundamental level of the body, ritual gestures enact the creative paradigm by uniting profane substance and sacred form. Bodies that touch one another out of affection or hostility gesture contagiously. Bodies that conform themselves more or less to one another in socially coded ways gesture sympathetically. Because they are transforming, contagious ritual gestures mark the point beyond which nothing is the same. They start and stop time. Sympathetic ritual gestures make time connected and continuous. They re-create the present in images of the past so life does not lose its moorings. Ritual power thus flows from the transformation and replication of bodies at key moments in the birth and death of the group.

Against ritual

Generals are always fighting the last war.   Aphorism

For better or worse, ritual in traditional societies offers the model to which we compare ritual in post-traditional societies. In the traditional model ritual is a significant group episode. Its meanings are shared by group members who are initiated into them early. Group members' private beliefs are thought to be congruent with the ritual worldview of the group. Ceremonial changes are imperceptibly slow. Ritual structures are coherent, consistent, and redundant in relation to one another. Ritual worldviews do not compete with alternative or dissident worldviews except during cultural breakdown, often from contact with societies like our own. This model seems far removed from the multiple, clashing elements of post-traditional life. But consider. In industrial society high totem rituals such as war and presidential elections are clearly marked. Throughout their lives totem group members are initiated and re-initiated into elaborate systems of patriotic practice. Though congruence between private and ritual world-views is always difficult to establish, what matters for the survival of the group is what we will do publicly on its behalf. And though to be modern is to be impermanent, successful totem rituals deny that change is chaos, framing it instead as an elaboration of fundamental group values. Our contemporary failure to find coherence in modern ritual systems suggests emic and etic bias.[5] To native observers of our own group it is hardly surprising that familiar social processes may seem more fragmented and less coherent than they actually are. By contrast, unfamiliar social processes that belong to others may seem unduly simple. We may not see their complexity.

Jack Goody has famously questioned the relevance of traditional ritual notions for post-traditional societies.[6] For rituals to function properly, he argues, congregants need detailed and frequent exegeses. Yet contemporary society has no apparent overarching myth system and no explicit initiation of devotees into ritual meaning. We argue that American nationalism is the overarching myth that patriotic rituals express and media endlessly elaborate. Goody considers mass media woefully inadequate for ritual instruction. The most powerful ritual meanings are undoubtedly conveyed body to body and in person. Still, mass mediated words and gestures play an important role. Together with blood sacrifice and a host of intermediate rituals they comprise a system of great stability, flexibility, and emotional persuasiveness. That system is never more than partially manifest at any moment, for totem meanings are always under construction, the full system is too rich and complex for any single presentation, and the totem secret must be preserved.

For Goody ritualized expression in industrialized societies is routinized, meaningless and ineffective. He fails to consider dramatically opportunistic and unpredictable rituals such as war. Still, predictability is no defect. Automaticity reinforces the status quo. As a kind of mortar for meaning, it so readily communicates what the world is that devotees have difficulty conceiving it differently. This status quo is punctuated by intervals of crisis that imperil routinized meanings that must then be ritually revivified or replaced. The most magical rituals are able to construct new creation–sacrifices when old ones no longer serve. In the process, exhausted meanings slip painlessly from sight. Not every ritual effort staves off crisis, of course. Some fail.

Goody argues that rituals must shed as well as preserve meaning. On Veterans' Day, William Pfaff describes such a mechanism while reflecting on the generational death of totem memory.

In the 1920s, one of my aunts, Catherine Burke, wrote a charming and subsequently much-anthologized story about a Boy Scout unhappily kept home from the Memorial Day parade to look after an elderly neighbor. The neighbor proves to have been a drummer present at Gettysburg when Lincoln gave his great address, and he gives the Scout a button from Lincoln's coat which the president had given to him.

My aunt and her sisters were only a little more distant from the Civil War than we are today from World War II. They experienced the Great War as adolescents or young adults. The man Catherine married had been gassed at the Argonne, and suffered from it for the rest of his brief life.

I write about this because the United States in which they lived, and into which I was born, now passes from the effective memory of Americans . . . There is no choice about this. History has simply closed a door . . . The country George Bush was born to is unrecognizable, even uninteresting, to vast numbers of Americans today. Clinton and Gore have another country to deal with. However, they were born to it, and know it. They too know no other.[7]

This example makes another point. Memory that motivates group-defining sacrifice does not originate in disembodied texts, as Benedict Anderson suggests, though texts may rehearse and refresh it. It takes a gassed soldier, a button, a holy relic that has touched totem bodies to sustain magic. It takes the memory of familiar bodies, or memories passed along by them. Magic weakens when bodies that loved sacrificial bodies are gone. Texts alone cannot sustain it.

For Goody the notion of shared meaning that lies at the heart of many ritual definitions contradicts common sense evidence that ritual interpretations vary. As a dimension of all human activity, ritualization is the process of imposing mythic order on bodies and events in order to make sense of them, though full ritual meaning never resides in any single act or interpretation.[8] In fact, the presence of competing interpretations directs attention to ritual obligations and the consequences of failing to perform them by making them a matter of interest and discussion. Our task will be to show the pattern to which even apparently oppositional interpretations belong and account for them.

Like Goody, Mircea Eliade believes that traditional ritual models have doubtful contemporary relevance. According to him, archaic men embraced an ordered, ritualized world of faith to which modern men have no access, though we are at least liberated from archaic fatalism.[9] In fact, Eliade's analysis of archaic ritual describes modes of thought and action that are perfectly familiar. For archaic men and totem supplicants alike, all meaningful gestures are lived through the gods. Archaic man "sees himself as real only to the extent that he ceases to be himself . . . and is satisfied with imitating and repeating the gestures of another."[10] "Everything that lacks an exemplary model is 'meaningless,' i.e., it lacks reality."[11] This exactly describes the totem system in which ritual gestures always refer to a model. Since ritual gesture is *only* a model, it is a source of profound anxiety. Though it imitates reality, it is not reality, which is ineffable.

Ritual types

I've seen the future; it is murder.   Leonard Cohen

Totem rituals may be *apostolic, priestly,* or *messianic*. Only apostolic and priestly rituals may be performed. In mythic doctrine, messianic ritual languishes untouched and untouchable at the beginning of the world, a lost and holy event. Apostolic and priestly forms derive their whole legitimacy from messianic ritual but cannot touch it. Though it is taboo with respect to them, preserving its numinous agency is their entire function. Ritual that structures the present is *apostolic*. It is a ritual of mission, transforming profane into sacred space. It guarantees totem succession. It is expansionist, repairing, reclamatory. Avowedly restorative, it constructs the present by reactualizing the past. It is uncertain and urgent. It aims to rescue imperiled totem order and could fail. Apostolic ritual may be routine and periodic, as in a presidential campaign, or occasional and situation-dependent, as in a military charge up a hill to take territory or a legislative proposal to ban flagburning. It is a redemptive effort in the name of messianic sacrifice, which it remodels. The flag advancing into battle marks an apostolic mission. Raised on territory sanctified by blood, the apostolic flag resurrects messianic sacrifice in order to re-establish a sacred center. Apostolic funeral rites consecrate the sacrificed sons, returning them as offering to their mother, the fertile nation. All transformative rituals (think only of induction, voting, and war) have this apostolic aspect.

Consider the raising of the Russian flag over the Chechen presidential palace in Grozny during an unpopular military action to prevent Chechen secession. American pundits observed its re-presentation in Russian media:

The way the Government treated it, the raising of the Russian flag over the black-ened hulk of the presidential palace in the rebel Chechen capital was akin to the Soviet flag going up over Hitler's Reichstag, an image graven in every Russian heart as the moment Nazism was beaten.[12]

The sacrifice thus apostolically recalled was the last to unify living Russians. Media dutifully recalled for congregants that this was the sacrifice to save Russia from fascism.

Some missions undertaken for apostolic ends appear foundational *in ret-rospect*. They are re-defined as singularly transforming or *messianic*. Messianic sacrifice is the central regenerative ritual of the totem system. It can never be consciously performed as such. It is recognized only in ret-rospect in other rituals that refer to it. Events retrospectively recognized as messianic are "saturated with reality" in Eliade's terms. Messianic ritual is the gesture of the mighty beginning and indispensable renewal. It over-shadows and replaces previous originary acts. It is the cosmogonic creative gesture after which nothing is the same. "They gave us our world," President Bill Clinton said of World War II veterans on the occasion of the fiftieth anniversary celebration of D-Day. Without it things would not be as they are. There may have been earlier sacrifices, but lived, real time for devotees begins with whatever sacrifice is utterly meaningful to them. Messianic sacrifice re-forms reality, creating new exemplars. It is the preg-nant gesture of the holy. From it the present acquires meaning and order, which is existence.

The final category of totem ritual is not primarily transforming as apos-tolic rituals are, or messianically creative. It is *commemorative*. Commemorative rituals re-present. They re-energize and re-dedicate sacred time and space created by acts of heroic predecessors. They inform devo-tees about models for apostolic missions and messianic sacrifices. Media presentations are the best-known commemorative rituals, but every totem ritual freshens up totem order. When a Gold Star mother says, "It is difficult to accept my son's death, but he's alive in my heart," she re-enacts a resurrection, remodeling the act that creates society, the violent blood-letting from which order emerges.[13] Living memory sustains sacrifice and thereby re-creates group life. In this sense every ritual commemorates and transforms, but to different degrees.

Consider Dwight D. Eisenhower's published memory of his induction into West Point, a narrative remodeling at once priestly and apostolic. As Supreme Allied Commander in World War II and later President, Eisenhower is a charged totem figure. His recollection is commemoratively valuable for showing how a messianic totem journey begins. It describes a seasonal rite of totem succession, the induction of new cadets. Here he recalls his own totem transfiguration, an apostolic moment of assimilation to the flag:

My first day at West Point – June 14, 1911 – had been rough. My classmates and I had been barked at and ordered by upperclassmen to do all sorts of ridiculous chores, on the double. All 285 of us were weary and resentful.

Towards evening, however, we assembled outdoors and, with the American flag floating majestically above us, were sworn in as cadets of the United States Military Academy. It was an impressive ceremony. As I looked up at our national colors and swore my allegiance, I realized humbly that *now I belonged to the flag*. It is a moment I have never forgotten.[14]

The acolyte signals to himself and the world that his doubts and confusions are cast behind him, beyond a temporal border. The military posture of his body signifies his new status. What has come before is discarded. Time stops and begins again. What was diffuse and ambiguous is ceremonially simplified and canonically refigured. According to his commemorative recollection, the embodied totem-to-be launched his life's calling in this model moment of merging with the totem.[15] This was no ordinary flagraising, but the apostolic embrace of a mission to redeem a founding sacrifice, to become one with the center. Both the lived ceremony and Eisenhower's memory of it condense apostolic initiation, the longer training to come in which young men from different tribes and allegiances strive for inner conversion through outer ordeals of ritualized suffering. Their new statuses are conferred in a moment of totem presence through mystical union with the flag that consecrates them for future sacrifice.

Recalling sacrifice

Solidarity is only gesturing when it involves no sacrifice.

Mary Douglas[16]

Reality is a condition of meaning enabled and sustained by successive creation acts that are known only in memory. If reality can be ritually apprehended only through memory, memory actually constructs reality by recalling it. Reality, so understood, remains tragically elusive and ungraspable. A defining feature of perfect creation–sacrifice, the utterly real, is that it has departed from the here and now. Existing only in memory, it is fragile. As a hedge against chaos, or forgetting, we can only imitate it. This anxious distance between model and reality provides the engine that sets the ritual cycle in motion. Though our models recall creation–sacrifice, we experience them as falling hopelessly short of the real event we cannot actually grasp. Guilt thus motivates believers to replicate the creation that chaos is in danger of dismantling. This replicative creation effort is ritual. Because the acted out model never *is* the creation to which it refers, efforts to reproduce it are undertaken over and over. In this manner the present aspires to reproduce the past that generates it. The present, urgently presented for repair, is never secured. This is how totem order regenerates itself, by endlessly seeking to close the gap between present bodies and the blood history that engenders them.

Though creation normally sets a temporal sequence in motion and renewal extends it, the temporal order of totem creation is different. Sacrifice does not set totem creation in motion. It retrospectively begets it. Totem order is created *after the fact* of a bloodletting retrospectively classified as sacrifice and invested with generative agency. Every important creation story begins with messianic sacrifice, the original and most important act in the totem system. To frame violence as originary sacrifice shapes it to a totem narrative. In the economy of totem order ritual not only constructs originary sacrifice. It is compelling evidence of its fecundity. How else could the ceremony that remodels it have come to be?

Roy Rappaport calls ritual "a communicative mode in which canonical messages are conveyed through indexical elements that specify the current state of participants."[17] Since canonical messages are immaterial, only the concrete behavior of ritual performers can actualize and validate them. By their presence in the ritual, participants cannot *not* be there. By their behavior they cannot *not* be publicly assenting to the ritual order, whatever their private beliefs. Combining formality and performance in this way makes ritual messages compelling. The canonical makes claims about the regenerative power of sacrifice. The indexical or ceremonial ties these claims to specific events and participants. Totem ritual weds canonical form to indexical substance by attaching mythic archetypes to present circumstances. Form encodes substance, and events substantiate form. As substance would be vacuous without form, form would be impotent without substance.

This model makes interpretable the anxieties of veterans who professed themselves unworthy to stand in for their dead comrades during D-Day fiftieth anniversary celebrations in Europe. Ritually, it does not matter if these men were scared during the invasion or behaved in a cowardly fashion, or if they remain unconvinced of their worthiness. By their presence and behavior they signify acceptance of the order to which they publicly conform. They will give honor and be honored as required, performing their roles in a liturgy they did not encode. Their self-doubts serve liturgy by recalling perfect sacrifice. These who bore witness to the sacrifices of comrades revivify them. Our existence as congregants further establishes the generative power of their creation–sacrifice. Their deaths engendered us, who are unarguably here. Our failure to do as they did, even as we model them, also establishes their generative power. We who were not present at the beginning of the world are less perfect than these witnesses, their comrades who were there. Our obligation to the totem dead who seek blood vengeance is also greater. If we fail to offer ourselves in imitation of their creation–sacrifice, the group will die, for only living sacrifice feeds the group.

Ritual models chaos to totem specifications. At its heart lies generative sacrifice, which invests blood with ritual form. Blood is the supreme ritual agent, the substance of group attachment and kinship. Each life in the community depends on it. Blood accompanies fertility (signified by menstruation and first intercourse), childbirth, and violent death. Unordered or uncontained, it unleashes chaos. Becoming ritually memorable, it acquires ordering power. Where disorder and chaos are greatest, ritual order will be pursued most fervently. The most dramatic site of regenerative sacrifice is the battlefield consecrated by human blood. Where battlefields are, much holiness is on display. Those who shed blood there are transfigured. Touching the forbidden taboo, they merge with the totem, which is death. This cosmogonic unity of substance and form is a religious mystery hidden from the group whose existence depends on it.

Ritual gestures materialize meaning by repeating acts performed at the beginning of the creation cycle by gods, ancestors, and civilizing heroes. Ritual re-enacts the beginning of cosmic time. Nothing that comes after is the same. There may be a past before creation–sacrifice, but lived, real time begins with it. Thus it reshapes mythic history. It is prophetic, directing future time back to itself. And not only time. Ritual space coincides with the cosmic center of the world. Places, gestures, and persons acquire reality through assimilation to a totem center, the *axis mundi* re-created in the flagpole. Mythic connections are struck between a centered present designated by the flag and an original creation in relation to which the present is consequence and renewal. But these commemorative acts are *not* the blood, they are *not* the sacrifice. They are not real *enough*, and this produces endless concern.

No ultimate sacrifice can be remembered by those who gave it, for they are dead. It can only be re-presented by those who were witness to sacrifice or become witnesses through commemoration. "If you weren't there, you'll never understand it, and we can't expect you to," explained a World War II nurse at D-Day ceremonies in France, "but we'd like to have your remembrance."[18] Messianic sacrifice, the holiest totem gesture, is defined in retrospect and imaginatively. "We are the children of your sacrifice," President Bill Clinton told World War II veterans in the summer of 1994 at Omaha beach, where the greatest American losses on D-Day occurred.[19] The historical Normandy operation was an apostolic mission to repair totem injury. Commemoratively, Clinton recalled its sacrificed soldiers as messianic and regenerative by describing them as parental.

How does commemoration effect totem survival? Remodeling focuses guilt. Compared to those who made the ultimate sacrifice, the sacrifices of survivors and descendants are naggingly incomplete. "Too few Americans know what that generation did," said Bill Clinton, articulating contemporary ritual guilt for World War II sacrifice.[20] At Portsmouth the Archbishop of Canterbury blessed the launch of commemorative invasion forces with these words:

Fifty years on, we commemorate the glory and sacrifices of the D-Day invasion. Many of you are only too well aware of what those words mean. It was your friends who gave their lives in the Normandy campaign. They fought alongside you. Their deaths could have been your own.

A key ceremonial element is acknowledging that ritual is not the sacrifice it models. This may be expressed as a longing to bridge the gap between remodeling and creation with new sacrifice. But ultimate sacrifice has no true re-presentation. The model can never be the full measure of the modeled unless it becomes a messianic sacrifice that future remodelings cannot in turn capture.

Guilt generates a wish and, when ritual works properly, an obligation to offer tribute for the world-creating sacrifices of bloodthirsty totem gods. "They were the fathers we never knew, the uncles we never met, the heroes we can never repay. They gave us our world," Clinton said.[21] Reminding onlookers what they and generations unborn owed to the dead of D-Day, the Archbishop of Canterbury recalled the guilt of a model member of the regenerative center:

The Archbishop said that all during the war Eleanor Roosevelt kept at her bedside a prayer that said: "Help me to remember, somewhere out there a man died for me today. As long as there be war, I must ask and answer, 'Am I worth dying for?'"[22]

Guilt harnessed by commemoration is a ritual engine for producing more sacrifice to generate further motivating guilt. Only memory generates sacrificial desire, and memory unreplenished by sacrifice fades. A year after the battle of Iwo Jima, the *New York Times* remodeled its memory by declaring the willing sacrifices of Iwo proof against totem division.

No one stopped to count the cost of what he did there . . . There was no question of color, or race, or creed. There was a bitter and bloody job to be done. All were valiant brothers in doing it.[23]

This remodeling was intended to provoke guilt and rekindle commitment to regenerative sacrifice.

What goals would be beyond the reach of this country if we could evoke again today the spirit of the men who fought and died on that alien shore? How much have we forgotten, in the twelve months that have passed, of the spirit of sacrifice, of all for one and one for all, of being fellow-members of a team engaged in the business of winning a war that every man might be free from the fear of aggression and per-secution, free to worship as he pleased and speak what he believed? It seems some-times as though we had forgotten much. The Iwos of our history will all have been fought in vain if we allow ourselves to forget them. The men who died on Iwo will have made their sacrifice in vain if we do not contrive to make a better world than any they had ever known.

Trooping the colors on TV

If it bleeds, it leads.   Newsroom saying.

Hegel observed that newspapers serve the national citizen as a substitute for morning prayers.[24] Television plays a similar role in American culture. Mass media share dramaturgical structures, formulaic incantations, and constant repetition with traditional systems of cultural authority. If earlier myth systems were timeless, changeless, and recalled for devotees their lot in the world, this suited those they instructed. Contemporary media systems are suited to us. They change as rapidly as the world, though their stable underlying message is a tale of violence. This makes the press a medium of totem themes. So do its claims to professional objectivity, which amount to an assertion that media messages are unassailably true. Media rivet attention on rituals of totem solidarity, especially at perilous moments. The link between totem ritual and media is more than a century old. Efforts to create patriotic consensus after the Civil War gave rise to lavish state occasions celebrating the wealth, power, and permanence of the re-forged American nation. Such occasions were directed at citizens and closely attended by the press.

The emergence of the press as a handmaiden of state ritual is related to the development of journalistic norms of professional objectivity.[25] Both the press's relation to the state and its pursuit of objectivity establish media presentations as ritualized. Objectivity is the belief that events drive cover-age, that professional mediators neither encode nor invent the news. If media reproduce only what gods enact, reporting is the ritual of remodel-ing the deeds of gods well. This requires that practitioners observe the litur-gical order of professional journalism, including a variety of procedures to re-create the illusion of bodily presence, the most basic of all ritual gestures. Source quotes, descriptors suggesting reporters are eyewitnesses, and locators that reference precise places, times, and relationships are part of this ritualized re-creation.[26] If even the most objective efforts to reconstruct events still change them more or less subtly, this is only what all rituals do.

Rappaport's operational definition of ritual as the communicative in-earnest "performance of more or less invariant sequences of formal acts and utterances not encoded by the performers" helps us understand media as a ritual mode.[27] Media are obviously *communicative*. By their own lights they are very much *in earnest*. Established conventions of re-presentation make them *formally expressive*. They re-present events *not encoded by performers* within a liturgical order they also do not encode. Journalists' ritual performances are less efficacious than the performances they re-present. A veteran who recalled coming ashore in the Normandy invasion described the pure performative condition. "There was nothing I could do on that beach except die," he explained.[28] In totem crisis members of the sacrificial class perform their sacred duty. They must for the group to survive. Photographers and reporters offer holy witness. Their presence is critical. Only through re-presentation and commemoration do apostolic missions become group-unifying messianic sacrifice.

All totem rituals remodel creation–sacrifice directly or by implication. Apostolic rituals remodel by promising, risking, or spilling new blood. Commemorative rituals remodel without spilling blood. "Nothing like it will ever happen again," wrote novelist Herman Wouk about the Normandy invasion, commemoratively re-presenting its originary capacity. "It belongs not with the great military memories of American history like Gettysburg and Valley Forge, but with Agincourt and Salamis."[29] "When these men were young," said Bill Clinton at fiftieth anniversary D-Day ceremonies, addressing not only the ghosts of the dead, but the youthful ghosts of many in attendance, "they saved the world." Mediators preserve and disseminate totem myth by bringing it *as if* to life once more. During D-Day ceremonies in Europe sacred relics and witnesses' tales revivified events half a century old.

The old planes, the parachutes descending again near Ste. -Mere-Eglise, on whose church steeple Pvt. John Steele dangled for hours before being cut down, the coffin-shaped boats back at Omaha Beach, the stories the veterans told – all rekindled the emotions stirred by the broadcasts of George Hicks, the radio networks' pool man on a ship out in the English Channel on June 6, 1944.[30]

By modeling and disseminating ritual events mass media contribute a crucial layer to totem structure. The most faithful congregants for totem rituals such as war and presidential elections are media audiences. Talk of media rituals troubles purists who regard them as impoverished or corrupt versions of more authentic ritual experience. This view is mistaken. Media rituals are as authentic as any ritual genre.[31] Every ritual is mediated since every ritual recalls absent, indeed, unrecoverable persons and events. The essence of all ritual is *to model* rather than *to be* the world-creating gesture. If the sacred gives ritual its form, its absence gives ritual its reason. To perform ritually is to recapitulate absent events and orders and so re-create them. Ritual genres are distinguished from one another not by levels of authenticity, but by degrees of magical efficacy. Though media constitute a genre of ritual action, they are not the most sanctified. Those that are construct the social directly from the body, transforming the sacrificed body in the presence of the holy. Such events are unique and, in a lifetime, rare. Though they cannot be replicated, they can be re-presented. And though performers subscribe to the fiction of making *as if* present what is absent, properly conducted rituals also confirm the distance between model and referent. Mediated by fictions of presence, participatory absence is no ritual defect. It characterizes all ritual performance, especially messianic sacrifice, which is recognized only in retrospect.

The most obvious difference between mass media and other ritual forms is how bodies are incorporated in them. In traditional rituals performers and congregants occupy one another's immediate presence. In media rituals, performers are separated from viewing and reading congregants, and congregants are separated from each other. Differences in bodily presence are matters not of ritual authenticity but ritual power. The most powerful magic is visceral. It is worked directly on the bodies of supplicants in the immediate presence of congregants. Battlefield death is more transformative for those who see it up close than press reports about it are for media audiences. Yet, if the press does not capture it or witnesses do not pass it along, blood sacrifice will not become ritually designated as creation–sacrifice able to perform its group-unifying function. The totem myth of blood sacrifice governs and organizes media coverage. "History is what hurts," Fredric Jameson has written.[32] Body language is necessary to describe it. The biggest history is about the biggest hurt, which is sacrifice. Media witness sacrifice and model it. Though they cannot perform real sacrifice, they scratch the itch in small ways and at regular intervals. They provide maintenance and memory until a big sacrifice comes again. Then they become the channel through which knowledge of sacrifice moves to the nation.

Media track the bodily engagement of congregants and participants in ritual events. Media show bodies performing ritual acts and observe congregants' bodily reactions. What is significant is conveyed with body language. "Hundreds of Israelis waiting outside a Tel Aviv hospital broke into screams and tears when a spokesman announced Prime Minister Yitzhak Rabin's death from an assassin's gun," reported CNN.[33] As voting returns came in for the referendum on Quebec's future, "separatists gathered for what they hoped would be a great victory party. They banged on drums. They stomped their feet. They cheered and whistled wildly."[34]

Media signal whether many bodies are ritually engaged or few. "Millions of people in millions of places seemed to spend ten spellbinding minutes yesterday doing exactly the same thing," the *Times* wrote about the audience for the verdict in the O. J. Simpson murder trial.[35] Ritual magic requires transformed bodies, so corporeal engagement must be apparent:

In downtown Montreal, a crowd estimated at 150,000 waved the Maple Leaf flag of Canada and the fleurs-de-lis flag of Quebec and sang the national anthem, hoping to convince the French-speaking people of Quebec to vote No in their independence referendum on Monday.[36]

Following the assassination of Yitzhak Rabin, a CNN reporter described the nation as "paralyzed with grief."[37] An Israeli citizen said "his pain was as searing as an ulcer."[38]

Other ritual elements are expressed in bodily terms. These include suspense around the ritual outcome and the outcome itself. As the referendum for Quebec independence approached, a newspaper headline proclaimed: "Canada Holds Its Breath as Quebec Votes." The more uncertain the outcome, the greater the ritual magic that must be deployed, the greater the transformation required, the greater the benefit to the group if the ritual succeeds, the greater the peril if it fails. When the verdict was read in the Simpson murder trial, the press reported that sobs sounded, audiences gasped, jaws dropped, people cheered and spoke. "I felt the verdict in my sinuses," Jeffrey Toobin wrote.[39] Television repeatedly presented the transformation of the defendant's face in the moment that determined whether the group would sacrifice him. The unifying effect of a triumphal World Series was remodeled in media by depicting all New York as one physical body. Body terms also portrayed the victory as time-stopping:

With its lungs and its heart, New York City . . . saluted the triumphant Yankees yesterday in a rousing ticker tape parade up lower Broadway's Canyon of Heroes.
For several hours in the middle of a splendiferous autumn day, work stopped, play stopped and the dog had to wait. It was Yankees and nothing else.[40]

Ritual is creative. It seeks the unity of form and substance, which is embodiment. Thus media are ritually driven to offer the illusion of bodily presence restored. Media also tidy up and polish events to make them mythically intelligible. They recall events that become something other than strictly real in the re-telling. Their failure is the failure of every ritual re-presentation since every re-presentation adds and subtracts elements in the service of group myth. A lump of guts becomes a consecrated body. Flagraising orders the disorder of unritualized death by re-framing the here-and-now as a world-creating event. But not, of course, without dissemination to a larger congregation.

Innovating ritual models

A formal ritual sequence satisfies by conforming to a previously established order not encoded by performers. A step down in ritual orderedness is the unanticipated event that elicits a known ceremonial response, but without advance planning. An example was the immediate and spontaneous lowering of flags across the country at the news of President John F. Kennedy's assassination. William Manchester describes the power of that gesture to transform observers and inspire replication. As befits a commemoratively proper narrative, the new First Lady registered its first effects:

Between pink lights on the way to Love Field the wife of the former Vice President, now the President, had glanced up at a building and observed there a flag already at half-mast. It was then, Lady Bird recalled afterward, that "the enormity of what had happened first struck me."[41]

Totem death and sacrifice, the utterly ineffable, is manifest only in the presence of the flag, though Mrs. Johnson had ridden in the doomed motorcade.

It was striking an incalculable number of Americans at the same time and in the same way. An irresistible, almost telepathic urge to lower the colors swept the country; banners were floating down outside schools, statehouses, prisons, stock exchanges, department stores, office buildings, and private homes. At the White House Commander Hallett sent a man out to reel down the mansion's ensign immediately after he had ordered the Cabinet plane back to Andrews Field, and since the Commander had access to the Kellerman–Behn line [the emergency phone link between the White House Secret Service Detail and agents in Dallas], the standard at 1600 Pennsylvania Avenue may have been the first to slide down its pole.[42]

As if directed by an invisible power, the gesture was spontaneously repeated. Manchester's re-telling imposes mythical order. He suggests that because a flag at the totem center should and could have been the first lowered, it *was*. The ritual performer of that gesture conjured up his own commemorative model of sacrificial totem death.

The motive of Hallett's swiftness lay in his own youth. He had marched in Franklin Roosevelt's funeral cortege as an Annapolis midshipman, and he remembered that there had been criticism then because several hours had lapsed between the announcement of Roosevelt's death in Warm Springs and the descent of the White House flag.[43]

Where models anchor chaos, more magical effects are observed.

In the nurse's station Steve Landregan phoned instructions to haul Parkland's flag down at once; at Brooks Medical Center in San Antonio Dr. Welch, who had no military role, dashed out to the spot where President Kennedy had stood the afternoon before and yanked in the halyard himself. Afterward neither man could explain why that had been his first thought. Whatever their reasons, such sights were to leave an indelible impression on those who witnessed them. Coming after a series of bulletins, each darker than the last, the spectacle of a falling banner was profoundly affecting. In Arlington Lieutenant Sam Bird, who had impetuously driven off to visit the Tomb of the Unknown Soldiers after hearing of the shooting, had just re-entered Fort Myer's grounds when he saw the post standard begin its descent. He drew over to the curb, alighted, and saluted. After this, he thought, nothing could move him so deeply again.[44]

Still other occasions invite ceremonial response where no organized ritual exists. Devotees are ritual bricoleurs, piecing gestures together to express their piety. Consider two examples:

1) A flier mailed to ratepayers by the Philadelphia Electric Company featured energy efficiency tips for homeowners, an article on electricity theft, notice of a charity walk for Alzheimer's victims, a reminder that May is Arthritis Month, and a request to "Pause For the Pledge":

Join all Americans everywhere to pause for a moment on June 14 at 7:00 p. m. (EDT) to say simultaneously the thirty-one words of the Pledge of Allegiance to the Flag. The effect of this simple ceremony is a stimulating patriotic experience at home and a sign of unity abroad.[45]

A Flag Day ritual is proposed and its effect prophesied. Though participants will be mutually invisible, outsiders will discern the meaning of their common activity. The sensibilities of performers will be transformed.

2) At the Philadelphia airport a citizen encountered a war casualty being shipped home from the Gulf War. He describes how he and others created a sacred zone in profane space.

One of the items loaded on the conveyer belt caught my attention. It was a pale blue cardboard crate, the kind that might hold grapefruit or other perishables. As I watched it move up the conveyer, I noticed it was larger than I expected. And then the conveyer stopped, and a flight attendant and a young Army private appeared from around the airplane. The private was carrying a triangular-folded flag.

The private came to attention; the flight attendant seemed to weep; the baggage handlers stood solemnly. The conveyer started again, and the young private saluted as the crate moved into the airplane's hold. Not knowing what else to do, I stood. I spoke to the private later. The crate indeed held the remains of a soldier killed in the war.[46]

Ritual elements may be assembled from multiple models. Consider Bill Clinton's first State of the Union speech:

You may catch a whiff of Ronald Reagan in President Clinton's direct approach to the television audience . . . but his public introduction of the Administration's economic prescriptions owes even more to the spirit of Frank Capra . . . On Monday night you could practicallly hear the big us-against-them speeches of James Stewart and Gary Cooper as the youthful-looking President pleaded, "We're all in this together," and perorated with an evocation of patriotism and the Almighty. All that was missing was a small boy looking on, aglow with admiration."[47]

Scattered across culture, elements and patterns of totem ritual are constantly circulated and re-worked. When occasion demands, they are gathered up and focused into new and powerful ritualizations of group unity. Media re-presentations keep a pool of useable models circulating and offer experimental arenas for new ones. Old models are refurbished; others drop out. Since the chain of mediated re-presentations is infinite, and re-presentation is a process of memory as well as a mode of cultural maintenance, there is no end to mediation except exhaustion, or a new crisis that rearranges the relationships of all previous models to that crisis and one another.

Rituals of media attending

The American people don't believe anything's real until they see it on television.   Richard Nixon[48]

Media assume a priestly obligation to undertake coverage on behalf of the group. Coverage is the ritualized re-presentation of totem deeds. It is revelatory, providing visions of citizenship and conveying totem will. Todd Gitlin has observed of television-toting college students that their sets are "their temple, their sense of being members of a nation. It's as if they're carrying their pews with them."[49] Media priests recognize their role in assembling ritual congregants. According to television critic Walter Goodman:

There are occasions that demand all-channel attention, as a certification of significance of acknowledgement of national togetherness . . . [National party] convention events like the [presidential] nominee's acceptance speech, and even a touch of the balloon and baloney partying, qualify as such occasions.[50]

Totem events fill up news programs and talk shows. By the end of the 1992 Democratic national convention:

> It seemed only viewers who had their televisions permanently tuned to the Weather Channel could have missed the shots of delegates hoisting placards or Bill and Hillary Clinton waving to the crowd or Al Gore talking about "change." And only those who had the volume control on their sets turned to mute could have failed to hear the Democrats' message: "This year we're unified!"[51]

By promoting the symbolism favored by the totem the press promotes its authority. This service may be compulsory in a totem emergency. Media also serve the totem spontaneously, as in this description of New York television during the Welcome Home parade following the Gulf War:

> On all the channels that carried yesterday's parade, emotions sprouted like yellow ribbons and patriotic phrases were waved like flags. Channel 7 announced that it was saluting "Our Heroes" and Channel 2 pasted the title "Heroes on Parade" on its coverage . . . Channel 9's Sara Lee Kessler reported, "We had the will to do it, and we did it," the "we" presumably being forces outside Channel 9. Another Channel 9 staffer wore a "Desert Storm" T-shirt with an American flag on it. "These colors don't run," the reporter said.[51]

Rituals of attending are practiced with special devotion during totem crises. Counting down to the American deadline for Iraqi withdrawal from Kuwait, nervous citizens practiced rituals of media-attending while spell-casting with flags and ribbons. "For many people, there was little but prayer, television and keeping an eye on the clock."[53] Others kept a vigil with friends "as they followed the late night news."[54]

The moral portrait of the world most citizens share comes from media. "The nightly message is that we're all in this together," Walter Goodman writes.[55] Somber high masses include state funerals or D-Day commemorations in Europe. There are seasonal rites such as presidential elections. Daily news programs offer regular devotionals. The World Series and the Superbowl present ceremonial-rich sagas within a totem-mythic framework. Humbler magic is found in the tabloid press. All provide narratives of totem sacrifice and affiliative aspiration, of sin and retribution, of healing and regeneration. Media vastly extend the reach and power of ritual modes. Their capacity for engaging emotion is high. Media accounts offer themselves in earnest. The stories they tell are meaningful to congregants.

What media rituals convey

> A true war story is never about war . . . It's about love and memory.
>
> Tim O'Brien, *The Things They Carried*

Ritual instructs congregants. Proper behaviors are rehearsed, key meanings elaborated. The dramatic climax of the funeral rites of one in totem service, for example, is presenting the flag that covers the casket to those with blood ties to the sacrifice. President Richard Nixon's daughter Julie Eisenhower wept on receiving a flag at her father's funeral, though she had been dry-eyed till then. "The symbolism of that folded flag being presented is so fraught with meaning," declared anchorman Ted Koppel. "Very, very difficult to maintain composure at a time like that. But as you have seen, the family has been quite extraordinary."[56] In his priestly duties Koppel directs the attention of devotees to an important ritual moment. He takes note of the transformative power of the flag – it compels mourners to weep against their will. He describes family members as heroically executing an apostolic mission in which self-control is the proper gesture. Additional lessons in composure ritually lost and regained come from a policeman's funeral:

The officers presented the flag to Barone's mother, Antonia, who took it, bowed her head and faltered a moment. Then she straightened and stepped toward the grave of her son.[57]

Instructing its readers in the formal elements of a Gulf War funeral, the *New York Times* signaled the importance of keeping one's body and emotions separate from the venerated object that could harm those who touch it. Contact requires procedures for ameliorating danger.

A sharp, cool breeze blew across the open spaces, carrying away the sharp reports of the 21–gun salute. Pine trees whistled and flags snapped at half-staff as a lone bugler played that simple sequence of notes that marks the end of a military life. Mrs. Stephen's face was still and expressionless when members of the honor guard handed her the folded flag that had covered her husband's coffin.[58]

On the other hand, ritual form must be sturdy enough to accommodate multiple conditions. A stoic mourner may be praised for ritual conformity. A weeping one is used to demonstrate the transformative power of the flag or the singularity of an event that justifies departing from protocol.

Ritual also may resolve tensions between private belief and public performance. At the 1992 Winter Olympics in Albertville, four-time Olympian and cross-country skier Bill Koch found himself at odds with totem protocol. Koch, the elected flagbearer for the US team, had stated his intention to break precedent and dip the American flag in the opening ceremony out of respect for the host country. "Olympics is a world event, and maybe it's not the place to have excessive amounts of nationalism," he declared, invoking the demons of political secularism.[59] In the end he deferred to the rule that the American flag does not bow to another totem. "There was a lot of pressure on me not to dip the flag," he explained. "I ended up going along with tradition."[60] Acquiescence signals where the actor's real commitments lie. Koch's submission strengthens the sacred postulate that America stands above all other countries in the eyes of its citizens, since one who professed heresy was unable to bring his own body to behave as if it were true.

Media highlight important totem themes. A narration of the funeral rites of a police officer killed in the line of duty that magically transforms him into a child drives home the regenerative power of the sacrificed body. A report that 4,000 police officers attended the funeral signifies its ritual importance and alerts readers to expect a well-conducted example of the genre. The description begins with two fire trucks lifting their ladders high over the roadway to form a traditional "flag-bedecked" arch for the funeral procession.

When the procession arrived at St. Patrick's a lone bagpiper played "Amazing Grace" as Barone's flag-draped casket passed through two facing lines of Norristown officers. To the side stood a platoon of out-of-town officers – at least 10 deep, at least 200 across – all saluting.

Father Ettore's final graveside words and prayers were brief. "Our brother Thomas has gone to rest," he began.

Three officers of an honor guard raised their rifles and fired a salute. Two buglers played Taps, and two officers slowly folded the flag from the casket into a tight triangle.

The officers presented the flag to Barone's mother, Antonia, who took it, bowed her head and faltered a moment. Then she straightened and stepped toward the grave of her son.

She kissed the polished wooden casket. She kissed the flag. Then she turned to leave, pausing to place a single red carnation atop the coffin.[61]

The story rehearses the death rites of totem sacrifice: the journey of the flag-covered casket to the grave, spells spoken and sung over the deceased to transform him and protect us, the honorific discharging of weapons, the flag presented to next of kin. The salute of weapons re-enacts death. Significantly, the shooters are not the enemy. They are ours, but shoot with blanks. The totem secret is glimpsed and denied. Recalling original totem sacrifice, the casket flag is folded into a triangular shape that remodels the hat worn by enlisted men in the Revolutionary army. The pace and precision of ceremonial folding suggests the danger and power of the totem object, which is the visible body of the god.

The bereaved family makes a show of accepting the flag as if it were the loved one. The mother of Officer Barone equates her son's body with the flag by kissing first one, then the other. But this flag is not a sacrificed body only. Ritual gestures and language re-present it as an infant with regenerative power. It recalls the pall that covers the Christian funeral casket, which remodels in turn the swaddling clothes of infants presented for baptism. The flagwrapped soldier becomes the infant child of the regenerative totem land. The flagwaving warrior answers the totem ancestor's call for more blood with sacrifice. The flag that wraps the casket transforms shed blood into the community seed ritually planted at the fertile center.

Tom Clancy, author of novels about totem intrigue, models the transformation of the sacrificial flag into the regenerative infant during a fictional funeral for a high-ranking totem official at Arlington National Cemetery. The deceased Director of Covert Operations for the CIA is a lifetime outsider, a "spook" with no family to receive the flag. His wife is dead. His son is a casualty of the lost war, Vietnam. The flag passes to the deceased's professional "son" in the agency, who articulates the infant-flag equivalence and the guilt of the regenerative center that profits from his death:

He still had the flag in his lap, holding it as gently as a newborn baby without knowing why – until he realized that if there really was a God, as the Baptist preachers of his youth had assured him, and if James really had a soul, he held its best legacy in his hands. It felt warm to the touch, and though he knew that it was merely his imagination or at most the residual heat absorbed from the morning sun, the energy radiating from the flag that James had served from his teens seemed to accuse him of treachery.[62]

Devotees need not understand every ritual element for totem order to be restored. Clancy's character connects the funeral flag to infancy "without knowing why." His account, like others in popular and official culture, helps furnish our understanding of nationalism even when we are not really paying attention.

Every sacrifice is an abnegation. The totem community deprives itself. Though the sacrificer gives up something, he does not give himself. "Prudently, he sets himself aside."[63] The gods take the sacrifice and leave the sacrificer to whom its moral and magical benefits accrue. Americans are the sacrificers of American soldiers. In the presence of witnesses a boon is conferred upon the family that is present to stand in both for the deceased soldier and the nation that has killed him. The flag is the benefit

6.1 World War II pietà. At wartime services flag is sacrificed son.

6.2 Patriotic pietà – Madonna with flagbody of her dead husband. First Arlington burial of Gulf War, 1991.

that passes from sacrificial victim to sacrificer, ensuring there will be no cause for vengeance by the family toward those who have caused its kinsman to die. Totem death rites place grieving female relatives at the regenerative core. Their sorrow both re-presents and conceals a guilt of magnificent proportions, the knowledge that the community sends its own to die.

Myth and history – creation stories

A tale of sacrifice is a creation story. Good creation stories are mythological, flexible, and retrospective. Loose ends are tied up, lacunae filled in. Whatever facts conform to a creation archetype are used. Others are discarded. Selection is echoic rather than linear, for the present must hear itself in what is selected from the past. The process is ongoing and experimental. Only the past that appears to the present as fulfilling a creative gesture or expressing a mythic rhythm well, is useful. Foundational sacrifice, for those who live it, is originary. The past predicted it. The present is in its debt. The future will repay it. By this means the nation is always constituted in the memory of the last sacrifice that counts for the living. This identity is a shifting one. World War II, the founding sacrifice of a generational cohort, is today a myth in transition. Those who lived it with their bodies are a declining fraction of the citizenry. While myths that are older than living memory may be more flexibly bent to totem uses, they are also less compelling. To re-create the totem myth in earnest, devotees need models as familiar as their own bodies. To remodel the past, mythic links must be struck between a centered present and a creation–sacrifice in relation to which the present stands as consequence and renewal. "The most holy thing a person has is memory," observed a veteran at Memorial Day ceremonies.[64] By re-framing the past the present explains what caused us, what we must attend to, and what we may ignore.

To lay groundwork for future sacrifice, the present must be found wanting. Former New York Governor Mario Cuomo bemoaned the loss of a group sense since the "last" sacrifice of World War II.

What is the basic mood? Here's what I believe it is. The biggest event in my lifetime was the Second World War and we have never been able to recreate it. Some people say thank God, but there's something we lost by not recreating what happened in the Second World War.[65]

Cuomo calls World War II the last meaningful creation–sacrifice for Americans. Pointing to his own life as a marker references his body, the medium that connects us to other group members. To reproduce old verities the nation must "recreate" war. "What happened" was the death of many Americans. This is the "lost" condition that engendered group life:

The Second World War was the last time that this country believed in anything profoundly, any great single cause. What was it? They were evil; we were good. That was Tojo, that was that S. O. B. Hitler, that was Mussolini, that bum. They struck at us in the middle of the night, those sneaks. We are good, they are bad. Let's all get together, we said, and we creamed them. We started from way behind. We found strength in this common commitment, this commonality, community, family, the idea of coming together was best served in my lifetime in the Second World War.

Unambiguous group borders sort good and bad violence. Collective violence strengthens group feeling and commitment. Starting "from way behind" provides another ritual lesson, since rituals that move to success from great uncertainty are most effective.

You never had a war quite like it. In the beginning of Iraq, you thought you did and a lot of people got excited. Hot dog, we've got another Hitler – Saddam Hussein. But then after a while, everybody got confused. Was it the oil? What the hell am I fighting the Emir for? Who is the Emir? What is an Emir? What's Kuwait? What did they do for me? Why is my son going? So that lost its luster as a cause. We haven't had another great cause.

Singularity is an attribute of originary sacrifice. An exemplary war is like no other. Even if the most satisfying ritual outcomes require the greatest suspense, the cause for which the ritual is undertaken must never be in doubt. Cuomo observes contemporary efforts to reproduce enemies as evil as those that once unified a country. Knowing that the Gulf War failed to do it because too few of our own died to create enduring unity is taboo.

We've not had a great hero or heroine since Martin Luther King, Jr. and John Kennedy. And they were taken down by fate. "Where have you gone, Joe DiMaggio?" It was perfect – [the singer] Paul Simon from Queens summed it all up. Where are our heroes, great causes? No cause. No hero. No heroine. Nothing big to believe in. Nothing to wrap your arms around.

Cuomo mentions two postwar heroes propelled by sacrifice to totem icon status. The para-familial links of Americans to King and Kennedy gave their deaths greater group value than the deaths of all Gulf soldiers taken together. Summing up, Cuomo describes a well-functioning totem. It requires something "big to believe in" to convince supplicants to sacrifice themselves, and a regenerative totem center "to wrap your arms around."[66]

Totem ritual locates the present in relation to a past that makes it intelligible. The significance of the present, which is tomorrow's past, will be reinvented by succeeding presents in light of their own opportunities and perils. The importance of our present will be estimated by its progeny. If they honor it, they will ceremonially re-present it. Contemporary actors may regret that their own foundational sacrifices have slipped in the estimation of those who come after, but authority to judge what counts as creation–sacrifice inevitably passes to new generations.[67] For the novelist James Salter, World War II "claimed us and became for me, at least, the reality against which all future things would be judged."[68] But not the reality against which the future itself would judge things present or past, including the war. When body memories fade and cannot resurrect the blood myth on which the group lives, new bloodletting is required. Each generation rejects the founding sacrifices of earlier ones for its own. The magical belief that proper sacrifice can renew the world once and for all is never dashed by the fact that every sacrifice has failed to do this. Each generation believes its own sacrifice will end time and give rise to a world in which everything will be different, and that its own meeting with destiny constitutes a singular turning point, a messianic creation–sacrifice.

A war to end all wars is the omnipotent fantasy of creation–sacrifice, unfalsifiable so long as each generation pronounces its own violent bloodletting utterly different from those on which it is, in fact, modeled. Renouncing blood lust, it makes its own violence taboo. Renunciation convinces us we deplore violence so that our embrace of some future call for blood will seem both necessary and exceptional. We have not wished for the death of our own; we have resisted to the last. Each generation proclaims that its own sacrifice will permanently satisfy the totem group that hates violence so much. This is the heartfelt cry, "Never again!"

Is messianic memory so flexible? Can any sacrifice displace any other? Was there a single moment in which American society announced itself as a god, to paraphrase Durkheim, an occasion when a distinctive American totem stood revealed as a transcendent nation? Is there any standard for assessing the mythic past with a grammar of cause sanctioned by historians? To ask the question is to show how much we want it to be true. So far as the creation and re-creation of national identity goes, the question of a true history is beside the point. Professional historians' narratives are not the memory that consolidates national identity. That role belongs to totem myth in its popular guise. In the face of new totem exigencies mythic or popular memory is more re-organized than corrected. Eliade speaks of "the anhistorical character of popular memory, the inability of collective memory to retain historical events and individuals except insofar as it transforms them into archetypes."[69] Efforts to replace myth with veridical narrative will have little impact without compelling totem reasons to adjust it in that direction, as the tenacity of the Betsy Ross myth suggests. That the documentary record casts doubt on Betsy's claim to have sewn the first American flag counts far less than whether devotees are mythically satisfied by this tale of maternal solicitude.

Evidentiary historical accounts are no less enchanted in the power they ascribe to a true beginning point, a "real" creation event. Milo Quaife, author of a standard reference work on the American flag, denounces flag myth as a "desecration" of patriotic sacrifice. The claim that historical events are polluted by professionally disfavored narratives displays the structure of every appeal to sacred origins held to be taboo and inviolable. Quaife comments:

There has developed about the flag a volume of myth and tradition which, by force of frequent repetition in numerous histories, popular addresses, movie films, and radio and television programs, has unfortunately been impressed upon the public mind as actual history. This a great pity, for the simple facts are far more dignified and inspiring than any fanciful narrative could possibly be.[70]

Quaife recognizes the remodeling role of media, but misreads the function of myth and tradition. These consecrate as real not what is veridical, but what is felt to unify the community, at least for the moment. Nor does Quaife argue for "actual history" on its own merits. He believes tales authorized by historians are more "inspiring," achieving patriotic unity more effectively than fanciful narratives and, he implies, with greater moral legitimacy. What unifies the community is truth in the sense of Durkheim's claim that religion is true because it constitutes the community. The purpose of totem myth *is* to dignify and inspire, as Quaife suggests. When veridical accounts are felt to do this, they are assimilated to national identity and thus to mythic models. What begins as accurate will soon be enhanced by dignity and inspiration, that is, by significance and structure. Whatever works for the community will select from, re-shape, and expeditiously discard accuracy. This is the process of re-framing, or tinkering strategically with the past. As powerful modelers of national identity, media practitioners daily embark on the quest to reveal totem gesture in the patent and sensible. It is their job to discover what best assimilates to a mythic model in unfolding events. As Rappaport says, "We judge the state of affairs by the degree to which it conforms to the stipulations of the performative ritual."[71] Our criteria for judging and remembering history are liturgical.

Group history is commemorative. It recalls apostolic and messianic events. Death is its subject, even when it is visited light-heartedly. Commemorative rituals take unexpected forms and are flexible enough to fit in small cultural spaces. "We were schoolboys and knew the armament and silhouettes of English and German ships and planes," novelist James Salter recalled about the early days of World War II. "We made models of them and fought battles."[72] Salter and his friends frequently re-enacted disasters reported from North Africa and Europe. "War comes naturally to boys: wounds, imitated gunfire, glory." Through commemorative rites young men anticipate future apostolic missions and messianic sacrifice.

Ritual failure: flagraising on the moon

A man who has a vision is not able to use the power of it until after he has performed the vision on earth for the people to see.   Black Elk[73]

Not every ritual is a success. The magic leaks, as this Memorial Day parade attests. "Behind the flags come more veterans, a mass of somebody else's grandfathers, all shapes and sizes, trying to look the way they remember the military looked."[74] Mythic imagination cannot reproduce in these old men the young gods of sacrifice. The order gets out of order. Believers grow impatient. The best models wear out. On a cold day in New York, James Salter happened on a lone figure staring at a pier where a docked carrier had become a priestly museum.

Without turning to me, he remarked that it was the Enterprise, if he wasn't mistaken.
"Do you know that ship?"
Yes, he said. He knew her. The last time he had seen her was off the Santa Cruz Islands in the fall of 1942. He had lost his wingman, and his own carrier, the Hornet, had been hit and was sinking. He landed on the Enterprise instead. He hadn't laid eyes on her from that day to this.
"Were you by any chance at Midway," I asked him.
"Yes, I was at Midway, too," he said.
He had been in many of the battles and had seen things I would have given anything to have seen, that are part of the annals. The ship he was looking at was in fact the Intrepid, launched a year after the battle of the Santa Cruz Islands, but as a former schoolboy I forgave him mere details.[75]

The chief impediment to ritual stability is the chaos of the world, which never lives up to ritual promises, especially to stop time. We cannot remain forever young and fresh in our achievements. When those who witnessed sacrifice no longer remember it accurately, how will those who did not?

Culture, meanwhile, rehearses mythic structure. It appropriates everything, honing its collective skill in anticipation of an orderable, group-forging moment – a moment like America's first walk on the moon. Even this apostolic triumph failed permanently to rearrange the mythic canon of the group. It came during the Vietnam era when media flags were associated with totem protesters. In *Life* magazine the sorts of heroic flag images that once ornamented *Life*'s coverage of World War II migrated to the space program, where effort and sacrifice were directed to securing new Cold War borders. Outer space was a site of territorial conquest. Buzz Aldrin, one of two moonlanding astronauts, saw himself as an apostolic successor to mythical civilizing heroes. "Since childhood," he wrote, "I'd been fascinated by explorers planting flags on strange shores. Now I was about to do the same thing, but on the most exotic shore mankind had ever reached."

Models are needed to take territory at a border where no man has been. The uncultivated zone must be given a form that invests it with reality. It must be "cosmicized," in Eliade's words. To repeat the divine act of perfect construction, a zone of the center must be created and animated. On landing, the first order of business was to assimilate the moon to a sacred center with a flagraising.[76] For ritual performers the stakes were high.

Of all the jobs I had to do on the moon, the one I wanted to go the smoothest was the flag raising. [Mission Control] had told us we were being watched by the largest television audience in history, over a billion people. Just beneath the powdery surface, the subsoil was very dense. We succeeded in pushing the flagpole in only a couple of inches. It didn't look very sturdy. But I did snap off a crisp West Point salute once we got the banner upright.[77]

What would perfect construction be without a waving, animated flag? In the airless atmosphere of the moon, only technology could engineer this necessity. A specially designed brace placed the flag in the ritual condition of being "alive" in the breezeless moonscape. Still, the flagraising was fraught with imperfection.

It was nearly a disaster . . . A small telescoping arm was attached to the flagpole to keep the flag extended and perpendicular in the still lunar atmosphere. We locked the arm in its ninety-degree position, but as hard as we tried, the telescope wouldn't fully extend. Thus, the flag, which should have been flat, had its own unique permanent wave. Then, to our dismay, the staff of the pole at first wouldn't go far enough into the lunar surface to support itself in an upright position. After much struggling, we finally coaxed it to remain upright, but in a most precarious position. I dreaded the possibility of the American flag collapsing into the lunar dust in front of the television camera.[78]

Preoccupation with ceremonial detail suggests a belief in consequences for ritual failure and awareness of the gap between one's own poor offering and perfect sacrifice. Despite these flaws, the astronauts transformed lifeless space into meaning-charged cosmos by hoisting the flag on the moon. Each was photographed next to the flag, as though the exemplary gesture of vivifying the sacred center would prove the moonlanding was real and that they had really been there. Armstrong's photograph of Aldrin saluting the flag in the classic gesture of ritual submission to a totem brought once more to life was the very image of apostolically renewed primordial crea- tion. As a familiar postwar icon, the lunar flagraising invites comparison with the raising of the flag on Iwo Jima. If the lunar version did not produce as enduring an image for the country, this is because the moon- landing was a victory only for the ritually bloodless Cold War. Though enormous treasure was sacrificed to achieve it, and three Apollo I astro- nauts perished in a freak fire during ground tests in preparation for it, these were not many deaths and did not accompany a visibly ceremonial execu- tion of the task.

Actors and congregants tell us when ritual works. Apostolically, the moonraising was a success. After President Richard Nixon conferred a totem blessing on the returned astronauts in the quarantine capsule aboard the *USS Hornet*, ABC anchorman Tom Jarrell offered this reflection:

As the President went down to see the astronauts, I couldn't help but think that he reminded me very much of a very proud father who had gone to the hospital to see a newborn child and discovered that he had triplets. It was the most enthusiastic thing I've seen in some time from him.[79]

The totem father surveys his totem newborns through the hospital window in the capsule womb. The world begins again. Seeking the group idea in the embodied totem, Jarrell's fellow media priest Jules Bergman invoked unity as a test of ritual success.

He's discovered, I think, that in this torn, tormented time of ours with a country that's searching to do the things it has to do, that this great thing that's been done here, this lunar landing is, if anything, a unifying factor, a moment of national triumph and dedication, and I think he feels it deeply, as all of us do.

The sacred history of the group is a series of repeating models of birth and death. Group time is echoic, not chronological. Richard Nixon pro- nounced the week "the greatest . . . in the history of the world since the Creation."[80]

For Buzz Aldrin the significance of the moonwalk was not in apostolic doing only. With his colleagues, he watched as apostolic substance was invested with commemorative form by media priests:

Our flight surgeon says to us, "I've got some [video]tapes of what was going on while you guys were up there. Would you like to see 'em?" I said, "Sure, sure." We watched 'em and all of a sudden an impulsive thought came over me, and I said to Neal, "Neal, look! We missed the whole thing!" I didn't realize the wisdom that I had when I said that. The significance of Apollo was not picking up rocks on the moon. It was not the science. It was the millions of peoples' lives who had value added . . . I think that was the payoff that we got from Apollo.[81]

Lives with value added; acts invested by congregants with ritual form. This is what makes a creation event. Ritual forms and precipitating episodes fuse in the minds of devotees. When ritual successfully conceals its fictiveness, ritual re-presentation *becomes* what it models, which is the ineffable. Anchorman Howard K. Smith spoke of this transformation hours after Apollo touched down on the moon:

I'm told that there've been sporadic protests from television viewers at not being able to see their usual and favorite television programs this weekend, and there will probably be more complaints later on. I beg to suggest to complainants that they're seeing what television is really for. Too often we consider this medium just another method of watching movies and seeing what used to be called vaudeville without having the trouble of going to the theater. But its real value is to make people participants in ongoing experiences. Real life is vastly more exciting than synthetic life, and this is real-life drama with audience participation.

When John Kennedy was assassinated, the nation was overripe for a burst of divisive bitterness. There's no doubt that by being made participants in that tragedy, Americans were purged of bitterness, and television was the cause of that. What the outcome of this participation of hundreds of millions of humans in an otherwise unbelievable human experience will be we don't know. But as one newspaper commentator said today, "We can be sure that things will not be the same again."[82]

The priest declares for the congregation that time stops and begins again with the moonwalk. Television frames life with totem form and meaning for participating congregants. Smith asserts that mediation bestows ritual power, even to the point of restoring totem order, as in the Kennedy assassination. Contemporary nation groups require mediation to enact the group idea:

Reporters who go to political conventions have discovered that if they stayed home and watched television they would find out more than by going to the convention. Well, you're watching on television and seeing things that one very important figure is not able to witness.

He's Michael Collins, circling the moon, nearer than anybody else to the landing except the men who've landed. And he has been witnessing less than you. *He* doesn't have a TV receiver in his module, and you've got one in your home.

The moonlanding was broadly interpreted as a nationalist response to the totem peril of the arms race. Its space version had begun with the Soviet

Union's first launch of an earth satellite in 1957. The resolution to this gloriously uncertain contest was the moonlanding framed by a signature flagraising that failed to re-shape public memory enduringly. An observer recalled:

Sadly, it turns out that what everybody thought would be a new epoch after the moon didn't last much longer than the moon walk itself. I have always been shocked by how little that moment carried forward. It's as though it was a big hoax shot on the back lot of a Hollywood studio.[83]

The ultimate insult. Not the real thing, a fusion of ritual form and pre-cipitating event, but a visibly contrived ritual.

It's as if the moonwalkers, with their wooden words and their awkward steps and their flags suspended on wires to simulate the Stars and Stripes waving in the wind, had reached the end of a long and brittle branch, and the branch had since broken off.[84]

Ritual memory may perish.

Doug Lynch, a systems analyst in Boston, was only five years old when the moon walk took place. But like almost every other American, he has seen numerous television reruns of the historic event and has given some thought to future space exploration. His conclusion? . . . "People look back and say, 'It's hard to believe that it happened.'" As time goes by, it loses its sense of realism.

And the ritual actors? An aerospace worker recalled a sacred time filled with heroic ordeals:

The headiest of his life, he said, month after month of 100–hour weeks, seeing the capsule take form right before his eyes, even under the guidance of his own hands. But these days, he often feels like a Vietnam veteran or an old high school football hero.

"You tell people that you're a space worker and helped put together Apollo and now work on the shuttle," he said with hurt in his voice, "and they say, 'So, what?'"[85]

What had been compared to Creation was now Vietnam, the unappreciated sacrifice, or high school sports, the pretend sacrifice. Though some believers called the moonwalk "the defining moment of the twentieth century,"[86] that sentiment was not broadly shared.

Totem creation stories

To be born again, first you have to die.   Salman Rushdie, *Satanic Verses*

Here is a totem creation story, broadcast as American soldiers entered Kuwait hours from achieving their objective in the Gulf War. Mythically useful in his anonymity, an unidentified Marine:

who refused to give his name, carried a US flag to the gates of the embassy compound. He said it had been given to him during the Tet Offensive in Vietnam in 1968 by a fellow Marine who died in his arms.[87]

The soldier proceeded to resurrect the embodied sacrifice of Vietnam as the living, fluttering flagbody of Gulf victory. Important totem stories always begin with a sacrifice, the original act of creation. Typologically, they are organized into female narratives of sacrificial birth and male narratives of regenerative violence. Among the former, which are taught especially to children, the story of Betsy Ross is the prototype. The latter are taught especially to soldiers. We will examine three: a filmic reconstruction of a controversial World War II episode, the most famous World War II image, and a filmic treatment of events surrounding that image.

Back to Bataan

Back to Bataan (1945) is a commemorative reconstruction of messianic sacrifice in World War II.[88] Aimed at an American audience struggling with the responsibilities and guilt of neo-colonialism in a postwar world, the film asks how totem groups are created and reaffirms the totem secret. The film poses the dilemma of Filipino identity in World War II: whether to join the invading Japanese or fashion a guerilla force allied with American troops who abandoned the Philippines after the greatest Japanese rout of Americans in the Pacific theater. Which is the right sacrifice for Filipinos?

Indigenous characters in the film argue that Filipinos should not join the American fight. Most reluctant is Captain Andres Bonifacio, grandson and namesake of the famous freedom fighter against the Spanish. Through Bonifacio, two totem identities, Filipino and American, are engaged. Filipino identity hinges on the choice between racial solidarity with the Japanese and social kinship with Americans who promise totem autonomy. The Japanese court Filipinos as lost "nieces and nephews" of the East Asian family, pledging to liberate them from the "exploiting and arrogant" race of Americans. The American appeal is made not on the basis of genetic kinship, but the social kinship of shared sacrifice. The historical resistance of Filipinos to American domination is acknowledged, but interaction between the two peoples shows only mutual appreciation and sacrifice. It is suggested that Americans may be better Filipinos at heart than Filipinos, for Americans champion a people that does not yet embrace its own identity, and so doubts itself. American characters display their commitment to Filipinos by providing an educational system and sacrificing American lives to protect them in the Pacific war. The most important American gift to the Filipinos, however, is modeling a totem identity.

The drama revolves around three characters: the motherly American schoolteacher Miss Barnes, who instructs Filipino children in their history; Colonel Madden, organizer of guerilla resistance to the Japanese, and school principal Buenaventura J. Bello, the perfectly colonized Filipino. By his sacrifice Bello calls forth the nascent Filipino totem to mate with the American totem against the Japanese. His character stands in for real Filipino heroes whose historical anti-Americanism cannot easily be incorporated into the mythology of the film, but who can be modeled and recalled in other ways.

The scene of interest is the last class in the village school of Balintawak after the fall of Bataan.[89] Miss Barnes shepherds her students through a lesson celebrating the legacy of European colonization in the Philippines, concluding with the American promise of independence. Asked to say what Americans have given Filipinos, the children offer soda pop, hot dogs, movies, radio, and baseball, signifiers of the exportable popular culture of the United States. Miss Barnes has something nobler in mind. She calls on the school principal, her first pupil. Buenaventura J. Bello has been intellectually and spiritually birthed by Miss Barnes, the American mother. He is a model to the assembled students. "America taught us that men are free or they are nothing. Since then we have walked with high heads among all men," says Bello, invoking the basic category for humanity in American patriotic myth. Without the American totem, Filipinos had no identification worth having. They were possibly not even human, a symbolic suggestion of American racism toward Filipinos. The film is at pains to deny such group exclusivity by assigning it to the Japanese or even the Filipinos who may be tempted by it, but who will prove their humanity by resisting it.

Miss Barnes recalls that Filipinos resisted American occupation. "And then what happened?" she asks. When a small girl answers that Filipinos were defeated by the Americans, a boy named Maximo asserts that Filipinos are unbeatable. He offers his brother's success in international athletic competition. Sports is the surrogate totem battle where colonial powers aspire to beat occupying ones, and where occupying powers indulge this symbolic defiance of totem authority. Contrary to facts, Maximo denies his brother's defeat with an American vernacular phrase, "We wuz robbed!" He has mastered the highest totem virtue: never give up. Miss Barnes asks about "a Filipino who wasn't beaten. What were the last words of General del Pilar to those who left him behind?"[90] Maximo struggles with the answer. Like his people, he has not yet mastered the symbols of his own history. The principal models the missing words of voluntary sacrifice: "I am surrounded by fearful odds that will overcome me and my gallant men, but I am well pleased with the thought that I die fighting for my beloved country. Go you into the hills and defend it to the death." The students cheer this statement as Japanese soldiers enter the classroom and Filipino soldiers led by Colonel Madden gather in the countryside.

Bello has ritually prepared for a martyr's death by repeating the words of General del Pilar, the Philippine sacrifice of most recent memory. The Japanese commander addresses the assembled school beneath Filipino and American flags flying side by side in the schoolyard:

Fellow Orientals, the hand of his Imperial Majesty, the Emperor, has put an end to your domination by an exploiting and arrogant American race. He will next put an end to a system of education designed to impress on you a sense of inferiority. Señor Bello, step forward please. As principal of this school, you will haul down the flag.

Señor Bello raises his eyes to the flag. It ripples across the entire frame. He sets his jaw and shakes his head no. The commander unwraps the halyard from the flagpole and thrusts it at Bello. Bello shakes his head again. "Señor Bello, unless you haul down the flag, you will hang in its place." Thus he prophesies the symbolic exchange. Again Bello refuses. The commander loops the halyard around Bello's neck and slaps him. Maximo rushes from the crowd and throws himself on the commander, whose lieutenant smacks the boy with a rifle. Maximo falls to the ground, the embodiment of a nation not yet strong enough to defend itself. "For the last time, Señor Bello, haul down the flag."

Now Miss Barnes releases her spiritual first-born from any forced obligation. "Señor Bello, haul down the flag. I speak to you in the name of every man, woman, and child in the United States." Señor Bello regards Miss Barnes with tear-filled eyes, squeezes them shut, and shakes his head in refusal. He is a willing sacrifice. The camera zooms in on his roped neck. The rope jerks up. The camera cuts to Miss Barnes, who averts her gaze in horror. Next it cuts to the assembled school. The horrified students also look away. A priest extends his arm in blessing, signifying the religious and transformative power of this death scene. Maximo, the next generation, returns to consciousness on the ground. We see what he sees: the flag wrapped around Bello's hanging body from which only his legs protrude. Bello and the flag are one. With his sacrifice, Bello has become the flag.

The camera has constructed an encounter with totem magic. The school has seen the unseeable god who demands sacrifice in order to regenerate itself when the Japanese threaten its power.[91] When the god reveals its sacred, or taboo character in the sacrificial event, the people acknowledge it in fear and falling back. "When society announces itself, it sets itself up as a god," says Durkheim. In a myth manufactured for American congregants, the god's appearance announces that henceforth, the American totem will be the god of Filipinos, the product of a messianic union between Philippine and American sacrifice. According to Durkheim, original taboos guard against contact.[92] Sight, which this horrified audience refuses, is contact. "The totem emblem is like the visible body of the god," says Durkheim.[93] "Dreadful actions" emanate from it. Taboo "comes from the respect inspired by the sacred object, and its purpose is to keep this respect from failing."[94] Viewers have witnessed the sacrificial offering of the Filipino totem to the American one. The sacrifice is made ready through Bello's language of identification with the American totem. But it is not his language that will galvanize Filipinos. It is his gesture.

Bello's sacrifice is symbolically once removed from American totem recreation in which the totem eats its own. In American eyes Filipinos are emerging from backward, read primitive, ways and tempted to return to them by the primitive Japanese. They gain a totem when it eats one of their own in a sacrificial feast. What remains unspoken is that the American totem also eats its own. Why the United States sacrificed its own troops in the Pacific is the unarticulated question of the film, since to ask the question directly is to expose the totem secret. Instead, the film constructs a parallel myth about Filipinos, a "primitive" people wrestling with totem loyalty. It is visually argued that the American totem is willing to sacrifice suitable others to restore totem order. The American totem needs the sacrifice of Filipinos, an adopted people, to survive. That the totem eats surrogate rather than "real" Americans is the mythic claim that conceals the totem secret.

To sacrifice oneself to the flag is the most magical totem act. The supplicant crosses the magical boundary between himself and the totem. To sacrifice is to merge with the flag, to be annihilated. Durkheim notes that sacrifice is typically the occasion for a repast. Here the sacrifice *is* the repast; the flag consumes the body. Alimentary communion produces "the same effect as a common origin."[95] Since relatives share flesh and blood, and food is the medium of re-making the flesh and blood of an organism, to eat is to join the substance of eaters and eaten, who thus become kin. Bello the martyr is a feast for totem divinity that visually ingests the sacrificial victim and makes him kin. The victim feeds the totem with his blood.[96] Bello is at once death and resurrection, the latter symbolized in his having literally risen, as though from the dead, to join the flag. His death is a messianic model for those who come after.

Faint from her encounter with the sacred, Miss Barnes remodels it for

Colonel Madden. She describes how the humblest of citizens may perform a sacrificial duty beyond language. Both its publicness and horror are requirements.

He was not a brave man. He was too terrified even to speak, but when they ordered him to haul down our flag he could only shake his head. And then they hanged him. In the schoolyard. In the presence of his pupils.

Miss Barnes confers on Señor Bello an epitaph by Jose Rizal, poet and martyr in the conflict with Spain. Miss Barnes instructs the guerillas to remember it, so "wherever men fight for freedom, there it may be said, "Here lies Buenaventura Bello, schoolteacher of Balintawak."

Evidence that the totem's transformative work has begun comes as Philippine resistance fighters discuss the fall of Bataan:

GUERILLA: "Why didn't the Americans send food and medicine, why didn't the Americans help?" (to Madden) "Maybe you can still get away, sir, there is no more army here. Now the fight will be down in Australia, sir."
MADDEN: "Maybe there will be fighting here. Maybe the people will want to fight."
GUERILLA: "Sure! The people will fight!"
GUERILLA: "Against thousands of Japs? After they've beaten our armies?"
GUERILLA: "We've fought that way before. We've never been conquered."
GUERILLA: "With bolos? Against machine guns?"
GUERILLA: "If a schoolteacher can die for the American flag, we can fight for the Philippines. We must have the hope. We cannot die for nothing."

Colonel Madden connects sacrifice to the Philippine totem father.

MADDEN: "You remember the name Andres Bonifacio?"
GUERILLA: "Every Filipino does."
MADDEN: "If he were alive and sent out a call, would the people answer?"
GUERILLA: "Bonifacio's dead."
MADDEN: "But his grandson is alive. Among those prisoners."
GUERILLA: "Maybe we'll be able to find him, sir."

Reality is created and sustained by the successive creation acts, each a gesture of hope, a ritual "repetition of paradigmatic gestures."[97] Ritual makes the world meaningful by repeating the creation act that transforms chaos into cosmos, profane into sacred.

Back to Bataan is full of sacred repetitions. When Colonel Madden is summoned to Corregidor to organize guerilla resistance, he hesitates to leave his Philippine Scout regiment. His commander points to the act of a more exalted totem model: "Joe, the President just ordered General MacArthur to Australia." "Well, then," replies Joe, "I guess I can leave the Scouts." As the unarmed Philippine resistance fighters evaluate their situation, they remind one another, and are reminded by Colonel Madden, that their fathers defended themselves with bolos. Lacking weapons and supplies, they repeat their fathers' acts. The new weapons of a new war are less ritually potent than the repetition of a sacred history.

As Balintawak is re-captured in the final sequence of the film, Miss Barnes enters her old school. She rips down the Japanese flag and uses it to erase Japanese writing on the blackboard. The enemy totem is de-sacralized with a gesture. Unlike the American flag, which has been able to summon sacrifice when its power is threatened, this totem cannot respond. In the last scene Andres Bonifacio and his fiancée embrace beneath American and Philippine flags now united in common sacrifice. Bonifacio presents her with a handful of "free Filipino soil," a fertility gift from a newly incarnated totem to his mate. They will populate the new nation together.

Iwo Jima

Among the chief disasters that can befall the clan is loss of the flag.[98] To lose it in battle is a special misfortune. Naval regulations once stipulated a maximum penalty of death for any serviceman "who strikes, or attempts to strike, the flag to an enemy or rebel without proper authority, or when engaged in battle treacherously yields or pusillanimously cries for quarter."[99] In *Halter* v. *Nebraska* (1907), which recognized flag desecration laws as constitutional, even the defense acknowledged that:

We apprehend that in all places where the flag is displayed by the sovereign power of the nation, the executive arm of the government has power to protect the flag in time of peace as well as in time of war, even to the killing of the person or persons who might haul it down, should it become necessary to resort to such harsh means.[100]

Surrendering the flag is tantamount to refusing to fight. Saving it in battle confers totem honor. Loss of the flag suggests loss of the will to perform the ritual activities necessary to preserve the group.

The best known twentieth-century icon of the American flag is a memory image about warding off loss of the totem. This is the Joe Rosenthal photograph of raising the flag on Mt. Suribachi during the battle for Iwo Jima in February, 1945. The image is both a creation story about restoring the totem in sacrificial conditions and a record that certifies the authenticity of the patent. Framing an actual event in a dramatic visual composition, the photo quickly achieved an iconic status that makes every ceremonial and photographic re-presentation of it another commemorative re-creation.

Never mind that the exact historical facts of the Iwo Jima flagraising are complex, distracting, and not possessed of the seamless heroic narrative that messianic myth requires. It has never been a secret that Rosenthal's photograph does not depict the original flagraising on Mt. Suribachi, the first Japanese soil captured by Americans at the cost of one-third of all Marine casualties in the war. Twenty-seven Congressional Medals of Honor were awarded for action there, the highest for any World War II battle. Flags are irresistible targets for enemy troops. They have not been routinely carried into battle by American soldiers since the Civil War. Raising or striking the colors marks a ritual border, such as the end of a campaign, by imposing unambiguous distinctions on ambiguous differences. Taking Mt. Suribachi, the highest point on Iwo Jima, was the first objective of four days of fighting during which devastating enemy fire rained down on American troops. The Allied command believed a flagraising would boost American troop morale and weaken the enemy's, while reassuring homefront congregations worried about Pacific losses. Flagraising was the apostolic mission. The messianic reconstruction that came to pass was unimaginable to the soldiers who undertook it.

Watching the flag go up to the cheers of soldiers below, Navy Secretary James Forrestal declared a successful renegeration. "The raising of that flag on Suribachi means a Marine Corps for the next five hundred years!"[101] The original flag was soon replaced by a larger, more visible one to reinforce ritual magic and protect the first flag from souvenir-hunters intent on individual commemorations.[102] Associated Press photographer Joe Rosenthal captured the second flagraising. He never imagined his "grab shot," caught on the fly, would register a mythic composition of the liminal moment before regenerative redemption. His picture showed a band of brothers striving together to resurrect the weakened totem father on a tree of life connecting heaven and hell at the center of the world. Reproduced everywhere, this image became the best known combat photograph of World War II. It survives as the anchoring image of a rapidly receding American memory of totem triumph and danger. The photo appeared a month later in *Life,* which described how:

Schoolboys wrote essays about it, newspapers played it for full pages and business firms had blow-ups placed in their show windows. There have been numerous suggestions that it be struck on coins and used as a model for city park statues.[103]

The *New York Times* called it "the most beautiful picture of the war." It was compared to Emmanuel Leutze's *Washington Crossing the Delaware* and Da Vinci's *Last Supper,* religious models national and sectarian.[104] Years later its creator described how the sight of the flag as he mounted

Suribachi "clutched" at his heart. "I still think of it as *our flag*. That was just the way I thought about it. I still don't have any other words."[105] That for which there are no words is holy. To authenticate the image's sacrificial claims, *Life* published Marine combat photographer Louis R. Lowery's dramatic account of the first flagraising, which had given rise to the famous second:

> As the flag was put up a Jap hiding in a near-by cave hurled a grenade, then charged out waving his sword. Marine fire cut him down and he fell in a bloody heap down the inner slope of the crater, his sword broken. A second Jap hurled a grenade which landed at Lowery's feet and he dived down the steep side of the volcano, rolling 50 feet before he could stop. The grenade blast missed him but he wrenched his side and broke his camera in his tumble.[106]

The Rosenthal photograph has been endlessly reproduced, imitated and parodied. Its most spectacular re-framing is the Arlington National Ceremony Marine Monument set on a marble pedestal surrounded by a carved border with the names of every battle Marines have fought in. Karal Ann Marling and John Wetenhall have written about the hyping of the icon, how five men who were not the original flagraisers were required to play that role for patriotic consumption, how they struggled to reconcile the public's godlike expectations of them with their ordinary lives and how the mythic machine set in motion by everything the icon touched would not let them. Rappaport describes how ritual participants such as these become "fused with the message:"

> In conforming to that which his performance brings into being, and which comes alive in its performance, he becomes indistinguishable from it, a part of it, for the time being. Since this is the case, for a performer to reject the canonical message encoded in a liturgical order that is being realized by his performance as he is participating in it seems . . . impossible.[107]

Among thousands of World War II photographs, this mythic portrait of sons redeeming an original sacrifice at great price combined circumstance and epic compositional elements into a single image of re-creating a sacred center. The ordeal of the band of brothers who resurrect the tree of life that connects heaven and hell is conveyed in the impression of muscular strain and effort. The apostolic mission is starkly rendered as men and the faltering totem alone in the universe. Like the sacrificial Christ redeeming the world, soldier sacrifiers carry their own tree of life, their cross, the sign of their willingness to die to restore the sacred center. The soldiers of the image are anonymous brothers in the same uniform laboring for a common end.

The photograph also conveys the earnestness of successful ritual. One can hardly take the obligations of public devotion more seriously than to risk being fired upon by the enemy. Since rationally it is better to shoot or take cover, there must be something very important about raising the flag, a most non-utilitarian act. Soldiers may complain about "the life," about officers, food, equipment, and snafus. They may not be gung-ho patriotic. But to be good soldiers they must publicly display acceptance of duty to a fault. Each of the Iwo Jima flagraisers was "participating in the order to which his own body and breath give life."[108] With body and breath the sacrificial band of brothers creates an order of totem rebirth from sacrifice.

Re-presentations of Iwo Jima emphasize facts that comport with mythic narrative. The flagraisers represent different son-groups in American society – "a son of immigrants, an Indian, boys from the Midwest, the plains, the East."[109] Facts at variance with the archetype – that this flagraising was not the first one, that the flagraisers were not under fire at the resurrection moment, that the individual re-enactors felt inadequate to the task of heroic re-presentation thrust on them, that they had faults of alcoholism and lying, that one of the principals in the picture was misidentified by the press for months – these facts fell out. Other facts evolved toward the mythical. Whereas the heads of the flagraisers in the Rosenthal photograph form a horizontal plane, the Marine Memorial alters this plane to model the triangular shape of the ancient magic mountain or ziggurat, which the flagpole, another *axis mundi*, amplifies. Located squarely in death and hell, Mt. Suribachi has become a magic mountain, an *axis mundi*.

Indignation and scandal have accompanied periodic rediscoveries that our national religious icon does not depict the first flagraising. This suggests how effective mythic reconstruction has been. The "second" flagraising is unable to resist mythic pressure to make it the original. "No Fiction, No Imagination," declared a prominent businessman promoting a statuette of the image weeks afterwards, "but real live marines exposing themselves to devastating fire that our flag might be raised above the enemy on the highest peak."[110] The mythicization of Iwo Jima is popular memory at its totem work. Eliade writes,

Historicity does not long resist the corrosive action of mythicization. The historical event in itself, however important, does not remain in the popular memory, nor does its recollection kindle the poetic imagination save insofar as the particular historical event closely approaches a mythical model.[111]

If the Rosenthal photograph had not existed, could another have replaced it as the defining image of World War II as effectively? We can only speculate. The transformation of the Rosenthal photograph into the national religious icon of World War II was the convergence of real circumstances with a mythic model persuasively offered. The facts of Iwo Jima alone did not determine the iconic fate of the Rosenthal photograph. If facts were determinative, other battles such as Okinawa, where American casualties were nearly twice those of Iwo Jima, or Guadalcanal or Tarawa, or D-Day or the Battle of the Bulge, should have produced images as famous.[112] Lacking visual re-presentations with the same mythic resonance, they did not. Like mythic narrative, mythic image begins with a less than mythic base of circumstance, that is, with the patent. The actual ordeal of Iwo Jima had mythic ingredients. The composition of the Rosenthal photograph provided a visual model for elaborating them. From this model of the resurrection of ancestral totem sacrifice, a generation's collective memory of World War II took both narrative form and the object of restoring totem order.

Sands of Iwo Jima

On the homefront, World War II was a mediated war, a press photograph its most famous re-presentation. Republic Studios released The *Sands of Iwo Jima,* a mythic elaboration of the events behind the photograph, in 1950. In the final sequence real battle footage of the assault on Mt. Suribachi was interspliced with fictive visual narratives. This is the mythicizing power of media at its most straightforward. The imposition of canonical form may be more obvious in feature film-making, but the same process makes the Rosenthal photograph ritually useful. Though *Sands of Iwo Jima* has not survived as an important re-creation of the Iwo Jima myth, its narrative is mythically instructive.

The title phrase, "Sands of Iwo Jima," was lifted by producer Edmund Grainger from a newspaper story, another media text. Conceived as a prestige project, *Sands* featured John Wayne, a then moderately-known star of low-budget westerns. The story of Sergeant John Stryker and his squad of Marines culminates in a commemorative re-enactment of the Suribachi flagraising. In the climactic scenes of the film Mt. Suribachi rises out of smoke and fire, hell and death. Stryker and his unit mount its slopes. Men on both sides die in uncharted territory without clear borders. The commanding officer, played by Lieutenant Harold Schrier, the real-life leader of the platoon that raised the first Iwo Jima flag, receives the filmic order to raise the flag over Suribachi. One soldier has planned on offering his own flag of homemade bits and patches. Its small size and humble provenance indicate its popular origins. At a word from Stryker, this flag is set aside for the general's larger flag handed down through the chain of command, that is, from a source with a heavier charge of totem magic. The popular totem defers to and is transformed by the high totem flag. With this device the film mythically encompasses the awkward fact of two flagraisings. Dispatched under armed guard to the movie set at Camp Pendleton, the filmed second flag was the Iwo Jima relic, the actual flag Rosenthal had photographed. This indiscriminate mix of newsreel footage, celluloid fiction, Iwo Jima warriors, actors, and authentic relics was calculated to increase the re-presentational magic of the film.

Schrier presents the flag to Stryker. Because it contagiously touches him in the act of accepting the mission to climb Suribachi's magical summit, we can guess he will soon be its sacrifice. Those who touch the ineffable totem are consumed by it or it would not be the totem. Stryker gathers his unit. He ritually prepares for sacrifice. He exchanges affectionate words with Private Conway, his favorite "son" in the unit. Conway has had a premonition that he will perish at Iwo Jima. He reports feeling better. The voice in his head must have been wrong. Stryker, whose own life will substitute, is glad to hear it. Taking the last cigarette of the condemned man who is about to die, he pronounces himself "happy," a willing sacrifice. In an instant he is shot through the heart. "Is he . . . is he . . . ?" his distraught men ask, unable to utter the taboo word.

The grieving soldiers discover a letter to his small son in Stryker's pocket. Read aloud, it becomes a letter from the ghost father-sacrifice to his warrior sons. "Be like me in some ways," he writes, voicing the totem command. He also laments leaving his own son to go to war. "I didn't want it to turn out this way." Stryker keeps the totem secret with his guilt. For he has not abandoned his son by going to war. Nor has he abandoned his unit sons by dying. He was sent by the totem to Suribachi as a sacrifice. He has been an exemplary father to his unit sons, preparing them well for the ordeal they face. Moved by the dead father's charge, Conway, the son whose life the father's life has bought, pledges to finish Stryker's work. He offers himself as sacrifice.

As men in the unit look on, the flag is raised, the dead father resurrected, the totem spirit re-animated. There are two separate shots of the flag. One re-enacts the Rosenthal photo. In the second, men gather around the flag as it blows straight out in the wind. Like the earlier combination of the popular flag and the general's totem flag, the presence of two flagraising images acknowledges two distinct flagraisings. Struck dumb in the presence of the holy, the men in Stryker's unit watch speechlessly. Magically transformed, they know what to do. Marching off together into the liminal fog of battle, they cross the border and disappear from sight.

7

Refreshing the borders

He's my kind of player. He comes to kill you.

Leo Durocher on Eddie Stanky[1]

Now Joseph had a dream, and when he told it to his brothers they only hated him the more. He said to them, "Hear this dream which I have dreamed: behold, we were binding sheaves in the field, and lo, my sheaf arose and stood upright; and behold, your sheaves gathered round it, and bowed down to my sheaf."

Genesis 37:5

The United States is first and foremost a nation of tribes. We use the term *affiliative* groups to designate them. Affiliative groups are the fulcrum of the totem system, an important resource for totem regeneration, a fallback when the totem fails, and the most dangerous threat to its unity. At its purest, affiliative behavior is coming to the aid of one's group by repelling the Other. This is not affiliative behavior only. It may be the most basic of all social behaviors. From affiliative identity comes our notion of ourselves as courageous, powerful, and strong, and able to meet the world on our terms. Not only are affiliative groups fundamental to American history and identity. Overcoming them by force and denying their aspirations to kill is a constant fact of political life, a historical achievement, and the key to totem success.

Every affiliative group is one of a number of son-groups striving to unbalance fraternal symmetry by seeking totem favor at the expense of other groups. Affiliative groups seek more than totem favor. They seek to topple and replace the totem. Affiliative groups are totem mimetic; they envy the totem and seek to do what it does. A group that enforces a defining taboo that others must respect knows it's a group. Totem groups take life to enforce their taboos. Denied full totem power, affiliative groups are continually in doubt about their status. All their organized efforts are in search of group identity. This is the pursuit of "pride," a term used by the military, an affiliatively structured group on which full totem identity is conferred; by sports teams, which ritualize the myth of affiliative conflict, and by individual affiliative groups. Pride connects group identity to a notion of shared achievement. The appeal and vitality of affiliative contests are evident everywhere. Affiliative behavior is a ceaseless contest for dominance in which affiliative borders are reproduced and fought over. Organized killing of outsiders is the most coveted source of affiliative identity. Since the totem forbids killing, coercion makes a temporarily acceptable consolation prize. The public is both attracted to and repelled by the violent aims and reputations of affiliative groups. They move in and out of favor with the public, which alternately admires and despises them.

Affiliative groups use the term *brotherhood* to designate their group collectively. Totem groups never do. Totem groups appeal to the father, the fatherland, our forefathers, the father of our country, and even the motherland. Affiliative groups are concerned with identifying real brothers, who are known by whether or not they were present at the struggle. Authenticity is the affiliative quest. *Were you there?* is the affiliative question. Affiliative groups embrace fraternal solidarity. Every brother must offer himself in defense of an injury to any member. Laying one's body on the line for the group enacts the affiliative organizing principle, its sacrificial ethic. A member of the Imperial Gangsters, rivals of the Vice Lords, one of Chicago's oldest predominantly black gangs, articulated this principle:

Black, white Mexican, gook, it don't matter to us . . . What matters is, "Is you down?" When we go out and mob somebody, you got to be out there with us, throwing blows, pulling the trigger.[2]

The United States was created for, settled and taken over by affiliative groups. The history of every town recalls their presence. Consider this description of a lumber and mining town in Washington State:

Roslyn has in fact never got along with itself very well. Its twenty-four or so nationalities distrusted each other. They drank at separate bars, joined separate fraternal lodges, and buried their dead in a dozen or so ethnically defined cemeteries, which today form an intricate necropolis on the western edge of town: blacks here; -ichs and -vichs there; -ellis and -bellos and -inis here; Masons there; New Knights of Pythias here; Old Knights of Pythias there; Red Men here; Cacciatori D'Africa there.[3]

A conglomeration of affiliative groups is not a nation, but a segmentary clan society, a stage for endless affiliative conflict. On the eve of World War I, Woodrow Wilson addressed newly naturalized citizens on the dangers of affiliative division. "You cannot become thorough Americans if you think

7.1 Affiliative segregationists march on totem border. Little Rock, 1959.

7.2 Affiliative member drives perceived invader from border. Boston, 1975.

of yourselves in groups. America does not consist of groups. A man who thinks of himself as belonging to a particular national group in America has not yet become an American."[4] To create a nation, affiliative groups must bow to the totem. The totem offers protection in return. The totem also needs affiliative groups as allies, to monitor one another, and as a point of comparison to show that the totem is right and proper, and affiliative groups are not. That is, affiliative groups offer serviceable enemies over which the totem may triumph. The totem flag trumps affiliative loyalties by definition. A small town in the Adirondacks debated whether a district attorney had an undue advantage from wearing a flag lapel pin at trial. "Anyone should be able to wear this flag," argued a World War II veteran. "You should be able to wear it to school, to your church or synagogue, to your fraternal organization. You can wear it to heaven or hell, too."[5] Totem magic must prevail over competing affiliative orthodoxies.

The totem task is to embrace all affiliative identities, to absorb all affiliative winning and losing. In the totem economy of desire and aggression, the totem seeks to level inter-affiliative striving. "We are just one race here," wrote Supreme Court Justice Antonin Scalia, declaring some ethnically targeted affirmative action programs unconstitutional: "It is American."[6] Though it professes to remain neutral in the delicate balancing act in which affiliative groups are always in danger of breaking away, the totem strategically sides with some affiliative groups against others.[7] Ambivalence thus characterizes the relations between the totem and its affiliative groups. This is because affiliative behavior is the natural expression of groups, and totem existence a contingency based on affiliative consent. A determined alliance of affiliative groups can topple a totem; a successful totem likewise requires affiliative cooperation. Where any affiliative group flourishes in defiance of the totem, the totem must kill it. This is what government prosecutions of the Mafia, or the Ku Klux Klan, or labor union racketeering entail.[8]

Though affiliative groups admire violence, not all pursue it actively. A striking instance of affiliative submission may be seen in a *Life* photograph depicting a proxy battle for control of Montgomery Ward.[9] Still-faced contenders in business suit armor face down one another in seated ranks at a stockholders' meeting. To the rear of the podium, where company executives look out over the group, stand American flags at rest. They symbolize death, the totem's privilege to kill any who offend it, and the withdrawal of that privilege from the contending groups in the photograph. Emotion creases the face of the leader of a takeover attempt. He waves his arms and angrily shouts at a rival, but does not and may not kill him. Within the bounds of totem law and order he recognizes limits to his predatory options. By claiming the stockholders' meeting for the territory of the United States, the totem enacts and expresses its relationship to this group of fractious men engaged in a contest for dominance.

Affiliative groups present themselves as practitioners of violence, as allies of totem violence or as allies of rivals bent on taking totem power. A gang member described his comrades' aspirations:

The biggest thing everybody is looking for is respect on the streets. It isn't money. They are just trying to make sure you respect them. People are just pushing each other to the maximum to get respect. And the maximum is death.[10]

Respect is a euphemism for the affiliative wish to kill, but respect is what affiliative groups must settle for. The more affiliative groups are aware of their desire to kill, the more dangerous they are to the totem.

The markers of affiliative belonging are totem mimetic. They include:

(1) **Exclusive membership based on blood affinity**. Affiliative groups share an exclusive sacrificial history. This may be the blood sacrifice of perceived biological kinship or shared blood ordeals that create social kinship. Both forms of sacrifice may be present in one group, and either may become the basis of a tight bond the rest of the world cannot fathom.
(2) **Enthusiasm for the fight**. Affiliative groups are always on a mission.
(3) **An unstable posture of totem affiliation manifest in an obsessive concern for the authentic**. Fealty to totem ideals is filtered through an affiliative lens ever-capable of rejecting totem ideology.
(4) **Strict group codes.** These may include secrecy, rules of behavior, codes of honor, and identifying bodily appearances, marks or clothing.

Every citizen has at least one affiliative identity. These may be enacted in affiliative *groups*. Affiliative groups that have fought the totem and lost include Jacobins hunted during the French Revolution; exogamously rebellious Mormons; nineteenth-century anti-Catholic Know-Nothings descended from the Sons of the Star-Spangled Banner; the Ku Klux Klan, self-proclaimed enemies of Jews, immigrants, Catholics, and blacks; the Scottish Rite of Freemasonry; the Black Panthers; Communists witch-hunted in the 1950s; the Weather Underground of the late 1960s and early 1970s; perhaps every religious sect or denomination at one time or another; the pro-life group Operation Rescue; paramilitary groups such as Posse Comitatus and White Aryan Nation; gangs such as the Gangster Disciples and the Mafia. Labor unions and veterans' groups have often jousted with the totem. The most threatening of all affiliative groups in American

7.3 Affiliative Boy Scouts model totem class violence.

history was the Confederate States of America, which bloodily challenged totem authority for five long years.

Affiliative groups are organized around kinship bonds, sectarian beliefs and even sports, and may encompass several of these identifiers at once. What affiliative groups always share is a sacrificial history. What they lack is totem identity, the authorized power to kill their own. By contrast, the totem possesses exclusive killing authority over all its members, who likewise possess a shared sacrificial history. These are the principal categories of affiliative groups:

(1) **Blood kinship**. Consanguinity is the classic affiliative marker. It refers to real or presumed blood ties expressed as ethnicity, race, gender or sexual orientation. The Black Panthers, La Cosa Nostra, and Act Up are all affiliative groups based on affinity by kinship. Labor unions were historically organized around craft skills cultivated by distinct ethnic groups. "Ethnic" is an acceptable contemporary term for genetic or blood affinity. It suggests an updated noble savage, a euphemism for "primitive." Though ethnicity now references race or nation, it once meant "heathen" or "pagan." If the social is indeed constructed from the body, such real or presumed blood ties constitute formidable social glue.

(2) **Fraternal groups and secret societies**. Where blood ties are weak or absent, bloodletting through common ordeals must accomplish the affiliative goal of shared commitment. Fraternally-based affiliative groups include patriotic societies, labor unions, veterans' and paramilitary groups, and street gangs. American Nazis, the Ancient Order of Hibernians, the Ku Klux Klan, the Mafia, the Women's Christian Temperance Union, Skull and Bones, the Nation of Islam, and Hell's Angels are embattled fraternal organizations whose members are ethnically distinct.[11] Veterans' groups are fraternities both of shared sacrifice and generational affinity. They have often been slow to admit new sacrificial warriors, withholding recognition from their sons' wars as worthy models of their own. Secret societies are a prototype fraternal organization. Regarded as primitive and anti-social, they are traditional instruments of political revolution and have always attracted the hostility of established authority.[12] For Lionel Tiger secret societies are elaborations of male hunting groups, perhaps the original affiliative bond, which the rapper Ice Cube describes as follows:

These brothers are looking for rites of passage. There ain't no lion for them to go out in the jungle and kill and come back and say, "I've killed the lion.

Now I'm a man." So they kill each other. They kill whatever is there, but there's a rebellious spirit that is in all of us.[13]

(3) **Sectarian religious groups**. Denominational faiths in the United States are affiliatively rooted in ethnic emigration. All have sacrificial traditions and exclusive codes of belief. Each bows down to its own violent authority. In the case of Christianity, that violent authority is a father who willingly sacrificed his son, himself a willing sacrifice. Abraham Lincoln, a martyr for totem unity, put the case for churches as affiliative groups by explaining why he had never joined one:

> When any church will inscribe over its altar, as its sole qualification for membership . . ." Thou shalt love the Lord thy God with all thy heart, with all thy soul, and with all thy mind, and thy neighbor as thyself," that church shall I join with all my heart and soul.[14]

(4) **Sports teams** are a distinct affiliative category that deserves separate discussion. We will treat them as having special functions in the totem order.

Though affiliative groups instinctively recognize one another, their insecure status makes them competitive and distrustful. "Will you join me in a declaration of war?" the Rev. Jerry Falwell, leader of the affiliative Moral Majority, wrote in a letter demonizing gay Americans, whom he perceived as seeking to bend the totem to their will.[15] The *New York Times* described the leader of the affiliative Nation of Islam, Louis Farrakhan, as "the black twin of David Duke," a former Ku Klux Klan leader, implicitly comparing the Klan and the Nation of Islam by their common affiliative enemies – immigrants, Jews, and racial Others, transposing only black and white.[16] In an affiliative comparison Christian Coalition leader Ralph Reed bragged that "the religious, pro-family community has reached a point of grass-roots effectiveness that rivals that of the labor union movement at its height in the 1940s and 1950s."[17]

Modeling the totem

> And what sort of soldiers are those you are to lead? Are they reliable? Are they brave? Are they capable of victory? General Douglas MacArthur[18]

Affiliative groups model the totem they envy. They stage initiating ordeals and cultivate sacrificial memory. They require, above all, a defining enemy. Among the most compelling is the totem. In short, affiliative groups do what totem groups do. The difference is the totem is the affiliative group in

7.4 Affiliative groups appropriate symbols of killing authority. Ku Klux Klansman with hangman's noose, cross, Bible, sword, Confederate flag, and the most powerful killing symbol, an American flag.

charge, with the power to kill its challengers and get away with it. Denied but coveting the privilege of enforcing the killing taboo, affiliative groups channel their aggressive aspirations into creating and breaking lesser ones. Imitating their totem models, affiliative members mark their bodies, dress distinctively, and adopt gestures that "dance" fighting. By the standards of polite society affiliative group behavior is often crude and repulsive. The more affiliative group members are at odds with totem authority or popular opinion, the more their bodily appearance and behavior mark them as outsiders. Ice Cube describes this sensibility among African–American teenagers with affiliative aspirations:

People started wearing different hair styles. People started wearing their clothes baggy, so they can let the system know that we ain't with this. We're our own people. And we gonna stand on our own . . . I try to make it clear to a lot of the brothers and sisters . . . that, you know, these are our warriors. This is our army.[19]

A trinity of descriptors may convey affiliative identity: hairstyles, head coverings or face markings; aspects of dress or body marking; and distinctive body behavior. A description of Hell's Angels as "long-haired, beer-bellied marauders clad only in denim and leather" indicates hair that exceeds civilized length.[20] Their overweight bodies are out of control from drinking, which produces dangerous behavior. Their uniforms are not respectable. They aggress against totem order.

Affiliative groups may imitate totem models explicitly. A founder of the Los Angeles Crips gang dreamed of erecting a model of the Vietnam Veterans Memorial with the names of all Crips and Bloods who had "given their lives for their neighborhoods." Like the Vietnam War dead, "They died for a cause. They died for their colors. They died for something they believed in and that was Crip."[21] An ex-Crip invited to a pre-inaugural luncheon for fifty distinguished Americans by President-elect Bill Clinton was proud the gang tattoos on his neck would be visible in his tuxedo. "This is where I came from. The Marines have tattoos with USMC What's the difference?"[22]

The Nation of Islam models and challenges the totem with its very name. Leader Louis Farrakhan has long instructed white majority America that African–Americans see a "different country." Members of the Fruit of Islam, the Nation's security force and training vehicle for young men, affiliatively display themselves as "bow-tied young soldiers."[23] Recognized by their stern visages, close-cropped hair and strict behavior codes, their mission is totem-mimetic and competitive:

"They want to operate outside the law" – but they are undeniably effective at chasing away crime and drugs in communities where nothing else works.[24]

A "former marine" with a rumbling voice taught members at a Harlem mosque to march:

As the men marched in place – arms swinging and knees pumping – and yelled in cadence – "One! Two! Three! Four!" – he would keep time by shouting the names of Islamic holy men. "This is not like in the white man's army," he told the marchers. "We want you to think."[25]

Here was the familiar trope distinguishing righteous discipline from coercive control by the Other of their own troops. Our soldiers think. Theirs are mindless robots without freedom, the defining characteristic of the human.

Gang culture likewise displays totem-mimetic features. In Dwight Conquergood's account of Chicago street gangs, killings are committed "for the nation," parlance for affiliative gangs. Gang conflict is the mechanism for defining turf. "Killing," Conquergood writes, "is the ultimate performance of negation for purificatory and generative purposes. Killing – for the nation! – is a profound act of both boundary clarification and mediation, division and merger."[26] It also places gang members at odds with totem law. Conquergood's informants articulate totem-mimetic rules for living. "You adapt to it or you die. That's the law of the street." You are either allied with a center, or a sacrifice.[27] There is no other place to be. Affiliative and totem groups alike understand the principle.

Though dissatisfaction with the status quo is a primary affiliative worldview, affiliative groups may admire and defend the reigning totem with pugnacious enthusiasm. Positive regard from groups such as the Boy Scouts, the Masons and Shriners, or hereditary patriotic societies may be deceiving since affiliative dissatisfaction is always barely concealed and easily elicited. Affiliative zeal to reform totem groups is as common as affiliative resentment and fear of a reigning totem or of rising affiliative competitors. A classic example is the nineteenth-century Nativist party, descended from the Sons of the Star-Spangled Banner and claiming totem blessing for its agenda of racial exclusion.[28] Affiliative groups are often openly jealous of the totem and bitterly competitive. At a 1939 German–American Bund "Pro-American Rally" to celebrate George Washington's birthday, thousands of fascist sympathizers packed Madison Square Garden. Cheering greeted the mention of Hitler and Mussolini. Laughter greeted references to "Franklin D. Rosenfeld."[29] The rally combined a characteristic affiliative appeal to the "true" totem with a rejection of the present one, in which affiliative groups are always disappointed.

7.5 Generative totem father George Washington presides over affiliative effort to mate with the totem. German–American Bund meeting, 1939.

Challenge as a way of life

Politics is the systematic organization of hatreds.   Henry Adams

Affiliative groups are not benevolent societies. Modeling their totem masters, they equate respect with fear. They unapologetically coerce those who refuse to do their bidding in bitter and often physical contests for dominance. "Nice guys finish last," was the classic affiliative comment attributed to Brooklyn Dodgers manager Leo Durocher.[30] He was "the personification of Dodger baseball: rowdy, brash, displaying lack of taste, but a fighter and a winner," inspiring passionate hatred and loyalty.[31] This is the quintessential affiliative personality, fighting, winning, always on the edge of losing – and affiliative groups do lose – in a society that wants winners.

Since legal coercion is unavailable to affiliative groups as an instrument of power, they seek to enforce respect for their traditions. They interpret all submission as a sign of their own moral superiority. Affiliative groups embrace pseudo-legal regulation, such as rules of athletic competition or the Ten Commandments, or these rules that bind a New York drug gang:

Los Solidos, like all self-respecting gangs, has a written charter, the membership's Bible. The opening page states that the book is to be handled with care "and never to be touched by hands that are dirty."

A new member has to sign a contract agreeing to abide by those rules. "Violation will result in termination, beat down and even death," the rules say.

"Once you become a member and have learned the family business," the charter adds, "there is no leaving, and you can't quit."

Members have to carry photo ID's, wear their red-and-blue "colors" and have a tattoo representing Los Solidos.[32]

For any exercise of force to which they are not totemically entitled, affiliative groups may be swiftly and harshly punished by the totem. During the trial of John Gotti, head of the Gambino crime family, the state prosecutor described Gotti's crimes as a usurpation of totem power:

Murder plays a central role in the business of this enterprise. It is the way discipline was maintained. It's the way in which power was consolidated. It's the way in which power was obtained . . . Murder is the heart and soul of this enterprise.[33]

The same could be said of the totem. The difference is that the totem is allowed and affiliative groups are not. "You know why he's dying?" said Gambino crime boss John Gotti about a murder he had ordered, "He's gonna die because he refused to come in when I called. He didn't do nothing else wrong."[34] This was incriminating evidence – that Gotti had presumed to sacrifice those who refused to declare themselves sacrifices to him. Affiliative appropriation of the right to kill is punishable by the totem to whom it is exclusively accorded.

Since affiliative groups lack the power of totem sanction, or border control, they are doomed to offer and answer challenge as a way of life. Even among themselves their identity is not secure. They impose disciplinary or symbolic killing rules on themselves and seek to impose them on whomever they cannot kill nor assimilate. Since infractions cannot legally be addressed with ultimate sanctions, group cohesion is always in peril. This results in a constant process of break-up and reassembly. The mechanism of group fracture and reconstitution in the absence of the decisive sanctions available to totem groups was described by an observer of the Ku Klux Klan, "The problem is that every Klan member wants to be a Klan leader and so they break off and start their own group, but the numbers of people involved overall changes very little."[35]

Affiliative struggles for identity are played out over and over in media texts. What did the Chicago Bulls basketball team want, mused a sportswriter? "A solid place in history. And if [Michael] Jordan has his way, they will seize it."[36] Battles are necessary to secure uncertain identity, and the advantage is always to the brave. "We won't get the respect that we want," said Jordan, "until we do what great teams in the past have done – keep winning until there is no doubt." There are never enough wins for affiliative groups, whose worth is always unsettled in public affection. Each win only makes them challengeable for the next game, the next season. Affiliative losses remind the totem group that affiliative groups are not the totem, but totem pretenders.

Totem ambivalence toward affiliative groups comes from recognizing that members covet totem power and wish to seize it. Affiliative ambivalence toward the totem comes from believing the totem class has betrayed true totem ideals. Bearing a history of dashed totem expectations, Vietnam veterans affiliatively registered their disapproval of Bill Clinton's first presidential visit to the Vietnam Veterans' Memorial. Clinton's crime was that he had not been there, had not been reliable, had not suffered the ordeal of his cohort. "Where was Bill?" read a sign asking the affiliative question. "You Lied, You Dodged, Refused to Go," read another. Some veterans turned their backs on Clinton and booed at each mention of his name. "Damn you, you coward," a protester jeered, engaging in the classic affiliative blasphemy of presuming to the totem.[37] How, wondered a columnist, could men who honored the military so disrespect the chain of command ending with the Commander-in-Chief.[38] "Forgive him, my rear end," a totem profaner jeered. "He didn't do anything that Benedict Arnold didn't do."[39] The protesters shared a fighting conviction that this embodied totem had wronged them. Their angry words were "like shots coming across."[40]

For blasphemously presuming to the totem, affiliative groups are admired and feared by turns. In Russia, Chechen secessionists appeared both dangerous and appealingly purer than their totem masters:

> Some of the worst people in the world live in this city [Groznya]; murderers, thugs, drug dealers and thieves . . . But anyone who looks at Chechnya and just sees a bunch of gangsters isn't looking very hard. There is an honesty and sincerity among the people here that disappeared from the cash-crazed streets of Moscow a long time ago.[41]

At odds with Russia for centuries, Chechen rebels embraced affiliative fatalism.

> Chechen soldiers have fought superior forces every time, with daggers, knives, rocks, even poison. They never win and they never stop.

Like all affiliative groups, Chechens admire violence. A reporter chose the "most striking piece of sculpture in Grozny, a huge stone fist with an enormous knife rising from it" to explain their "messianic, nihilistic, half-baked" commitment to fight. Equally affiliative was their shared sacrificial history. "Everyone remembers the day they took us away," said the Chechen Foreign Minister, recalling the deportation of half a million Chechens to disease and death in cattle cars in 1944. "It will never happen again."[42]

Totem control of affiliative breakaway

When the totem lacks strength or will to enforce its borders, affiliative competitors strive for ascendance. The end of Soviet totem authority in Eastern Europe unleashed rivals striving to reform totem borders through the extermination policy called "ethnic cleansing." Serbs confiscated property, expelled non-Serbs from the villages they had seized, rounded up unarmed citizens, herded them at gunpoint into trains bound for the nearest border, or killed them outright and burned their villages. "They are ready to kill everybody who is not of the same nation," a Croat refugee said.[43] A description of the outsider was not far behind. It came from a Croatian military commander. "It's a war of ordinary people against primitive men who want to carry us back to tribalism."[44] The level of carnage was the greatest in Europe since World War II. It modeled creation–sacrifice among partisans who saw the dismemberment of the Soviet Union as an occasion to redeem the bitterly remembered sacrifices of their own groups. Affiliative labels such as Tigers, White Eagles and Chetniks remodeled units that had waged guerrilla war against the Nazis.

In Western Europe the loss of the restraining Soviet border brought out skinheads and other groups pursuing an extreme nationalist vendetta against immigrants. As Europe watched the Balkans in turmoil, Germany in racist conflict, and the succumbing of the Maastricht treaty to nationalist ambitions, a leader of the German opposition commented, "People are worried and disoriented, and they don't trust the Government any more. They are looking for a scapegoat."[45] Just as affiliative groups feed on a collapsing totem, a totem group with nothing to feed on at the borders feeds on itself. Affiliative groups are available for this purpose since they never go away. They provide a reserve for creating necessary strangers if the totem wavers and needs new enemies. The totem may cast them in the role of outsider to consolidate and renew its power, or they may cast themselves or one another in this role in a struggle to overthrow or support the totem.

When totem groups feed on affiliative groups, their shared ordeal may become the basis for a strongly forged identity. Even losing to superior totem force can unify the group so long as it is willing to sacrifice its own to resist an encroaching totem group. When an affiliative group is perceived by its members as not having fought back, as in the case of the Jewish Shoah or the European enslavement of Africans, this is a source of unease and disunity. Was the sacrifice willing or unwilling? Group identity will remain in doubt until members are willing to resist with blood and forge their own totem group, as Israel has done for the Jewish nation, the vehicle for unanimously sacrificing its willing own. For affiliative groups the alternatives are to sacrificially resist totemic Others and unify as a group, or surrender affiliative ambitions and join the larger totem group. At this moment in history, American Jews have largely assimilated to the American totem group, retaining their sectarian identity, but willing to sacrifice their lives for the nation–state. Martin Luther King, Jr. made it possible for African–Americans to offer willing blood sacrifice around affiliative identity in so-called non-violent protests without violating totem killing authority. This outcome invokes the distinction between affiliative and totem groups. Both share sacrificial histories but only the totem group is authorized to kill its own. The civil rights movement was a historical marker of affiliative identity for African–Americans who remain ambivalent about joining the larger totem group. Thus the first black major league baseball player, Jackie Robinson, signaled an affiliative posture in a bitter memoir about his experiences, "I cannot stand and sing the anthem . . . I cannot salute the flag; I know that I am a black man in a white world."[46] Once an affiliative group is willing to resist an encroaching totem, it can use incomplete, which is to say, unwilling sacrifice to search for new sacrifices to redeem further challenges to its affiliative identity.

Affiliative groups may press totem authority to the point of takeover or breakdown. When Abimael Guzman Reynoso, the imprisoned leader of the terrorist group Sendera Luminoso (modeled on the totem-toppling Khmer Rouge of Cambodia), offered to negotiate peace with Peruvian president Alberto Fujimori, the latter refused on totem grounds. "A peace agreement," he declared, "implies a negotiation between two belligerent groups equal not only militarily, but morally and ethically. This is something that cannot be accepted."[47] When the totem retreats or dissolves, the ruling principle of force that is always *in* force, but variably visible and admissible, becomes explicit. After a campaign of Mafia attacks on Italian law enforcement, the chief prosecutor of organized crime in Sicily lamented, "Democracy does not govern. What governs is terror and death."[48]

Affiliative borders are constantly reproduced and fought over. Even under a strong totem affiliative strife is a continual process of refreshing the borders. By eliciting unending hostility, affiliative groups re-direct conflict from one set of boundaries to another. This may serve or threaten totem interests. In 1939 *Life* magazine depicted Communists and Fascists, two affiliative groups vying for popular affection, as structurally indistinguishable:

Each of these groups wins its converts by summoning patriots to "save America" from the other, but at bottom they are no more unlike than the red and the black on a roulette board. They hate and fight each other precisely because they are rivals for the same power . . . Each calls its doctrine Americanism and skulks behind the symbols and heroes of America while working to destroy the American democracy which it despises.[49]

So long as the totem is strong, affiliative groups are commanded to respect it. Warner Brothers' film *Magnum Force* (1973) portrays an affiliative rebellion within the totem class.[50] Renegade cops start killing citizens. Though they appear to be defending a totem code against criminals, they are unauthorized by the totem and cannot stand. Clint Eastwood is the hero who flushes out these affiliative rebels for totem retribution. The theme line, "A man must know his limitations," is a warning to affiliatives in the context of totem myth not to seize the totem power of sacred killing. One must serve the totem, one must not usurp its power.

Subgroups within the totem class are especially in danger of becoming affiliative groups capable of moving against the totem, particularly if they can muster popular support. Totem control of affiliative competition includes forcing candidates for totem class membership to renounce affiliative allegiance. Army recruits must swear they do not belong to any organization that "advocates or engages in the disruption or halting of US government activities through force." Even groups that have cast off previous loyalties to swear allegiance to the totem may revert to affiliative type or move back and forth between totem and affiliative allegiance in border-porous circumstances. Under pressure, will the police behave as totem class members, or are will they run affiliatively amuck? "Who's going to catch us? We're the police. We're in charge," a policeman who regularly beat up suspects and innocent bystanders explained in hearings on New York City police corruption.[51]

Such concerns emerged from the thirty-fifth annual Tailhook Association convention in Las Vegas in 1991 where rowdy attendees assumed a predatory affiliative posture toward female naval personnel. Tailhook members were retired and active-duty elite naval and Marine Corps aviators. Tailhook thus comprised both totem class and affiliative members. The group identity of the organization was blurred. Participants displayed the uncontrolled affiliative rule-breaking that is feared from totem class members lapsing into affiliative loyalty. There were scenes:

"streaking," "mooning," "butt-biting" and other events . . . The report characterized the suites at Tailhook conventions over the years as "a type of free-fire zone" where aviators could behave "indiscriminately and without fear of censure or retribution in matters of sexual conduct and drunkenness."

This description suggests the attributes of male hunting groups:

Hundreds of officers – lured by the prospect of free drinks, free food and a chance to share war stories with old buddies – roamed the third-floor "hospitality suites" rented by aircraft squadrons. Strippers and scantily clad bartenders worked the 20 suites, where Navy and Marine Corps pilots watched pornographic movies. Male streakers dashed about, and in one suite, officers goaded female guests to drink from a dispenser shaped like a rhinoceros penis. The alcohol bill per suite was as much as $7,000 during the three days.[52]

Aviators recently returned from Gulf War victories were said to have felt threatened by military downsizing, a move especially affecting junior officers, and by a command decision to allow women to become combat fliers. This was the most talked about topic at the convention.[53] But a report by the inspector general also noted that recent conventions had been characterized by an escalating "can-you-top-this" atmosphere of affiliative competition.[54] When Navy Secretary A. Lawrence Garrett III failed to discipline affiliative insubordination in the ranks by active-duty Tailhook offenders, he was dismissed.

Veterans' groups also may move affiliatively against the totem. During its 1937 convention in New York, *Life* magazine devoted twenty-one pages of pictures to the American Legion, "its parade, its high jinks, its history."[55] *Life's* description of the 110,000 conventioneers as "a peacetime army of middle-aged men in vari-colored uniforms behaving like boys and marching like heroes up Fifth Avenue," conveyed the mixed regard in which Americans held the Legion and its play-war affiliative status. *Life's* flag-drenched pages depicted a highly ambivalent view of legionnaires. In some pictures conventioneers delivered food boxes to needy children; in others, they assaulted female pedestrians "with electric shocking devices generally applied to the rear."[56] *Life* characterized the Legion's affiliative platform of position statements and enmity toward other affiliative groups as "resolved for peace, for a Big Navy, for neutrality in Labor disputes, against all alienisms. '"[57] It speculated on the Legion's record of public approval and disapproval:

In 18 years the Legion has grown great and million-strong . . . It has been revered as a legion of heroes, earned just praise for its work in disaster relief, child welfare, civic betterment. And it has been fiercely denounced as a greedy Treasury-raiding machine and potential Fascist nucleus.

Observers conscious of history have wondered whether the Legion is to become another such self-seeking political incubus as the Grand Army of the Republic, which took a quarter-century after the Civil War to reach full bloom. To a broader question, no nation has found an answer since Alexander's legions marched back from Carmania. That question: can a body of men uprooted, toughened and disillusioned by war ever be returned to normal citizenhood?[58]

This is the affiliative temptation presented by totem class membership. Can men who have exercised totem prerogatives be expected to relinquish them when borders are re-secured? Will they regroup as an affiliative threat? Against such an eventuality society constructs elaborate rituals to convert border-crossers back into obedient observers of the totem taboo. That the pleasures and dangers of exercising totem power with permission are partly re-captured and re-experienced in affiliative conflict is one of the great attractions of affiliative groups and one of the great risks to the totem.

Affiliative flag practice

The characteristic flag of totem authority is a resting flag that surveys its rightful domain. It is stationary. The usurping flag is the emblem of agitated affiliative son-groups on the move to seize the totem father's power. The characteristic posture of affiliative brothers is marching together behind the flag on a quest to seize an elusive object before them. This is a journey to the border. Where this flag leads, its clan follows. Affiliative groups display the totem flag to model a totem with which they wish to ally, or to offer dares or launch mock battles for power that may turn real in an instant. At Brigham Young University, a Mormon institution, it is a "campus tenet to salute the flag whenever it is raised or lowered."[59] The institution signals that it yields to totem authority amidst its pursuit of dominance over other affiliative groups. By contrast, Bob Jones University in Greenville, South Carolina, a sectarian school that bans interracial dating as contrary to God's law, affiliatively defied totem directives about displaying the flag after the assassination of Martin Luther King, Jr.:

> In April of 1968 we had had a Bible conference that included Ian Paisley, the militant northern Irishman, and at the end of a Saturday night, Bob Jones, Jr., got to the podium and said "Martin Luther King, Jr. has just been shot in Memphis, Tennessee. The President has asked us to fly the flag at half-mast. We will not fly the flag at half-mast for an apostate," at which time the audience clapped and cheered. I had never witnessed such a racist act.[60]

Filtered through an affiliative lens, the totem always falls short of expectations. Confederate disillusionment with the United States totem was recalled by Admiral Semmes, the captain of the Confederate vessel *Alabama,* who maintained that the true totem idea was re-presented in the Stars and Bars.

> I have always cherished an affection for the principles of the . . . old flag; and it was only when the old flag became a new flag, and ceased to represent those principles, that I consented to war against it . . . The stars and stripes that I hold in my hand were no longer, in our judgment, the stars and stripes of the revolution of 1776, or of the war of 1812.[61]

In the admiral's view new creation–sacrifice was needed to salvage a corrupted totem identity. By referencing the Stars and Stripes in its new name and new design, the Stars and Bars sought to appropriate the "old flag's" authority even while defying it. The Stars and Bars retained the "true republican colors" of red, white, and blue. "There was a very general desire to depart as little as possible from the old flag," recalled an editor of the *Savannah Morning News.*[62]

In competition with the totem, affiliative groups may create flags that are pointedly not the American flag. A case in point is the MIA–POW flag flown by former prisoners of war and their supporters. Though the soldiers commemorated by this black mourning flag were totem class members, its design conspicuously lacks all totem reference. Its supporters resent the totem's lack of commitment to its lost sons, and their flag portrays an affiliative withdrawal of totem loyalty. (The white flag of surrender is relevant in this context. In the West white is a not-flag, the explicit absence of the sign of those who are ready to sacrifice themselves. Who surrenders under a white banner marches under no flag. He is no willing sacrifice. He wants to quit, the prime affiliative and totem sin.)

Affiliative flags lack agency compared to the totem flag. Occasionally, a giant heresy elevates an affiliative flag to a magically profane level. If sacrifice creates totem sanctity, totem sacrilege is affiliative defiance magically transformed. Its power is directly proportional to the size of the totem sacrifice that has been summoned to repel it. In American history no affiliative challengers have acquired the profane magic of Confederate and Nazi flags. Not even the Soviet flag radiated such blasphemy during the Cold War. We have argued that this is because the Cold War lacked significant blood sacrifice.

A flag controversy in the Panama Canal in 1964 illustrates affiliative challenge and totem response. In response to demands from Panamanian nationalists in 1959, the US granted titular sovereignty to Panama within the Canal Zone and the right to fly its flag equally with the American flag at the US Canal Zone building. When President John F. Kennedy extended this directive to the entire Zone, resident American students protested. Kennedy then ordered that no flags would be flown at schools inside the Zone. This action precipitated a sacrifical crisis, a peril to totem distinctions. Empty flagpoles equalized affiliative aspirations within a disputed territory and engendered a competitive quest to lay exclusive claim to the killing power that flags signify.

Flag-carrying American students marched around Balboa High School and disobeyed a direct totem order by running up a flag for two days. "The Stars and Stripes is our identity with home," they argued. They invested it with magical agency. "When it flies alone, we feel that the zone is American, that it *is* home." According to *Life*:

On the third day, demonstrating Panamanian students entered the school grounds and sang their national anthem, but the Balboa students blocked them from raising their flag. There was a scuffle – and the Panamanians retreated in outrage, claiming their flag had been ripped by the Zonians. A few hours later when the Panamanians returned, it was no student demonstration. It was a mob – out for blood.[63]

Panamanians ripped up an American flag and carried their own dishonored flag to the president of Panama. Zonians and Panamanians, rival brother groups, wrestled for affiliative dominance. Violence predictably followed an escalating trajectory. Panamanians gathered in the streets and "snipers began to attack US-owned buildings." When US Canal Zone police fired directly into a Panamanian crowd, American troops rushed to the scene. This superior display of totem arms ended the melee.

Here was a border zone of uncertain claims between rival affiliative son-groups with presumed equality. Rioting Panamanians were one totem-protected son-group, unruly American students another. Each sought dominance in ritualized contests in which striving by each side was taken as a justification for equal or greater affiliative resistance in an escalating call and response to perceived injury to their respective totems. "The next step, if they have their way, will be just to fly the Panamanian flag," explained an American girl at another Canal Zone school where US flags were defiantly raised. She named as a transgression by the other side what she wished for herself, to fly her flag victoriously, appropriating totem authority. A ceremonial quest became a real quest for totem succession. Peace required a sacrificial submission, a reassertion of distinctions.

The Branch Davidian disaster

Every cult is a kind of nation.   *Time*[64]

A deadly conflagration broke out when federal agents moved on the Branch Davidian cult in Waco, Texas, on April 19, 1993. Seventy-five lives were rapidly consumed. In the confrontation a religious cult refused to bow to the totem and defied it with armed resistance. Here is what happens when an affiliative group defies the totem to the death. Immediately after the disaster, Davidians were portrayed in press accounts and public opinion as having got what they deserved. Fifty-one days earlier, cult members had fired on agents of the Treasury Department's Bureau of Alcohol, Tobacco and Firearms during an unsuccessful raid on the cult, which was suspected of being in violation of federal firearms statutes. Four agents and at least six cult members were killed.

What were the Davidians guilty of? "These people had thumbed their nose at law enforcement," explained an FBI official.[65] The sin of totem blasphemy was re-stated by another, "This man believed he was God."[66] An ex-cult member prophesied, "They will kill for him."[67] These reasons for violent totem retaliation rang truer than vague allegations of child abuse within the compound or fatigued hostage negotiators, reasons that were officially advanced. The true national god is manifest in the sole right and power of the nation-state to kill. False gods may not claim it. Nor may they be worshipped with sufficient enthusiasm to place in question who has legitimate killing authority, which it certainly was in the case of the well-armed, highly committed Davidians.

"Which of your two children are you prepared to sacrifice?" Koresh had asked a follower.[68] The remark was repeatedly quoted for its emblematic demonstration of behavior forbidden and condemned within totem borders, as was Koresh's claim to be the Messiah, a sacrificial savior.[69] The exact parallel with the demands of the American totem for the sacrifice of its own children went unremarked. Likewise, sinister intent was ascribed to Koresh for structuring the lives of his followers without acknowledging the resemblance to American totem practice:

> To equip his flock psychologically for the battles to come, Koresh reportedly played and replayed videos of his favorite movies about the Vietnam War: *Platoon, Full Metal Jacket* and *Hamburger Hill*. His followers prepared themselves physically with weight training, military-style drills and obstacle-course runs. To acquaint them with the experience of famine, their vegetarian diet was strictly rationed. Daily life was a harsh mix of work and Bible study.[70]

Life in the compound resembled military boot camp. Diet was controlled, bodies and minds disciplined, pleasures rationed. The latter included popular feature films also used by the US military to entertain troops. The Davidians also aped the totem class in "fights between the boys [that] were staged possibly in preparation for man-to-man combat in an apocalyptic war."[71] Only the example of holy writ was different, replaced in military life by training manuals and patriotically inspired texts.

A psychiatrist reported that the surviving Branch Davidian children portrayed Koresh as "an ambivalent shadow," a ghost associated with violence and death.

> In their drawings, the compound is both riddled with bullet holes and depicted as the kingdom of heaven. In other drawings, they surrounded the words I LOVE DAVID with hearts. "They learned to substitute the word love for fear," Perry told the *New York Times*.[72]

The final observation is the most telling. The children deny Koresh's killing power just as citizens deny the killing power of the national totem. Respect is rendered as love instead of fear.

Before the second raid *Time* magazine called the Davidians a "Cult of Death" in an essay about the havoc wreaked in the world by religious conflict. The essay was deeply committed to the unspoken proposition that the United States was a different kind of community, transcending religious strife. "If you scratch any aggressive tribalism, or nationalism," assayed the editorial with no ironic self-recognition, "you usually find beneath its surface a religious core, some older binding energy of belief or superstition, previous to civic consciousness, previous almost to thought." In the familiar association of "primitive" and Other, *Time* failed to discern any parallel to American nationalism or any Eastern European ethnicity locked in struggle with its neighbors. The pattern of distancing Western nations from the residual primitive was noted by a former Peace Corps director in West Africa:

You, and most of the Western news media, routinely portray neotribal primitivism, murderous old clan feuds, and warring racial fiefs – whether in Somalia, the Sudan, Kenya, Nigeria or Burundi – as exclusively African . . . Aren't there also warring clans and tribes in Eastern and Western Europe, as well as in the former Soviet Union, with more than enough Western warlords or tribal chiefs killing, raping, and starving rival clans and tribes? Not to mention bloody clan feuds multiplying in America's own urban highlands and lowlands.[73]

The fiery end of the FBI–Davidian confrontation was recorded on television. Tanks flying the American flag battered the flag-defended Davidian compound and lobbed tear gas, as fire accelerated by gusty winds consumed it. Both sides, the mother of a cult member said afterwards, were "bent on survival."[74] What was at stake in each case was the group idea. Since the totem tolerates no other nations within its borders, whatever acts, walks, and fights like a nation must die. After who was entitled to kill and who was not was resolved by force, the state took back its rightful authority. Media described the demise of the flag of affiliative authority, now deposed, in almost magical terms.

On the flag pole front of the compound where the Branch Davidian Star of David flew until it disappeared in a swirl of black smoke on Monday, the state flag of Texas and a blue-and-white flag from the Bureau of Alcohol, Tobacco and Firearms flapped at half staff today.

Four stars on the ATF banner signified the agents killed here on Feb. 28 in the shootout that began the 51–day ordeal.[75]

Having reimposed totem authority, law enforcement raised its own flags over conquered territory, advertising and commemorating its own sacrifice as the more worthy.

Affiliative cases: Hell's Angels

Our discussion so far has drawn on a number of different affiliative groups. We now explore three specific expressions of affiliativeness in more depth. We examine an unassimilated veterans' group, the Hell's Angels; a nativist vigilante group, the Ku Klux Klan, and Queer Nation, exogamously irregular by traditional totem rules. Each shares an identity perceived to be based in blood and a mythic history of ordeal, and each engages in totem-defying behavior. It happens that the origins of all three are related to wartime sacrifice. The Klan's roots lie in the Reconstruction South. After the Civil War re-established the American totem, the Klan held out in affiliative defiance. Its ethnic origins were Celtic and Protestant – *klan* referred to the Celtic ancestry of its original members. *Kuklux* alluded to the Greek "kuklos" for *circle*, invoking borders.[76] The Klan's defining program is blood exclusivity, or racism, which it calls "100% Americanism." The Hell's Angels originated as military veterans from World War II. They are domestic soldiers of fortune, adventurers and general delinquents known by their outlaw personae. The gay rights movement, whose affiliative aspirations are expressed in the phrase "Queer Nation," traces its history from communities of gay veterans who settled in coastal centers after World War II and forged a political identity modeled on the civil disobedience battles of the 1960s. They are organized around sexual practices that at this writing are constitutionally unprotected and even criminalized in many localities.

Hell's Angels are a classic affiliative group to which others may be compared, though few are as uncompromising as the Angels, who present the unsullied paradigm. The Angels are largely the offspring of Okies, Arkies and hillbillies from Appalachian America, poor Scotch–Irish stock who migrated west during the depression years of the 1930s. Hunter S. Thompson writes of them:

It would not be fair to say that all motorcycle outlaws carry Linkhorn genes, but nobody who has ever spent time among the inbred Anglo-Saxon tribes of Appalachia would need more than a few hours with the Hell's Angels to work up a very strong sense of *déjà vu*. There is the same sulking hostility toward "outsiders," the same extremes of temper and action, and even the same names, sharp faces and long-boned bodies that never look quite natural unless they are leaning on something.

Most of the Angels are obvious Anglo-Saxons, but the Linkhorn attitude is contagious. The few outlaws with Mexican or Italian names not only act like the others but somehow look like them. Even Chinese Mel from Frisco and Charley, a young Negro from Oakland, have the Linkhorn gait and mannerisms.[77]

While Scotch-Irish blood provides the genetic stock, the addition of motorcycles and the love of adventure came from World War II and then Vietnam. When soldiers return from war and jobs are scarce, they face the problem of survival. Having exercised the totem prerogative to kill, they return to a world where such tasks are no longer theirs to execute. Hell's Angels are a solution to the economic predicament of a class – unemployment among working-class white men who know something about mechanical work and engines – and the spiritual predicament of those who have learned totem behavior they may no longer practice. They have taken the option available to every totem group member. They have become affiliative.

The Angels are social outcasts who know it and don't care. "We are complete social outcasts – outsiders against society," says one. "That's the way we want to be . . . We're bastards to the world and they're bastards to us."[78] More, the Angels are violent. Their "casual acceptance of bloodletting is a key to the terror they inspire in the squares."[79] Bloodletting may occur in response to any perceived wrong to an Angel under any circumstances. The organization's creed of honor is total retaliation for any insult or offense. "In any argument a fellow Angel is *always right*. To disagree with a Hell's Angel is to be wrong. And to persist in being wrong is an open challenge."[80] This ethic gets the Angels continually in trouble. It makes them a problem to totem authorities and a subject of fascination to the public. Angels claim to be regular guys who have been wronged by journalistic image-makers. "We're hard-working people," explained an Angel sporting a knife holster at a benefit to raise legal fees for them. "We're people who go to work at 6 o'clock in the morning. People with children. The image of a Hell's Angel is totally Hollywood."[81]

Angels are a secret society. A reporter had this exchange with an Angel-in-training:

How long before he would get his colors? "You never know," he said. How long had he been hanging out with Hell's Angels? "I'd rather not say." How many members are there in the New York charter? "Ask a member," he said, then added with a smile, "In other words, don't even ask."[82]

Their larger politics are totem-affiliative, also in the classic sense. Behind the stage at the benefit at the Marquee biker club, a Manhattan warehouse space, "hung a black banner depicting the Hell's Angels insignia – a skull in profile with a wing growing out of its brain – and an American flag that seemed as big as the White House lawn on one wall."[83] Angels apply to their country the same exclusionary standards of ideal community they apply to themselves.

The Angels, like all other motorcycle outlaws, are rigidly anti-Communist. Their political views are limited to the same kind of retrograde patriotism that motivates the John Birch Society, the Ku Klux Klan and the American Nazi Party. They are blind to the irony of their role . . . knight errants of a faith from which they have already been excommunicated.[84]

They fail to understand how little use the totem world has for them as long as they seek identity through violence:

Their reactions to the world they live in are rooted in the same kind of anarchic, para-legal sense of conviction that brought the armed wrath of the

Establishment down on the Wobblies. There is the same kind of suicidal loyalty, the same kind of in-group rituals and nicknames, and above all the same feeling of constant warfare with an unjust world . . . The main reasons the Angels are such good copy is that they are acting out the day-dreams of millions of losers who don't wear any defiant insignia and who don't know how to be outlaws. The streets of every city are thronged with men who would pay all the money they could get their hands on to be transformed – even for a day – into hairy, hard-fisted brutes who walk over cops, extort free drinks from terrified bartenders and thunder out of town on big motorcycles after raping the banker's daughter. Even people who think the Angels should be put to sleep find it easy to identify with them.[85]

The important point is this. Put a military uniform on a Hell's Angel, cut his hair, and he'll act the way he always does. But now he'll have totem authority. Take away the American flag, and everyone becomes a member of an affiliative group. Nor is this transformative effect lost on affiliative groups who aspire to totem status. The affiliative lesson is likewise appropriated by the totem, which divides its soldiers into competitive services further subdivided into regiments, companies and platoons, all with affiliative identities and behaviors constantly bent to totem purposes. Such strategies produce groups with clear and well-defended borders. Put differently, the military elicits and channels affiliative bonding for totem ends. As Admiral James B. Stockdale, the highest-ranking Vietnam POW, said of those who faced death as prisoners of war:

In the end, the prisoner learns he can't be hurt and he can't be had as long as he tells the truth and clings to that forgiving band of brothers who are becoming his country and his family. This is the power of comradeship.[86]

Totem groups cultivate loyalty, but affiliative bonds hold comrades together through great ordeals.

The invisible empire of the Ku Klux Klan

Following the Civil War conflagration that officially resolved the question of totem authority in the United States, the Knights of the Ku Klux Klan were one of the first groups to organize in affiliative reaction. The Klan found its mission in punishing carpetbaggers and scalawags, border trans-gressors from outside who came to reconstruct the South. It also targeted white allies of these groups and blacks attempting to exercise new citizen-ship rights. The Klan's posture was classically totem-mimetic. It sought to control borders by expelling agents of a totem it regarded as illegitimate, along with whomever was perceived to have violated antebellum codes governing sexual relations between the races. "We are the law itself," the Klan boasted. The brutality of its vigilante violence moved the victorious totem to crush it with military force in the 1870s.

Klansmen were united by ordeal and kinship. Membership was limited to native-born white Protestants sworn to embrace its racist, anti-Semitic, anti-Catholic creed. Confederate veterans of a shared sacrificial war took leadership positions in its quasi-military hierarchy. The Klan developed a full panoply of affiliative ceremonies adopted from Catholicism and Masonry including a specialized language, secret oaths and emblems, a paramilitary chain-of-command and its own calendar. Its distinctive mask and robe were said to be "as sacred to [Klansmen] as the fez and the plume are to the Masons, as other religious regalia are to the church, and as uniforms and flags are in governmental functions."[87] According to an original-generation Klansman, the organization's spook-like garb was intended to suggest Confederate ghosts risen from their graves to wreak vengeance.[88] Soldier Klansmen were called "ghouls," symbolically recapitulating the border guards of totem myth. Every new member was hazed and tested in acts of lawlessness.[89] Ritual passwords hallowed the affiliative bond in the name of the idealized totem:

> *Who comes here?*
> A friend.
> *A friend to what?*
> A friend to my country.[90]

The Klan elicited the usual love-hate fascination with affiliative groups. "Ku-Klux Fever" entered popular culture alongside anti-Klan denunciations in Congress. Consumers were urged to use Wickes' accident-proof kerosene because Kommon Kerosene Kills. Ku Klux Kocktails became a popular drink. Music stores featured "The Kluxing of the Ku Klux Klan."[91] The most ambitious tribute was the extravagantly produced film *The Birth of a Nation* (1915) based on Thomas B. Dixon's *The Clansman*, a popular racist romance that helped spawn the Klan's twentieth-century revival.

Though the Klan is an affiliative villain in contemporary culture, a composite sketch of sympathetic sources suggests the flavor of a more ambivalent era:

At first the Klan directed its energies "against local incidents of radical misrule." Later, it began to "silence or drive from the country, the principal mischief-makers of the Reconstruction regime . . ." The Klan "accomplished much good in reducing to order the social chaos." It "kept the negroes quiet and freed them to some extent from the baleful influence of alien leaders . . . property was more secure; people slept safely at night; women and children were again somewhat safe when walking abroad – they had faith in the honor and protection of the Klan."[92]

A Klan apologist, Congressman Philadelph van Trump, linked it to a romantic and honorable tradition of revolutionary and secret societies:

Bad government will produce bad men among the best people on earth; and that has clearly been the cause of Ku-Kluxism . . . It has been so in all ages of the world. It produced the *Carbonari* in Italy; it gave rise to the *Free Companions* in France, in the bad reign of Louis XI; and it filled all England with *Moss Troopers* under the iron rule of the Normans, who reappeared in Scotland against the tyranny of the English Crown prior to the Union. Even *Robin Hood* and his burly followers, whether mythical or real, whether their exploits were matters of mere romance or of veritable history, serve to "point a moral" in the philosophy of government; for they stand both as the representatives and the exemplars of the indisputable fact that good as well as bad men will band themselves together in resisting the aggression of tyrants wielding political power.[93]

The Klan was fiercely loyal to the totem by its own lights. In the words of Grand Wizard Nathan Bedford Forrest (who eventually repudiated the organization's lawlessness):

[The Klan] is a protective, political, military organization. I am willing to show any man the constitution of the society. The members are sworn to recognize the Government of the United States . . . Its objects originally were protection against [Union] Leagues and the Grand Army of the Republic.[94]

The Klansman's creed holds "my allegiance to the Stars and Stripes next to my allegiance to God alone."[95] Treason against the United States is the first "major offense" in the Klan constitution, violation of the oath of the order the second, and disrespect of women the third.[96] Cards distributed on street corners and in churches and lodges in Indiana during the 1920s focused on protecting the fertile center:

Remember, every criminal, every gambler, every thug, every libertine, every girl ruiner, every home wrecker, every wife beater, every dopepeddler, every shyster lawyer, every K of C [Knight of Columbus], every white slaver, every brothel madame, every Rome-controlled newspaper – is fighting the KKK.[97]

A different view of the totem-mimetic Invisible Empire was offered by Govenor William Holden of South Carolina. Requesting troops to defeat the Klan from President Grant, he wrote, "This organized conspiracy is in existence in every county of the State. And its aim is to obtain the control of the government. It is believed that its leaders now direct the movements of the present Legislature."[98]

The Klan sought totem accommodation during the 1920s and 1930s. It espoused a "100% American" ideology of Anglo-Saxon purity, ascribing its own ideals to the totem it had defied. It stood pledged "to restore and then to preserve and develop the old, fundamental ideas on which the nation was founded and which have made it great."[99] A re-born midwestern Klan sought to bend the totem through electoral means to Protestant chauvinism, militant patriotism, and hostility to ethnic minorities during the 1920s. Typical was this Klan border rhetoric:

America must close the door to the diseased minds and bodies and souls of the peoples of foreign lands . . . [The] present horde of immigrant invaders are [sic] composed of "Italian anarchists, Irish Catholic malcontents, Russian Jews" . . . They are "ignorant and unskilled, covetous and greedy"; they maintain "loyalty to the lands of their birth . . . they preach their own religions – mostly Roman Catholic or Jewish; they read their own newspapers, printed in foreign tongues; they deride America and its ideals."[100]

The Klan has routinely alleged affiliative conspiracies by blacks, Jews, and Catholics against the totem. It circulated thousands of copies of a purported Knights of Columbus blueprint for a Catholic takeover of the country in the 1920s in which Catholics were said to be stockpiling guns and ammunitions for a massacre of non-Catholics. According to one sturdy story, every time a Catholic boy was born, a rifle was buried under the local church to arm a papal takeover of the United States before he grew to manhood. The 1950s Southern Klan deployed themes of African–American sexual menace by detailing miscegenation plots to weaken the native white stock for Communist and Jewish takeover.[101]

In totem-mimetic fashion the Klan alternated beatings, lynchings, and night-riding vigilanteism with community picnics, barbecues, fish fries, school reform, and hospital building. It endorsed politicians and sponsored local legislation. It built Protestant-only hospitals in communities dependent on Catholic ones.[102] Periodically, it sought to alter its image as a "loosely knit and highly secret vigilante terrorist network in the defeated Southern states" composed of "wild and lawless elements," and "gangs of night-riding hoodlums, probably criminal and certainly crazy, along with a scattering of feeble-minded people who had been hoodwinked."[103]

A 1924 book affiliatively titled *The Challenge of the Klan* trumpeted the organization's reformed status and increasing electoral strength while throwing down a totem gauntlet:

It controls, in a way in which no political party has ever controlled, hundreds of cities, towns and counties, a few states; it has elected its picked men mayors, sheriffs and judges, legislators and governors, representatives and senators in Congress. It is reaching for the presidency.[104]

An apologist claimed the reconstructed Klan was entitled to "dignity and respect – yes, respect even if joined with fear and nervous ridicule – which belong to such movements."[105] This describes exactly the regard in which affiliative groups wish to be held.

Queer nation

"Queer nation" describes a collection of loosely organized groups within the gay rights movement during the late 1980s and early 1990s. The use of the term was hotly debated within the gay community and reflected its ambivalence toward a totem it both envied and defied. Totem-mimetically, the movement acquired a sacrificial banner, made claims on the totem and sought popular approval.[106] Whether or not they embraced the term "Queer Nation," politically engaged activists portrayed gay citizens as a sacrificial community sharing blood bonds of sacrifice and perhaps genetic ties as well. Assimilationist wings welcomed heterosexual supporters as allies while more radical pockets wished to exclude straights as movement members. This posture exactly mirrored the totem's official ambivalence toward gay citizens. Sacrificial milestones chronicle American movement history. According to John D'Emilio, the earliest important gay organization in the United States was the Mattachine Society, named after "mysterious medieaval figures in masks . . . [who] might have been homosexuals," and whose organization "was modeled on the Communist party, in which secrecy, hierarchical structures, and centralized leadership predominated." World War II marked the birth of the modern gay community in the United States by bringing together young gay men from across the country who settled after the war in enclaves on both coasts.

The *founding* sacrificial crisis of the American gay rights movement was the 1969 Stonewall riot, when gay men defended themselves from police during a bar raid in Greenwich Village, an occasion subsequently commemorated in Gay Pride marches on every anniversary of the event. This sacrifice to defend borders marked the birth of the movement as politically self-conscious and possessed of an affiliative identity and mission. Its *defining* sacrifice, in which members act to save an imperiled community, was the arrival of AIDS in epidemic proportions during the 1980s. It "felt like war" as people, especially young people, died in devastating numbers while the country remained largely indifferent.

At the same time, a growing belief that self-disclosure of sexual identity is essential for individual well-being, and the best means for securing tolerance, challenged an earlier rhetoric of privacy as the best means for accommodation by straight society. In reaction to all these events, some community members began to "out" others.[107] "Outing" was the act of publicizing the sexual orientation of prominent but closeted gay individuals, a forcible sacrifice of public reputation justified by totem-mimetic logic as a right and necessary return on privileges bought and paid for with the blood of brothers. The logic of outing was indistinguishable from the logic of the draft board, since outing was an unwilling sacrifice unless the outed individual welcomed the event as some, in retrospect, did.

The gay community compared its bodily and spiritual sufferings to those of Jews and African–Americans, other affiliative groups struggling with assimilation and boundary maintenance in a hostile body politic. Immigrants and African–Americans had offered themselves in war to establish legitimate claims to totem membership. The gay community likewise struggled to achieve eligibility for military service. Its members sought to become totemized by sacrifice as fiercely as they sought to define themselves as a distinct affiliative community. Additional goals included endogamous legitimacy – the rights of same-sex marriage and child-rearing.

On April 25, 1993, several hundred thousand demonstrators marched on the capital to demand totem rights for gay Americans. Some chose this day to out themselves willingly for the movement. In the *New York Times*, Allan Gurganus articulated the totem aspirations of gay citizens by comparing their sacrifices to those of the totem class.

To have lived in New York for the last 12 years is to understand more about war and triage and foxhole conversions than any of the decorated vets of the Grenada Beach Trip or the Persian Gulf Media Action.

Only one-third of our Civil War's Confederates were wounded or killed. Fifty percent of the gay men in New York City are H. I. V. positive. We, the other half, the witnesses, have been waging a battle that would have impressed Lee himself . . . The gay community lives its efficient, directed trench warfare, defending a community under an epidemic seige that's run eight years longer than the Second World War.[108]

Gurganus confessed his own closeted military service, recalling that he had witnessed the sacrifice of a buddy caught sexually touching another soldier, but done nothing. The offending soldier was shaved, imprisoned, and transformed into a sacrificial outsider. He escaped from the brig when their carrier put ashore. In this manner, he crossed the border. "I somehow guess he's dead, and if he is, then it's for him and thousands like him, not just caught but killed, that I march, we march." Gurganus wanted the full totem measure. "To run our banner up a portion of the flagpole means you risk leaving us – and our justified rights – flying at half-mast." Without full totem rights, gay men and women were as good as dead, permanent outsiders to the totem group.

During the march on Washington, the multicolored stripes of the Rainbow Flag were given a field and stars to mimic the totem flag, and rainbow fabric was styled as bunting. The affiliative flag sought to mate with the totem or bend it to its will. Borrowing an affiliative sports metaphor, the march was billed by Torie Osborn, head of the National Lesbian and Gay Task Force, as "the kickoff for the gay nineties." Osborn conceded that the major effect of the march was energizing the "troops" to go home and organize.[109] Media discussion spent time on whether the gay movement was well-served by its theatrically flamboyant "boom-boom girls" and "leather boys," often the most visible members of groups like Act Up. These were the foot soldiers of the gay movement's struggle, expanding the borders for members more identified by appearance and manner with mainstream America.

Parables of the totem

If nationalism or statism is the high church version of the new dispensation [created by the historic decay of Christian faith and practice], then sport may be looked upon as its low church manifestation.

Wilbur Zelinsky[110]

The highest respect you can pay to any player is that you fear him.

Magic Johnson[111]

Religion organizes killing energy. More precisely, it organizes men who wish to kill so they will kill the right people. The religious question sports addresses is this: if groups of men are inclined to act violently, how can this violence be contained when it is not needed to run off neighboring tribes? Specifically, how can warriors be kept from slaughtering everyone inside the tribe while waiting for bigger and better wars of sacrifice? Such questions must be posed and answered in the most intense and widely shared experiences, for they are critical to the welfare of the group. How to manage affiliative aggression is in fact endlessly re-enacted in ritual lessons woven into the religious fabric of the culture. Sports contests offer the most visible arena for ritual action and reflection, particularly among males, for playing out the affiliative myth of striving under totem authority.[112]

Sports organize and display male force by replaying as ritual dance the hunting myth that pervades totem culture.[113] What is permissible in the dance of professional sports is to hunt men down and kill them *within limits* set by the totem. What is not permitted is to kill the totem, which remains taboo. The lesson is twofold. If the totem did not exist, affiliative groups would kill one another. At the same time, affiliative groups must cooperate

7.6 Affiliative brothers unify in opposition to the totem.

to protect totem authority. To play ball is to call for blood, to have the dancers and devotees feel the blood rise, to celebrate moves and strategies, triumphs and losses in what could be war but isn't. In sports the acted out death of men is felt as joyful ecstasy at spilling the enemy's blood, or wrenching fury and despair at one's own sacrifice or the sacrifice of one's comrades. It feels real, even if it isn't.

Sports do what religion always does. They teach values. These include effort, teamwork, and fair play. Effort is sacrifice. Teamwork is identification and cooperation with the group. Fair play is abiding by totem rules. Though the lessons are identical, each game is grippingly different, the better to capture the interest and involvement of believers. Sports remind affiliative competitors of their subservience lest they be tempted to usurp the totem's killing prerogatives. The most important lesson of professional sports is that affiliative groups are disciplined by a violent totem authority. In deference to it they agree not to kill each other and never to disobey the totem. Sports contests play out the myth of affiliative conflict by repeating the pattern of all affiliative groups governed by the totem: teams ready to kill one another and referees determined to control them. Teams share an affiliative history of ordeals, enthusiasm for the fight, disciplinary rules, and a willingness to sacrifice their own. What they do not share with other affiliative groups is the political desire to kill and take over the totem.[114] We classify them as affiliative groups because of how they are framed by popular culture. Author Robert Creamer, a Brooklyn boy, explains:

You'd say to somebody, "What are you, a Dodger fan? Giant fan?" I mean, there was an identification. "Are you Catholic? Protestant? Jewish? You a Giant fan? Dodger fan? Yankee fan?" It was a *thing*. That's what you were! It was part of your life.[115]

Having a favorite team is like having a sectarian faith; the comparison is affiliative. Compare this with the question totem recruits must swear to. That question is, "Are you an American?"

In sports the flag reminds us we're Americans. What we share is that we bow down to a violent authority. Professional sports are a way of practicing war without real killing while doing honor to the exclusive prerogative of the totem to kill, which the contending sides fear more than they fear each other. In this context the flag is both the all-powerful totem and a limp female cloth, the regenerative center that can only be protected or preserved with affiliative cooperation. This is because affiliative behavior is the constant condition, and totem existence the contingency based on affiliative consent. The ritual order of sports reduces real affiliative tensions to symbols, prepares for the rigors of totem conflict, rehearses the ultimate sacrifice of war, and regenerates the totem by restoring our belief in it.

Consider how the affiliative rivalry between the Pittsburgh Steelers and the Cleveland Browns was played out through a surrogate flag:

Brentson Buckner, a Steeler defensive end, entered Three Rivers Stadium waving a gold Terrible Towel similar to those that thousands of Steeler fans were waving. But when Buckner accidentally dropped the towel, Earnest Byner, a Browns running back, stomped on it, provoking other Steelers and Browns to mingle. Not affectionately.

"Don't disrespect us like that," Buckner was saying now after the Steelers' 29–9 rout. "The towel wasn't bothering him. After he stomped on it, he yelled: 'We don't care about your towel. We're going to beat you this time.' It added fever to the fight."

To the Steelers and their black-and-gold-clothed loyalists, stomping a Terrible Towel is a crime that ranks only below that of stomping the American flag. And as it turned out, Byner's stomping would be the Browns' finest moment. Their only moment . . .

All the Steelers also were quick in reacting to Byner's stomping of the Terrible Towel during the introductions. "That," said Ray Seals, "is the type of thing that motivates you."[116]

The desecration of affiliative emblems always takes second place to the desecration of the totem. But the significance of the former transgression is in modeling the greater taboo. So understood, affiliative disrespect must be punished with defeat within the totem rules of fair play. This is what sports teach: how affiliative groups ought to behave in the presence of the totem.

War and sports are closely linked. Each is steeped in metaphors of the other. "For thirty years we've relied on the metaphors of war to tell football stories," explained Steve Sabol on *This is the NFL*, a popular game-day show filled with ritual commemorations and moral lessons about football. He recalled the war talk of the game's great generals: "George Hallas looked for men who had the light of battle in their eyes," and "Lombardi sounded the trumpet that would never call retreat." War talk returns the favor. An Iwo Jima veteran recalled that when American troops first saw the Stars and Stripes raised in the wind on Mt. Suribachi, it was "like a touchdown in a football game."[117] World War II soldiers encountered a Japanese battle cry, "Fuck Babe Ruth!"[118] Explaining how he sprinted through a hail of enemy fire to aid wounded comrades in Somalia, a Special Forces medic compared the experience to "stealing a base in baseball."[119] Commenting on the passing of the men's figure skating torch from an old guard to a newer and hungrier generation, sportswriter George Vecsey commented, "That's why the best soldiers are nineteen. Their knees are good and their memories are blank. They don't ask questions."[120]

Recalling athletes who made the ultimate sacrifice in World War II, Steve Sabol reminded fans that, "Football is, after all, just a game, and not a matter of life and death."[121] On the contrary, football and other sports are perceived as a matter of life and death and framed in these terms. "I remember the Brooklyn Dodgers. I remember living and dying on Sundays," recalled a fan who grew up on Long Island.[122] The liturgy is interrupted only when real sacrifice is in progress, for example, when the San Francisco earthquake of 1989 postponed the World Series. Only war threatens Superbowls, and rarely then. The Gulf War turned the 1991 Superbowl into a flag-filled media dedication to the troops. During World War II, President Roosevelt decreed that baseball should continue in order to strengthen citizen and soldier morale.

The connection of sports to the group idea is as deeply felt as it is ritually denied. "If [the Olympics] is sacred," mused sportswriter Ira Berkow, "then it's as sacred as the World Series. Or the Super Bowl."[123] Sacrificial games observe a rhythm of ceremonial days and seasons. Devotees may experience the liturgy live in the stadium or played out in media texts. Different denominations – football, baseball, basketball, hockey – suit the doctrinal preferences of different believers. Some faiths sprinkle, others immerse. Some sports carry the ball, others bat it. The contagious and sympathetic magic of a system of relics – caps, shirts, pennants, and autographs – is cherished by devotees. There are saints whose ordeals and miracles are known to all believers. There are uniforms reserved for authentic members of the order. There are debates about whether ceremonial changes to revitalize the faith threaten ritual purity:

> So far, most things baseball has tried in recent years to keep the game exciting and saleable have not hurt the sport, as disgusting as they were: artificial turf, designated hitter, domed stadiums, late-late-night playoff and World Series games, moronic mascots.[124]

Not just anyone is authorized to perform the ritual of professional play, and not every player may take part in the seasonally climactic World Series or Superbowls, though everyone may piously model his or her own observance with friends and teammates. Those selected to perform the holiest, most celebrated dances around which religious emotion swirls most intensely are specially picked and tested. These players most perfectly model the sacrificial hunter. They have shown themselves to be courageous, physically flawless, and strong of character. They also may be labeled as savage, the sign of all who go beyond borders on a defining mission.

The most important contests take place in the ceremonial presence of the totem. The President throws out the first ball of the baseball season; a totem color guard marches the national colors onto the field during the national anthem before all professional league games; the flag flies in every ballpark; halftime ceremonies celebrate patriotic themes. The seventh-inning stretch is thought to have originated when President Taft stood at a ballgame and the crowd stood with him. The *Star-Spangled Banner* became a popular game opener with fans during the 1918 wartime World Series. It soon became a tradition for Opening Day, the World Series and other patriotic occasions. By 1945 it was the traditional prelude to every professional league baseball game.[125]

The sporting life is filled with spells and magical artifacts. Its holy writ is the rulebook that controls play. A system of totem parables is piously guarded, joyously repeated, amended and modeled by players, fans, and media priests. Particular games and plays are fondly re-visited as skirmishes in war. There are martyrs to the faith whose sacrificial stories are central to the system of parables. There is the visiting of the sick and distressed and laying on of hands by professional athletes whose healing powers come from mastering their own trials. There are rites of keeping the faith, as in Lou Gehrig's and Cal Ripken, Jr. 's records for most consecutive games played. There are spells and charms for killing the enemy and protecting oneself in battle. There are curses. The most famous in baseball descended on the Chicago White Sox for throwing the World Series in 1919.

Sports teams elicit the usual public ambivalence. Fans see athletes as heroes or bully boys. An observer recalled the rowdy St. Louis Cardinals of the 1930s, the "Gashouse Gang," in affiliative terms. "They came around there. Most of 'em needed a shave, and every one of 'em had a dirty uniform on. What a bunch of bums!"[126] Charles Barkley, *enfant terrible* of the National Basketball Association, declaimed in a Nike television commercial, "I am not a role model. I am not paid to be a role model. I am paid to wreak havoc on the basketball court."[127] A skilled practitioner of non-lethal force, Barkley's success as a master of controlled brutality is defined within sports rules. This is what makes him attractive and dangerous, the affiliatively shifting object of public affections, for he always threatens to go beyond his place in the totem hierarchy, to presume to the totem. "Jock 'tude," a sportswriter called it: "Look at Michael Jordan's eyes, not his smile, and you'll see how close he is to killing you if you don't get out of his way."[128]

Defining "Jock 'tude," as "crimes of manner, of posture, of attitude, an excess of the very same attitude that lifted them to the major leagues in the first place," sportswriter Robert Lipsyte elaborated the affiliative virtues of never quitting and enthusiasm for the fight, traits both condemned and admired. He called for a distinction

between the Jock 'tude that stays positive in the bottom of the standings, that pushes you back on the field after a humiliating performance, that finds permanent lessons in temporary failure, and the Jock 'tude that revels in its adolescent jerk-hood, that bonds with other boys by dominating women and creates a hostile Other world from which all the problems come.[129]

This is the affiliative paradox. We do not admire unchanneled aggression except when we do. We admire aggression channeled by group norms except when we don't. "All the great ones had Jock 'tude, or you never would have heard of them." Accompanying the lesson that we choose to live together under the totem is the lesson that we choose sides and must. "Taking sides is one of the basics of sports," declares George Vecsey. "Most fans are not doing anything as complicated as watching the artistry of the athletes or critiquing the strategies of the coaches. They are rooting for 'us' against 'them.'"[130]

Rites of connecting men to a totem lineage

A stock scene in American war movies is the extraction of sports knowledge from a character who must cross a military checkpoint to be admitted inside a totem border. Even if he wears the correct uniform, he must prove his true colors by answering a pop quiz improvised by the border guard about American sports. The assumption is that as members of the same totem culture, all American males without exception learn identical affiliative rituals and parables. Baseball "connects American males with each other," explained an observer. "Not only through bleacher friendships and neighborhood loyalties, but most importantly through generations."[131] The narrative of sports, replaying the totem struggle without the ultimate sacrifice, is what American males share. Ira Berkow has written that baseball can be viewed as a "mystical bond between boyhood and fatherhood, between its constituents and the Constitution (at least the enduring elements of the Republic)."[132] He concludes with a regenerative metaphor from one of the game's totem fathers, baseball commissioner and "symbolist supreme," Bart Giamatti, for whom baseball was "all about coming home."[133]

Sports attracts the support and interest of males at every demographic level. They constitute the shaping place of young men's identity before war and marriage, those group-assigned tasks of sacrifice and fertility that define male totem group members.[134] Sports train them and show them what they fight for. Playing touch football for the cameras, presidential candidate Bill Clinton remarked that such games were "a precondition of citizenship for young boys" in the South.[135] Initiation by older hunters is a crucial feature of sports rituals. As Clinton remarked:

American men, not all of us, but a great many of us, think back to baseball in connection with our fathers, maybe our grandfathers, with uncles, with people who played particular games sometimes, but also people with whom we went to particular games, or people we played catch with.[136]

Fathers do not so much tame violence in boys as elicit it for the sake of channeling it. Boys are transformed into men by fathers who push them to the borders. "My old man told me that if you give up once, you'll give up again," said Buffalo Bills linebacker Darryl Talley, rehearsing advice he took into every game.[137] "Champions may be beaten," explained another father, "but they never, never give up."[138]

The playwright August Wilson offers insight into other affiliative lessons, especially the uncertainty of winning and losing. Wilson depicts team loyalty as a component of affiliative identity in Hazelwood, the working-class neighborhood of his boyhood. His community was:

made up mostly of steel workers who worked at the Jones and Laughlin steel mill. On Saturdays, they drank beer and cut their lawns, and on Sundays, they took their wives and daughters to church. Their sons, it seemed for the most part, were left to their own devices. The numerous events and sports teams sponsored by the local Knights of Columbus and the Moose and Kiwanis Clubs served better than the church for the molding of their character.[139]

The devotional routines of sports are male rituals faithfully observed. They exist alongside church, or female rituals, and are passed on by fathers hoping to teach the totem lessons of life.

Sports in Hazelwood was a pretty serious proposition, and almost every kid had the opportunity to play for one team or another. These teams were started and sponsored and supported by stout men with large hands and broad backs who sought ways to teach their sons rules of conduct and ideas of fair play, and to instill in them a competitive spirit that would serve them well when they grew up and became lawyers or shoe salesmen or advertising executives. Sports might even lead to college and a job other than the arduous and all-consuming work of making steel.

Sunday, a holy day in sports culture, was given over to Pittsburgh Steelers' games. The sons understand well the group-defining lessons taught by the totem fathers. "To a 14–year-old in a world of rapidly shifting values and expectations, sports is a way of discovering and defining yourself, of exploring the limits of potential. A way of being and becom-

ing." In this world heroes are terribly important. Young boys commemoratively model them. "You lived through your heroes' flesh and sought to
reenact their accomplishments, whether in a pick-up touch game or on the
playing field of the local high school or in the world of your imagination."[140] On a day when Wilson's school was set to play the best high school
team in Pittsburgh, four best friends scaled the stadium wall to watch the
great running back Jim Brown play the Steelers. This day he was losing. Not
only was Jim Brown stopped just before the goal line on a 73–yard run, but
he fumbled the ball two yards from the goal on the next play. The young
devotees were crushed. What could it mean?

We walked in silence and gradually it came to us: The possibility of failure carried
with it the possibility of success. If the great Jim Brown could fumble the ball, then
maybe just maybe, the great Westinghouse High School football team could
stumble on its way to the championship. It was a thought where there had been none
before.[141]

The affiliative lesson is that groups may win *or* lose and that one's own identity shifts back and forth between winner and loser. The religious resonance
of this lesson of the fathers is underscored in Wilson's end scene: "We
turned onto Second Avenue, the wind at our backs and the road home welcoming us as heaven welcoming a saint."

Different sports highlight different facets of the affiliative myth. Football
is framed as war. "Football ha[s] the same entertainment values as
'Terminator' and 'Rambo' movies: plenty of blood and flaming crashes,"
observes Russell Baker.[142] By contrast, baseball's contemporary lessons
relate to its nostalgic status as a regenerative rite. In a changing world, it
"somehow reassured us every year with its return on the warm winds of
spring," recalled the poet Donald Hall. Baseball is a source of regenerative
connection. In John Sayles' *Eight Men Out* (1988), the case for ritual fertility is made by the character Bucky Weaver of the Chicago White Sox, the
team banned from baseball for throwing the World Series to the Cincinnati
Reds. In the film a small boy, emblematic of the regenerating presence of
youthful acolytes, asks, "You didn't do nothin' wrong, didja, Bucky?" He
replies:

Guess I never grew up. I still get such a bang out of it – playing ball. Same as I did
when I first came up. You get out there and the stands are full and everybody's cheering. It's like everybody in the world come to see you. Inside the [dugout] players are
yakkin' it up and the pitcher throws. You look for the ball. Suddenly there's nothin'
else in the ball park but you and it. Sometimes when you're feelin' right, there's a
groove there, and the bat just eases into it, and meets that ball. When the bat meets
that ball you can just feel that ball just give and you know it's gonna go a long way.

Damn, if you don't feel like you're gonna live forever. Couldn't give that up; not for nothin.[143]

The ritual of regeneration and connection is played out over and over. Players mate with the crowd, the hitter mates with the bat. Faultlessly executed, these events refresh the spirit with the possibility of never losing, never dying, with always being young and able to win again.

8

Dismemberment and reconstruction: the domain of the popular and its flag

Saying anything negative about Mickey Mouse in America is tantamount to being insulting about the flag, or the national anthem, or a Big Mac.

Ira Berkow[1]

Transcendance defines the sacrificial totem. It is death to touch it. As a presence it is ghostly. By contrast, the popular totem manifests immanent divinity. It expresses itself in the messy, rutting, shoving people. It resides in the popular domain, which includes mass media. It is grounded in the immediate living world where citizens re-create the whole material and social existence of the nation-group. If the sacrificial totem is defined by death, purity, and exclusion, the popular totem is grotesque, fecund, teeming, chaotic. Not definition and separateness, but connection and multiplicity count in the popular domain. Totem sacrifice is the task of one domain; totem creation the task of the other.

The popular totem does what the totem in its ethereal sacrificial aspect cannot. It furnishes and builds the community. Next to the male principle of border sacrifice and death the popular domain stands as the female principle of home and community life. In the popular domain there are no forbidden boundaries between sacrificial hero gods and ordinary citizens that forever transform those who cross them. Stories about the popular flag distinguish the creative totem substratum, the people, from totem killing authority. A citizen explains:

Patriotism is the love of the land, the country, the people. It's our bond with the past and an appreciation of a whole way of life. Patriotism is making the country great from within, not being tough with the rest of the world.[2]

If the totem priesthood is a sacrificial class that cultivates pure totem hearts, the people are an impure class of feast, riot, and indulgence. The community is the structural inversion of the totem class. Its emblem is the vernacular or *parsed* flag, which is every non-regulation flag. A parsed flag is any flag that refashions the size or color or design of the standard flag in a way that refers unmistakably to it. Remaking the standard flag remodels the act of regenerating the community. Popular culture appropriates the vernacular flag for this purpose. If the totem flag designates boundaries, the popular flag designates the fertile center. The totem sacrificially consumes the people to renew itself. The people sacrificially consume the totem to replenish themselves as a community.

Consider the popular presentation of a flag-wearing Uncle Sam in a speech by Governor Robert L. Taylor to the Fourth Tennessee Volunteers, a regimental hometown unit, in 1897:

The most striking and picturesque in all history is the picture of a lean and sinewy old man, with long hair and chin whiskers, and wearing an old-fashioned plug hat. His pantaloons are in stripes of red and white, and his blue swallow-tail coat is bespangled with stars. He is the personification of the United States, and we call him Uncle Sam.

He is the composite of the wild-cat and the cooing dove, the lion and the lamb, and "summer evening's latest sight that shuts the rose." He is the embodiment of all that is most terrible. The world stands appalled at his wonderful power, and bows in admiration to his matchless magnanimity.

He is the tallest figure on this mundane sphere, and when he steps across the continent and sits down on Pike's Peak, and snorts in his handkerchief of red, white, and blue, the earth quakes and the monarchs tremble on their thrones. From the peaceful walks of life he can mobilize a mighty army in sixty days, and in ninety days he can destroy a powerful navy and demolish an empire. He is boss of the Western Hemisphere, Sheriff of Cuba, Justice of the Peace of Porto Rico, and guardian *ad litem* of the Philippine Islands. He is as brave as Caesar and as meek as Moses.

He is fierce as a tiger, and as cool as a cucumber. He wears the tail feathers of the eagle of France in his hat, and the scalp of Mexico in his belt. He laughs at the roar of the Russian bear, and is always ready for a schooner of German beer.

All that is left of Spain is her "honah," since her combat with Uncle Sam. No longer the lion of England roars at our door, but the twain now stand together for liberty and humanity.[3]

Uncle Sam displays the combination of opposites that defines the popular domain. He is a collection of ragtag contradictory pieces. He is brave and meek, cool and fierce, humorous and serious, generous and stern. He is not ethereal or pure but visually grotesque, a hirsute old man in an outlandish, colorful costume. In contrast to the sacrificial transcendent totem he is immanent, rooted in nature, connected to animals and earth. Wearing a cut-up flag, he is the community visibly reconstructed from its own pieces. A flag that so gaudily decorates bodies must be happily social. Uncle Sam blows his nose profanely, depositing the impure excrescence of his orifices into a flag handkerchief. Like the flag he wears, the flag he uses is not taboo and dangerous but homely and helpful. He is humble and expansive. He embodies the people.

Unlike totem and affiliative groups, popular groups are chaotic. They are of indeterminate size and duration. They have open boundaries and overflow borders in search of connection. Their regenerative impulses are expressed as mating and joining, eating and incorporating. The popular domain is promiscuous and non-exclusive. It is connected to popular *movements*. Totem, affiliative, and popular groups may combine in mateable pairs. Any two domains can accomplish social work by coming together and excluding the third. A popular movement is an alliance between elements in the popular domain and the totem class or between the popular domain and affiliative groups. Properly mated, the chaotic, creative, flagwaving people may be harnessed for totem sacrifice or affiliative competition. A totem class that joins with the popular and excludes affiliative division can wage successful war. An unpopular totem can put down popular insurrections with the help of affiliative legions. Popular groups led by affiliative usurpers can end an unpopular war and even overthrow the totem.

Sites of vernacular flag expression

Set up a pole, crowned with flowers in the middle of the public square, have the people assemble – and you will have a festival. Better still, let the spectators partake in the spectacle, make them actors themselves, let each person see himself and love himself in the others, and they will be more closely united.   Starobinski[4]

Popular flags grace the *homefront*, the *carnival*, and the *marketplace*. In a totem crisis the homefront is the near side of the boundary with death. The *homefront* flag waves from the porch of an idealized white clapboard house in small-town America that contains a family, the regenerative core of the community. This is what the fighting border protects: the center, a place of women and children who guarantee the future. The homefront is a domestic arena. "All the way through a Sousa program, wrote the *Topeka Daily Capital* in 1902, "you can see the old flag waving, hear the clothes flapping on the line in the back yard, and smell the pork and beans cooking in the kitchen."[5] This flag evokes home and intimate bodies. It brings to mind clothes that touch and wrap the regenerative body as the totem flag wraps

8.1 Popular protest: antiwar movement waves the parsed flag.

the sacrificial one. It flaps like washing, it presides over a home-grown feast of meat, the sacrifice raised on the farm. "Flags and Barbecues: Two Sure Signs of the Fourth of July," declared a caption on a newspaper photo of flags gaily flying over holiday celebrations at Liberty State Park in Jersey City. Beneath them a family tends the barbecue as children play ball.[6] The popular flag is also a renewing flag of planting and fertility rituals. The gardening columnist of an Arkansas newspaper greeted spring with the headline, "It's Time to Fly Flag, Plant Beans."[7]

Citizens may be introduced by their flags alone as *dramatis personae* in journalistic narratives such as this: "On the other side of this middle-class suburb of tidy lawns, wooden porch swings and American flags almost as common as curtains . . ."[8] Connecting citizens to flags makes them Americans, voters, totem-creators. This flag identifies a citizen who stands in a fertile tradition of totem-creators.

Rose Slavick, 65, was making her lawn neater when she stopped to talk politics. An American flag was flying from her red-brick porch.

"I have my flag out everyday except rainy ones," she said. "I'm a patriot and a Democrat from way, way back. So was my father."[9]

The small town where ordinary people live is a main character in the regenerative American myth. Small towns have creative power:

Hometown (population 4,769) is an unpretentious, aluminum-siding kind of town, where houses have pickup trucks out front and basketball hoops out back, where adult children live a few doors down from their parents and where the mayor has hung a poster in his office that says, "I Am the Flag."[10]

When flags are waving, borders are in transition. At presidential inaugurations, at war's conclusion, when campaigns are in full swing or soldiers leave for battle, shamanist flags liquefy borders. This is the *carnival*. Its classic form is the street parade. Flagwaving makes community boundaries permeable, the necessary ritual condition for turning insiders into sacrificial outsiders and reassimilating those who have touched death. Popular participation signifies unanimous victimage. Ceremonies of expulsion register the community's consent to kill its own. Flagwaving also removes the death aura from those who return from beyond the border. By thus symbolically mating with returning soldiers, the community resurrects them and becomes fruitful again.

In the *marketplace* the shamanist flag blesses consumption and exchange. Here the vernacular flag is the progenitor of a vast totem-creating bounty. Popular piety is uneasy about connecting the flag to commerce. The civilian flag code, for example, expressly forbids buying and selling with the flag. Imaginative and bold uses of the flag in the marketplace, along with more subtle presentations, testify to its regenerative power and fertile effect. If death is a sacred taboo, promiscuous engendering is a popular one, which we shall have occasion to treat in a later chapter. In fact, what is fertile can never be pure and isolated, taboo and contained.[11] It must be generously overflowing and reformable. The marketplace must be free to do with the flag as it wishes. A vast and irreverent range of flag products and advertising suggests it is. The union of fecundity and contamination is modeled in vernacular rituals, including media rituals that connect the popular domain and its flag to each other.

Elements of vernacular flag expression

> The sacred thing is *par excellence* that which the profane should not touch, and cannot touch with impunity. To be sure, this interdiction cannot go so far as to make all communication between the two worlds impossible; for if the profane could in no way enter into relations with the sacred, this latter could be good for nothing.   Durkheim[12]

The agent and focus of the vernacular flag is the body. Not the pure sacrificial body is at issue, but the fertile body of the people, an amorphous, shifting, ill-defined agglomeration with totem-creating power. The vernacular flag is talismanic. It lies along a plane of symbolic inversion in relation to the numinous flag. A flag of connection and attachment, it is anything but taboo. To touch it is to give and receive life. In contrast to the numinous flag that demarcates borders, the popular flag conveys festive anti-structure. Whereas the numinous flag conveys sacrifice and singularity, the popular flag conveys feast, abundance and multiplicity. Whereas the numinous flag is patrolled by protocols that protect it from transgression, the popular flag thrives on chaotic variety. If the totem domain is concerned with killing, the popular domain is attentive to mating. It is promiscuous and improper, unlike the proper and self-contained totem flag.

The popular flag is *touched, multiple*, and *dismembered*. Each of these regenerative properties distinguishes this flag from its sacrificial progenitor. The *touched* flag is a contagious spellcasting flag, transforming what it joins. In this homecoming ceremony the touched flag confers regenerative blessings on whomever unites with and consumes it:

"Great job, guys," said volunteer Linda Zee, 35, of South Philadelphia, as she and a half-dozen others clapped and waved small flags. "Welcome home! Welcome home!"

Two pre-teen volunteers squealed and cheered and other Red Cross helpers directed the equipment-laden troops to a long counter, festooned with red, white, and blue bunting, white balloons, and a "Welcome Home" banner.

There, more volunteers were cooking hot dogs, busily preparing bagels and drinks and filling up bowls with snacks. A huge cake decorated with a flag and yellow ribbons was waiting to be cut.

Training for the 100-meter freestyle in the Olympics, world record holder Jenny Thompson treated the flag as a personal talisman. She summoned it with the same regularity and intensity with which she exercised her muscles and for the same regenerative reason: to increase her strength and her power to bring home victory. Touching the flag familiarly transfers its magic.

Jenny Thompson wraps herself in the American flag every night when she goes to bed. Her comforter is all stars and stripes and quilted padding. Her pillow, her lampshade, are both decorated in red, white and blue. She tried to hang an over-sized flag on the ceiling of her dorm room at Stanford so she could go to sleep dreaming the American dream about medal stands and national anthems. The flag wouldn't stick. It went on the wall, instead . . . While the sophomore majors in one of the social sciences at Stanford, she will continue to collect her red-white-and-blue memorabilia. She will wear American-flag dresses and blouses and swimsuits. She will complete her practice laps.[13]

In contrast to the magic of male sacrifice that characterizes the taboo sacred flag, the female magic of intimate connection characterizes the fertile, accessible, multiple flag.

The touched flag has *multiple* avatars. Unlike the standard flag that is jealously one flag, the designs and versions of the popular flag are infinite and fertile. It reproduces itself in endless variety. Forests of small flags at street parades, sports events, and election rallies are quintessentially popular. A long-standing principle of flag retailing testifies to the fertile multiplying power of popular flags. If one neighbor shows the flag, so will others. In Albany in 1890, the inauguration of a morning flagraising ceremony at Public School No. 7 inspired the boys of the town to imitation:

Not long ago a youngster living on that throughfare went out into the back yard early one morning armed with a spade and a long pole. With the former he dug a hole in the ground, in which he placed the latter, and firmly fixed it there. Then he rigged a sort of rope and pulley to the pole and hoisted a "sort of a kind of" an American flag. This he lowered every evening and hoisted every morning with great regularity and much evident satisfaction. The small boy who lives next door soon looked over the fence and saw what his youthful neighbor had been doing; and forthwith he became seized with a desire to do likewise.[14]

Soon there were "eight or nine alleged American flags" fluttering from poles in as many backyards, raised by morning and lowered by evening. A "sort of a kind of" American flag is the very definition of a popular parsed flag.

The multiple touched flag is a *dismembered* flag, dissected and reassembled by a community that regenerates itself in the act. The red, white, and blue logos of American professional sports organizations – the NFL, NBA, NHL, National League, American League, and USGA among them – are dismembered parsed flags. For example, the familiar emblem of the National Football League, a heraldic shield with a horizontal border of white stars on a blue field from which the red letters NFL descend in stripe-like fashion, constitutes a parsed flag in a commercial frame. Recombined and reconstituted, the cut-up flag is revitalized by the participatory faith of the people. Its reconstruction is the hope of the community.

Acts of totem regeneration are plentiful in popular culture. They are syncretistic and need not observe codified procedures. In a magazine feature about the state of the country gleaned from stories of travelers on a Greyhound bus, a multiple, touched, dismembered flag appeared as a flag bandanna worn by a homeless drifter and veteran from the Kansas heartland. He had this to say:

> I love my country, no matter what happened in my life. This whole country is mine as far as I'm concerned. I got a piece. I got a right to go anywhere I want to go. And so that's what I do.[15]

The notion of a country fashioned of pieces that belong to all the citizens is regenerative totem talk. The community thus imagined is flexible and mutable, and in need of every believer. It is different and richer for each citizen's contribution.

Rigid protocols communicate the taboo status of the numinous flag. The riotous, constantly shifting vernacular flag communicates bountiful mutability. Compared to the numinous monotheism of the high totem flag, the popular flag is ecumenically multiple. Dismemberment desecrates numinosity but revitalizes the vernacular flag. The numinous flag may not be touched. The popular flag is nourished and vivified by touch. To touch the numinous flag is to be consumed by it, since the totem it symbolizes exists apart from the people. It may be regenerated only through consubstantive merging with sacrificial victims whose blood nourishes it. The popular domain regenerates itself by dismembering and consuming the totem flag.

War and popular flags

During war, popular and totem domains mate in order to create consensus about killing. The popular domain also undertakes the ritual work of transforming insiders into outsiders. Popular flagwaving places the

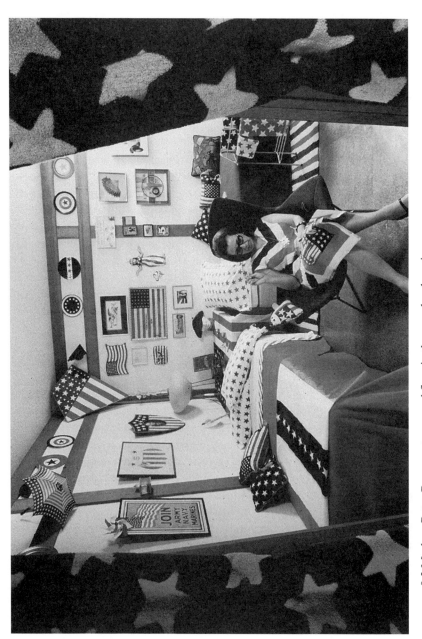

8.2 Modern Betsy Ross creates parsed flags in the popular domain.

sacrificial mark of death on departing soldiers. The community does it together, for victimage is a group responsibility. When the killing mission is over, the group has a new ritual task. This is to re-create outsiders as regenerative community members. This ritual is also conducted by the whole group in the presence of popular flags. Flagwaving removes the death mark from those who have been beyond the borders and mates returning death-touchers with the body of the community.

When flags are waving, borders are in transition. Standing behind the flag on the symbolic inside of the group, every flagwaver remodels the relationship of the regenerative center to its sacrificial borders. Popular flagwaving prefigures the border transformation of ritual sacrifice. The totem mark of death is conferred on departing soldiers at the symbolic border. It will be withdrawn at the same place from those who return. Because every flag is a link in a chain of signifiers to the totem that symbolizes the sacrificed body, even popular flags ultimately refer to the dead and about-to-be-dead. Waving flags invigorate and resurrect the dead to whom they refer. Modeling these dead as upright and alive and vividly in motion, waving popular flags bring them to life. Flagwaving is a spell that creates border-crossers, that keeps the dangerous dead from bringing death to the group, that keeps the totem secret by denying the existence of sacrificial death at the same time as sending soldiers to it. It disguises our blood lust while enacting it.

As the Gulf War geared up in January, 1991, military censors created a "hard-news gap." News organizations scrambled to fill it with "experts, maps, and props," the *New York Times* wrote. And flags everywhere, it might have added. For a month after the first bombs fell on Bagdad, rare was the televised news program without at least one lingering flag shot in at least one emotionally charged story weaving charms against the anticipated sacrifice of Americans. At every moment print and electronic media reminded Americans that their flag existed and instructed them in using it to mark and create the events of which they were part. The popular flag was faithfully rendered as a conjuring instrument for those who love common soldiers. Though citizens lack direct power to move armies or withdraw them, they love bodies so moved and withdrawn and must consent to sacrifice for the ritual to work.

Bargaining for totem favor with homemade spells, families on the homefront conferred contagious blessings on the popular flag by decorating it with ribbons, stars and hearts. They re-created it in cakes and bouquets, in living flags of their own bodies, and in red-white-and-blue embellishments of personally significant artifacts. They adorned their dwellings with it and placed it at doors and windows, points of vulnerability to spiritual invasion. Contagiously, they lent it vitality. Wire services carried the story of a fireman who shaved his hair in a flag pattern dyed red, white and blue after he was forbidden to wear a flag on his uniform. A local skating rink colored its ice in a flag design for delighted skaters who scored its surface. A pro-war patriot marched to the rhythm of his drumsticks on a flag-patterned drumface. The flag was painted on fingernails and grease-painted on faces. It was a $4.95 keychain, a $9.95 sweatshirt, a $2,000 cashmere stole.

Sympathetic spells imitate the effect to be achieved. In the case of the popular totem, the effect to be achieved is life. "If you don't flaunt your yellow ribbon and proudly wave your flag," a newspaper reader explained, "you are undermining those brave men and women fighting for you."[16] On the eve of the President's ultimatum to Iraq to withdraw from Kuwait the *New York Times* reported,"Some people said they would tie yellow ribbons on trees or put American flags in front of their houses after midnight."[17] Pledging to fly it, they promised to model sympathetically the lives it re-presented until the possessors of those lives returned. These spells of animation gave loved ones life and breath. Every handheld flag fluttered vigorously after departing soldiers was a magic wand to protect men in battle if only the entreaties of flagwavers were powerful enough. And of course they were.

Sixty of the 2,100 residents of Gate City, Virginia, were on active duty in Saudi Arabia. A journalist wrote, "Gate City wears its patriotism proudly. Yellow ribbons – as well as red, white and blue ones – decorate the entrances of shops and homes, and flags fly from many doorways."[18] In Palatka, Florida, 450 citizens gathered in the town's amphitheater for a vigil to support the troops:

Veterans of past wars mingled with relatives of troops stationed in the Gulf alongside fountains illuminated in red, white, and blue. They sang patriotic songs, lit candles and prayed aloud for peace before they discussed the need to prepare for war.[19]

Children at one parade toted signs bearing messages of support for their fathers. "Some carried tiny flags. "Hold that flag high, baby," yelled a spectator instructing them in effective magical procedures. "Hold that flag high."[20] Ostentatious demonstrations of sentiment fuel popular magic. In high totem magic, faultless ritual observance mandates the disciplined disguise of feelings that must be kept at a distance from the untouchable flag. Totem protocol distances citizens from the flag, mediating taboo power through right gesture, perfect posture, and sentiment denied. Popular flag practice embraces feeling. Creativity, variety, and individuality mark

authentic sentiment. Violations of law or the flag code are routinely over-
looked in popular usage wherever right sentiment abounds.

The high magic of a totem declaration of borders, that is, a declaration
of war, combines with "a million tiny, private gestures" of spellcasting to
transform insiders into sacrificial outsiders. Both high and popular totem
rites must set sacrifice in motion. Here are popular rites at work in the Gulf
War:

As the news swept through this area last week that military convoys were moving
along the Interstates carrying soldiers bound for the Middle East, clutches of
people waving flags seemed to appear magically along the highway overpasses to
salute them.[21]

This media passage renders the popular magic that transforms insiders into
sacrificial outsiders as automatic, unanimous, and potent.[22] One citizen
testified to being in the presence of a religious miracle, experiencing the
"overwhelming" response of his countrymen to the war as a "humbling
experience." At Norfolk Naval Station a flagraising ceremony drew devotees as if by magic. Other examples surfaced in newspapers, radio, and television programs across the country:

They stood on a cold and windy hilltop here Tuesday, holding hands and singing
God Bless America to honor the men and women of Desert Storm.
    More than 200 people were at the 9 a. m. ceremony, hurriedly organized the day
before. People like 23–year-old Deborah Wall, who heard about the flagraising on
her car radio and headed for Mount Trashmore despite the flu and freezing tem-
peratures.[23]

By gesture and incantation, a Belmont, Vermont, citizen acted out the
community's relation to its sacrificial borders, transforming insiders into
outsiders:

Allen Devereux took his American flag out of winter storage today and put it on
the pole in front of his mountainside home in this tiny snow-covered hamlet.
    "We want to show people we're behind the boys," said Mr. Devereux, a veteran
of World War II who for 40 years ran Belmont's only store and served as post-
master.[24]

This incident occurred in Philadelphia:

As I was about to pull out of the Elkins Park Library parking lot, three cars rolled
by with their headlights on. One of them had a small American flag strapped to its
antenna. When I turned onto a busier street, about five out of every six cars on the
road had their lights gleaming in the late hours of the morning.
    It came to me right away. There was no need to turn on the radio or run home to
watch the news on the television. It was just like the yellow ribbons.[25]

Patriotic amulets were summoned to protect the lives of soldiers. The owner of Rocket Rick's Tattooing near Fort Benning, Georgia, noted a surge in business from Gulf-bound soldiers. "I put some beautiful stuff on them, too," he added. "I want them all to come home safe."[26] Mickey Messineo, a World War II veteran, hung two flags and a yellow ribbon on his screen door. "We kept them up until we thought all our Nebraska boys were home."[27] The owner of the San Francisco "49ers distributed 65,000 miniature flags to fans at a conference game "to show support for the nation's military efforts in the Persian Gulf."[28] Arizona kindergarteners recited the Pledge, "so those people will come home safe."[29] Fearing for her husband's safety, Debbie Hughes hung a flag upside-down on her door as a sign of distress and righted it when she heard Kuwait City had been liberated.[30]

Noisemaking signifies spiritual transformation in many cultures. Organizers in Philadelphia combined flagwaving and noise to perform ceremonial magic.

"We want people to fly the flag, honk their car horns, and, hopefully, church bells will ring and fire alarms sound . . . We want to make some noise to show our troops we care. And then everybody can gather and sing "God Bless America" and "The Star-Spangled Banner.""[31]

On the first Sunday of the war in Westchester County, New York:

Gentle winds streaked thin clouds into chalk marks across the sky and explored the winterbare landscape, tugging at yellow ribbons and American flags set out on porches and the lapels of Sunday worshippers to show support for American troops in the Gulf.[32]

On the third day of the war two stories on one page of *USA Today* instructed citizens in flagwaving, prayer, and blood sacrifice: three potent spells. One headline described dramatic increases in flag sales. "All anyone can do is 'pray, give blood'," exhorted a second.[33] Giving blood not only sympathetically models soldier sacrifice. Blood contagiously vivifies soldier bodies by merging with them. Blood banks across the country soon faced a surplus.[34] A Red Cross spokeswoman described "one man, an executive type, [who] told us that he felt powerless to do anything else to support the troops, so he came to donate blood."[35] With an earnestly magical intent, citizens asserted that giving blood and showing the flag would influence the war. Consider these spells sampled from local news shows in Philadelphia:

- A gas company supervisor displayed two fists stuffed with talismanic flags: "I think it's about time everybody showed patriot-

ism, and there's not enough patriotism. Every desk in the gas company's gonna have a flag on it."
- Late this afternoon, the [Terry Dreyer] family put out an American flag on the front porch. They say it will stay there until Joseph Dreyer and the other American soldiers come home.
- Flags are flying along several SEPTA routes tonight in a show of support for American troops in the Gulf . . . It's the idea of SEPTA general foreman Bernie DelGieudice. He says he wanted to do something to counteract flagburning he saw on TV.
- Of a front porch: "It's bedecked with flags and ribbons. In the window a picture of an Army PFC, Frank Goff, now on the front lines in the Gulf. Inside a worried mother and father sit glued to a TV set, concerned but encouraged by flags and ribbons all over the Delaware Valley."
- Along with other nursing home residents Mary Powell tied yellow ribbons to small paper flags and recalled a neighborhood ritual from World War II: "We would have a flag in the window with a star for each boy that was in the service. And then in the middle of the block we had a huge flag. Almost all the blocks in the city did that."[36]

A week into the war, media mogul Al Neuharth declared that popular flag magic would bless the community and cause it to prosper. He prophesied fecundity as the magical outcome of flagwaving sentiment:

Across the USA, more and bigger flags are flying. Miniversions of the stars and stripes are worn as lapel pins, arm patches, on T-shirts.

At public events, people actually are singing *The Star-Spangled Banner*. They're not just moving their mouths but really reciting the words to the Pledge of Allegiance.

It's unfortunate that it took the Gulf War to bring out this bubble of patriotism. Will it burst when the war is over, or can we keep it alive?

I think it will continue to grow and glow. Because of your attitude. And ours.[37]

Outsiders define the border. Social freaks are distanced from the center by illness, deformity, misfortune or deviance. During a totem crisis social freaks re-unite with the community in popular gestures of solidarity. In a totem crisis, those on the margins are socially re-positioned. They are drawn close to the group as a poignant reminder that communities consist in the common sacrifice of many citizens. Their crisis-induced mating with the center may be visually mediated through the flag. How these outsiders earn their keep as insiders was a recurring Gulf War story. Local and national television featured stories of social freaks drawn from the blind, the retarded, the elderly, and prisoners, all symbolically creating the community by sewing, pasting, and assembling flags for the group to use in its magical rites. Victor Turner writes:

Here the anomaly, the "stone that the builders rejected," is removed from the structured order of society and made to represent the simple unity of society itself, conceptualized as homogeneous, rather than as a system of heterogeneous social positions, surmounting in this way the contradictions of the group.[38]

In a totem crisis stories about social outsiders who aspire to join the center inspire guilt in those who are not freaks. Their plight arouses the center to reach out to them as Same and not Other. Stories of sacrifice by outcasts to a community prepared to give little in return are a ritual means of provoking in non-freaks a heightened sense of group responsibility in a crisis. Vernacular flags and ribbons mediate this effort:

Outside the Gallery, Mary Valletta sold candy for a penny and pulled her tattered green sweater around her bent body. She works the street corners seven days a week and makes about $4 a day. She worries about her next meal. Still, she bought a flag early on to pin to her knitted cap, and she found a scrap of yellow plastic that she fashioned into a yellow bow and tucked into her cap.

Despite her social alienation from the fertile center, Mary Valletta sacrifices to display totem piety. Her wishes are all for regenerative order. Her hopes are for the group and not herself. "I'd like to see our boys come home, get married and have babies," she said. "They're too young to die, too young."[39]

Carnivals of union – lifting the taboo

The blessing of God makes the land possible for men to live in.

Mary Douglas[40]

Soldiers are transformed by the totem journey to the borders. Fathers make the ritual pronouncement: "We sent a boy, and we're getting back a man."[41] That the boy was sent conveys the totem secret in coded language. Soldiers become men by touching death. This distinguishes them from women and children. "Why are we celebrating all that death?" asked an observer of the New York parade for returning Gulf War troops.[42] The answer is that this is how we get men. Once men touch death, they must choose between it and the group. They may rejoin the group only by rejecting death-touching power. Reciprocally, the community forgives them, both for coming back and for breaking the killing taboo. It opens its borders, ritually purifies them, and renders them lifegivers. The fertility rite that reassimilates them is a parade. A working definition of transformable border-crossers appears in this account of who rates ticker tape parades in the nation's largest city:

Ticker-tape parades have usually been short lavish bursts of adoration on lower Broadway for lone heroes or a few world-class athletes, political or military victors, astronauts or foreign leaders.[43]

All are figures of totem sacrifice who have been to the border to touch real or symbolic death, except for foreign leaders who have always lived beyond the border. The popular domain takes them to its heart and makes them insiders by mating with them in four ritual steps.

Flagwaving purifies death-touchers

The primitive mark of the outsider is visible on returning soldiers and makes them proper subjects for homecoming rites:

[Major Ted Pusey, adjutant for First Brigade, 24th Mechanized Infantry Division:] "Today is the first day I have eaten with a metal fork in seven months," he said. "The stewardesses are the first women I've seen in skirts. It's good to see green grass and drink real milk."[44]

The whole community must be in on the ritual:

People feel it all over – from West Virginia's tiny mountain towns, where flags and yellow ribbons adorn every front door, to big cities like Dallas and Dayton, Ohio, where huge homecoming parties are planned for the troops.[45]

Like the touched, multiple, dismembered flags that identify them, homecoming ceremonies are all different and all the same. In North Carolina:

Thousands "dressed in red, white, and blue" lined a two-mile path to cheer troops returning to Fort Bragg and Pope Air Force Base in early March, 1991.[46]

In Philadelphia:

They were greeted as heroes by crowds waving a sea of fluttering American flags and singing boisterously along with patriotic music played by military bands.[47]

In Savannah, Georgia:

A great cheer went up as the plane landed. The soldiers gathered their rifles and gear and walked down a runway to a crowd of cheering relatives waving flags and yellow ribbons.[48]

In Washington, DC:

For the hundreds of thousands at the Mall it was a day to feel part of a winning team – to wear, wave, and salute the flag. They did it the American way: picnicking on fried chicken and beer, posing for pictures and clapping in time to the march music.[49]

At Robert Gray Army Airfield, Texas:

Several miles of roadway leading from the airfield to the entrance of Fort Hood were lined by thousands of people honking their car horns, cheering, and waving flags and banners.

Trees, bushes, telephone poles, and highway overpasses were covered with yellow bows and wrapped in red, white and blue crepe paper.[50]

> *Flagwaving is accompanied by hugs and kisses, handshakes, and gifts that symbolize mating between the community and its border-crossers.*

Regenerative expressions accompany peace. Following President Truman's declaration of Japanese surrender in August, 1945, Americans began celebrating. In New York the merrymaking was natally described as "ten New Year's Eves rolled into one."[51] In addition to general disorder and transformative noisemaking ("a cacophony of church chimes, air-raid sirens, honking horns, blaring bands, singing, shrieking and shouting"), there was an outbreak of kissing. Soldiers are not only waved across the border by flags. They are kissed, a token of reassimilation to the fertile women at the center of the community.

When peace news was confirmed, Americans, full of the same high spirits they had displayed abroad, put on a spirited display of public kissing at home. News photographers had long trained servicemen to assume ardent poses for the camera but there was little posing in last week's coast-to-coast frenzy of kissing. From city to city and block to block the purpose was the same but the techniques varied. They ran the osculatory gamut from mob-assault upon a single man or woman, to indiscriminate chain-kissing. Some servicemen just made it a practice to buss everyone in skirts that happened along, regardless of age, looks or inclination.[52]

Touch is a blessing. It liquefies borders. Back from the Gulf War,

Lieutenant Col. Howard L. Pope . . . reached out to embrace his wife, Phyllis. The other members of his family and several neighbors crowded in, some of them holding aloft American flags so large that when they fluttered down they all but covered the airman and his wife.[53]

The flag itself is a gift.

A woman walked by handing out little American flags.
Free.
In Manhattan.[54]

Businesses, agents of the popular domain, offered scholarships, employment, free weekends in the country, dinners on the house, day care and other blessings to returning soldiers.[55] At Camp Pendleton:

8.3 Orgiastic reunion of totem class and fertile center marked by flag.
Celebrating peace on Hollywood Boulevard, 1945.

Rounds of drinks are bought by strangers, signs of welcome adorn the stores, and homecoming parades have been thronged by cheering spectators.[56]

The language of homecoming is fertility. Paradegoers in Washington, DC, watched "soldiers atop tanks wave like beauty queens on floats."[57] At Pope Air Force Base regenerative gestures flowed to the 82nd Airborne:

Young men wrenched from home to fight in the desert held new babies for the first time. Reunited couples wrapped each other in sweet, lingering embraces. A loudspeaker blared out the names of the waiting relatives, as disoriented soldiers wandered the tarmac. Even strangers pumped soldiers' hands, thanking them for a job well done.[58]

Navy Petty Officer Dennis Hohman of Pittsburgh declared, "It felt great to come home and have this response. It was almost as good as sex."[59] A reporter at the New York City parade described an especially fruitful coupling, a transformative totem mating:

It was a kick to see General Powell, the Bronx boy, sending kisses along the route and to hear all those people saying nice things about the city for a change. It would take a mighty television critic not to be affected by the appearance of so much friendliness on streets that have a reputation for anything but.[60]

Mating restores the community. To break the spell of death-touching, homecoming talk included babies arrived and babies to come. At Hunter Army Airfield:

As Sergeant Brian Christensen looked out into the crowd he smiled tightly and said there was only one thing that could make him happier. "My wife's back in Minnesota, and she's going to have a baby in nine days."[61]

The touch of the people breaks the spell of death on the faces of returning outsiders. The regenerative gifts of children welcome conquering heroes.

A bold little girl ran out into the middle of the street. She handed a small flag to Vice Admiral Stanley R. Arthur, who commanded American naval forces in the war zone and led Navy personnel in the parade. Similarly emboldened, another child ran up and handed him a yellow flower.

Before the parade had advanced another hundred feet, enough children had run up that Admiral Arthur's left fist clutched a brace of flags and flowers. Behind him, his four staff officers tried hard to look serious and not break stride as they accepted flowers and flags from still more children.[62]

Returning soldiers are unmasked as insiders after all. A soldier loved and charmed by a small girl is no babykiller, the epithet applied to Vietnam veterans whose mark of outsiderness was never removed by ceremonies of

8.4 Flagwaving removes death mark from returning Gulf War soldiers who reunite with popular domain.

touch and regeneration. The fear that death-touchers may return to kill insiders, especially women and children, the totem hope and future, must be staved off by ritual:

By the end of the parade, most of the marchers waved flags, grinned broadly and shook hands with spectators who spontaneously broke out with chants of "USA, USA"[63]

Soldiers must accept the community's invitation

Destroyers become deliverers by consenting to come back to life. Homecoming ceremonies address the guilt of those who have come back without being sacrificed. To one paradegoer, returning prisoner of war Lieutenant Jeffrey Zaun was "the spirit of the war. He's a hero. He represents all the prisoners." As Zaun rode in a white convertible, fertile blessings and gestures rained down, removing the mark of outsider and connecting him to the center:

People reached to shake his hand and give him flowers . . . People ran to the car, hugging and kissing him. "Thank you, thank you," a smiling Zaun said repeatedly.

The testimony of returning soldiers measures the efficacy of celebration:

You come home with your head held high and your chest out. You have people honking their horns and waving their flags all along the expressway. It's just a terrific feeling.[64]

Less sanguine views exist, but rarely appear in mass media, which have the job of declaring group spellcasting a success. A contrary account is this by a combat pilot returning to a small farming town at the end of World War II. Knowing the totem secret prevents him from joining the festivities:

On the one-block main street of the village I had known as my hometown all my life, they had built a bonfire. While some in our town thanked God for ending the war, others chose to vent emotions in a ritual that closing the village taverns could not inhibit. Parked around the corner, I got out and approached a scene that struck me as one from an old movie, in which barbaric tribesmen were whipping themselves to frenzy. They had sacrificed their young men to appease the demon and ward off dark evils. Now, celebrating their success, they were giving their thanks to the Great God War for sparing them.[65]

This death-touching outsider sees the celebration as a primitive appeasement in our sense of constructing the social through blood sacrifice of our own. In the end he decides for the group and crosses the border to join it:

What are they celebrating? . . . Among them I recognized some I had known well when the decisive battles were still to be fought. They had not seen those as their battles. They had not sworn to obey any orders. They had taken no oath. They had pledged not their lives, their fortunes, nor their Sacred Honor. Yet they accepted the victory as theirs, as if by Divine Right, attained, by them, simply by waiting for it. Now they celebrated peace, their peace . . . I had known these people. I could put names to all their faces. But now they were strangers to me, living in a world apart from mine. I wanted their silly celebrations no more than their pious prayers. I wanted to run away.

I wanted to run away, but to where? Turn my back because they prayed, or celebrated? Should I condemn them for not seeing a world I saw? I had been raised among them, with them, as one of them. By what right could I now say I was not one of them? If not one of them, who could I be? . . .

The war was over – I had survived. I was home, safe in the land of my birth. Only my innocence had died, and with it my youth. Fair or not fair, right or wrong, whether I wanted it or not, whether anyone liked it or not – I had a life to live. I . . . stepped off the sidewalk into the crowd.

I joined the survivors.[66]

The transformation to which soldiers and citizens must agree re-attaches sacrificial exiles to the community. In the end there is no choice, except between death and the group.

The ritual must be declared a success

Standing at the Tomb of the Unknown Soldier, President Bush certified the transforming effect of the war: "There is a new and wonderful feeling in America."[67] A reporter wrote:

It remains unclear what the Persian Gulf War will do to the political geography of the Middle East, but so far it has transformed the psyche of the United States.

The sour, deeply divided nation of a few months ago, worried about economic decay and political paralysis, has received a remarkable lift from the war. Despite the presence of a sizeable minority opposed to the fighting, there has been a surge of patriotic rallies, flag-waving and professions of unity unmatched by anything in this generation.[68]

Citizens declare that community time has started again:

Laveta Wetherington, 39, of Greenville, was wearing a sweater dyed to resemble an American flag. "I think this is going to be a real turning point for our country," she said. "It's about time."[69]

When the totem is renewed, old enmities can be resolved. Affiliative groups may make an enthusiastic public show of submission to the totem. The high point of the St. Patrick's Day parade in Philadelphia, a few months after the Gulf War, came when the "O'Mahoney Association lowered its Irish flag and raised the Stars and Stripes while breaking into 'America the Beautiful.'"[70]

Assembling for the president's postwar State of the Union address, legislators expressed the people's approval of the latest totem achievement by adorning themselves with vernacular flags. Since lawmakers are both members of the totem class and representatives of the people, their gesture signified an embodied mating between the people and the totem class in a popular war with a successful outcome.

The House chamber [where the President spoke] was awash with red, white, and blue from 600 small American flags lawmakers waved or stuck in breast pockets.

Republicans were more inclined to wave theirs frantically at certain applause lines.

They also sported large yellow buttons adorned with American flags that read, "I voted with the president!"[71]

The President completed the war ritual by declaring the Gulf War a creation–sacrifice, the bloodletting that guarantees the future. A typical headline was "Bush looks to lasting peace." The feeling would not last. One hundred hours of ground war and 148 Americans dead from half a million called up, was too weak a sacrifice to endure. The epitaph of the Gulf War with its disappointing blood offering was soon penned by media priests: "A bare six months after the shooting and bombing stopped, the memory of the war has faded more quickly than most national crises."[72]

She wore a yellow ribbon

Tie a yellow ribbon round
The old oak tree
It's been three long years
Do you still want me?   Erwin Levine and L. Russell Brown[73]

Yellow ribbons were an emergent popular symbol during the Gulf War. Spontaneously added to the numinous flag, the yellow ribbon transformed it into a vernacular flag. Together, the ribbon and warrior flag made a fertile union of the homefront and the border, the male and female principles of mating and death-touching that are indispensable parts of a fighting community. Yellow ribbons were identified with the home and hearth symbols that constitute the central reference of the vernacular flag. To an anti-war essayist they symbolized "the fires kept burning at home for friends and relatives in the Gulf. When I see a yellow ribbon that I take to be such a tribute, I am moved."[74] Through a process of condensation yellow ribbons came to stand for the vernacular flag itself. Substitute the American flag for every yellow ribbon in this *New York Times* editorial about its populist significance:

8.5 Regenerative center wields popular magic to protect Gulf War soldiers.

In Rome, Ga., they stream from car antennas, and in Jacksonville, Fla., they decorate the lampposts. A florist in Pound Ridge, N. Y., is giving them away, and a few days ago, on the Massachusetts Turnpike, a long line of tractor-trailers flourished them on their hoods. All across the United States the streamers flutter in the winter air. Yellow ribbons, miles of yellow ribbons, for every American man and woman in the Persian Gulf.[75]

Ribbon and flag equivalence are implied in the mention of sacrificial soldiers. Further populist themes are at work in this account:

Yellow ribbons, wrapped around trees, telephone polls, satellite dishes, pinned to lapels, or fluttering from car radio antennas, mail boxes and shopping carts, have blossomed into a national reminder of combat in the Gulf. All around the country, small towns have smothered themselves in yellow ribbon, looking a little like captives of the wrap artist Christo.[76]

Yellow ribbons are not new. They were the romantic symbol of domestic fidelity to frontier soldiers depicted in a John Ford western, *She Wore a Yellow Ribbon* (1949), released soon after World War II.[77] Its theme song came from a lyric infantrymen still learn:

> Around her neck she wore a yellow ribbon
> She wore it in the winter and the merry month of May
> And when I asked her why the yellow ribbon
> She said it's for my lover who is in the cavalry.

In the traditional cavalry scarf yellow symbolizes sulfur, an ingredient of gunpowder, as black in the cavalry uniform stands for charcoal, and blue for saltpetre. The combination is a mnenonic of killing power and sacrifice inscribed on the body. A memory token in a yellow hue is thus the soldier with a missing body, the departed soldier. In the larger culture yellow is also the traditional color of non-combatants and cowards. By implication it represents women, non-combatants who nurture children. Women and children are what death-touchers are not. Ribbons, of course, call to mind hair bows and gift wrap, feminine symbols of fertility and bountifulness.

Media accounts traced the Gulf War yellow ribbon to its immediate ancestor, yellow ribbons for American hostages held for fifteen months in Iran between 1979 and 1981. That crisis revived a popular hit about a sweetheart's fidelity to a returning lover who the song vaguely implied was an ex-convict. The song, "Tie a Yellow Ribbon 'Round the Old Oak Tree," was released in 1973, the same year 590 American prisoners of war returned from Vietnam after years of captivity. Gulf War media rendered the commemorative genealogy of yellow ribbons as a composite model of Gulf War soldiers, Iranian hostages, Vietnam prisoners of war and ex-convicts who had served their time. All were outsiders associated with unredeemed and even shameful sacrifice now made honorable by the publicly esteemed Gulf soldier.

If white is the chromatic sum of the primary colors red, blue, and yellow, the addition of yellow to the flag's red, white, and blue completes a chromatic circle. The addition of the female yellow ribbon to male fighting colors thus makes a chromatic as well as regenerative whole. Ribbon and flag make a coherent union in the same way that combatants and non-combatants make a nation. "To me it stands for hostages," insisted Undis Foltz, who claimed to have created the yellow ribbon symbol for the Iranian hostages. The flag, she felt, "is more patriotic to servicemen."[78] Her remarks recognized the symbolic division of labor between the male warrior flag and the yellow ribbon of feminized hostages unable to defend themselves. In an era of feminist sensibility the Gulf War was celebrated as a war to which women also went. The union of flag and yellow ribbon could be interpreted either as the cooperative efforts of male and female soldiers together, or as the traditional arrangement in which male warriors go to the border while women keep the home fires burning. American culture had room for both contributions to the preservation of the group.

There was more to the symbolism of yellow ribbons. They invoked knot rituals as old as antiquity, time-honored techniques for sacred ties that bind. Ribbon tying relates to leaving "something to placate or thank a deity or as a reminder of what is desired." The *New York Times* compared yellow ribbons with other leaving customs, including:

prayers scribbled on bits of paper and poked hopefully into the chinks in Jerusalem's Western Wall. The discarded crutches at Lourdes. Turkish trees hung with small white rags, each the prayer of a barren woman. The ex-votos in Latin American churches, each tiny image a testament to recovery. And now, the yellow ribbons.

Like other charms against death, yellow ribbons petitioned for safe passage. "We dread the messenger and try to forestall him by striking bargains with the gods. They're no frivolity, America's yellow ribbons, but pleas, prayers and hopes, made visible."

Yellow ribbons also conveyed support for the war by little people enacting a popular democratic consensus. "Yesterday in Miami's Little Havana," wrote the *New York Times* soon after the ground war started, "yellow ribbons were as commonplace as cups of cortaditos – Cuban coffee mixed with steamed milk."[79] Yellow ribbons were ideologically flexible, more useful for demonstrating solidarity than framing precise meanings.

In Concord, Calif., a tattoo artist is busy applying peace symbols topped by yellow bows. Hawkish veterans in Greenwich, Conn., passed out yellow ribbons tied to lapel pins in the form of olive-green plastic soldiers crouched over bayonets. "I don't know what it means exactly," said Peter Rosengard, a visiting Englishman, "but I decided to wear it."[80]

Writer Russell Banks invested yellow ribbons with regenerative attributes:

Yellow ribbons have signified our desire to bring home Americans who were being held against their wills in foreign lands (which, since Vietnam, is how I have regarded enlisted men and women anyhow). We would keep dinner in the stove, sheets on their beds, until our kids were brought home again.[81]

This was the anti-war movement speaking a female language of nurturance that doubted that soldiers were a willing sacrifice. In this respect the Gulf War yellow ribbon signified a reconciliation between the American people and two traditions they had not always been easy with: the Vietnam anti-war movement and the women's movement. The yellow ribbon was a sacred knot tying together disparate parts of American political culture. It said, we Americans acknowledge peace-making and grief as deserving of regard by the patriarchal warrior culture signified by the flag.

Pennsylvania's Allegheny Trails Boy Scout Council inscribed the yellow ribbon in a parsed flag shoulder patch designed as a keepsake for Scouts marching in the Pittsburgh Welcome Home parade for returning Gulf soldiers. The patch was a vertically divided circle. One half was an embroidered blue field containing four white stars. The other half was embroidered with horizontal red and white stripes. A circular border of blue letters on white read, "Welcome Home Parade '91 Allegheny Trails." Superimposed on the parsed flag of the two halves was a yellow bow with streamers and a knot shaped like a Boy Scout trefoil. Whether to combine the unofficial yellow ribbon with flag symbolism had been a dilemma for the totem-mimetic Scouts. Council executives decided America had voted with its feet. "The Scouts don't lead, they follow," one explained. "When the Boy Scouts use it, you know it's part of society."[82]

Symbolically associated with the yellow ribbon was the oak tree it sometimes encircled. In a divided country the yellow ribbon was a token of grief, a bandage for a wounded society. Presented in the female shapes of bow and vagina, the source of life, and in a traditional female gesture of binding, it wrapped the symbolic color of women and not-fighting around the wounded totem of the old oak tree. It feminized and recalled men who were absent from the arena of warriors. The old oak tree is the aged phallus, not the young and vigorous one. It is the symbol of Zeus, who is old and sad. The yellow ribbon in the Gulf War was the sign of a society tired of fighting itself, a society mourning a generation of casualties of war and division, hopeful of finding itself unified and wiser at last.

Rebecca saves the flag – female initiation

An allegory of female totem-creation appears in a turn-of-the-century novel for young women called *New Chronicles of Rebecca*, sequel to the popular *Rebecca of Sunnybrook Farm* by Kate Douglas Wiggin. Two chapters tell the story of an Independence Day celebration in the fictional community of Riverboro, Maine. Flagraising is its centerpiece. Creating a flag, a symbolic body nourished and treasured by the community, and guarding it to fruition are accomplished by cultivating traditional female skills. The effort coincides with Rebecca's transformation from child to woman the summer before her entrance into a female seminary. Flagmaking and raising furnish a symbolic initiation rite into adult female responsibility.

An adored female role model, the minister's wife, proposes that the women of the community make the flag for the girls of the community to raise:

"It may not be quite as good as those manufactured in the large cities," she said, "but we shall be proud to see our home-made flag flying in the breeze, and it will mean all the more to the young voters growing up, to remember that their mothers made it with their own hands."[83]

This is a feminine statement of totem-creation. When Rebecca's turn comes to sew her star on the flag, she receives the bundle of bunting "as if it had been a child awaiting baptismal rites." She asks what stitch to use, that is, how to employ her female skills. The minister's wife replies:

"Look at all the others and make the most beautiful stitches you can, that's all. It is your star, you know, and you can even imagine it is your state, and try and have it the best of all. If everybody else is trying to do the same thing with her state, that will make a great country, won't it?"[84]

If the mission of men is to separate from the group and cross the border to defend it, the mission of women is to do what others do, to hew to a cooperative vision of a connected community. Rebecca consecrates herself to the labor of star-sewing, symbolically bringing forth offspring. Her role is Betsy Ross's. As Betsy is a widow in the American totem-creation myth, a spiritual madonna who brings forth a flag from her own lap without a mortal mate, Rebecca is a future seminarian. Her fecundity is spiritual.

She composes a poem with a "kind of magicness" for the occasion. She recites it prayerfully to the minister, ritualizing her creative effort. She claims not to have consciously composed it: "I didn't write it, I just sewed it while I was working on my star." The regenerative destiny of women is not chosen but realized. The poem, "My Star," describes her relationship to the community flag:

> For it's your star, my star, all the stars together,
> That make our country's flag so proud
> To float in the bright fall weather.
> Nothern stars, Southern stars, stars of the East and West,
> Side by side they lie at peace
> On the dear flag's mother-breast.

Rebecca explains that "the flag is the whole country – the mother – and the stars are the states" and have to lie somewhere.[85]

The day before the festival Rebecca spots the finished flag bundled among white sheets in the back of a wagon driven by the town scoundrel, Abner Simpson, a ragman. Hoping to rescue the flag in its swaddling without humiliating its kidnapper, who is also the father of a friend, she asks for a ride. Her task is to resolve division in the community without tearing its social fabric. Rebecca explains that the children of the town will be disappointed without a flag to raise. She pleads for its return. When Simpson denies stealing it, Rebecca threatens to fight: "I can't fight like the boys, but I can pinch and scratch, and I *will* scratch, just like a panther – I'll lie right down on my star and not move, if I starve to death!"[86] The mother's role is giving sustenance to offspring. Witholding nourishment is her most potent threat. Simpson gallantly surrenders the bundle he thought was clean washing when he stole it.[87]

The pageant day arrives. Male roles are assigned according to the wartime exploits of one's male ancestors in the town. Female roles are assigned by virtue, an attribute of female regenerative worth. Rebecca has a starring role. The morning of the flagraising, a favorite schoolteacher acting as Columbia initiates her into womanhood by dressing and arranging her hair. The festival begins.

The brass band played inspiring strains; the mayor spoke eloquently on great themes; the people cheered; then the rope on which so much depended was put into the children's hands, they applied superhuman strength to their task, and the flag mounted, smoothly and slowly, and slowly unwound and stretched itself until its splendid size and beauty were revealed against the maples and pines and blue New England sky.[88]

The outsider Abner Simpson watches from the edge of the crowd, the community border. He wonders who would value a flag, worthless for swapping. Then he hears Rebecca's poem:

He looked curiously at the rapt faces of the mothers, their babies asleep in their arms; the parted lips and shining eyes of the white-clad girls; at Cap'n Lord, who had been in Libby prison, and Nat Strout, who had left an arm at Bull Run; and the friendly, jostling crowd of farmers, happy, eager, absorbed, their throats ready to burst with cheers.[89]

The poem and flag transform him. He goes home and declares to his wife that he is not so low a man as to steal a flag. Thinking how he would court the beautiful Betsy in different circumstances, that is, imagining a regenerative connection to the community, he resolves to reform his thieving ways. He vows to cross back into the community as a contributor.

The story portrays women as totem-creators whose bodies bring forth the flagchild that rejuvenates the community. The Rebecca story replays the Betsy Ross myth as initiation into womanhood through childbearing. It specifies the importance of female beauty and virtue and the role of women in inspiring men, border travelers who may threaten the community, to re-attach themselves. In this case feminine socializing saves the flagchild on whom totem-creation depends. Initiated females, the minister's wife and the schoolteacher, take charge of Rebecca and teach her to be a woman. Through the exercise of traditional female skills Rebecca makes the flag, protects it with a spell of her own devising and defends it without damaging community cohesion. Indeed, she creates more community. By bringing its divisions together, its outsiders inside, she shows she is a competent adult female. Women traditionally do save the flag. It is to them that commemorative flags are given when soldiers are buried. They preserve it because they embody the community.

Living flags

Flagwaving is the reconstitutive gesture of the popular domain. A lesser known reconstruction ceremony is the "living flag," a traditional display of homefront support for soldiers at war. Each "human flag" participant displays or wears an element from its design. In a kind of stationary dance, participants coordinate their bodies to make a complete flag design. The living flag dramatizes the lesson that people construct the community. Like the living flag, the community lasts as long as its participants are willing to enact it. The living flag ritually reconstructs the touched, dismembered, multiple flag. A flag of living bodies is by definition touched. Each person is a detachable element; thus it is a dismembered flag. Living flags are multiple because every living flag is different from every other, constituted from the unique bodies that compose it. A living flag of 3,500 school children on Flag Day, 1985, was the subject of a *Washington Post* story, a parable about creating a nation out of disorderliness, especially the disorderliness of children, the flag's future. Fort McHenry, the site of this living flag, is consecrated ground. During the British bombardment of 1814, Francis Scott Key was moved to model in poetry the flag's endurance under fire. The battle for the death-defying *Star-Spangled Banner* was ritualized as a creation-sacrifice guaranteeing the nation for eternity and illuminated by the regenerative dawn.

> O say can you see, by the dawn's early light,
> What so proudly we hail'd at the twilight's last gleaming,
> Whose broad stripes and bright stars through the perilous night,
> O'er the ramparts we watched, were so gallantly streaming,
> And the rockets' red glare, the bombs bursting in air,
> Gave proof through the night that our flag was still there.
> O, say does that Star-Spangl'd Banner yet wave,
> O'er the land of the free and the home of the brave.

The *Post* account chronicled the Fort McHenry living flag ceremony from its unpromising beginning. Emphasizing the disorderliness of the process and participants, the story projected an uncertain ritual outcome. Solemn pronouncements by organizers and dignitaries about the importance of this creative act alternated with anecdotes of disorganization and disruption. These concerned eighty busloads of participants aged between ten and fourteen, arranging themselves on a 255' x 135' field divided into 3' x 3' squares. The adults spoke to their charges of beginning the country's future at that place. "You are making history," urged the Mayor of Baltimore, investing the children with totem-creating powers. "Fifty years from now you will tell your grandchildren, "I was at Fort McHenry when they made that human flag.""[90]

The threat of chaos was contrasted to the goal of creating ritual order. The *Post* story harped on procedures for ritual efficacy. It discussed the sacrificial discipline that would be needed, the proper sequence of ceremonial events, the sizeable degree of ritual uncertainty and the devotion of the participants. All the elements of ritual were present. *Formality* showed itself in the goal of the ceremony to reproduce the flag's design. The adult discussion of the ritual's importance was *in earnest,* as were the children's efforts. A helicopter observing the proceedings enacted the link between *communicativeness* and *performativeness* by signaling to the organizers the moment the ritual was successfully completed. Communicativeness was also found in the way the witnessing press made sense of the proceedings. Popular sacrificial performativeness was present in the disciplined attentions and postures wrested from unruly children by harried adults.

The children were the most important ritual performers and the most unpredictable. "They assembled over the course of an hour, trying to stay in their squares, while their teachers hoped no one would have to go to the bathroom," an implied desecration. The story described broken styrofoam stars and children reluctant to stay still. Most had not been picked for patriotic devotion, but for how obediently their teachers thought they would behave. Ritual conformity was prized above private belief since many children seemed unsure what was happening. Commerce had played a regenerative role in making the ceremony possible. American Airlines flew in students from every state. Packets distributed to the children contained a history of the *Star-Spangled Banner* and a $5 gift certificate for the Merry-Go-Round clothing store. The variety of children offered an emblematic microcosm of the multiple and diverse national community.

There were tall gangly kids and short runty kids, pimpled kids and dimpled kids. Some wore their Sunday best, but most wore pants and T-shirts or jackets with "Orioles" on the back. The girls played hand-clapping games and brushed their hair, and the boys made telescopes and bopped one another with them.

The greater the difference and disorder, the more uncertain the outcome, the more impressive the achievement of ritual order:

The placards were passed out, red, white, and blue. "Red, RED!" a teacher yelled at two confused students, who were holding the wrong side up, looking like marshmallows on the end of a red line. The big moment was getting closer.

At the critical moment, participants stood and sang "America the Beautiful" and raised their placards for hovering helicopters to see. The children accepted their ceremonial obligations; the living flag was a success. It held until the cannons of Fort McHenry boomed, the children squealed distractedly, and orderly squares broke up. The last moments of the highly human flag and the return of the landscape to normal from sacred time were depicted in a closing narrative.

A small boy danced his own boogaloo as the Stars and Stripes milled around him, cuffing each other and rolling their placards into telescopes. Adams [an organizer] was shouting at them to line up when he called the number of their bus. The helicopters roared away, leaving the sky to the birds and the clouds and the replica of Mary Pickersgill's flag [the widow who made the Fort McHenry flag that inspired Francis Scott Key] flapping in the breeze.

The story taught that the flag belongs to the people, not the authorities. When authorities try to discipline them, the people are likely to be their irrepressible, childishly buoyant selves. The thing gets done, nevertheless. In their clumsy, creative way the people construct a community by following the rules. If they depart from them, they do it innocently. In the end they will form themselves into a cohesive, respectable, rule-following clan doing their duty.

9

Fresh blood, public meat

> When I asked the [savage] visitor what advantage he gained by his superior position among his own people – for he was a captain and our sailors called him the king – he said, the privilege of marching first into battle.
>
> Montaigne, "On Cannibals"[1]

In the cycle of sacrifice, feast, and rebirth, rites of war act out totem crisis. War mobilizes the community for a blood sacrifice to stop time and re-create the group. Not all wars achieve this aim. Those that do are risky and opportunistic. War is risky when the substance of the nation is in danger of being irreparably consumed. Opportunistic war must appear to be unprovoked by the group. It preserves the totem secret by seeming contrary to the peaceful desires of the citizenry. To be messianic and group-transforming, war must be popular, it must masquerade as defensive, and it must consume valuable lives and treasure. Besides all this, its outcome must be nail-bitingly uncertain. Unpredictable in its origins, uncertain in its prospects, costly to the group, ritually successful war is the most powerful national ritual because the greatest amount of blood magic is required to overcome the serious odds against its successful prosecution.

Magic wears out, as Durkheim knew. The group must constitute itself again and again. Because creation–sacrifice is costly, it is rare. If it happened often enough to dissipate murderous group tensions, the group would soon exhaust itself. Apostolic missions and commemorative remodeling must substitute for blood sacrifice. To a degree, they do. Mostly, however, contrived group crisis fills in. Between wars and other forms of messianic sacrifice, contrived group crisis places the group regularly at risk, but in a more limited fashion than war. The most important American example is the quadrennial election of a president, a seasonal rite to regenerate the totem for future sacrifice. Elections are contrived fertility

9.1 Mating ritual between totem suitor and symbol of fertile center who wears flag in her hair like a flower, 1992 presidential campaign.

rites of mating between the people and a leader. They parallel the ritual structure of war, though they lack the impact of ritually successful blood sacrifice. The conditions of ritually successful sacrifice may be compared to ritually successful elections as follows:

1. In war blood must touch every member of the group. Electoral mating must also touch all the people. Voting accomplishes this.
2. War requires willing sacrifice. During electoral campaigns, suitor–candidates declare the life of the group to be the cause for which they are willing to give everything.
3. In war victimage must be unanimous. The group enthusiastically tests suitor–candidates' promises to give themselves utterly to the group.
4. There is uncertainty about the fate of the group in war. In successful election rituals there is uncertainty both about group survival and how the election will come out. Uncertainty heightens ritual by investing it with consequence. It also teaches that whatever the outcome, there is not just one solution to the problem of survival. Groups must be able to manage many outcomes: the life or death of a leader, a Democratic or Republican victor. The lesson of contrived group crisis is that the group will prevail so long as members are ritually faithful.
5. In war outcomes must be dramatic and definite. In elections citizens choose a victorious candidate to mate with. The more decisive the victory, the more effective the ritual, provided the result has been genuinely uncertain. Should there be any doubt, inaugural rites enact all outcomes as unambiguous, rendering them certain.
6. Only new rituals repair a failed war. These could be new wars, but are not limited to them. Likewise, only new rituals repair a failed election. A successful election transforms the group by renewing the group idea. Not all elections achieve this or can achieve it for long.

War unifies the nation through totem sacrifice. Election unifies it through totem creation. As its religious etymology suggests, the end of election is raising up a chosen one. The drama of sacrificial devouring and regenerative courtship constitutes the campaign, the prelude to electoral mating. In the process candidates "wrap themselves in the flag," displaying their regenerative potential in the image of a nurturant body. Ritual eating and mating locate nourishment and fertility in the body of society and primitively construct the social. Feast and fertility model consumption and reproduction, the defining activities of the regenerative center. A victorious coupling between the people and their chosen candidate, who is transformed by the election ordeal, brings forth a newly incarnated totem. Ritually, elections consist of these elements:

Feeding

During the campaign the people metaphorically tear and consume the flesh of candidates who thereby nourish the profligate, riotous body of society. Feasting on the future totem, the people invert the sacrificial order in which the totem eats its own to live. This reversal creates a contrived crisis that threatens group order. This ritual disorder is anxiety-producing and creative. It signifies that the slate can be drawn afresh. Pledging to give the people what they want, candidates are figuratively ripped from limb to limb and served up to an insatiable electorate. "If I throw my hat in the ring, does my head go with it?" asks the candidate in Frank Capra's film about an American presidential election, *The State of the Union* (1948).[2] The ordeal in which the community savages those who would lead it foreshadows the sacrificial responsibilities of the re-embodied king who must offer himself to the community when it calls. His death in office may be physical or constituted in the loss of political authority through scapegoating.

Courting

Primaries and nominating conventions mark the stages of a stormy romance between candidates and voters in which suitable fertile pairs are created to regenerate the totem. Metaphors of wedding, mating and courting dramatize the regenerative goal of election. Candidates are said to "flirt" with political allies, particularly those trying to become running "mates." Proclaiming their mating potential, candidates become grotesque and fertile doubles of the people.[3] By successfully mating with willing supporters in each primary contest, reinvigorated winners offer themselves as totem suitors. These are paired with surviving competitors in their own parties for successive contests of elimination, and finally, with opposite-party candidates. In an emotionally accelerating choreography of mating and sacrifice, a Democratic and Republican candidate are chosen during two national conventions to face one another. Each has been tested by ordeal and betrothed to a large group of followers. From this fertile pair will come a new president.

Consummation

Etymologically, voting means taking vows. It is a ritual act of faith. Its devotional character is apparent in the patriotic belief that every vote counts. Who wins matters less than that every citizen express dedication to the totem. To vote is to choose a betrothed. The community gives itself to

9.2 Regenerative courting between disordered popular domain and taboo embodied totem George Bush, 1992 campaign.

one who will be a deferred sacrifice, who will offer himself to the community when it calls. As war produces a totem transfigured by death, the consummatory embrace between a candidate and the people in the presence of the flag, the transcendent totem god, produces an embodied, promised child. Voting ritually regenerates the community. Elections may also produce totem fathers, avenging sons or other typifications. The vocabulary of totem themes is flexible enough for a variety of avatars so long as there is a fertile union between the people and the candidate.

Sacrificial promise

In return for the people's vow of fidelity, the newly raised up totem offers himself at the inauguration. His is not the only gift. The losing candidate is an immediate sacrifice. The inaugural includes the ritual death of the old king whose willing submission defines democratic procedure. As the deferred sacrifice, the victor will pay the blood debt that guarantees the future of the group.[4] This is the purpose for which he is made leader. The election pair of winner and loser resembles the goats of sacrifice described in Leviticus. Two goats are offered on behalf of the group. One, the ritual sacrifice, is killed immediately. The surrogate sacrifice takes on himself the sins of the people and goes into the wilderness, beyond the border. By sacrificing the loser and deferring the winner for future sacrifice, the people make one offering and hold another in reserve. The election ritual is complete.

Flags are transforming agents in totem regeneration. They signify that borders are at issue, that social energy and treasure are expended, that groups are being defined and the community renewed. Their power is conveyed in the sheer density of banners waving and on display during the campaign and inauguration. Three points are especially marked by forests of popular flags. Each is a specific ritual moment of regenerative sacrifice. The first is when candidates announce and offer themselves for feasting. The second is when political parties choose candidates to do battle in the campaign. The third is when the victor offers his inaugural pledge. The parsed flag is an electioneering flag, a high flag brought low within a system of structured desecration, a cut-up and reassembled version of the flag that symbolizes the body of sacrifice. It appears in bunting, campaign buttons, posters and other election paraphernalia.[5] It signifies the creative impulse of the people to rend and dismember the totem. It is reformable, symbolically remaking the community through electoral mating.[6]

There is a well-known pattern to election proceedings. Certain outcomes are expected by participants and engineered to that end. Much care, observation, and comment accompany the ritual unfolding. Predictions are made about the skills of performers. Comparisons with previous rituals abound. With a sufficient commitment of social energy and treasure, a totem will always be created, though some electoral couplings are more successful than others. A ritually successful election will end in unity and *hope*, the word of pregnant promise and reproductive outcome. Often uttered as a political refrain, it signifies the readiness of candidate and electorate to connect in a mating dance. Hope, a pundit wrote during the 1992 presidential campaign, "expects success, and deferred, sours with nearly the violence of spurned love."[7] Here was a prediction by which to chart the course of relations between a president and the people.

The totem is known by the radiant face on his flagstaff of a body. He awes, he is more than human. A political observer said of General Colin Powell, the fantasy candidate who refused a presidential run in 1996, "You look at Powell and you think about saluting the flag."[8] A journalist described presidential "mystique" in bodily terms:

Ordinary folks who came in contact with his person – skin to skin, in a handshake, perhaps – couldn't help but shudder at the thrill of it. As head of state, he was the personal embodiment of the United States of America – the Stars and Stripes made flesh.[9]

On the eve of the 1991 New Hampshire primary callers to National Public Radio discussed the magic of aspiring totem faces, beginning with Paul Tsongas. A listener commented: "I'm not sure what people are looking for, I think it's stamped right across [Tsongas's] forehead that this fellow is trustworthy, intelligent, and I hope he gets it." "I love your image there," the moderator chimed in. "It's kind of like Superman, he goes into the phone booth and puts on the glasses and then he looks presidential." "I've been healed!" 15-year-old Ronda White shouted after brushing against the governor. "I touched Bill Clinton!"[10] "I was kind of hoping to get close enough so the President could kiss my daughter," explained Paul Imbimbo in Garfield, New Jersey. "Oh my God, oh my God – I looked right at him!" said Janet Duffy, reacting to George Bush.[11]

Recombinatory mechanisms – election exogamy

Richard Scammon describes elections as "a mercenary kind of game in which armies march and counter-march and threaten each other, but eventually compromise without blood being actually spilled."[12] Despite the sacrificial rhythm of party against party and candidate against candidate, what makes elections regenerative is that the electorate chooses the winner by uniting with him. One party may not physically crush or eliminate another as in totem sacrifice and affiliative conflict. Nor do parties determine presidents. The people must bestow their affections, choosing suitors who court them. "If it weren't for you," Bill Clinton declared to thousands of supporters at a rally in his home town towards the end of a bruising primary season, "and the hundreds of thousands you represent, I wouldn't be up here about to be the nominee of the Democratic Party."[13]

The production of fertile mating pairs is central to the election. A fertile pair consists of two partners whose purposive association produces a desired outcome for the group. Fertile pairs are everywhere in a presidential election. The competing candidates make a pair. So do the parties they represent. The most important fertile pair is the electorate and the victorious candidate. Others include candidate and running mate, candidate and spouse, candidate and party, and victor and departing incumbent. "No one is playing the mating game any harder, or enjoying it more," the *Times* reported as Clinton pored over vice-presidential possibilities.[14] Comedian Dennis Miller joked about the fertile pair constituted by the Democratic candidate and his running mate: "They're young. They're handsome. They're on the same ticket. Can America afford even the shadow of a doubt?"[15] "The American people want to see a candidate and his wife campaign together," explains a character in *The State of the Union* (1948), a film that compares elections with marriage. "It's an American tradition."[16] Exogamous systems form critical mating pairs across clans rather than within them. Electoral exogamy is manifest in the two-party system in which two presidential candidates from the same clan, or party, may not constitute a final mating pair. One candidate must be Republican, the other Democrat. There are exceptions, as when only one party fields a candidate for office. But well-conducted rituals require two. The more powerful the office, the more important the rule. In a successful election, not only candidates but voters mate across clans. To produce a victor who ritually unites the group, substantial numbers of voters from one party must unite with the other party's candidate.

The ongoing cry by press, public, and candidates for substantive discussion of election "issues" keeps the collective focus away from deeper ritual themes of sacrifice, creation, and renewal. Totem talk about these themes is plentiful and informative, but its audience is distracted by the belief, which is part of the talk, that it is beside the point. Totem talk of fertility and combat is presented as tangential to the meat and potatos of political discussion. "The evening news has become more and more irrelevant to the civil conversation, because it's all blood and guts," an observer complained.[17] (Is there a ritual difference between the act of killing and election talk about it? Both remodel the cosmogonic act, but with vastly different degrees of magical efficacy. Shedding real blood, it goes without saying, is more magical than talking about it. Does one cause the other? When it comes to killing and regeneration, talk models action, and action models talk. They give rise to each other.) Totem talk ritually instructs even as it is set aside with useful fictions. One of the most enduring is that election shaped by totem talk is a bad election.

Totem talk, as opposed to talk about issues, is most prevalent when ritual suspense is highest. This includes periods when the leading candidates have not yet emerged, just before the vote and in the buildup to the inauguration. On the eve of the 1992 election journalist Howard Fineman characterized the indecision of the American people as "the-night-before-the-wedding" jitters.[18] His compatriots on the television program *Washington Week* laughed to distance this sexual metaphor from the serious issues of the election and to move this discussion of ritual uncertainty to safer ground, the volatility of the late polls. Joking is a strategy for dealing with taboos, as Freud knew. The comic façade of jokes, he wrote, conceals "the fact that they have something – forbidden – to say."[19] A humorous essay in the *New York Times* used totem talk to portray the candidates as suitors in a stormy romance:

The American people: so fickle and unimpressed. What do they want? As I watched them being courted these many months, it occurred to me that the three candidates really were suitors . . . They were trying to get a date – Nov. 3 – with the American people.[20]

The dirty campaign

During a totem crisis such as war, national borders must be tight and impermeable. The borders of totem-creation are symbolically inverted. The fertile center, which is the body of the people, is in a disordered borderless state. The community feels endangered. Resolution requires fertile union between the people and a leader who will draw borders and make the group secure. Borderlessness is a contrived crisis since, for regeneration to take place requires an orificed, profligate, grotesque body. This last term is Bakhtin's, for whom bodily boundaries reflect social structure. The grotesque body – low, corpulent, devouring, permeable, disgusting and fecund – may be contrasted with the classical body – smooth, noble, unorificed, bordered. The grotesque body is transgressible and communicating. The classical high body is inviolable and remote. The grotesque body of the candidate may be violently devoured and noisily mated. The classical body of the victor is worshipped and feared.

The campaign in which the grotesque body disports itself has a setting. This is the fair and the marketplace, carnival settings characterized by crossroads and extremes, the antithesis of order, civility, and decorum. A reporter described Bill Clinton's grotesque appearance in a Milwaukee hotel, ritually descending from his suite to the lobby where "lunching grandmas yank throwaway cameras from their purses" to consume the candidate with their eyes.

As the glass capsule glides to eye level, we get a crotch-up view of the Comeback Kid. From that angle, Clinton looks like a grinning balloon, his cheeks enormous, his trademark hair a brillowy nimbus around a florid face.[21]

The *New York Times* editorialized:

[Clinton] had hardly presented his fresh face to New Hampshire primary voters before it was defaced with one mud pie after another – accusations of adultery, ducking the draft, fudging about marijuana, improving on the truth.[22]

The fair is wherever the candidate pitches the people. It is the realm of the profane, the counterpoint to the holy. In campaigning, totem talk describes a movement from disorder to order regenerated. All sides express concern about the impact of the dirty campaign on the community. Press, populace, and candidates decry a campaign that fans group flames. "All that doom and gloom just to get themselves elected," commented a truck driver.[23] Fears for the death of the group are central to contrived group crises. Only if the integrity of the community is placed seriously in doubt will reunification achieve its effect. The 1992 primary season produced large doses of disorder and chaos. Not only was the polity at risk, but politicians might be swept into the maw of the popular searching for its defining sacrifice. "People talk as though our political system had been taken over by alien beings," observed the Kettering Foundation.[24] Electoral chaos was the theme of a William Safire column:

The politics of resentment is being covered – and of course, exaggerated – because enough people are persuaded that it is more fun to sound off than to sign on. As a result, the nation's most visible product is steam, which is being let off at a great rate.[25]

Grotesque bodies are exaggerated, overflowing, amorphous masses exuding steam. "Outrage bestrides the stage." Garry Wills wrote, "The crazies are in charge. The fringe has taken over."[26] The nation was in a mood for sacrifice. Perhaps it came in three days of civil unrest in Los Angeles at the end of April, a prologue to the sacrifice of a sitting president. As one voter put it, "Bush can't be the only one who can do this job. We need some fresh blood."[27]

9.3 Popular grotesque flag display. Presidential candidate Ross Perot embraces supporter, 1992.

The feast

The campaign is a carnival of dissolution and indulgence. It cannibalizes the candidate for its own nourishment. It is the scene of public orgies. It was said of Democrat Gene McCarthy's supporters in 1968: "Many people in the liberal community had both arms and both legs around Gene McCarthy, and were kissing him on the neck and biting him on the ear."[28] "This is a party hungry for victory," explained Tom Brokaw as Bill Clinton wound up his quest for the Democratic nomination.[29] His grotesque body personified the food feast of the campaign:

At best, political campaigns are diet disasters, with spreads of nibbles at almost every stop. Within weeks of hitting the 1992 campaign trail, Mr. Clinton ballooned well beyond 200 pounds and his suits began to bulge noticeably in the shoulders and waist.[30]

At the Democratic convention, food was a carnival sideshow.[31] Delegates traipsed to elegant restaurants. Lavish spreads were funded by lobbyists. The *New York Times* decorated a front page of its food section with bunting and lavished ink on convention comestibles. It was as though candidates were being plumped up for sacrifice. "Once you're running," explained talk show host Larry King about voter anger toward politicians, "you're public meat."[32] Texas Governor Ann Richards made the metaphor more pointed after Bush's weak performance in the first presidential debate: "He's done, and stuff a fork in him."[33] Clinton also came in for fantasies of alimentary violence. "Joan Didion has a word for the liquid center that oozes out of Clinton whenever you bite down: personalismo," wrote Richard Goldstein. "It may be the defining trait of our presidents from now on."[34]

In the wake of Bush's loss, a comedy writer accused him of being insufficiently grotesque:

Dear President Bush,
    On the eve of your leave-taking, you should finally be told the truth about why you lost the election.
    You were too skinny.
    Presidents can't be thin. Presidents are supposed to be round and kind and fatherly . . .
    We want public figures. Like Tip O'Neill and Ted Kennedy and Lyndon Johnson – people who eat too much and get us into trouble and embarrass us.[35]

Advising that lunch was a family value, he concluded:

George, you can make a comeback in four years.
    Here's the plan: any chance you get – grab a sandwich. Have a malted. Carry

cheese balls in your jacket. Tomorrow, call a breakfast meeting; have the breakfast, skip the meeting.

Pudge up. Call yourself "Georgie-Porgie," and live up to it. Your overriding political rule has always been, "I will do anything to be elected." From now on make it, "I will eat anything to be elected."

The carnival of disorder

Campaign combat takes place before a bloodthirsty crowd. An observer describes the "vicious cycle" of media coverage. Media accounts are issue-oriented "before the public begins to focus." Once the public pays attention, "the horse race and the scandals" – the fair and the grotesque body – move to center stage. Voters "see the slash and burn and nothing else."[36] The analysis suggests a consumptive public slowly bringing its monstrous bulk into "focus" to lay waste what it touches. The incumbent totem tried not to touch the down and dirty campaign. "I have to do certain things that the attackers don't have to do," George Bush explained. "One of them is be President."[37] A Democratic strategist observed the president's reluctance. "In the Bush–Baker world view, you do ugly, distasteful things to get elected."[38] Voters were angry. The *Times* spoke of the "volcanic nature" of the political season in which "ethnic and cultural passions [were] boiling," of "a year when politics trembles with rage and dislocation, when the campaign trail has become the wild earth."[39] The "thin-skinned President" was upset that voters had "turned on him, when he was expecting a coronation, not a crucifixion."[40] An adviser called the campaign "a three-ring circus." Campaign officials dealt with threats from Republican challenger Pat Buchanan by "running around like chickens with their head cut off." Attacks on the president were "tarring him." The campaign faced "meltdown."

Regular party candidates faced an "untested wild man" in challenger Ross Perot.[41] Republicans portrayed him as the profane animal of Western culture. Press secretary Marlin Fitzwater described him as "a pig in the poke and a dangerous and destructive personality."[42] Perot urged his supporters, "If you've got the stomach for it, let's do it."[43] Bill Clinton came in for his own status reversal ordeal early in the campaign. The *Village Voice* described him as a "draft-dodging, weed-toking, Commie-loving fornicator," a man whose "sins resonated with our aspirations."[44] "I didn't inhale," the candidate insisted, defending his grotesque, orificed body as a classical one, when detractors painted him as polluted by marijuana.[45] Charges that his body had also engaged in illicit sexual congress with other women and that he had shielded it from the purifying sacrifice of totem combat, portrayed him as defiled. Clinton bowed to the ritual order of status degradation, philosophizing "that political life could be unfair and denuding, and that running for public office is a trade-off in which enduring low blows and pitiless scrutiny must be endured in order to have an opportunity to lead and change."[46] Candidates' bodies are prepared for sanctification by the ordeal of the campaign. Vice-presidential candidate Al Gore reflected on an incident in which his own and Clinton's entourage had collided at a campaign stop:

He turned to a reporter with a look of reflection on his face. "Did you ever see that Woody Allen movie where there are these six guys dressed in black coming down a street and they're carrying this guy on a cross, and they're looking for a parking space? Then, just as they're backing into a space, these six other guys in black carrying a guy on a cross come in from behind and take the space. You remember that scene?

"That's what this is like for me sometimes," Mr Gore said.[47]

The Gore remarks appeared below a photograph of Clinton addressing a night rally, his body reflecting the light, his arms outstretched in an unmistakably messianic pose.[48]

In some African rituals, says Victor Turner, the future chief separates from the community and undergoes debasement before he may be reaggregated and installed as king. This 1868 account of the enstooling of a king in Gabon bears more than a passing resemblance to presidential campaigns. As the future king walked through the village:

He was suddenly set upon by the entire populace, who proceeded to a ceremony which is preliminary to the crowning and must deter any but the most ambitious man from aspiring to the crown. They surrounded him in a dense crowd, and then began to heap upon him every manner of abuse that the worst of mobs could imagine. Some spat in his face; some beat him with their fists; some kicked him; others threw disgusting objects at him; while those unlucky ones who stood on the outside, and could reach the poor fellow only with their voices, assiduously cursed him, his father, his mothers, his sisters and brothers, and all his ancestors to the remotest generation. A stranger would not have given a cent for the life of him who was presently to be crowned.

Amid all the noise and struggle, I caught the words which explained all this to me; for every few minutes some fellow, administering a specially severe blow or kick, would shout out, "you are not our king yet; for a little while we will do what we please with you. By-and-by we shall have to do your will.[49]

The *New Yorker* described the combined roles of suitor and sacrifice for candidates in not dissimilar terms:

All right. Here was a guy who endured a non-stop thirteen-month coast-to-coast ordeal of schmoozing, speechmaking, and handshaking perhaps more arduous –

9.4 Totem suitor Bill Clinton offers himself as sacrifice in 1992 presidential campaign.

more barbed, baited, and booby-trapped – than any other in the history of American Presidential politics, a man who submitted himself to more questions and attacks and psychological dissection than the average politician (to say nothing of the average human being) would experience in ten lifetimes, a suitor who courted the public with an assiduousness and complaisance unexampled since Lancelot.[50]

Threats to ritual purity

The great totem drama of the 1992 campaign was an exogamous irregularity: the entrance, withdrawal and re-entrance of independent candidate Ross Perot. Perot's candidacy was said to have been derailed by his unwillingness to subject himself to the degradation ordeal of the campaign. Perot proclaimed himself reluctant to disrupt the election with an inopportune third-party challenge following the revival of the Democratic party, one of the proper members of the mating pair. Later he charged that a fertility violation, an alleged plot by opponents to ruin his daughter's wedding, had precipitated his withdrawal. Pundits blamed the fury of the campaign process. "There is just so much of the process that is wretched and onerous and appalling, and what happens is that this causes an exclusionary effect, a sort of natural selection process, so that there are only a very few people – Bill Clinton, for example – who are prepared to go through this," explained a Perot adviser.[51] Other analysts decried the man who lacked ritual strength. "All those people who thought Ross Perot had guts – and he don't – must go back to the obvious choice, who has guts," offered a New York State organizer.[52] Journalist Ed Bradley described Perot's failure:

They took pot-shots at him, and just when you had him lined up in your sights, he went back in the house and you had to put your gun away. So then he came back and you had to find your gun, you had to go find your ammunition and re-load, and then they started taking shots at him again, and he got real testy.[53]

Perot had committed the unpardonable totem sin. He had given up. *Newsweek* ran his picture on its cover with the single word "Quit" over his head. Perot's departure contrasted with Clinton's sacrificial tenacity. Linda Bloodworth-Thompson, a media adviser to the Clinton campaign, prepared a short film with resurrection overtones:

a bunch of clips from pundits talking since January, all of them saying, "Clinton is dead. He'll be out of the race tomorrow. He's hemorrhaging. He's swimming around with three harpoons in him." They don't know this guy. You can't kill Bill. He'll be dead when he's embalmed, and even then I'd suggest an airtight casket, to be on the safe side.[54]

If ritual order had gone awry with Perot's candidacy, the solution lay in reinstituting proper mating procedures. Perot's candidacy had "turned the race, and the campaign calendar, on its head."[55] His withdrawal wiped out all thought that the changes he and his followers "craved could come outside the turf of the two political parties," that is, through irregular mating procedures.[56] His quixotic candidacy had given the public more "respect" for party regulars, a term of sexual as well as battle honor. He had made the parties "pull themselves together," a phrase of mating and ordering. One commentator claimed Perot had revived the belief that popular will and government could fashion a fertile union. "He restored to politics something of the joy of participation that has been largely missing from national campaigns for generations."[57] Columnist A. M. Rosenthal wrote that past campaigns of cliches and epithets "strung together like sausages" had provided only "bellyache," but the 1992 campaign "gave us some nutrition – insights into our national self." In the end, "The old lumbering American political system that we are instructed so often to despise produced exactly the right Republican and Democrat to face each other this year."[58] His metaphor hinted at mating and battle, regeneration and sacrifice.

Fear that voters could not distinguish the major parties was a ritual concern about mating pairs.[59] The oppositional, exogamic structure necessary for regeneration was at risk. Republican Charles Rangel of Harlem suggested the Democratic candidate should court minority supporters more ardently:

I told Governor Clinton the rough thing about this campaign is, when you turn on the television set and you see these massive rallies and all of these wonderful white faces with the little American flags, you really don't know right away whether it's a Bush rally, a Clinton rally, or a Perot rally. And America is not like that, and I hope, and I trust, and I'm confident that before Governor Clinton leaves New York he's got to say something that's tantamount [to], I love ya and I don't want to be President withoutcha.[60]

Each party was cast as a different member of a symbolic mating pair. The Republicans were male defenders of borders, out of a job since the end of the Cold War. The Democrats were the female partner, soft on border control, strong on domestic concerns. An observer described the official poster of the Republican National Convention, in which a star-spangled cowboy rode a huge bucking bull, as "blatantly phallic. The positioning of the cowboy's left arm holding the reins can leave no doubt of the intention. It seems the Republicans equate vitality with masculine virility, expressed in purely sexual terms," exactly those appropriate to a mating ceremony.[61]

Blood sports

Candidates talk totem talk, beginning with the name of it all, a "campaign." "It's a wide-open race. This was the starting gun, not the finish line," declared the Democratic National Committee chairman after the New Hampshire primary.[62] *Time* magazine called presidential politics a blood sport for paid professionals.[63] "Mr. Bush's bloody nose" excited pundits when challenger Pat Buchanan did better than expected in New Hampshire.[64] Every Democrat spent time "beating on George Bush."[65] Republicans wondered whether Perot's "kamikaze candidacy" would spoil Bush's chances.[66] In Buchanan, Bush was calling "a proven street fighter outside."[67] Bill Clinton liked "to remind everyone that he has already shown he can take a punch."[68] Exhorting supporters, Perot declared, "You have got to stay in the ring shoulder-to-shoulder with me."[69] Surveying the infighting, former Vice-President Walter F. Mondale observed, "It's five High Noons at once."[70] As his campaign faltered and recovered, Clinton dubbed himself "the comeback kid." The primaries were "headed toward a showdown, somewhere."[71] The press predicted Democratic hopefuls would "bring out their heavy artillery" in the New York primary.[72]

The prophet of totem crisis was Ross Perot, regeneratively described as "the heartthrob of millions of disillusioned voters," and sacrificially as "an authentic American folk hero."[73] Whatever his shortcomings as a traditional candidate, he was an unmatched practitioner of totem talk. He adopted a Texas Rangers slogan with totem overtones: "One riot, one ranger." The riot was the campaign, the ranger the totem aspirant.[74] He had a gift for totemically apt comparisons. He accused General Motors of taking longer to design a new car than the United States had taken to win World War II. He claimed the business community lacked sacrificial commitment to overcome new border threats.[75] Regeneratively, he promised that he and Congress would waltz together "like Ginger Rogers and Fred Astaire."[76] Denying rumors that he had improperly investigated the President's children and his own, Perot called the flap "tossed salad." The implied comparison was to red meat, the hunter's quarry.[77]

The public identified him with prisoners of war, a lingering raw nerve of totem sacrifice in Vietnam. He accused the government of abandoning these border ghosts. He criticized the embodied totem's proudest achievement, the Gulf War, by challenging presidential virility. "I don't have to prove my manhood by sending anyone to war," he said.[78] He charged that Kuwait, the damsel in distress of the Gulf War, was guilty of exogamy violations. He suggested the holy sacrifice of American soldiers was pro-

faned by the irregular sexual practices of a religiously primitive people led
by the Emir of Kuwait.

"Now, if I go knock on your door and say I'd like to borrow your son to go to the
Middle East so that this dude with 70 wives, who has got a minister for sex to find
him a virgin every Thursday night, can have his throne back, you'd probably hit me
in the mouth."[79]

He called for apostolic "fair-shared" sacrifice to remodel World War II.
"Ross Perot says it all. Sacrifice has to start at the top."[80] There it was. An
election that successfully re-creates the totem must raise up a sacrificial
leader. Perot declared himself willing to become a quixotic sacrifice to the
mess the government had become. "Some still see him as a potential savior,"
an analyst explained.[81]

Perot claimed the totem class was his largest base of support. "I do this
for you," he pledged, "because you fought and won the hot wars and the
45–year-long cold war for us. And in many cases, nobody ever even said
thank you. This is my tiny little way of saying thank you." He promised to
placate ghosts of sacrifice past to guarantee the future.

When I think of all the sacrifices my parents and all the generations who came
before them made in the earlier times for us so that we could live the American
dream, certainly we all dedicate ourselves to seeing that you, the young people in
our country, will have the American dream passed on to you.

He had a totem talisman, a Purple Heart sent by a Vietnam veteran, who
wrote:

Let it also remind you of the army of ordinary citizens that has mustered to your
call and looks to you to stop the hemorrhaging of the American spirit, to unite once
and for all our diverse citizenry under a single American banner, and to restore
honesty, integrity, and responsibility to our Government.[82]

In the end Perot entered and left the campaign in an exogamously irregular way. Strategist James Carville's description of his withdrawal as "the
most stupid single act of masturbation in the history of American political
campaigns" recognized the ritual goal of election as a mating between a
hopeful candidate and his supporters, and the Perot candidacy as a failed
ritual act.[83]

The party begins (again)

A political convention blows in and out like a 90–mile gale.

James A. Farley[84]

The Democratic National Convention was held in Madison Square
Garden. "Not politics-as-theater so much as politics-as-half-time-show, as

pep rally, sing-along, circus," wrote Stanley Elkin.[85] Media lead-ins empha-
sized the festivity of the proceedings. "Good evening from inside the
biggest show on or off Broadway tonight, the Democratic National
Convention, here in beautiful but jammed-to-the-rafters Madison Square
Garden," said CBS's Dan Rather, introducing the event as a "dance of
democracy."[86] The podium looked as though waving flags were marching
up either side of it.[87] "The whole thing is like a flag billowing in a breeze. It
both embraces you and defines the space," explained the convention architect. "Like a big hug?" inquired a journalist. "I think of it that way," the
architect replied. "It's like a mother's arms saying, 'You're welcome.'"[88]

Frustrated by the scarcity of "issues" at an orchestrated convention
where the nominee was a foregone conclusion, reporters wondered if
conventions were obsolete. Governor Ann Richards demurred with the
certainty of a performer who knows a fertility rite when she sees one.

RATHER: Are you presiding over the last real Democratic convention?
RICHARDS: I don't think so. I think this is a rite of passage. It's one of those
wonderful kinda ceremonial things. It's like christening your baby. It's one of
those things that you really need to do because it's a tradition. It's American. It's
the way we choose and announce and communicate with the public.

A campaign of family values was the predictable epilogue to a Persian
Gulf War. To build themes of natalism, the Democratic party championed
women, a favored constituency. A woman chaired the convention, women's
rights were a major focus, and women were rhetorical objects of concern
and caring. The chair's opening remarks celebrated the promise of America
for her five-year-old granddaughter.

Lily is a conscience for me. And those of you who have held that first grandbaby
know what I mean. You get that feeling of continuity of your actions being tied to
the future in a way that you never ever felt before, and you understand how important it is to do right now so that that grandbaby, that grandchild is going to do better
later.

Richards contrasted the unifying promise of childhood with the fall of
affiliation.

Now Lily is at the stage where she's getting excited about school. I bet you can
remember anticipating that first day of school . . . No one had made an A or an F,
no one had been chosen first or last for basketball. It didn't matter if you were rich
or poor, you could be a fireman or you could be a movie star, or you could be an
astronaut. Everything was out there just waiting to happen. You remember that
feeling? Well, that's the feeling that we need all over this country, in the first grade
classrooms and on the shop floor and in the board rooms of the businesses of
America, is that eagerness and excitement that we can do it in this nation. It's that
feeling that all the possibilities are out there, that we can do it. Because they are,

Lily. That's what this country is all about, that's what this election is about. It's about the possibilities, it's about the chance to do better. It's about the opportunity for change in this country. Because we are a great nation, we are a great people.

And then the mating call:

And just imagine what we could do for Lily and for all our children if the people of this country and their government actually work together.[89]

Governor Zell Miller of Georgia expanded the regenerative theme, declaring, "When a child has no hope, a nation has no future." Hope was the mating currency, a recombinatory spell chanted by candidates and party regulars. As Edward Kennedy said the next night, "Whatever the winds of the moment, carry high the banner of hope."

Sacrifice was a sensitive subject. The Gulf War had proved an anemic offering to the gods, and Democrats had offered ritually faulty sacrifices in five of the past six elections. The only agreed-to sacrifice was the nominee's. His mission was to carry the party to victory or die trying. He was nominated by the party's favorite orator, Mario Cuomo, who spoke of his regenerative powers:

He does not believe in the cynical political arithmetic that says you can add by subtracting, or multiply by dividing; but instead, he will work to make the whole nation stronger by bringing people together, showing us our commonality, teaching us cooperation, making us not a collection of competing special interests, but one great, special family – the family of America![90]

Cuomo closed with a vision of another fertility rite, a great national parade celebrating domestic victories just as the nation had celebrated the Gulf War homecoming. It was time for the totem, its borders secured, to look within. "So step aside, Mr. Bush," Cuomo intoned. "You've had your parade." He called for the party to send "the comeback kid" from a town called Hope off to campaign war. This was not the scripted climax of the convention. That was scheduled to be the candidate's acceptance of his sacrificial role. It was the emotional high point, nonetheless. Reporter Cokie Roberts described the delegates' warm reactions to erstwhile suitors like Jerry Brown, Ted Kennedy, Paul Tsongas, and Mario Cuomo in nuptial terms:

What you're hearing here is that Mario Cuomo, Ted Kennedy, who spoke earlier, and to some extent, Jerry Brown – as one person said to me – "speak to the heart and soul of the party, but Bill Clinton will lead us to victory." And that's what's really going on here. You have a party that's about to walk down the aisle with the man that mama and daddy have said is going to make the best husband for you, but they are having a last minute romance with the boys they're really in love with,

Mario Cuomo, Teddy Kennedy at the top of their list, and it's always hard to say goodbye to those people, but they know it's not really a good marriage.[91]

State delegations cast their votes, engineered so the first were cast by Clinton's own mother for Arkansas's "favorite son, and my son." When the nomination was secured, Clinton and his wife danced off-site. The delegates danced, too, bobbing signs and waving flags while balloons rained down like manna, the gift of gods. The nominee appeared briefly. Standing with the virtual parsed flag of his family, he promised to unite the country.

When one watched Mr. Clinton, in a blue suit, hug his daughter, Chelsea, dressed in white, and his wife, Hillary, wearing red, and the three made their tricolor way onto the streets of Manhattan, one could not help thinking that there was something stirring about the American political process after all.[92]

Parsed flags showered down and transformed him:

When Mr. Clinton finally emerged onto the podium under a blizzard of red, white, and blue confetti and took the microphone, he seemed to have finally acquired the aura of a potential President, an aura that comes from having millions of people watching thousands of people watch just one man.[93]

The following night, the embodied totem-to-be and his running mate leaned heavily on personal sacrifice stories as evidence they had been to the border and back. Gore said his son's near death had changed him forever.[94] In the absence of war records such signs of being transformed and, therefore, worthy to mate with the people were important.[95] Clinton spoke of a "New Covenant," an agreement binding himself and voters. Both *covenant* and *convention*, Willim Safire noted, come from the Latin *convenire*, to come together.

Speeches done, the flag dancing began in earnest. Signs bobbed, pennants waved, flags fluttered. Delegates clapped as the candidates stood in fertile pairings – presidential and vice presidential nominee, and each nominee with his wife and children. The candidates' wives embraced and did an impromptu jig. Regeneratively, they "hopped up and down like pep squad leaders whose team had just won the game."[96] Flagwaving marked a border crossing by sacrificial warriors off to battle Republicans. It seemed to work. "I feel he's going to bring the country together," said a citizen. "They seemed more unified. There isn't all the bickering," approved another.[97] What did the television audience remember when it was all over? Not the speeches, but the candidates' wives doing a jig on the victory podium. The ritual message had gotten across.[98]

The Republican national convention

> Conventions have been . . . televised since 1948 – and thus have attracted
> tens of millions of spectators who had no way, before, of really savoring
> . . . those flash-lit minutes in which candidate and candidate's wife stand
> – teeth bared, eyes fixed on the farthest rafters, outer arms upraised; inner
> arms lovingly entwined – while . . . acres of folks from Kankakee stand
> roaring like seals during the mating season.   *Life*[99]

Conventions focus the exogamic differences a good ritual requires. "The
goal of the [Republican] platform was to draw distinctions between
Republicans and Democrats," explained Senator Dan Nickles of
Oklahoma.[100] Potlatch competition is one arena for such display. An official
explained:

The Republicans will drop four times more balloons (250,000 balloons, or 113 per
delegate, a world record, he said). The Republicans will have two, not one, high-tech
video walls, each with 40 televisions, behind the podium. Even the shards of confetti will be much bigger than those at the Democratic convention.[101]

The podium was a parsed flag display with decorative stars scattered
across the proscenium of the nine-foot-high, red, white, and blue stage
lowered to "look less like a barrier between the President and the
people."[102] The Astrodome was a tented carnival of patriotism, a Big Top:

Think 16 vertical banners 52 feet tall and 16 feet wide hanging outside from the
grillwork. And two dozen 12-by-18-foot banners suspended from the lampposts
around the stadium. All in bright red, white, and blue with stars, stripes, and ele-
phants, to leave no doubt that the 1992 Republican National Convention was going
on inside.[103]

The description continued:

In all there will be more than 300 vertical and horizontal flags and banners. The
largest are 50–by–30–foot American flags that will hang inside around the top of the
Astrodome; the smallest are still big, 5 feet by 9 feet. For just the decorations outside
the Dome, about 6,000 yards of fabric will be used.

Outside the Astrodome a giant topiary elephant next to "a live one, with
feet painted red, white, and blue," grasped a small flag in his leafy trunk.[104]
With a nod to the transforming power of popular flags, designer Robert
Keene explained, "An event like this is all about inspiring people, getting
them enthusiastic, excited. That's what we hope to do with our American
classic flags and banners".[105]

Fertility metaphors were abundant. "The Republicans have called a love
fest in Houston," wrote Garry Wills.[106] "Already there is sort of a rarefied
air about it, like Christmas or New Year's," said a chef hosting the party's

most prominent supporters, comparing the convention to other natalistic rites.[107] Lacking a cold war, Republicans bickered over domestic exogamy issues including homosexuality and totem-authorized killing through abortions. The living totem father, Ronald Reagan, played mediator to affiliative warlords, reminding delegates:

We are all equal in the eyes of God – whether we come from poverty or wealth, whether we are Afro–American or Irish–American, Christian or Jewish, from big cities or small towns . . . We must all be equal in the eyes of one another.[108]

Pat Buchanan declared Republicans the winners of the Cold War and predicted new defining battles. His vision of a religious war against gays, pro-choicers, and feminists was echoed by a platform in which the regenerative center was at risk: "Today, more than ever, the traditional family is under assault."[109] In one of the more remarked pronouncements by a party official, Republican National chairman Rich Bond thrust Democrats beyond the borders, declaring, "These other people are not America."[110] Buchanan cast the Los Angeles riots as an affiliative parable of Americans fighting Americans:

The troopers came up the street, M-16s at the ready, and the mob threatened and cursed, but the mob retreated because it had met the one thing that could stop it: force rooted in justice and backed by moral courage! Greater love hath no man than this, that he lay down his life for his friends . . . And as those boys took back the streets of Los Angeles block by block, my friends, we must take back our cities and take back our culture and take back our country.[111]

The incumbent president leaned heavily on his administration's role in slaying the "Red Dragon" but had trouble getting the electorate to notice.[112] Epochal struggles require sacrifice to let people know there was a fight and ceremonies to nail down its meaning. No American ceremonies marked the end of the Cold War. No visible sacrifices had defined its boundaries for Americans, and no soldiers were welcomed back across them. The Soviet Union had sacrificed Gorbachev and the Communist Party, but the United States had not even offered much treasure to the cause in a visible, ceremonial way. The end of the Cold War was marked by the fall of the Berlin Wall, a border. Many had been sacrificed there to Communism, but none was American.

The post-convention campaign

In keeping with its military label, the "campaign" begins as a totem journey to define borders. On a cross-country bus tour the Democratic candidates promised to "Take America Back." Their aim was to "get this country on the right road again," said Al Gore. "We need to lift this country up and go forward," said Bill Clinton in the language of sacrifice and conquest. But the Democratic theme focused more on the ascendance of the regenerative center. "When the Republicans raise the old flag of fear," urged Clinton, "you tell them, "No thanks. This time we're going to vote on our hopes.""[113] Holding out the promise of fertile pairings, he declared, "You are here for yourselves, your children and your future because you want your country back. And Al Gore and I are going to give it to you."[114] Clinton accused Republicans of interfering with the generative process "by dividing the people, by terrifying the people, by convincing the people their opponents are aliens from outer space somewhere."[115]

Republicans portrayed Clinton as lacking boundaries, a grotesque, shapeless body. "Bill Clinton is always on both sides of the issue," accused George Bush. "You cannot define yourself by being all things to all people," charged the Bush campaign's political director. "[Clinton]'s a pastel water-color with all the hues running into each other. There are no hard edges to this guy."[116] Republicans contrasted this image of grotesque promiscuity to George Bush.

Here's a guy who fought in one war, who led the world community in a war against an aggressor in the Middle East, which was a crisis of unique proportions in modern presidencies and one in which he was tested under fire and performed extremely well.[117]

The candidate debates launched the phase of the campaign when voters began to ask seriously, "Do I really want to marry this guy?"[118] Mating potential was measured in fighting qualities. "I've listened to all their macho talk," complained Bill Clinton when George Bush dithered over scheduling, "but when it comes time to go man to man, plan to plan, where is he?"[119] Clinton said Bush should run for First Lady instead of President. Bush described "Clintonesia," in which the sufferer showed "weak knees, sweaty palms and an incredible desire to say anything on all sides of any issue."[120] Republicans worked to feminize their opponent. He had dodged the draft, he wanted to open the military to gays, he couldn't control his wife.

The Bush campaign made its final appeal on the issue of trust, a concern of lovers and comrades. It was too late. As Joe Klein of *Newsweek* observed, "People all year said they believed George Bush just didn't care about them very much, and in our exit polling, that shows as one of the major reasons why people voted for Bill Clinton."[121] Clinton had the fertility symbolism wrapped up. The soubriquets "Sweet William" (a flower favored for its vivid, fragrant blossoms) and "Slick Willie" suggested

SIGNE
PHILADELPHIA DAILY NEWS
Philadelphia
USA

Cartoonists & Writers Syndicate

9.5 Marriage between affiliative women and totem suitor "delivers" newly incarnated infant totem. Cartoon parody of 1992 totem creation rites.

womanizing. Reporters dubbed the photo opportunities in which the candidate hugged women, "clutch shots." "I like strong women," said Clinton, the candidate close to his mother. "Clinton puts all of us in touch with our sexuality," observed a *Village Voice* reporter. Norman Mailer thought he had "the capacity to warm the country up." A *Spy* magazine poll showed that 70 per cent of readers thought Clinton would make a better lover. Only 6 per cent chose Bush. Clinton led early among women:

because of his commitment to choice; because his marriage seemed more emblematic than his adultery; and perhaps because of the way he said, "I really need your help."[122]

A week before the election, polls showed Clinton with 45 per cent of the vote, well ahead of Bush. He was said to have the power to fertilize other Democratic candidates. Expressing her willingness to unite with the candidate in an act of political reproduction, California Senate candidate Barbara Boxer declared, "If he has coattails, I'll take them, and if I have skirttails, he can have them."[123]

Election night – wedding and consummation

Consider the language of death and rebirth in a Chicago precinct captain's preparations to raise up a president: "I've been buried alive by Reagan Democrats for 12 years, but not today." While voters "slept as quiet and still as the grave of the legendary machine boss, Richard J. Daley," this precinct captain

arose as the generations before him had done: his grandmother, Anne Murphy Lyons, precinct captain at the turn of the century; and his father, Joe Lyons, Sr., now retired but once a captain among captains.[124]

Fertility overtones in election narrative strike even children. "The last time I remember such tension, I was a kid," said a voter, recalling the 1960 contest between John Kennedy and Richard Nixon. "When I went to bed, Nixon was ahead and when I woke up Kennedy had won. It felt like magic."[125] Children sense the electricity in the air, the sexual tension around the anticipated mating ceremony. Something happens at night when the children are asleep in their beds. When morning comes, there is a new reproductive outcome. This is the Christmas story. The holy couple comes to the inn on Christmas Eve. On Christmas Day the promised child-savior appears. Comedian David Letterman complained about the onslaught of television advertisements toward the end of the campaign, "Election Day has gotten to be so commercialized that people forget it's about Jesus."[126]

On election night Democratic National Committee chair Ron Brown sounded the code words of electoral fertility:

One of the reasons why Bill Clinton's message has resonated so strongly around America is it's a message of unity, of bringing our people together, of making us one nation, of forgetting about these so-called wedge issues that Republicans love to identify that splinter and tear us apart, but rather to build bridges so that we look to the future with hope and optimism.[127]

As priestly messengers declared a Clinton victory, 40,000 supporters at the governor's mansion in Little Rock cried,"We love you, Bill." The president-elect articulated their hopes for a fertile outcome: "In massive numbers the American people have voted to make a new beginning." His thankyous conjured up mating pairs: himself and his wife; himself and his daughter whom he thanked "for reminding us what this election is really all about;" himself and his running mate ("I want to tell you that Al and Tipper, Hillary and I have become friends"); himself and his staff; himself and the outgoing president who, in a sporting phone call, offered to work with Clinton in effecting a smooth transition. Clinton welcomed "the new blood" in Congress. He appealed to opposition voters to mate with his administration. "I know you love your country . . . I ask you to join with us in creating a re-United States." On-scene reporter Chris Bury described supporters shouting and hugging one another. "There's a great sense of bonding, and a great sense of continuity here." The *New York Times* described the "kissing couples and conga lines on the lawn of the Old [Arkansas] State House" following the main event.[128]

For Ross Perot, with 19 per cent of the vote, more than the polls had predicted, the night was also cast in victory terms. Perot, the suitor, urged his supporters on with promises of mating and sacrifice:

We will stay together, and you will be a force for good for our country and our children . . . I want you to know that our love for you and my love for you is permanent, and I will carry the memory of these past few months with me the rest of my life, and I am available to you any time, any place, anywhere, as long as I'm around.

Ritual uncertainty

Following the New Hampshire primary, an episode of the television sitcom *Northern Exposure* portrayed a mayoral election in Cicely, Alaska, an idealized small town whose fictional doings were the subject of the series.[129] The episode narrates a totem creation myth. Visually packed with popular flags, it depicts election as a contrived fertility rite. Cicely has never had an election, but Edna Hancock, one of the town's earliest settlers, is vexed at

Mayor Holling Vincoeur's failure to erect a promised stop sign. She challenges him to an election. Here is a contrived group crisis full of ritual uncertainty. Ed, an "honest" Indian character, confides to the doctor his symptoms of bodily "tension" brought on by divisions in the town around the election. Only fertile union will resolve these divisions and permit the community to move forward.

The contrived crisis is a battle of the sexes played out in sniping between the romantic leads, Joel and Maggie. Joel compares elections to baseball, the male regenerative sport. He offers sports-like statistics about winners and losers. Maggie offers a woman's perspective:

MAGGIE: For your information, Fleischman, elections are more than just statistics.
    It's emotions, people, ceremony.
JOEL: You make it sound like a wedding.
MAGGIE: Well, it is like a wedding. Sort of. Well, look, we come together in the sight
    of God to commemorate an important event, and in that respect it's like a
    wedding. And like a wedding there should be a certain decorum. I mean, Mother
    said the appearance should always be memorable.

By election day, even the mild-mannered incumbent is earnestly engaged in contrived sacrificial strife against his female challenger:

HOLLING: Two days ago, if Edna Hancock had been elected mayor, I might have
been able to live with it. Today, I'd rather be treed by hounds. I don't just want to
beat Edna Hancock. I want to destroy her. I want to fold her in two.

Ed has the last word. He describes how voting makes him feel to the town's wise woman:

I feel manly. Like a man. Ruth Ann, do you realize I did something today that I've
never done before? And it was kinda like the first time I was with Lightfeather. Well,
only that was just between me and her but afterwards, I felt kinda light. But this.
This was between me and Cicely and I don't feel light at all. I feel bigger.

The battle of the sexes is resolved in a regenerative union of the community.

Uncertainty is ritually present in elections. It is found in the dual system of sacrifice and regeneration. In election myth it presents the group as poised to disintegrate and in need of re-ordering. The final uncertainty is the election result. If voters doubt the election is free and open, that it is fundamentally uncertain, it will fail as a unifying ritual. Narrow voting margins engineered by Lyndon Johnson in Texas and Richard Daley in Illinois threw the 1960 presidential contest to John F. Kennedy, who triumphed with a mere tenth of 1 per cent of the vote. The "most celebrated, and the closest Presidential election of modern times" was rigged.[130]

Closeted with advisers, the losing candidate Richard Nixon considered whether to challenge Kennedy's victory. In the end he submitted to the appearance of a ritually uncertain election process. To cast in doubt the integrity of the election would create a genuine rather than contrived group crisis, tantamount in its destabilizing effect to exposing the totem secret in war. As in war, the secret is rarely concealed from combatants; only from the group as a whole. Collective uncertainty makes an efficacious outcome possible, but this must be expressed in a ritually proper way. The time for uncertainty is before the vote. To introduce it at the moment of ritual completion would profoundly imperil the ritual process.

Transforming magic

The night after Bill Clinton's victory, ABC aired a documentary about the "magic moment" of his transformation to president-elect.[131] Those it featured were interviewed the day before the election and during the early hours of Election Day. Though polling had convinced journalists and campaign personnel of Clinton's approaching victory, this was a ritually liminal time, the moment of maximum public uncertainty before a candidate is transformed into the president-elect. Commentators were "telling audiences less than they [knew]" by way of responding to criticism that media had disenfranchised voters in previous elections by projecting final results while western polling booths still remained open. Their restraint allowed the ritual to unfold in its appointed course. The networks knew the ritual outcome but believed they must not spoil it for the people.

Advance polling did not keep campaign operatives from ritual spellcasting. Chief strategist James Carville displayed the black gloves he intended to wear to the end: "These gloves are my lucky charm . . . I got to keep my hands clean and pure so I touch the victory." Paul Begala displayed a tie figured with "Mexican death signs." It signified the campaign's determination to give and take "no prisoners, no mercy, no quarter. We don't want to coast into this, man. We just want to drive a stake through their heart." Borders must be unambiguously defined. The enemy must be killed. Mandy Grunwald detailed another taboo observance:

How many dinners have we been out to where somebody starts thinking past November 3, and you know, what'll happen with this? Or, who'll have what job? And, literally, it doesn't take us sixty seconds for everybody to – " Don't say it! Don't say it!"

Spellcasting had taken the candidate to ten cities the last day of the campaign. Koppel described the sacrificial promise of this marathon.

It is as though Governor Clinton has made a compact with the American people. If they will only vote for him tomorrow, he will subject himself to one more day of as much pain as humanly possible.

The candidate spoke of regenerative magic:

The energy, that's what I was getting out of that crowd, you know, and they believed in me, and they had all that hope, and I somehow wanted to grasp it and take it home with me and keep it always.

Staffers signaled the approach of victory with private embraces. A fertility dance had begun. Even the candidate was "a little giddy." Ecstatic states trumpet success. "Elvis lives!" declared a staffer aboard the campaign plane, referring to Clinton's well-known interest in the dead rock star, a resurrected popular totem.

Would there be a "magical transformation" of the candidate following his victory, Koppel asked? Those closest to the president-elect certified his newly taboo status and magical powers:

I'm scared to see him the first time.   (James Carville)

He's about to pass from the role of regular human being into the role of legend . . . We're going to win, and that means that more people are going to have better jobs, people are going to pay a little less for health care, get better care, and more kids are gonna go to better schools.   (George Stephanopoulos)

It will be different. [Will you still call him by his first name?] I won't. No, not any more. He's "President-elect Clinton" as far as I'm concerned.

(Mickey Kantor, campaign chairman)

I don't know what to call him.   (George Stephanopoulos)

Asked days later if his friends were treating him differently, the victor who had cultivated a self-consciously populist image replied, "Not yet, but they're acting like they wonder if they're supposed to." At the point of totem elevation even men of the people have limits:

He turned a bit starchy when he was asked if his populism would extend to having his staff call him "Bill" rather than "Mr. President. "
"No," he said, "I don't think that's appropriate. I think that at least during working hours, we should follow the protocol. All of us should."[132]

On Election Day journalists scolded the outgoing president for touching the new totem too familiarly. The observation telegraphed who was newly taboo and who was no longer.

When Clinton showed up at the White House a couple of hours ago, George Bush was clapping him on the back saying, "Welcome, son," and now he's the President, you don't clap the President of the United States on the back, I don't think.[133]

When Clinton had been president for several weeks, observers discerned totem aloofness emerging where once a candidate had bounced high and low at the whim of the electorate. "During the campaign, the events of the day would affect his mood. His mood doesn't seem to be affected by the events of the day anymore."[134]

Incarnation

The Incarnation took place, of course, at the moment of conception in the Virgin's womb . . . The Incarnation was manifested – "revealed" only later, when the Child was manifested to the world at his birth, held in his mother's arms, shown to the Magi for their adoration. John O'Malley[135]

The day after the election, a front page photograph in the *New York Times* showed the President-elect standing before a white frame house in Little Rock.[136] A flag flew jubilantly from the porch in a perfect popular tableau. To the viewer's right was the president-elect, his mother's arm around him. He was off-balance, his left foot upended as he leaned into her for a hug. She seemed to be holding him up for all to see. This journalistic pietà revealed the totem incarnation at the moment of fullest promise, before the president-elect had sullied the hopes he represented with a single word or act. The totem nativity, or rebirth, is the outcome of a successful mating between the people and candidate. The totem restored and made flesh displays himself as the press plays the role of wise men, or symbolic Magi. Drawn by the brightest star, they take word of what they have seen to the world while pundits sing tidings.

The white frame house was a popular symbol of home and hearth, the fertile womb of the people cast as the female element in this fertility rite. In contrast to the contrapposto posture of the president-elect his mother stood with both feet firmly planted on the ground. Was he hugging her, or was she scooping him up in her arms to show to the world? The son's posture recalled the upraised foot of countless Madonna and Child portraits. The visual effect re-presented the theme of Clinton as boy savior, untested in war and even childless, according to poll research about voters' beliefs.

Leo Steinberg argues that Christ the Heavenly Bridegroom who chooses Mary as his eternal consort is iconographically descended from classical depictions of Cupid and Psyche, in which Cupid gestures affectionately toward Psyche to show erotic attachment without sexual union. Historically, this ambiguity allowed some later pietàs to be read both as the Virgin with her dead son and as a young woman grieving for a lover.[137] Such

9.6 Newborn totem presented for sacrifice in popular pietà.

maternal and erotic associations were present in a post-election political cartoon by Signe Wilkinson of the *Philadelphia Daily News*. The women's vote is depicted as a young matron cradling the president-elect, a smiling happy baby (one foot upraised!), as she steps across the threshold of the White House, wedding-style, for the consummatory act. Pietistically, the image combines natalism and fertility. Clinton is child and bridegroom.[138] At a dinner for the president-elect at the home of Pamela Harriman, the Democratic matriarch whose political protégé Clinton was, the scene was ritually resonant:

Clasping his hand firmly in hers, she led Mr. Clinton, pink-faced and smiling, from group to group, introducing him to those few he did not know.[139]

In the *Times* photo of morning-after celebration, the flag flapped gaily next to the re-embodied totem in a nativity portrait proclaiming the humanation of divinity for the task of redeeming the group. We know the savior's divinity is expressed in ultimate sacrifice. But this was a moment of thanksgiving to the transcendent totem who is known by his son who becomes flesh and dwells on earth. The people hope the re-embodied totem will renew the country, save it from corruption, and re-create it through sacrifice.

The morning after the election Clinton offered himself for feasting. Regretful at not having seen everyone at his victory party, he remarked, "That's the first thing I thought, that I wish somehow there had been more of me to go around."[140] The new president was a delectable dish, the feast at the people's table, who is brought down to nourish them when the time is right. He reminded his audience of ghost fathers demanding their due in an unbroken cycle of sacrifice and regeneration:

America has called upon me to be our next President. But our forebears call on all of us at this moment to honor their efforts, their sacrifices, their ideals and their lives by working hard and working together to improve this good and great nation as much for our children and our children's children as those who preceded us did for us.[141]

The process of messianic reconstruction had begun, not because Clinton's presidency was messianic, but because this is what groups seek from totem leaders. A Clinton coordinator recalled the "biblical sense of mortality" that had gripped supporters in the last week of the New Hampshire primary. "Talk about walking through the valley of the shadow of death," said the organizer. "He was in an inferno. And he absorbed it, stood in the middle of it like frozen granite."[142] What was being out of power like? "It was like having been a member of a religious minority in a country with a state religion," explained an aide to the Democratic House majority leader.[143] This fate awaited Republicans, predicted a GOP consultant. "The party will be searching for its soul in the wilderness for several years at least."

At Bill Clinton's church the Sunday after the election:

The Rev. Rex Horne preached from the Book of Genesis today, telling the story of how Abraham survived God's test of asking him to sacrifice his son, Isaac.

The white-haired man in the fourth row listened carefully, and if he failed to make the biblical connections to his own life, Mr. Horne explained it for him in his sermon.

"Life is a succession of tests," he said, looking directly at Bill Clinton.[144]

The immediate sacrifice also was ritually addressed. A conservative group gathered at the Heritage Foundation to discuss the Bush defeat.

Suddenly two pranksters bearing on a platter a rubber mask of George Bush, stuffed with red crepe paper to resemble gore, and an instructional sign, "AVAILABLE FOR BEATING AND MUTILATION," marched into the Heritage auditorium and up the aisle – and post-election dejection gave way to frenzied ecstasy. By performing the pagan rite of symbolic beheading, the disinherited scions attempted to exorcise the Bush curse.[145]

Rites of renewal

At these times Washington is like an old courtesan taking a new lover.
Russell Baker[146]

What range of roles may an embodied totem play? The entire totem holy family is available, but particular roles reflect the opportunities of circumstance. In 1992 the bridegroom presided over voting, the infant graced the inauguration. Media framed Clinton as a small boy, his campaign a children's crusade.[147] Clinton and Gore were "the political offspring of John F. Kennedy and the spirit of the New Frontier," said Tom Brokaw.[148] In a musical variety show staged for the president-elect and the nation on the eve of inauguration, traditional "patriotic flagwavers" were recast as "lullabies," according to a critic's description.[149] It was said the new president would take the oath of office on a childhood Bible. He was celebrated in T-shirt souvenirs of "Bill and Al's Excellent Adventure," a reference to a popular comedy portrayal of immature adolescents. "Infant Administration Tackles Full-Grown Workload," was a headline the day following the inauguration.[150]

Commenting on Clinton's relationship to his wife, journalist Sally Quinn evoked the image of mother and child. "Clearly he is very dependent on her in a lot of ways."[151] When Clinton's health care plan foundered, R. W. Apple Jr. wrote, "The question . . . is how long the President, whose attention can wander like a teen-ager's on Saturday night, manages to keep himself squarely on target."[152] As Republican challengers pondered the next presidential election, epithets of childishness abounded. "If we've learned anything in the last two years," former Vice-President Dan Quayle declared, "it is that the world's only superpower can ill afford to elect a President who needs training wheels."[153] Columnist David Broder spoke of the image of a "loquacious, self-centered youth who somehow slipped into the Oval Office."[154]

The inauguration, a popular carnival, provided the occasion for "Washingtonians and visitors [to seize] what seemed like a good excuse to paint the town red, white, and blue." Grotesque and fertile elements of destruction and reconstruction were abundantly present. Russell Baker described a regenerative feast of political patronage fueled by:

> Greed for money, influence, jobs, taxpayer-subsidized cars, promotions, unlimited expense accounts, partnerships, real-estate killings, titles, servants, retinues, private-plane privileges, invitations to dine, chairmanships, cabinet positions, for seeing onself praised by notorious newspaper columnists as brilliant, for being introduced to members of the opposite sex as powerful.[155]

The Democratic Party issued joke presidential seals bordered in white with a red and blue legend, "The Inauguration of Bill Clinton: Inhale to the Chief." Parsed flag T-shirts, hats, buttons, balloons, and other keepsakes dotted the inaugural Reunion on the Mall. Over two days 700 groups entertained 600,000 people.[156] Wearing an enormous blue taffeta ballgown with a red and white sash, Diana Ross sang at the Lincoln Memorial. Patriotic fireworks followed her performance.

Pre-inaugural partygoers "braved traffic jams, interminable airport taxi lines and other inaugural hazing rituals, all the while clutching their white chocolate White Houses and other party favors."[157] Citizens came from around the country for "a bite and a hug" with the president-elect.[158] Slick Willie's, a new Washington restaurant, offered Big Willieburgers, Arkansas Chicken, and Sloppy Al's.[159] The new president was described as a junk food addict, a clear grotesque body. He was said to have reformed with the election, a grotesque body no more. The notion of a "full plate" for Clinton appeared early and often.[160] "Mr. Clinton and those who work with him are about, in a way, to get fried in history's frying pan," warned Reagan speechwriter Peggy Noonan.[161]

At the climax of the regenerative inaugural eve gala, "An American

Reunion," pop diva Barbra Streisand licked her lips over the president and vice-president and offered "grace" for the repast America was about to enjoy:

I know that grace is something said before a meal. But I feel that America has a great feast before it. And so perhaps a grace of sorts is appropriate. I'm thankful . . . especially for the new leadership that will take us forward to a time of hope and healing.[162]

A feast song in this context, her remarks introduced, "God Bless America."

"Let us begin anew"   John F. Kennedy, 1960

The inauguration christens the chosen son. It is the ceremonial dedication of a promised child conceived in the fertility rite of election. To Jimmy Carter this moment was "the ultimate in mutual commitment between our people and our government."[163] Speechwriter Ray Price called it the "supreme sacrament of the democratic process." The newly embodied totem sacrificially promises himself, and there is a killing of the old king. Walter Cronkite called the inauguration "the satisfaction of two apparently contrary desires, for change and for permanence." Rituals resolve contradiction.

As the day dawned, radio and television kept up a running commentary. Reporters told anecdotes, recounted precedents and "re-capped" events to accomplish the priestly task of instructing devotees and locating the latest ceremony in a long line beginning with George Washington. As the old and new presidents journeyed together from the White House to the Capitol, network anchor Dan Rather was mindful of his responsibility to instruct the television audience in proper religious feeling:

As you watch it on television, you sometimes don't absorb the emotion of these moments as people do who are watching live along the parade route. If an American inauguration can't bring a lump to your throat and a tear to your eye, if you don't feel as corny as Kansas in August, maybe you need a jump start and some vitamins.[164]

Anchor Tom Brokaw rekindled memories of totem successions past as the Clinton motorcade traveled its appointed route.

So many triumphs and tragedies here on Pennsylvania Avenue – the site of the funeral of John F. Kennedy; the triumph, of course, just a few years before, of his arrival in this capital. The street down which Franklin Roosevelt proceeded to the White House for his inauguration, and it was down this street as well that his casket was borne. I remember vividly the night that Richard Nixon was forced to resign from the presidency, a great mixture of solemnity and and sorrow and celebration on the part of a lot of people who were happy to see him go. Jimmy Carter walked down this street, Ronald Reagan came down Pennsylvania Avenue after having happily announced that the hostages were free. George and Barbara Bush four years ago, and now the turn of Bill and Hillary Clinton.[165]

Other commentators repeated inaugural folklore beyond the living memory of viewers. Based on frequency of mention, Kennedy and Roosevelt remained the most significant totem avatars for living Americans. Speculation about the upcoming inaugural speech inevitably recalled Kennedy's sacrificial invitation, "Ask not what your country can do for you; ask what you can do for your country."[166] In the campaign Clinton often compared himself to Kennedy, the totem forebear who, a pundit observed, had been "haunting the presidency."[167] By remodeling Kennedy, Clinton offered himself for renewing sacrifice. The *New York Times* mythically commemorated the Kennedy inaugural:

For many Americans the inauguration of a new President calls to mind the flickering, black-and-white images of that bitterly cold day in 1961 when John F. Kennedy took the oath of office and Robert Frost recited a poem . . . [Michael] Blimes, who was a sixth grader in Ridgecrest, Calif., when Kennedy was inaugurated, said he remembers a time when people believed "all things were possible."

But if the old sense of idealism is gone, the words of another young President, as well as the words of another poet, Maya Angelou, helped bring back the sense of possibility.[168]

"The best word to describe this day," said a reporter, was *hope.*[169] Regeneration was in the air, "a great national revival meeting," said Daniel Schorr.[170] Invited to speak at the inaugural ceremony, poetess Maya Angelou spoke of feeling like "a seed rolling around in somebody's hand."[171] In morning services at the Metropolitan AME Church, the president-elect was told, "You have invited all who will to be partners in forming a more perfect union . . . We can, we must, and we will say, 'Yes! Yes! Yes!'" Fertile pairings were on display: the new president and his wife, the president and the people, the president and vice-president, the president and Congressional leadership.

The new and departing president formed a final critical pair. The *New York Times* described them as the ceremony began: the president-elect whose "wide grin" suggested a grotesque, orificed body and the outgoing president who walked to his seat "hardly acknowledging the lawmakers, Supreme Court Justices and others already seated,"[172] dressed in a dark suit and tie as if "for his own funeral,"[173] an invisible, departed ghost already. The key to the day's "magic," said journalist David Gergen, was those "few moments when both the outgoing president and the incoming president together give everybody a sense of reassurance that power is peacefully transferring."[174] This is the language of fertile pairing. It is worth noting the founding fathers envisioned a presidential election in which the winner would be president and the loser would be vice-president.

The main events of the inaugural ceremony are the installation of the newly embodied totem in the presence of the witnessing nation and the sharing of the totem vision. On the inaugural stand in front of the Capitol vertical red and white panels were topped by draped clouds of bunting with white stars on a blue field. Above the stand and behind it were seven American flags from different historical periods to suggest the continuity of the nation. At exactly noon, halfway between the sunrise of a new presidency and the sunset of a departing one, the presidential oath was administered. The Marine Band played "Hail to the Chief" to the accompaniment of twenty-one guns, the highest totem honor. Promising not to "betray" his supporters, Clinton presented himself as a suitor whose bride was the people. He spoke of celebrating "the mystery of American renewal" and "embracing" the time.[175] "There isn't anybody on the platform who hasn't gotten a Presidential hug," said editor Hendrik Hertzberg.

Four years earlier George Bush had said, "This is a day when our nation is made whole, when our differences for a moment are suspended." A ritual task of the inaugural is to heal divisions in the electorate and unify the president and the people. Its efficacy was evident in pilgrim testimony:

REPORTER MARGARET LARSON: Cathy was a Bush supporter, and has changed her mind, and what is the reason for that?
CATHY: I'm excited. I like what he has to say, the unity, I feel it with the people. I'm out here today. I've been here since 8:30 this morning, and I'm really excited.[176]

This citizen, who had voted for another candidate, told of waiting patiently for the newly embodied totem in an act of piety, and of religious ecstasy in comtemplating him. Another flagwaving devotee had come because, "This is the man that we voted for and put into office, and we'd like to welcome him." Her husband chimed in, "She wants a kiss from him." A third echoed traditional myths of holy impregnation through spirit or breath. "I'm looking for a fresh wind to blow in and better days for our country."[177]

The inaugural parade is marked by lavish displays of parsed flags and flagwaving that signify the people's embrace of the sacrificial compact.

Then the flags began to wave, first for a moving van that rolled down Pennsylvania Avenue, then for police cars, motorcycles and the color guard. Then they swirled furiously, like leaves in a storm, for the new President.[178]

Reporters repeatedly described the ritual:

We're seeing a lot of American flags being waved. There've been [Navy Seabees] who've come by earlier passing these flags out. People have been very generous in passing them back to the folks who didn't have such great seats so that everyone could pay homage to this country and to the new President . . . Everybody here, as you can see, waving the flag, letting out a cheer, waiting to greet the new President.[179]

There are millions and millions of little miniature flags being waved all over the place . . . a sort of sea of little American flags and a lot of very excited people.[180]

The announcer here locally just said that Bill Clinton was on his way and the crowd literally went bananas, just an explosion of American flags, and red, white, and blue pompoms, everybody waiting to see the president.[181]

The people bring the kingship to life by waving totem wands. Re-creating him, they re-create the group. The reconstituted group symbolizes itself. At the inauguration spectators carried flags, wore parsed flag buttons, starred and striped bows, flag shirts and hats, and partook of a huge red, white, and blue layered cake offered on the Mall. Along the parade route every crowd shot featured waving flags and parade barriers draped in red, white, and blue bunting.

In the evening inaugural balls attracted the famous and powerful to "rub shoulders" with the president, a veiled mating metaphor. Film stars from the pantheon of popular fertility gods and goddesses were prominently featured. "We elected this man. He is of the people. We chose him," said Barbra Streisand.[182] Lauren Bacall echoed her: "I'm so thrilled to see two young guys. I think it's exciting. I have tremendous hope; I haven't been this excited in years."[183] At a White House reception the next day Clinton laid hands on the young, the old, the sick, and other awestruck wellwishers. A Los Angeles couple brought their infant son because, "We wanted to have him shaking your hand for his infomercial when he runs for President."[184] They hoped to model the magical anointing of the boy Clinton, himself the recipient of a priestly laying on of hands by a totem avatar. Regeneration is, after all, for regenerates. "It's a very good for kids every four years to watch something like this," said Peggy Noonan.[185]

Disemboweling the totem

The sovereign . . . exists only for his subjects; his life is only valuable so long as he discharges the duties of his position by ordering the course of nature for his people's benefit. So soon as he fails to do so, the care, the devotion, the religious homage which they had hitherto lavished on him cease and are changed into hatred and contempt; he is dismissed ignominiously, and may be thankful if he escapes with his life. Worshipped as a god one day, he is killed as a criminal the next.   Sir James Frazer[186]

Inauguration invests the president with magic powerful enough to cure what ails the people. Central to this process is the willing sacrifice of the outgoing president. His reununciation prepares the ground for what Bill Clinton called the "forced spring" in his inaugural rendering of the vision accorded him as totem. While willing sacrifice is contrived in the four-year election cycle, the people adjust these intervals by sacrificing or embracing incumbent presidents or parties as their mood demands. An important inaugural theme is the suffering and death of the outgoing president. Until more dramatic sacrifice comes along, the painfully visible abdication of the leader helps restore the community. A trio of NBC newsmen observed that there had not been so many living ex-presidents at an inauguration in years. John Chancellor recalled *Louisville Courier-Journal* editor Henry Watterson's proposal for ex-presidents: "Take them out and shoot them."[187] Presented with this taboo, the group laughed uproariously. Theirs was at once the joyful, celebratory dance of a community unifed by an aggressive act against the body of the deposed king and a denial that any such sacrifice was permitted.

Since ex-presidents are not shot and are well-cared for at public expense, the media must work to establish that surrender of power is wrenching and a price is being paid. Ritual efficacy increases with the sacrificial measure. Much was invested in tokens of the suffering George Bush. The deposed president was said to be "deeply depressed."[188] For Bush "the publicly painful, personally public part of this loss cannot be underestimated," said Mark Shields.[189] Commentators speculated about the prospect facing a rejected suitor of the nation.

Consider George Bush, who has just lost an entire country. At sixty-eight, George Bush is experiencing what is difficult to endure at any age: a broken heart at the hands of people who he had reason to believe loved him as much as he loved the post they had elected him to fill ... There is something cruel about a ceremony that compels the loser, like a discarded spouse, to watch the remarriage of his partner to another.[190]

The ex-president was beyond the reach of the living. Referring to George and Barbara Bush, commentator Jim Lehrer speculated, "The pain that these people must feel must be beyond anything that ordinary mortals like you and I can even imagine."[191] Acknowledging the deadly price of leadership, several commentators recalled that "Jimmy Carter has shown that there is life after the presidency."[192] A guest at a small dinner in the family dining room on George Bush's last night in the White House called it a "kind of a last supper, I guess."[193] *Life* magazine described the Bushes receiving the consoling cheers of the White House staff.

The camera caught them standing like figures in a wax museum, arrested in a frieze of defeat . . . George Bush waving numbly, like a man recovering from electroshock therapy, Barbara Bush grim, a face at a funeral.[194]

Poll ratings showed Bush with a 62 per cent outgoing favorability rating compared to 51 per cent during the election, suggesting that the public appreciated his sacrificial performance.

Current suffering was compared to legendary totem degradations. "When Lyndon Johnson left at the end of his term and flew to Texas in Air Force Two," recalled David Brinkley, "they took his baggage off the plane, set it down on the ground and flew away. He was infuriated! Because prior to that they'd had limousines and people to move his baggage, and so on. They put his bags on the ground and left!"[195] The story depicted the literal deposing of a totem leader, the depth of his descent symbolized in the physical distance between the heaven-bound plane and the earthbound ex-president, an unimaginably impotent ghost totem whose wrath until then had commanded legions. "It must be one of the most difficult transitions a person could make . . . everything is done for you," observed Peter Jennings, describing the special treatment accorded those who are called to die.[196] A *Newsweek* reporter recalled the "feeding frenzy" by a dozen handpicked reporters and photographers who rode on Air Force One with the departing Gerald Ford to California. Symbolically cannibalizing the deposed president, the reporters looted notepads, matchbooks, menus, cigarettes, pillows, blankets, silverware, napkins, candy dishes, a set of tumblers bearing the presidential seal, even the fruit basket.[197]

Defeated after three terms, Governor Mario Cuomo of New York depicted the sacrifice of losing in religious terms.

[Campaigns] start with conjecture and hope, they are filled with unexpected gifts, undeserved rejections, inexplicable pain, incredible joy, confusion, vindication, everything . . . How do they end? I come from a religion where the whole symbol of the religion ended in condemnation and crucifixion.[198]

To surrender power is to relinquish a sacrificial burden.

When a rabbi, a longtime friend, called to tell Mr. Cuomo that he would find his defeat liberating, Mr. Cuomo said: "Rabbi, thank you very much, but who wanted to be liberated?"

"It's like we're all putting this weight on his shoulders," mused a citizen observer about the president-elect.[199] "We have chosen him freely," said Jimmy Carter. "He owes us a lot."[200] As media priests reviewed the recent trend of one-term presidents, Charles Kuralt said, "We are pretty hard on our presidents, I think, Dan, and this one, who is now performing his first duties of office in the Capitol building may as well know that we're going to be hard on him."[201] The transition having been made, the new sacrifice had begun. It was led by the press "before the groom had got to the church, before he'd bought the ring, before he'd even made the proposal."[202] A president must deliver on his promises. Bryant Gumbel reminded viewers, "Part of the reason George Bush is flying back to Texas right now is because he broke his pledge." "Welcome to power, Mr. Clinton," said Tom Brokaw. "The honeymoon is over."[203]

Four months into his presidency, when Clinton had a 48 per cent disapproval and 41 per cent approval rating, a reporter wrote:

Part of Bill Clinton's problem is that the citizens of the United States are ... well, to say they are vicious, backbiting cretins might be too strong. They can be selfish and whiny and supremely ungrateful, and right now they've had it up to here with these bozo politicians.

Bill Clinton would never subscribe to this unsanguine view of the public, but the fact remains that if he gets on people's wrong side they'll kick him in the ribs until they see blood on his lips.

"The people have been in a nasty mood," said Gordon Hoxie, president of the Center for the Study of the Presidency. "What was aimed at Bush is now aimed at the present president."[204] Hugh Sidey's evaluation of the Bush presidency in August, 1992, applied as well to Clinton shortly after his election:

What have we done to our Presidents? ... We have ... invested the poor fellow with godly power – then raised our expectations accordingly and vented almost every human frustration and anger at him.[205]

"Did the nation still respect him in the morning?" asked the *Philadelphia Inquirer* about the candidate the electorate had "married." It expected him to fulfill his "promises" and make sacrifices. "He's taking on a job that will make everybody want to kill him," a voter predicted after Clinton pledged himself and his party to reduce the deficit.[206] "He's doing something that so many other men would never try to do."

In April, 1994, with his health care plan stalled, scandals about real estate investments dogging him, and sexual harassment charges gathering steam in Little Rock, historian David McCullough described the American habit of "making our kings and then killing our kings."[207] Of the "sniping" and "growling" directed at Clinton he observed:

It is so hard, it is so unimaginably punishing, so unimaginably draining of energy and physical and intellectual vitality, to be president ... The president carries the world on his shoulders.

Ross Perot once described the presidency as "equivalent to getting up every morning, climbing in a barrel and having everyone in the world beat on the barrel with a stick."[208] "Clinton is meat on our table," said conservative satirist P. J. O'Rourke.[209]

An election, a primary season, a nominating convention. All are set pieces, contrived dramas of sex and death, symbolic disruptions of the family healed, exposed once more to disintegration and healed again, at least for the "honeymoon" after a successful electoral mating that selects and recombines appropriate ritual elements. The flexible reach of totem myth extends to a limitless variety of circumstances. Few cannot be reconstructed to reflect fundamental totem themes. In this way every election becomes a critical election that defines the country. The presence of these elements is more critical for successful totem-creation than the particular candidate elected. This does not mean that who wins the election is unimportant. But the re-creation of the group does not depend on his unique identity. The structural uncertainty of election ritual enlists public effort and attention. It also enacts a message about the long-term resilience of the community. Not one but many solutions to group problems are possible. If it is ritually faithful the group will flourish, whichever candidate is elected.

Though elections are historically specific, the totem themes they present are familiar, standardized, and in earnest. They convey what the group cannot afford to forget and do what the group must do to survive. Election brings the newly embodied totem to life in three clearly marked rites. The selection of a symbolic mating pair of candidates establishes the conditions of fertility for reproducing a ritual king. The people offer vows of fidelity to the totem. The totem's reciprocal gift is a vow of fidelity to the people. The inauguration is the dedication of a promised child, embodied and partly divine, the deferred sacrifice who will pay the blood debt that guarantees the future of the group.

In addition to these regenerative rites, there is everywhere present in the election their shadowed and inadmissible opposite. As insubstantial as an ancestral ghost, this atmosphere of talk and metaphor pervades every structured element. It is talk as regular as a drumbeat of sacrificial death and carnage, conveying the deep knowledge that the renewal of the community depends on the violent death of the king. It shows up in talk about ripping the candidate to bloody shreds and feasting on him, in talk about the destruction and suffering of the losing candidate, in talk about the symbolic death of the departing incumbent. Sacrifice holds the election together, provides the connection among its distinctly marked parts and guarantees the life of the group.

10

One size fits all: the flag industry

If sacrifice is the most important border ritual of the nation, regeneration is the ritual focus of its fertile center, which we call the popular domain. Here commerce reconstructs and nourishes the community. Without it, the community would die. But just as the community denies the sacrificial demands of the totem, the totem group denies the essential reconstructive function – and attendant sacrificial implications – of commerce. Commerce demands the surrender of money and labor to establish each member's place in the group. Elaborate and richly patterned, commercial rites confer social shame on whoever fails to participate earnestly and successfully. The result feeds and furnishes the tribe in its popular aspect. If the greatest taboos keep the group from knowing it sacrifices its own, somewhat less well-guarded taboos disguise the intercourse of the fertile center. Thus the totem is felt to be tainted by commerce. This motivates the prohibition enshrined in the civilian flag code on using the flag in advertising, despite the long and robust history of this practice.[2] Laws distancing the taboo totem from commerce have never been strictly observed, but flag emblems routinely grace products and populate advertising. Nor is advertising the sole arena where the flag has a commercial life. Another is the manufacturing industry that physically creates the flag.

As befits a popular domain enterprise, flag manufacturers are family concerns. Annin, Chicago, Collegeville, Dettra, and Valley Forge, account for more than 90 per cent of all flag manufacturing. Annin & Co., in Roseland, New Jersey, is the oldest continually operating manufacturer. By all accounts, it is also the largest. No one knows for sure because of the secretive character of the industry. Alexander Annin, a ship's chandler, founded the business in Manhattan in 1827. The Mexican War provided enough business for his sons Edward and Benjamin to devote the company exclusively to flags during the 1840s. Annin's largest competitor, Dettra, started in 1901 with a Wrigley company contract for carnival and exposition flags. All five manufacturers sell mainly to dealers, the next tier in the industry structure. Annin claims about 2,000 dealer-customers. Most buy from several manufacturers. Both dealers and manufacturers sell to K-Mart, Wal-Mart, Sears and other mass merchandisers. Some dealers dabble in direct consumer sales. A small portion do some flag manufacturing of their own. The final component of the industry consists of specialty companies that sell flag paraphernalia, such as eagles and flagpoles.

Despite occasional industry rumors of foreign-made American flags flooding the country, there is little evidence the totem product is anything but homegrown. When American inventories were depleted during the Gulf War, dealers bought from whoever would sell to them, foreign suppliers included. But there was no permanent loss of markets to overseas manufacturers. Annin president Randy Beard speaks totemically of global competition, "We have made an effort to remind the American buyer that you should draw the line somewhere, and the American flag is where you should draw the line."[3] Foreign competitors have been successful with novelty items such as parsed flags and patches, flagpole attachments, and flags for boats. Of the big five all but Chicago are located in the northeast, the heart of the nation's textile industry. Most flag industry workers are unskilled, low paid, and female. Flag shops are rarely unionized. Since flag industry workers are often first-generation immigrants, there is a romance of transformation attached to media stories about flagmakers who become Americanized through their work. There are also guilty tales about the difficult circumstances of many of these flagmothers.

Except during patriotic periods such as popular wars, volume in flag sales comes from government agencies and private business.[4] Among the big five, Annin is thought to command the largest share of government contracts. The Department of Defense, the Veterans' Administration, and the General Services Administration purchase the largest number of flags. An average order to outfit a single aircraft carrier on a fifteen-month cruise is 5,000 to 7,000 flags. Some 600,000 or 700,000 flags a year go to sea, where flags out in the weather need replacing every 96 hours.[5] Flags manufactured to totem rather than commercial specifications are more costly, since multiple regulations cover manufacturing materials, measurements, and procedures. But government work is steady and keeps plants running, and Annin even maintains permanent office space for a federal inspector who passes on all flags before the government buys them.

Flag manufacturers are famously proprietary about sales, profits, markets, and techniques. Insiders say this is because each company makes virtually the same product the same way. Flagmaking has altered little since Betsy Ross. Its last dramatic innovation was screen printing, introduced in the nineteenth century. Even this technique avails little when ceremony or durability count and only sewn flags will do. Because there are few ways for companies to differentiate or improve their products, innovations are carefully guarded. This is one competitive strategy. Finding a special market niche is another. Amidst such uncertainty, theories of sales cycles abound. One manufacturer hypothesizes that saturating a given display market takes about five years in which sales rise for two and a half years and then decline. War and the admission of new states have been the major means of channeling large numbers of individual and household buyers into their own flag purchasing cycles. Demand in response to changes in flag design or groundswells of patriotic feeling comes less from government, which buys on a steady schedule, than from households, businesses, and event organizers who respond to the publicity and excitement of particular national events and crises. Otherwise, flag demand is seasonal, accelerating in April and building to three patriotic holidays, Memorial Day, Flag Day, and Independence Day. After Labor Day, Americans take down their flags and go inside until the following year.

During the past two decades the flag business has grown steadily if incrementally. The president of Annin, Randy Beard, predicts that American flags will occupy a declining proportion of the flag business as Americans become more globally focused and ethnic identity becomes more celebrated. But Brian O' Connor of Humphrys Flag next to the Betsy Ross House in Philadelphia argues that growing restrictions on commercial urban signage have drawn entrepreneurs more and more to flags and banners as inexpensive, visually appealing advertising.[6] According to Dettra president Bill Spangler, growth in the institutional and commercial market has more than outpaced declines in fraternal and community flag display.[7] Veterans' organizations have been politically eclipsed by the ageing of World War II veterans and the emergence of new affiliative struggles. Commercial flag display has supplanted local patriotic celebrations in small towns swallowed by urban sprawl. Finally, population and household growth have increased the number of schools, post offices, real estate offices, banks, and other places that display flags.

In the twentieth century the greatest jump in flag demand came at the end of World War II when President Eisenhower took the military out of the uniform and flag manufacturing business. The Korean War stimulated demand but was neither a peak or valley. The admission of Alaska and Hawaii in short order visibly reinvigorated demand that had languished after World War II. The Vietnam War accelerated demand both among protesters who carried the flag and those determined to outwave them. The 1976 Bicentennial and Desert Storm in 1990 were bookends on a decade of growth that also ratcheted up the demand floor. Ronald Reagan gets credit from manufacturers for being "a real drum major, he got in front of the parade and pumped everyone up," according to Bill Spangler. The kidnapping of American hostages by Iran "excited" rather than changed the market. And finally, says Spangler, "During the buildup of troops for Desert Storm, flag sales were very good, but the minute the war started, flag sales went through the roof."

Nothing in recent memory matches the flagbuying craze of the Gulf War. The weekend before hostilities began, Annin's fax machines were pumping out orders twenty-four hours a day. On what became known as War Thursday, the third day after the American ultimatum for Iraq to withdraw from Kuwait, Dixie Flag Company of San Antonio had the biggest day in its thirty-year history, selling 5,000 flags.[8] Day in and day out, war or no war, the perennial large-volume sellers are handheld 4" x 6" flags and their cousins. At Dixie Flag the most popular Gulf War item was an 85–cent Stars and Stripes designed for car radio antennae. At Dettra, 3' x 5' flags for householders were especially popular. Elevated everywhere, flag demand lasted from the buildup preceding the war to July 5 when it simply died.

Though Americans often sewed their own flags during the nineteenth century when there was no codified flag standard and no urgency about enforcing one, the flag business has always flourished. With fifty stars and thirteen separate stripes in two different colors, American flags are difficult to make by hand if someone will do it for a fee. With a taboo artifact for a product, however, the symbol-conscious flag industry has unique marketing problems. For one thing, excess inventory must be carefully disposed of. At Annin, it is dismantled with special shears. But mistakes occur. We heard several versions of the following story from industry insiders. The existence of different versions suggests the value of a cautionary tale about what happens when ritual procedures to ameliorate dangerous magic are neglected. This version comes from an industry executive. After the Gulf War many flag vendors were left with large inventories. One wholesaler of printed goods ended up with thousands of yards of cotton fabric printed with 4″ x 6″ flags. Such printed sheeting is usually disposed of by dyeing it black and selling it at a loss for furniture ticking. This merchant neglected to convert his stock to black goods before selling it. It ended up in Haiti as stuffing for furniture that was eventually shipped back to the United States. A minor scandal occurred when consumers discovered their pillows were stuffed with hacked up American flags.

Flag decorating

A unique niche in the flag business is occupied by a dwindling number of entrepreneurs who decorate communities with flags and bunting for patriotic holidays and civic events. One of the oldest continually operating enterprises is Rojee Decorating Specialists of Medway, Massachusetts. Medway, population 11,000, lies halfway between Providence and Boston.[9] Joseph Rojee, its founder, is the patriarch of a clan that includes twenty-nine grandchildren and thirty-four great-granchildren. For a lark in 1935, Rojee drove an old-time "raghanger," his neighbor Frank Phillips, to Maine to decorate a small town there. Traditional American raghangers were itinerant decorators who followed warm weather and patriotic holidays on a Maine to Florida circuit. They were fabled characters, colorful individualists and artists who bought from manufacturers and dealers wherever they found them. When Phillips died the next year, Rojee bought up his stock.

For fifty years the family business he founded has deployed its artistry across the country, decorating as many as eight towns a year. The labor force is whatever family members are available. Friends and relatives begin training as children to help out. A decorating stock of 10,000 pieces is stored in a barn on the patriarchal property. New and replacement pieces are regularly built or sewn by the family. Float trailers and vehicles to haul them surround the barn. Inside is a workshop filled with float bases; stacks of red, white, and blue flat stock; bundles of bunting from long ago decorations; hundreds of display letters; a wall mounted with municipal centerpieces; rolls of floral sheeting, sequins, and glittering accessories, and tools of every description jerry-rigged by the Rojees for their needs.

The decorating business illustrates the affinity of the popular domain for commerce. For a single community celebration, local businesses generally underwrite the costs of decorators like the Rojees, of events such as centerpiece contests, and of items such as floats. Each investment may run any-where from $750 to $10,000. Since parades and celebrations draw crowds even in cold weather, local businesses consider these costs worthwhile. Though floats constitute about half their business, the Rojee family's stock in trade is its long experience decorating town halls, streets, reviewing stands, houses, and local businesses. The simplest decorative elements are bunting lengths known as "pieces." Half-fans are made from accordion-pleated lengths of flat stock stapled at the top and pulled out at the bottom. Two half-fans mounted side by side and spread in opposite directions make a half-circle, or full fan. Pull-downs are vertical strips of decorating cloth with a square field of stars at the top from which three vertical red and white stripes descend. They are often bunched and tied at the bottom. Half-fans and pull-downs may be combined to create a curtain effect. Side by side two full fans become a "butterfly." Each mounted piece is $10.00. Centerpieces cost $30.00. A typical "storefront," the term for each deco-rated building, runs around $100.00, though merchants and homeowners may opt for more elaborate or pared down embellishments. Centerpieces, the focal design element of most celebrations, are individualized for each town. These are generally 3′ x 3′ flats bearing seals or special logos designed by local decorating committees in contests that draw community partici-pants at small cost.

The decorating business works best in a small-town world where people know and trust one another. The best clients are communities where every-one knows everyone, and competitive and cooperative pressures may be brought personally to bear, where the maze of formal and informal permis-sions goes more smoothly because it can be socially lubricated. The Rojees negotiate for a basic guarantee with a local committee of merchants and citizens. A typical contract is 15 per cent of the price of each contracted storefront rebated to the committee and charged against additional decora-tion for streets, buildings, and reviewing stands. Efforts are made to drum up as much additional business as possible before the Rojees come to town. This strategy pulls in community leaders who can attract more business and collect more receipts than the Rojees could ever manage on their own. When the Rojees finally arrive about a week before the event, they move family members and friends into local motels and cottages, buy out local bakeries and patronize local restaurants. If all goes well, decorating conta-gion takes over and spreads from place to place and neighbor to neighbor. Local police, fire, and construction crews may help out with cranes and other equipment to hang pieces. The Rojees drive the floats and party with the locals when the parade is over. To support this way of doing business, word of mouth is the only advertising required.

The most important rule is preserving the family reputation for delivering the contract. This means getting the job done on time, removing it in a timely fashion, and never running out of stock. In a business of slim profit margins, entrepreneurs are generally loathe to invest in surplus stock. The Rojees relate hair-raising accounts of competitors with insufficient stock who welshed on contracts and stole into the night. They have often been called in to salvage such jobs or assist decorators whose volunteer labor failed to materialize. Running out of stock or labor is not so much a problem for the Rojees, with their years of accumulated stock and a returning clientele with familiar needs. In the early days Rojee men took bunting off the sewing machines as fast as Rojee women could produce it. Today the family relies on carefully cultivated relationships with manufacturers like Dettra, which has more than once opened its plant in the middle of the night to outfit Rojee for an unexpectedly large job. The family record is 1,000 pieces up at one time, a total that represents several jobs hanging at once.

Few competitors can mount a labor force as reliable, flexible, or well-trained as the Rojees. The children and grandchildren of Joseph Rojee are firemen, policemen, teachers, and nurses active in the civic life of Medford, a proud town in the New England tradition. They combine a community service ethic with rotating responsibilities in the family business so that someone is always available to fill in. The result is a client tradition of towns like Millis, Massachusetts, decorated by the Rojees on its 50th, 75th, and 100th anniversaries. This continuity has not been without change. Joe Rojee remembers doing twenty pieces on a storefront for $1.00. Today a center-piece and two half-fans costs $50.00. Where gas stations, barbershops, and local businesses once were first to invest in community decoration, these businesses are now owned by absentee conglomerates who may be last. Where fraternal, hereditary and veterans' organizations once were substantial underwriters of flag decoration, businesses now assume most of the responsibility. The Rojees speculate that this is because of the disappearance of World War II veterans from the scene, the relative inactivity of Vietnam veterans' organizations, and a general decline in volunteer activity. Other things are different, too. In the old days no one would touch decorations. Now merchandise not promptly removed may be stolen.

The other flag industry

The other American flag industry consists of every commercial use of flags or flag images. Officially, this industry does not exist. Its legality was ambiguous for years. It is believed to threaten the purity of patriotic emotion, but it has been in business as long as there has been a country. A primary field for articulating popular flag meaning, it combines familiar traditions of flag representation with remarkable conceptual, gestural, and visual invention. It is where most Americans encounter the flag despite denial and resistance on both moral and legal grounds. The commercial flag appears on supermarket shoppers. It flies from banks, funeral homes, insurance companies, and auto body shops. It graces clothes, sports equipment, department store windows, and every kind of advertising. It blossoms around all patriotic holidays. It is characteristically accessible. Rarely does it deliberately offend perceived limits of acceptable totem treatment, though miscalculations do occur.

Commercial flag display is flexible in its symbolic execution and interpretation. It is carnivalesque and grotesque, for it indiscriminately combines domains. It dissolves and reconstructs familiar flag meanings and practices into new ones. By no means the sole source of innovations in flag meaning, commercial flag display is nevertheless an important site. Still, resistance to such practices, and denial that they even exist, are social commonplaces. To distance itself from the taboo it violates, commercial flag display often treats itself as invisible. In the early 1990s the Resolution Trust Corporation both distanced itself from and used the flag in a striking advertisement in which the earth appears as a distant half-lit planet seen from the lunar surface on which the Apollo 11 flag flies against the dark universe. The barren lunar landscape of the foreground is broken by astronaut footprints and tractor treadmarks. "One Of The Few Properties You Won't Find When You Call The RTC," reads the caption. The reference is studiedly ambiguous. Though the property you won't find is the moon, the flag also cannot be sold in the symbolic sense. It can only be paid for with blood. The Resolution Trust Corporation was organized to buy up failed mortgages – other peoples' sacrifices. There is no sacrifice it will not repossess except the ultimate sacrifice. The Resolution Trust Corporation has a heart and conscience after all. It would not sell the flag.

Americans are not unaware that the flag occupies a prominent place in their commercial culture, but they do not like to be reminded of this fact. A *Philadelphia Inquirer* columnist wrote:

When I think of the state of patriotism in the United States of America, I think of a couple of billboards on the Schuylkill and Delaware Expressways. One is for a Top 40 radio station in which the slogan, "What the hell, here's another hit," is punctuated by an American flag displayed prominently in one corner. The other is for a casino in Las Vegas in which passing motorists are told in stark white letters on a black background, "Not since Philadelphia in 1776 has so much freedom been found in one place."[10]

10.1 Commerce shows its affinity for the parsed popular flag.

Musing on what art might emerge from the Gulf War, Vietnam novelist Robert Stone remarked, "When I think of the cultural impact of the Persian Gulf War, what I end up with literally is commercials on CNN, some of which became noticeably more patriotic."[11] In their skepticism these observers tell us the fact: the flag comes to us primarily through commercial display.

What does it mean?

"Would I buy American? Don't you see the Stars and Stripes scattered all over my body here?"   Click and Clack, the Tappet Brothers[12]

Despite efforts to distinguish them, patriotic flag display and advertising resemble and structurally complement one another. Both attach signs to motivated action. In totem practice the flag inspires killing and dying. In advertising it spurs buying and selling. The sacrificial totem imperative is to leave the group and die. The popular totem imperative is to be fertile and multiply by engaging with the group in mating exchanges, especially commercial exchanges. Both patriotic and commercial flags transform audiences into participating congregations. Both attempt to transcend mere signs and animate ideal action. Both are concerned with worth, value, and exchange; one for sacred purposes, the other for profane.

Since it is ritually required to keep the totem away from what injures it, popular discomfort with flag advertising suggests felt peril to sacred boundaries. Popular belief, legislative statute and the civilian flag code assert that advertising contaminates the flag. Since the American "way of life," the domain of cultural reproduction and creativity protected by sacrificial borders, is largely created by commerce in its material aspects, this is tantamount to saying the people sully the flag in their pursuit of domestic life. Whatever patriotic pronouncement says, popular practice reveals something different. Since the barrier between patriotism and commerce is so regularly breached, what violation occurs from their contact? What flag advertising is unproblematic, and what counts as perilous?

Commercial advertising is a carnival site where cultural forms are mixed and produced. By providing social experimentation in a licensed environment, the carnival is a permissive crucible of cultural destruction and reconstruction within an overall stability of social structure. Advertising conveys joining, revivification and nurture. It invites consumers to mate with products to furnish and rejuvenate culture. To maximize the effect of its courting behavior, advertising seeks the largest consensual space. Thus it upholds the regenerative values of family, work, and community even as it respects no particular culture and relentlessly dissects and recombines established cultural patterns. Uneasiness about the flag in commerce comes from viewing it as profane and grotesque, the very qualities that make it culturally fertile.

Notions of right action toward the flag model the distinction between sacred and profane work in traditional societies. For Durkheim work aimed solely at providing life's necessities is "an eminent form of profane activity."[13] What is universally obligatory is ritual or sacred work. In sacred work, Victor Turner explains:

> the work of men is . . . the work of the gods, a conclusion which would have delighted Durkheim, though it could be construed as implying a fundamental distinction between gods and men, since men cooperated in ritual the better to enter into reciprocal, exchange relations with the gods or with God."[14]

Soldiering is the most sacred work in the totem system. Though military service is optional in peacetime, it may be required for all fighting age males during a totem crisis. What Turner writes of tribal society – "the whole community goes through the entire ritual round, whether in terms of total or representative participation" – describes military communities and communities at war.[15] Since sacrifice governs the exchange relation between men and the totem, apprehension about commercial flag use often comes down to whether totem sacrifice is properly referenced and deferred to. Where it is, advertising will pass muster. Where it is not, fears of violation arise and action may be taken. The free and uncontrolled play of totem representations in the carnival of commerce provokes ritual anxiety for the totem's due. Only visible sacrifice appeases. When the totem benefits commerce but receives no proper offering in return, or when sacrifice is too lightly regarded, this may be of concern.

Successful consumption requires large amounts of time, effort, and capital. If all are to eat in a complex society (of which industrial capitalism is one form), everyone must consume something it would be unnecessary for them to consume just to live. Only thus does society maintain its differentiated, optative complexion. The sacrificial pursuit of consumption is thus ritually obligatory. Advertising is an ally of social structure and articulates its values. It connects consumption to the productive mainstream of society while disguising the way in which it manifests the coercive and regulatory aspects of the profane work from which consumption is said to be a reprieve. What the flag in commerce is at risk of exposing is that consumption is obligatory sacrifice in the popular domain. Group harmony requires convincing consumers that consumption is voluntary, just as soldiers must be convinced that their sacrifice is willing.

Shopping is a transaction between private identity and social convention for the sake of equipping oneself as a group member. Its sacrificial dimension makes it potent popular magic. In patriotic shopping citizens choose what suits them personally from the stock of patriotic symbols, which they in turn make available for public display to reinvigorate the stock of public symbols. This story appeared in the *Philadelphia Inquirer* shortly after the outbreak of war in the Persian Gulf.

In New Jersey, 11-year-old Ariella Jones of Westville Grove . . . [didn't] have the words to explain why she was there with a paper bag filled "with my own money." She just knew she wanted to do something. So, she marched to the most expensive shirt in the small store at Deptford Mall and pointed.

"The one with the American flag," she said, not caring that the item had a $28 price tag. "One of my friend's dads might go over there. I want this for our country," she said.[16]

The story observed that many people "were buying shirts, pins, posters and pinwheels to show their support for the troops." The generous, uncontained rhetoric of popular flag retailing contrasts with the fixed protocols and narrow specifications of totem flag practice. Commercial vocabulary conveys a vernacular appreciation of the abundantly improvised, multiple popular flag:

Step into the squat bungalow that serves as the Nebraskaland Flag shop and find any kind of flag you want: desktop, porchfront, lapel-size, room-size polyester, rayon, nylon, with or without the gold fringe. The shop will even order the 20–by–30–foot flag, for $895.[17]

If the touchy relationship between advertising and the flag retreats from public inspection, so much the better for totem dynamics. At least three strategies disguise the totem in the popular domain in order to conceal its taboo presence:

(1) Language spells inveighing against the peril to flags from advertising may simply divert attention from widespread violations.

(2) Images that reproduce standard flags may be counted as pure design distinct from "the flag itself." These images become flags once removed, or text flags. The flag on a stick that is waved, that engages the body, is designated as the only "true" flag. Parsed flag images are safer still, since they signify the reconstructed popular flag and not the taboo totem. But threat is possible even from this quarter.

(3) Finally, public sentiments wax and wane, investing more or less interest in totem protocols and observances.

Crossing boundaries – taboo artifacts for sale

The commercial flag rarely rises explicitly to public notice. It creates a ritual stir when it does. Consider two examples:

Firstly, as noted, parsed flags participate in a system of popular desecration in which the flag is dismembered and reconstructed. Since the line between permissible and forbidden desecration in the popular domain is ever-shifting, even parsed flags may cause concern. In 1991 the Office of Patent and Trademark (OTP) denied trademark protection to a condom company's logo because it would "scandalize or shock the conscience of a substantial composite of the general public."[18] The logo was an unfurled, waving condom pennant exhibiting an American flag design. It appeared in the packaging and promotional campaigns of Old Glory Condom Corporation, whose name the Trademark Office also refused to protect. The relevant section of the Trademark Act refuses protection to any mark that

Consists of or comprises immoral, deceptive, or scandalous matter which may disparage or falsely suggest a connection with persons, living or dead, institutions, beliefs, or national symbols, or bring them into contempt, or disrepute.[19]

Old Glory is the brainchild of artist Jay Critchley.[20] His company sells hundreds of thousands of condoms in an American market where hundreds of millions are sold annually. Critchley's idea began as an entry in an art show using patriotic symbols to show how Americans could fight AIDS. Backed by investors, Critchley launched his product at a press conference on Flag Day, 1990. Besides providing a high-quality condom and promoting safe sex, Critchley says his purpose was to redefine what it means to be patriotic in the 1990s. Each package of solid red, white, or blue condoms contains the Old Glory "Pledge":

We believe it is patriotic to protect and save lives. We offer only the highest quality condoms. Join us in promoting safer sex. Help eliminate AIDS. A portion of Old Glory profits will be donated to AIDS related services.

At some other time the association of Old Glory condoms with the profane disease of AIDS and non-procreative sex might have produced a vigorous popular outcry. Instead, Critchley's audiences were sympathetic and interested. Even military bases have ordered Old Glory condoms and T-shirts bearing slogans like "Worn With Pride Countrywide."

Critchley appealed the refusal. The decision of the Appeal Board to grant protection was based on the interpretation of the Trademark Act over the previous decade, during which only two marks were denied protection on "scandalous" grounds.[21] The symbolic conflation of a flag with a condom, each image individually unobjectionable, had constituted OTP's claim that the logo was scandalous. The Appeal Board noted that the examining attorney never explained why the association was scandalous. Logically, to do so would have required acknowledging the totem as sacred. The OTP attorney did describe the flag as "sacrosanct," citing totem panics such as the proposed constitutional amendment against flagburning, Chief Justice Rehnquist's claim in the flagburning case that Americans have an "almost mystical reverence" for the flag, and news stories about the reaction of veterans' groups to rock singer Madonna's public service video.

Critchley's attorney argued that among more than 1,000 marks the Trademark Office had registered for condoms, many were sexually suggestive and possibly scandalous. The Office had also granted protection to more than 1,000 marks featuring the American flag.[22] To refuse this logo was to deprive it of protection because of its political content. Critchley insisted the logo was meant to reinvigorate the concept of patriotism and use humor to overcome embarrassment about using condoms. Why did the Old Glory logo fail to produce a totem scandal? Perhaps because Critchley succeeded in associating it with sacrificial patriotism. Disciplined condom use saves lives. Such discipline constitutes a sacrifice that justifies pleasure.

Secondly, the 1992 Winter Olympics took place as the Soviet Union dissolved. The International Olympic Committee designated former Soviet athletes as members of a Unified Team symbolized by the Olympic flag. The collapse of Cold War rivalry spawned sympathy for what was no longer the Soviet team, but was not quite something else. Commercialism rushed into the vacuum of border-defining patriotic conflict. In the standard media critique the Summer Olympics was too commercial. Controversy developed around the American Olympic basketball team, the Dream Team, when superstar Michael Jordan let it be known he would not observe a US Olympic Committee regulation requiring American medalists to wear parsed-flag Reebok warmup jackets on the medal stand. Raising their arms in victory, athletes wearing these official jackets became embodied parsed flags of white stars on a blue field draping one arm, and red stripes draping the other. As the possessor of a lucrative contract with Nike, a Reebok competitor, Jordan epitomized the commercial persona of the Dream Team, which existed only because Olympic restrictions on commercially sponsored professional athletes had been lifted.[23]

The Dream Team won every game it played. There was no ritual uncertainty and little interest. The only suspense was what Michael Jordan would do on the medal stand. When the time came for the Dream Team to collect its gold medals, each of its members emerged in Reebok jackets. The three team members contracted to Nike – Jordan, Magic Johnson, and Charles Barkley – had also draped American flags over their jackets and around their shoulders. The superior magic of the totem flag either shielded the athletes from angry Nike sponsors, or purified the commercially profane Reebok logo beneath them. The one thing powerful enough to trump the magic of a parsed flag jacket was the totem flag itself.

thirtysomething

Uneasiness about commercial flag use was the focus of an episode of *thirtysomething*, a popular dramatic series about the tribulations of yuppies.[24] Michael Steadman, a principal character, is incensed by his advertising firm's efforts to piggyback a client's product on the Gulf War. Though his character has weathered many workplace conflicts, selling beer through an unearned association with flagwaving sacrifice moves him to resign in protest.[25] His sacrifice will pay for the regenerative benefit provided by the flag.

The episode chronicles Michael's agony over his decision. In a dream he conjures up a woman from the advertising campaign. She is a parsed, wrapped flagbody who wears "a one piece swimsuit, cut high on the hip. The body of the suit is red and white stripes. The bra is blue with white stars." Michael watches her gyrate suggestively, disrobing to reveal her flag bathing suit.

GIRL: Tell me this isn't brilliant. Tell me they won't eat this up with a big wooden spoon. [. . .] That St. Pauli Girl can kiss my butt. Right here you got your patriotism, you got your wholesome sex, and if that's not enough.
[She's very close to Michael as she reaches for something below the frame line. Michael instinctively flinches, but what the Girl comes up with is a burning Fourth of July sparkler which, under the circumstances, refers to the same thing.]
GIRL: Rocket's red glare. Well? How's it hitting you? What do you think?[26]

Commercial entrepreneurs devote limitless resources and skill to imitating ritual forms. Everyone knows commercial mass media performers are "just acting." They are not true ritual sacrifiers. Nevertheless, the entire perlocutionary force of commerce seeks to convince congregants that vicarious spectatorship is as good as genuine ritual behavior (itself also a model, ritually speaking), and that commercial modelers are ritually in earnest. Though advertisers profess loyalty to the established order, totem anxiety reflects a fear they will imperil it:

ANGEL: I can't believe you guys don't see the danger in this.
MARK: This isn't politics, it's commerce.

ANGEL: So, you think this is right?
MARK: No, it's not right. It's business.[27]

Miles, the advertising director, trifles with ritual practice:

MILES: It lacks . . . flags.
MICHAEL: Flags?
MILES: We should put in more flags. It's always a good idea to put in flags.
MICHAEL (to Miles): Durstin wants something patriotic, we can do that, but there's more to patriotism than flags. We can get out ahead of all that bunting if we want to.
MILES: We could do that, I suppose. But how much more beer would it sell?[28]

Michael considers the carnival, where meanings are mixed up and reassembled. He fears that totem re-ordering is dangerous without proper sacrifice, and wonders if he has profaned ritual order.

MICHAEL: The thing that bothers me is the circus. The bumper-stickers, the T-shirts, the Gulf War trading cards; all the stuff that isn't just pro-American, but anti-everybody else. We pulled [the war] off. Barely got our hair mussed. What does that mean? What are we going to do with that? I hear a bunch of rich white guys talking about a "New World Order" and it gives me the shakes. Am I one of those white guys? Am I selling the "New Order"?[29]

After Michael proposes a loftier, less commercial message, and Miles rejects it, he has a second dream.

MICHAEL: Ah, where am I?[30]
GIRL: America, pal! Where the hell did you think you were?
MICHAEL: Who are you?
GIRL: I'm the ideal. I'm what all the fighting's about. The strawberry blonde with corn-flower blue eyes and a Miss America smile. My hobbies are cooking, sewing, and helping the poor. My heroes are George Bush and Julia Roberts, not in that order. I believe in the traditional family, old fashioned Christmases, and I make love like a crazed animal . . . but only if we're married.[31]

Where the totem is concerned, sex must be paid for through the sacrifice of marriage and family at least, and from time to time, much more.

Sacrificially correct flags

Television commercials often feature the flag. In 1991 Dean Witter Financial Services used it to dramatize the company's bailout of Harley-Davidson, the only American-owned motorcycle company, which had been on the verge of takeover by Japanese investors. The advertisement is a narrative about transforming affiliative villains into team members. In it, black leather-jacketed bikers ride down Wall Street to the temple of the New York Stock Exchange. Sidewalk spectators include a blond child waving an American flag, a pointed contrast to the bad company of black leather jackets. The bikers ride into the New York Stock Exchange. They pass beneath a large American flag that licks the transom over the entrance. The flag marks the border these death-touchers have been outside. A living flag-in-motion, it also transforms and resurrects them as insiders. His helmet off, his jacket exchanged for a business blazer, the president of Harley-Davidson smiles at the assembled stockbrokers, who clap. Church music swells. A narrator declares that Harley-Davidson was brought back to life "three days from extinction." There may be money-changers in the temple, but they are agents of resurrection and rebirth like the blond child. Not only Harley-Davidson is transformed, but business itself.

A 1990 Maxwell House Coffee television commercial portrayed a small town café with black and white men in suspenders and fedoras drinking coffee while flags and veterans pass by in a local parade. Everyone drinks coffee, just as everyone is a citizen under the flag. The message is that Maxwell House traditions are as rooted as patriotic ones and indistinguishable from them, in any case. The commercial is filmed in the sepia tones of American nostalgia, except for the flag, which appears in color at the first mention of the product name. A Marine wearing a contemporary uniform sits inside the coffee shop. Outside, an African–American Army soldier leads a column of veterans in uniforms from two world wars. Though civilian clothes recall the 1940s, black and white men sit together in the coffee shop, and a black soldier leads the parade. A motherly waitress serves coffee to male patrons while a white cheerleader twirls her baton behind the black soldier who bears the flag. Civilian marchers carry a large, billowing flag horizontally. Bystanders include avuncular white men and a small boy who doffs his hat when they do, just as he will drink coffee one day because they do, for this is an advertisement about rituals and modeling. The shamanistic vernacular flag is associated with the democratic coffee that everyone can drink, whatever their race, creed, or color. The setting is utopian America, timelessly locked in small-town values, though with reference to contemporary notions about the sacrificial equality of race, symbolized by war veterans (but less contemporary notions of gender, since a waitress serves the men and a drum majorette is on sexual display).

The missing war in this advertisement is Vietnam, which marks it as pre-Gulf War. Its imagined target audience is described in a newspaper article about Lincoln, Nebraska, citizens anticipating a Fourth of July parade:

Vera Sautter, a volunteer at a senior citizens' center in this parched prairie town, remembers when people bought war bonds and followed serials on the radio and when grown men took their hats off when the flag passed by in a parade.

Those were the days before Vietnam and Watergate and assorted crises surrounding anything from oil to the hostages in Iran, the days when people were not embarrassed to say they were American and patriotism was right up there with Hula Hoops and apple pie.

Now radio has largely given way to television, grown men are more likely to wear earrings than hats and protesters are as quick to condemn the flag as to salute it. But the Persian Gulf War and its afterglow have revived a 1940s kind of patriotism among many and made what was perhaps mawkish and unthinkable twenty years ago acceptable, comforting, even fashionable.[32]

The Maxwell House parade is not real, but neither is it false in any simple sense. "Real" parades are rarely composed of people one actually knows except in the smallest towns, and patriotic parades always refer to events not actually present. Just as effective advertisements model what is meaningful to audiences – respect, status, love, security – what is any ritual but a model of what is meaningful? What is any flag but a replica? Is meaning diluted for being remodeled and repeated? Not for this reason alone, since memory is the backbone of tradition. The problem gets to the heart of what a flag is. By now, we know it is a model of ultimate sacrifice. Whatever remodels or refers to that sacrifice has totem significance.

Commercial rituals

Four "Vietnam Wall" replicas designed by Habitat, Inc. of Tempe, Arizona, have toured the country since 1990. Roughly half the size of the original, the replica Walls are an enterprise of a Houston-based cemetery and mortuary corporation. Cemetery companies pay up to $5,000 to bring one to their communities. Each models the real Wall, which itself models the sacrificed dead whose names it bears. Each is presented as having its own ritual power. Promotional literature explains that duplicates of the plates for the original memorial were used to sandblast the names of the dead onto the faux reflecting granite surfaces that constitute the replicas so visitors may make rubbings, "which are taken as mementos of those lost in the conflict." Magic is thus contagiously and sympathetically transmitted from the dead soldiers to the original Wall, from the Wall to replicas, and from replicas to rubbings.

Media coverage of the replicas is characteristically respectful, offering endless examples of pious acts they have inspired and describing ritually proper reactions in detail. A well-furnished media packet contains press clippings and a complete ritual service for those who seek assistance in transmitting replica magic. So perilous to presumptions of ritual earnestness are these commercial reproductions of the authentic memorial that sponsoring companies may not use the replicas in advertising or place sales personnel at display sites. This has not kept other entrepreneurs from seeing them as natural sites for commercial activity. "Peddlers have hijacked the monument for use on everything from belt buckles to balloons."[33]

Because of its commercial nature, the ritual authority of the replica remains unstable. This columnist denounced it as false magic:

It struck me as grotesque to take this monument on the road – like a rock band, or a carnival.

I also couldn't understand how a scaled-down, ersatz monument could evoke any feeling of sympathy among visitors. To be satisfied with a fake, fiberglass Vietnam Wall is like going to the French and English pavilions at Disney World and telling yourself you've been to Europe.

Furthermore, it seemed heresy to remove the monument from its setting on the Mall in Washington, where its austere beauty and profound dignity temper the bumptiousness of other monuments.

For him the original memorial is a source of transformative magic unusual even for war memorials.

None of our public monuments – not even those paying homage to the dead of other wars – summons our deepest emotions in this way. And certainly none has the power to heal the political and private pain that wells up with the tears.

A faux "Vietnam Wall Experience" struck the columnist as absurd. "Pilgrimage is ancient and universal, an integral part of every religion. Coming to the monument is the first act of reverence toward it."

Jan Scruggs, the driving force behind the Vietnam Memorial, insists that a measure of the power of the original monument is sympathetically transferred through the replicas. "There's no way it's like seeing the real thing," but "its hold is so strong that even when it's just an imitation, it still has this strange power." Not even commercialism can overwhelm it, for commercialism is its essential vehicle.

"It's hard to believe," Scruggs says, "But people have the same reaction for a replica as they do for the real memorial. They come to the traveling wall and they leave flags, letters, poems, Father's Day cards, flowers. They stand there and they touch the names and they cry.

"You know, I'll never understand the power of this memorial, not really."

Here is proof of ritual authenticity. The replica engages not only the feelings but also the bodies of congregants. They make offerings of flags and flowers that speak to the senses. They write letters directly to the dead. They touch the sacrifices modeled in carved names and weep.

In a culture where religion is officially optional and deprived of the prestige of ultimate truth claims, denying that flag belief and practice are religious helps distance them from second-class truth carriers. The totem guarantees its sanctity by separating itself from what is conventionally religious but polluted by the onus of partial falsehood. Living religions require both sacred and popular forms. Each form requires the other to define it, but each also has essential functions. High totem traditions guard and perform the most sacred rituals, especially death rituals. Popular forms of totem religion, including commercial ones, provide places where flag meaning and practice are joined, elaborated, remembered, re-invented and discarded. Like the popular domain to which it belongs, patriotic commercial activity is an arena of fertile mixing, a contrast to high totem order. It is the hybrid marketplace, "where limit, centre, and boundary are confirmed and yet also put in jeopardy."[34] Commerce distributes the bounty of popular totem spells. It remodels totem traditions accessibly. It proves the bloodthirsty god has a beneficent face. It demonstrates that citizens embody the otherwise immaterial god in themselves, just as they also are subject to its sacrificial hunger.

11

Epilogue

> I hate women who in preference to the common good, choose for their
> own children to live.   Praxithea, *The Erechtheus*

In the creation myth of the West, Greece is the "first" Western civilization.
The Parthenon, a shining exemplar of Greek architecture, plays a special
part in it. This famous temple to the goddess Athena was built during the
Periclean golden age at the very moment that Greek culture was experi-
menting with remarkable new forms of art, thought, and politics. What our
fondest interpretive traditions see in the Parthenon – clarity, serenity, and
calm beauty – are taken to be the qualities of the civilization that conceived
it. The Parthenon proclaims the harmony and high-mindedness of the
West. Admiring it, we admire ourselves as members in good standing of a
tradition whose success we believe our very existence confirms. What it was,
we believe we are.

Good myths are rarely as simple as they seem. A continuous series of low
relief sculptures on the frieze around the interior wall of the Parthenon was
long thought to depict a tableau of joyous civic duty, the annual
Panathenaic procession celebrating the birth of the patron goddess. Now it
appears the frieze depicts the ritual sacrifice of the youngest daughter of
King Erechtheus to Athena to save the city from defeat by Eumolpos, who
launched the first attack on Athenians.[1] Fragments of a lost Euripidian
drama establish this as the founding myth of Athens. "To think that this
iconic structure of grace and just proportion could turn out to have been
dedicated to the glorification of a practice as primitive, cruel and irrational
as the sacrifice of children!" an observer has written.[2] If the Parthenon tells
us the creation myth of Western civilization, our appetite for the bloody
slaughter of our own children lies at its heart. It is a hard lesson.

Our myths tell us civilization is built on violence. Violence demands a moral response, a group-defining set of "oughts" that connect us to or separate us from the bodies of others. This is the mechanism by which we take sides or, in totem terms, form bordered groups. Violence is a central dynamic of nation–state groups insofar as all societies are notions of order imposed on bodies, expressed ultimately through the explicit or implied exercise of force on these bodies. Sacrifice disciplines groups. It keeps violence from escalating out of control. This is what we mean by saying it forms bordered groups. Indeed, despite our conviction that violence is morally repugnant and should be eliminated, it creates the groups to which we feel the strongest attachments. If this is so, are we forever doomed to suffer violence and inflict it? Is there nothing we can do? The tempting comparison is to weather systems. Wind, fire, water, and earth shape the world we live in and may wreak havoc on any of us. Violence is a kind of social weather that shapes the fate of all in its path. However much we hope to bend it to our purposes, it is stronger and sturdier than we are. It can turn on us in an instant. When we think we can beat it, it will thrash us.

The difference between social and natural violence is that men are not complicit in the breeze or the rain, but social violence is entirely the action of men. That said, people rarely accept responsibility for violence. They even more rarely admit to profiting from it. To own or enjoy it is taboo except in the most ritually circumscribed conditions. As a general rule, actors identified with violence are socially and physically thrust to the margins. Fearing contagion, the group expels them. But if violence is the action of men, these men are not border dwellers and strangers only. We are all violence users, all complicit in its exercise. Our violent history makes us possible by organizing social kinship. Even those who decline to use their own bodies to exercise force, defined as physicality escalated to a level necessary to control someone else's behavior, benefit from society's use of other bodies to control group-defined disorder. Enduring groups are defined *by* violence. They are known for organizing violence in a distinctive way. The question is never how to get rid of violence, but which set of killing rules we will submit to. The religious believer who refuses to send his children to war because he submits only to God submits no less than the patriot to a power more violent than himself. He differs only in the killing authority he recognizes as legitimate. If every enduring group creates borders that contain and expel violence with more or less success, this is not the same as eliminating violence. We can change groups, but we cannot remove ourselves from a system of totem violence so long as we are members of any group. Wherever we are, killing rules are in effect.

This view will not satisfy readers who hope an analysis of violence will explain how to defeat it. Violence dramatizes and promises death. Since the final purpose of ritual action is to keep the group alive against all odds, our denial of the necessity for violence is partly a refusal to believe in the death of our group. To keep the group alive, we must stop time. This is the primitive magic our most important rituals perform. To demand that a theory show how to stop violence is to misunderstand what theories do. It is to look for a ritual to stop time and death, instead of exploring how groups organize themselves in a world structured by time and death. Rituals do not describe reality. They deliver us from it by re-creating it for a while. So long as we belong to a nation that denies its religiosity, our efforts to make rituals of our theories come as no surprise. In a disbelieving age, if nothing else provides deliverance from death, perhaps our theories can. We look for religious solutions because we are social beings. Religion, Durkheim knew, is the highest form of sociability. We enact our sociability by collectively denying death.

To reject violence is to be morally alarmed that people desire the brutal dispatch of others. But when it comes to violence, what counts is where our bodies are. Failing to intervene directly in violence, we facilitate it. Intervening to stop violence, we repeat it. There is also the disquieting evidence of our fantasy lives, only apparently removed from the moral ambiguities of violent practice. Consider any film audience that cheers when the bad guys get their just desserts. Who has not felt that thrill? The argument that this is not the same as enjoying real violence is not altogether convincing. If pleasure at the bodily coercion of others were not available to all of us, it would not be available for fantasy any more than real life. If we admire ourselves for responding to expressions of the noble virtues in fantasy, why are we unappalled by our delight in a bad end to a fantasy villain?

Violence that we regard as justly inflicted elicits a sense of entitlement and righteousness. It keeps the moral and cognitive boundaries of our group secure. Properly organized, sacrificial suffering dissipates hostile impulses and re-establishes connectedness to group members. We don't mind when the Wicked Witch melts in the film classic, *The Wizard of Oz,* decidedly against her will. Neither does Dorothy, a small-town girl of the regenerative center who embodies decency and care for others. Nor do we mind that our children enjoy this violent body-transforming death. Though witches are supposed to be fictions, the Wicked Witch of the West has very human characteristics. We permit ourselves to enjoy the violent demise of humans who can be transformed into witches just as we admire ourselves for loving the Scarecrow, who is no more or less human than the witch. Those who are violent are not only no less human than those who are loving, they are utterly human.

By owning the monopoly on legitimized violence, nation–states have organized the destiny of peoples for two centuries. If organized violence is intrinsic to social life, will nationalism always be its primary vehicle? There is no good reason to think so. The totem structures that organize nations have organized empires and tribes for centuries. While there is a wishful disposition to imagine that technology can bypass these violent energies, we doubt it. Where blood is not at stake, groups are not enduring. Communities based in electronic communication alone are textual communities unsupported by sacrificial bodies. Electronic communities may thrive in the service of enduring groups based in blood. But without armies or willing sacrifices of their own, these communities cannot generate the religious intensity that causes groups to cohere. The violent energies that fuel nationalism are not likely to wither away in a brave new technological world. It is wholly conceivable that empires or tribal warlords may replace nations. Communities based solely in electronic communication never will.

To return to the tornado and the flood. We can learn about them. We can build houses that shelter us from them for a while. We can avoid or defer them in some cases by making good use of them in others. We cannot eliminate them. Neither can we eliminate violence, as elemental as weather. As well try to eliminate sex, the partner and complement of violence. Even non-violence is no more than another way to distribute violence. For political purposes, the most effective non-violence is the kind that gets people hurt or killed, that results in violence. A military general who orders troops into battle knows they will die as they rush up the ridge, even with guns to defend themselves. He is not so different, in that way, from a non-violent general who also urges his troops into battle, as it were, to sacrifice themselves without guns. Both generals correctly believe that the exercise of a sufficient amount of superior force will bring conflict to an end.

Non-violence powerfully reveals the secret that we kill our own, but generally only to reimpose it on behalf of a different group idea. In the language of sectarian religion, our dilemma is that we are never without sin, which is violence, even when we willingly offer our bodies or those of our children to appease or resist violent Others. Whether we inflict or submit to violence, we choose a side it defines. The question is whether we recognize our complicity or deceive ourselves that our support is anything but deferring to the killing rules of the side whose part we take. The traditional esteem in which we hold non-violence is misleading. It obscures the violent authority that demands sacrifice and thereby perpetuates violence against supplicants and their perceived enemies even when both offer themselves willingly. We are meant not to notice. The secret keeps us together.

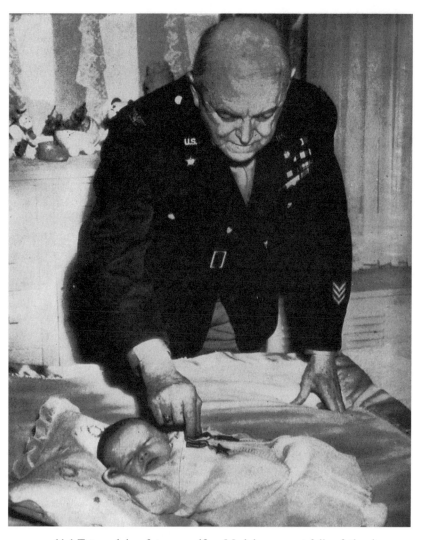

11.1 Totem claims future sacrifice. Medals resurrect fallen father in
infant son.

Appendix 1

The flag in life: representational politics of the stars and stripes

Since flags carry potent political meaning, we might expect them to occupy a central place in the literature of political communication. In fact, investigations of practices relating to displays of flags and other national symbols are rare.[1] Difficulty in collecting representative data from the field may play a part, but it is more likely that scholars have not expected to find interesting patterns in such data. If everyone knows what the flag means and how it is displayed, there is little for scholars to say. The totem taboo may also be at work. In a culture conditioned not to examine its flag religion too closely, scholars may be no different from other citizens in subscribing to the notion of a sacred flag with an ideal, unvarying appearance and a meaning so sublime it resists full or final articulation. Variant forms are marked as messageless or non-communicating at best, profane and threatening at worst.

Two broad scholarly approaches to flag study suggest that scholars have operated in terms of a totem logic. Both presume that only "correct flags" communicate. One approach is found in studies of flag history that begin with the notion that the flag once was not itself, and has become itself through a temporal process of design change, special sanctifying events, or both. An example of this genre is the classic *Flag of the United States of America* by Rear Admiral George Henry Preble, published in 1872.[2] The second approach addresses flag protocol, the proper use of the proper flag.[3] Both history and protocol models imply a set of conditions including properly executed design, sanctifying gestures, and procedural taboos that make the flag real and potent, and a set of contrasting conditions in which the flag is not its effective or proper self.

Our model of flag display is a social field in which both regulation (standard) and non-regulation (parsed) versions of the American flag have symbolic significance. To investigate it, we examined American flag display over three and a half decades in *Life* magazine, a national media arena. *Life* offers a uniquely systematic record of American cultural imagery. For years the largest circulation news magazine in the United States, *Life* was a major disseminator of news to Americans long before television, and an important arena for advertising display.[4] Through an industrialized ritual of weekly publication, it represented American life and culture to a mass audience from its inception in 1936 until it ceased continuous publication in 1972. Its presentations included nationally received images of flag display in advertising and news.

We identified the entire universe of patriotic images in *Life* between 1936 and 1972. Of these 5,220 images, 4,898 featured one or more flags.[5] Of special interest to us were rhythmic exchanges of flag imagery between editorial text and advertising, and rhythmic shifts of flag imagery associated with conflict and consensus in public opinion. We postulate that advertising is an arena of representation that emphasizes unifying issues in the culture and mobilizes citizens for war or peace as each moves into view. Editorial matter, by contrast, is a frame in which threats to the social fabric are monitored.[6] We expected flag representation to vary depending on its location in text or advertising, and according to whether the country was at war or peace. Specifically, we expected more totem display in periods of threat to national borders or integrity. In peacetime, greater internal divisions in the community should be manifest in greater variability in flag display. We also expected that flag display associated with conflict should be manifest more in text, an arena for presenting conflict, than in advertising, an arena for presenting unity. To test these hypotheses, we coded flag images along four dimensions: *frame, domain, type,* and *history.*

Frame

Life magazine is a system of editorial and advertising matter. Each has distinctive semiotic functions in the representation of American culture. *Advertising* is a representational arena, or frame, in which commercial concerns publish words and images of their choosing. Editorial matter consists of words and images produced by *Life* editors, writers and photographers. We use the journalistic term *text* for all editorial, or non-advertising matter that includes both words and pictures.

Domain

Flag display falls into three domains of activity that we label *totem, affiliative,* and *popular.* Each domain constitutes a kind of flag activity with characteristic visual attributes. We briefly highlight the attributes of each domain. The totem domain constitutes the flag as a symbol of society in its highest, holiest form. It is the Durkheimian totem, the collective will and agreement of the social body. The totem flag symbolizes the submission of the people to the totem god who demands sacrifice. It occupies a condition of ritual separateness. Special ceremonies guard against its profanation or loss. Special rules prescribe possibilities for communicating with it. The totem authority of the flag confers killing power on agents of the totem class, the police and the military.

By affiliative, we mean the flag held high by any freemasonry of broth- ers or sisters with a common cause and set of beliefs, joined by bonds of sentiment and experience, striving together for recognition and power before spectators who consider them with mixed emotions. Affiliative groups practice exclusive membership and aspire to totem status. That is, they aspire to respect and power as broad and unquestioned as that due the totem, preferably at the expense of other affiliative groups and even the totem itself. Their triumphs are temporary and never secure, for though they aspire to totem status, they may not kill to achieve it. Labor unions, the Ku Klux Klan, and religious denominations exemplify affiliative groups. Affiliative activity may challenge totem authority actually or symbolically.

By popular, we mean the disorganized, creative flag-waving substratum of the people, a fertile body of social matter and energy to be harnessed for totem sacrifice or affiliative competition. The popular domain sends sol- diers to war and welcomes them home again. It is the domain of popular elections. It is also the domestic arena in which commercially organized groups re-create society through economic and cultural exchange in pro- duction and consumption. This domain includes art as well as commerce. Flag art is the popular representation of the flag in artistic media, includ- ing paintings, clothing, movies, theater, and dance.

Type

Flag type refers to how design elements are arranged in flag images. The *standard* type is the familiar American flag in its whole integrity. The *parsed* type rearranges any of the first type's elements – stars, stripes, colors, or proportions – by abstracting, dismembering or recombining them. The result must refer unmistakably in presentation or context to the standard flag. Flag bunting is the best known parsed flag. The shield of the National Football League is another well-known parsed flag with its white stars on a blue field and its red letters simulating red stripes on a white field. The parsed flag is a flag of connection and association with the people. In contrast to the distant, untouchable, standard totem flag, it is accessible and reformable.

History

History refers to bounded periods within which flag display may be observed. *War* and *peace* are our periods of interest. War years were defined for World War II (1942–45) [though the war began in December, 1941, few photographs were available for publication until 1942], Korea (1950–53), and Vietnam (1965–72).[7] Peace years were all those remaining.

Hypothesis

We hypothesized that type and domain in flag images vary according to whether that imagery is found in text or advertising, and whether it occurs during war or peace. Our null hypothesis was that type and domain in flag display vary independently of frame and history, that is, that domain and type in flag images have nothing to do with whether these images are displayed in editorial matter or advertising, and nothing to do with whether the country is at war or peace. Our hypotheses were confirmed; the null hypothesis was disproved. We suggest the meaning of these results in our discussion.

Method

We examined every page of *Life* magazine from 1936 to 1972. Every editorial photo and advertising image containing one or more standard or parsed flags (N = 4,898) was coded by frame, domain, type, and history. (For representative coding examples by frame, domain, and type – history being self-explanatory – see Appendix 2.) Three coders were trained on three different sets of fifty flag images selected for relevant variables. Differences in coding on two sets of flag images were discussed to eliminate as much intercoder difference as possible. The final set of flag images was used as the baseline test of intercoder reliability. The mean level of agreement was 0.92 (range 0.89–0.95).

We also recorded every occurrence of five non-flag patriotic symbols: George Washington, Abraham Lincoln, the American eagle, Uncle Sam, and the Statue of Liberty. This was to establish a baseline contrast for comparing flags to other regularly occurring patriotic symbols (N = 661).[8]

Using a chi-square test, we analyzed these interactions:

(1) (Frame) How does flag imagery shift between text and advertising?
(2) (Type) How does flag imagery shift between standard and parsed flags?
(3) (Domain) How does flag imagery shift among totem, affiliative, and popular activity?
(4) (History) How does flag imagery shift between war and peace?

Results

Distinctive patterns of flag imagery emerge in *Life* over thirty years of war and peace. We observed these trends:

(1) Flag imagery dwarfs other patriotic imagery, including George Washington, Abraham Lincoln, the American eagle, the Statue of Liberty, and Uncle Sam. Even added together, the total number of patriotic non-flag images is equal to only 13 per cent of the total number of flag images. Though it is a shadow of the flag's volume, the symbol that behaves most like the flag in its rhythmic distribution over time is the American eagle.[9] In *Life*, flag images outnumber American eagle images by roughly 20 to 1. Eagle images occur twice as often as images of Abraham Lincoln, the next most frequent symbol. Flag imagery is also strongly associated with war and presidential elections.

(2) Parsed flags appear in 2,425 images, 49.5 per cent of 4,898 total flag images. Parsed flags are an enduring and systematic form of flag display that harmonically echoes the overall pattern of standard flag display in text and advertising taken together. A symbolic exchange of parsed flags takes place between text and advertising. In text, the number of standard flag images exceeds the number of parsed flag images in every domain (totem, affiliative, popular). An exact reversal occurs in advertising, where parsed flags exceed standard flags in every domain. (Chi-Square = 4897.99 [15, n = 4,898, p<. 0005].)

  While state and federal statutes for the observed period forbid the use of flags in advertising,[10] this does not entirely explain the pattern of significantly fewer standard than parsed flags in advertising, since standard flags do appear in *Life* advertisements, however infrequently. According to the civilian flag code, the only thing more taboo than using standard flags in advertising is dismembering, rearranging, writing on and otherwise modifying the flag. Such prohibitions

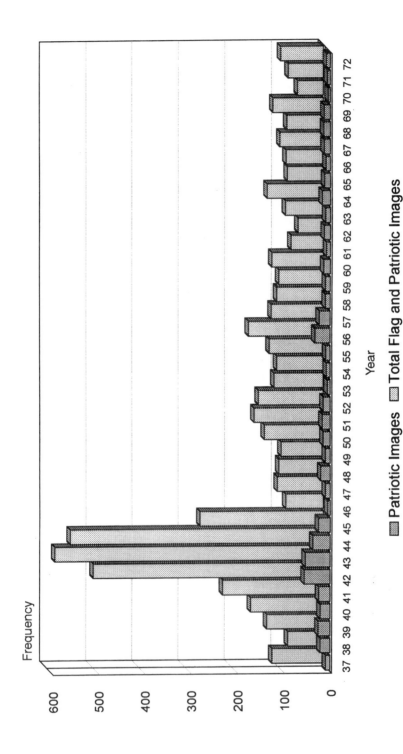

Graph 1 Total flag and patriotic images.

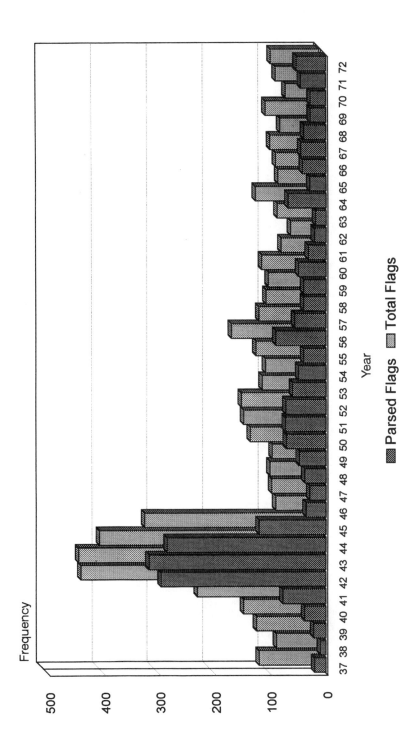

Graph 2 Total and parsed flag images by year.

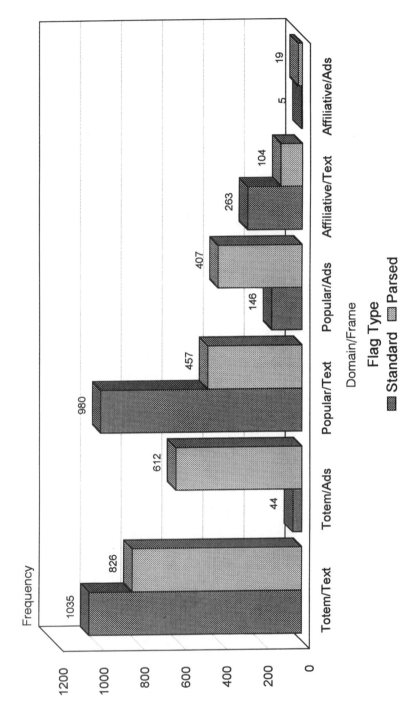

Graph 3 Parsed flag images by frame and domain.

notwithstanding, this modified flag is in fact the parsed flag of every-day experience and the flag most frequently found in advertising. If the taboo against standard flags is violated comparatively infrequently in advertising, the taboo against cut-up flags is honored not at all. Advertising, the frame of popular effort and activity, is strongly asso-ciated with the reconstructable, parsed flag. The reconstructable, parsed flag emblematizes the regenerative activity of commerce.

(3)   Domains of flag activity populate text and advertising in significantly different ways during war and peace. In text during war, the totem domain commands the largest share of flag images (at 59 per cent, by far the largest) compared to affiliative and popular domains. (The ratio is roughly 10 totem flags to every 1.5 affiliative flags and 6 popular flags.) When peace comes, the number of flag images in the totem domain shrinks 52 per cent. Even in its reduced peacetime state, the totem domain commands the largest share of peacetime flag repre-sentations. But something different happens to the other domains. During peacetime, all domains increase their proportional representa-tion of flag images relative to their occurrence in war, except the totem domain, at whose expense this increase occurs. Non-totem flags are suppressed in text during war, it appears, to re-emerge during peace-time.

Whereas popular text flags increase in frequency by 33 per cent in the transition from war to peace, affiliative flag activity increases by 60 per cent. Put a different way, the ongoing surrogate war of affiliative groups declines during war within the frame of the text, which tracks social conflict. When the official totem is at war, affiliative combat is suppressed to re-emerge in peacetime. Still, just as totem groups command the largest overall chunk of flag images in text both in war and peace, affiliative flags represent the smallest overall chunk of text flags both in war and peace. Second in frequency to totem flag imagery in the text environment are popular flag images, both in war and peace. In the text environment, which tracks threats to group borders, totem vigilance never ceases, though it relaxes a bit in peacetime. (Chi-Square = 75.01 [3, n = 3,665, p<. 00005].)

A different pattern emerges in advertising, which we treat as a frame that locates unity in the culture. In war and peace, affiliative percent-ages are roughly the same; 3 per cent of advertisements in war feature affiliative flags; 2 per cent do in peace. Totem and popular flags reverse their respective proportions in advertisements in war and peace. In war, totem flags constitute 62 per cent of advertising flags. Popular flags constitute 36 per cent. In peace these percentages are roughly

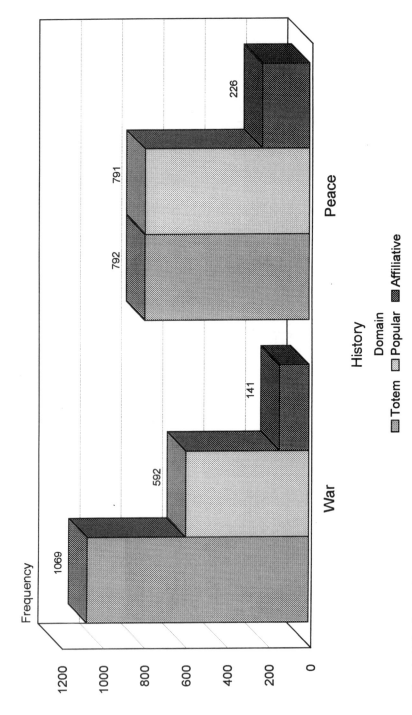

Graph 4 Flag images in text during war and peace.

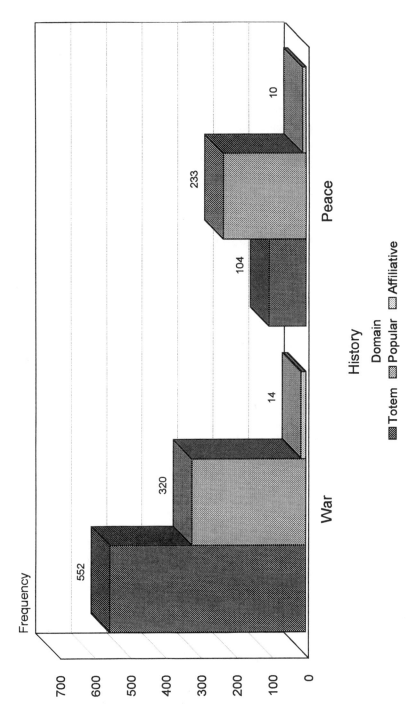

Graph 5 Flag images in advertisements during war and peace.

exchanged. In peace, popular flags constitute 67 per cent of advertising flag images, and totem flags constitute 30 per cent. In the totem emergency of war, the entire society bends its efforts to victory, and the totem flag reigns supreme. In peace, the people's flag asserts itself. (Chi-Square = 167.69 [3, n = 1,233, p<. 00005].)

(4)   Other patterns emerge in comparisons of flag imagery in text between specific wars. As a percentage of flag images in the three wars examined, the affiliative domain is proportionally nearly twice as large during the Vietnam War, accounting for 13 per cent of all Vietnam War text flags. Affiliative flags in the Korean War constitute 6.2 per cent of text flag images, and 5.2 per cent of text flag images in World War II. This increased affiliative percentage for Vietnam comes at the proportional expense of the totem domain, which accounts for 62.2 per cent of all World War II text flag images and 58 per cent of Korean War text flag images, but only 48.8 per cent of Vietnam War flag images. In three wars, affiliative groups who wished to seize totem power were most visibly manifest during the Vietnam War. (Chi-Square = 122.12 [9, n = 3,665, p<. 00005].)[11]

Each of the three wars has an even more distinctive advertising profile. Among all advertising images with flags in World War II, totem domain images account for a massive 76.1 per cent. Affiliative flags are a tiny 0.2 per cent, and popular flag advertisement images account for 18.5 per cent. In the less popular Korean War, totem flag advertizing images account for 53.5 per cent of advertising flags, affiliative flags are invisible (0 per cent), and vernacular flag images account for 46 per cent. But during Vietnam, the least popular of these three wars, totem flag advertising images have shrunk to 11.7 per cent, and affiliative images have risen to 8.4 per cent. Most striking of all, popular flag images account for 66.9 per cent of flag advertising images. It appears that during the Vietnam War, advertising compensates for absence of social consensus by projecting the popular domain – the people – as custodians of flag imagery rather than the totem, about whose war the people disagree. (Chi-Square = 343.98 [9, n = 1,233, p<. 00005].)[12]

Discussion

In the symbolic system of *Life* magazine, flag display is highly patterned. We explain the exchange of flag images between text and advertising during war and peace by postulating that advertisements are the symbolic repository of immediate and historically specific themes of social unity – what the

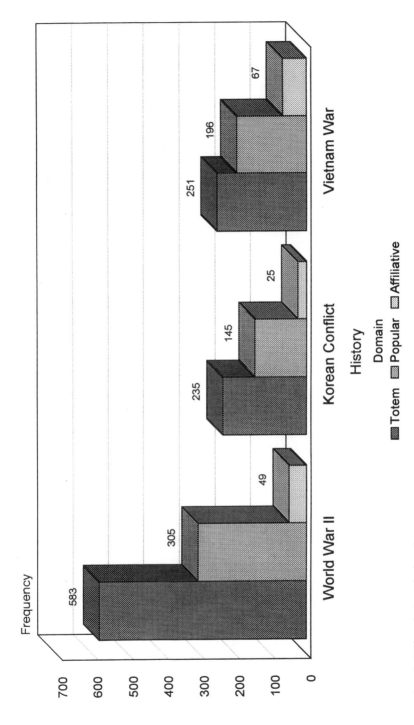

Frequency

700
600
500
400
300
200
100
0

583
305
49

235
145
25

251
196
67

World War II

Korean Conflict

Vietnam War

History

Domain
■ Totem ■ Popular ■ Affiliative

Graph 6 Flags in text during three wars.

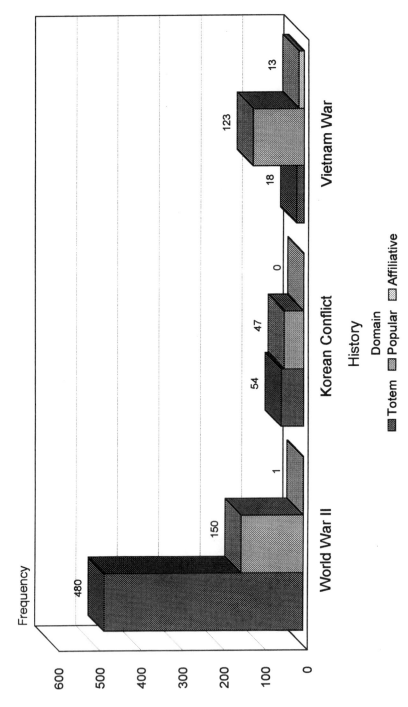

Frequency

Graph 7 Flags in advertising during three wars.

community can agree on in public at a particular time, as well as themes about future states of social effort that must be mobilized for the core symbolic exchange of money to go forward in production and consumption.[13] Advertising in *Life* addresses themes such as the value of familes, health, neighborliness, work, and consumption. During war, advertising themes also celebrate the war effort at home and at the front.

Text, on the other hand, tracks and displays conflict. By highlighting affiliative antagonism during peacetime, text indicates where unity may be breaking down in the social compact. In war, editorial attention shifts to external border threats. Advertising imagery in war is strongly totemic. In peace, and when war is unpopular, advertising focuses on popular activity at the expense of totem authority. Finally, far from being a degraded kind of flag display or random noise around "true" flag display, non-standard parsed flag display is a distinctive and sturdy form of flag imagery that is responsive to changes in frame and domain.

Homicide rates in war and peace

At least one other class of empirical measures bears on the totem system of flag meaning we offer here. We have argued that wars unify or divide the totem group in response to several important criteria, among them the proportion of war dead to the total population. All other things being equal, large sacrifices unify more than small ones, at least up to the point at which the group can no longer sustain itself. All other things are not equal, however. The unifying effect of war also depends on its popularity at home, the uncertainty of its outcome at the beginning, and the certainty of the result at the end. The more such factors are present, the more unifying the war will be, measured in terms of what citizens say about their identification with the war effort and satisfaction with the war as a group experience, and how long the memory of the war as a motivating sacrifice can be meaningfully invoked by the group.

It is worth asking what light totem theory sheds on a long-standing problem: the significance of changes in homicide rates in war and peace, specifically, the effect of war on crime rates. Reviewing the relevant scholarship in 1976 and again in 1984, Archer and Gartner found that measurements of decreased crime rates during war are subject to severe bias.[14] During major wars, crime rates are likely to be depressed by the massive removal of young men from the civilian population. Convicts may be prematurely released on condition that they join the armed forces. Employers are reluctant to prosecute scarce workers who remain on the homefront; crimes that would have been reported and prosecuted in peacetime become invisible. Parolees who are too old for conscription, but in peacetime might have returned to crime because of difficulty finding employment, become more employable because of labor shortages. Other wartime shortages include alcohol, which may accompany crime, and policemen, who may be unable to arrest malfeasers at rates associated with higher staffing during peacetime. It is also possible that family disruptions and long workdays in wartime increase crime rates. Abandoned and unguarded property and blackouts provide more criminal opportunities. New types of crime are created by wartime regulations. Measurement of changes in crime rates during wars are also complicated by changes in the boundaries of warring nations and interruptions in record-keeping.[15]

To avoid these biases, Archer and Gartner compared mean homicide rates in different countries for a fixed prewar (five years) and postwar period (five years) to gauge the effects of war on homicide rates. They compared changes in a total of 101 combatant nations and control nations not at war over seventy years of the twentieth century. They also paid attention to whether combatant nations were victors or losers, and the number of military casualties as a proportion of total population. Two indices of change were computed for every nation. The first was the ratio of the mean postwar to mean prewar homicide rate expressed as a percentage comparing postwar to prewar levels. This measure provides an index of the overall magnitude and direction of change in homicide rates from prewar to postwar. The second index was a t-test comparison between mean prewar and postwar homicide rates. This measure takes into account the variance of prewar and postwar rates, and provides an index of how unusual the postwar change is compared to the variability of the prewar rate.

Combatant nations in both world wars were more likely to experience postwar homicide rate increases than control nations that did not experience war. In control nations, homicide rate changes were evenly directionally distributed. Among twenty-five combatant nations in these two wars, postwar increases outnumbered decreases by nineteen to six. Nations with large combat losses were more likely to show homicide increases than those with fewer losses. Finally, victorious nations experienced more rate increases than defeated ones. The study finds that the war most likely to produce increased homicide rates is one that is both deadly and won.[16]

The United States does not follow this model for World War I and II, or for Vietnam (through 1967), the wars for which American homicide rates were measured. Though victorious in both world wars, the United States was not among nations with the heaviest combat losses. American war casualties were 0.3 per cent of the total population in World War I. Deaths alone constituted 0.1 per cent of the population. In World War II, these percentages increased. American casualties were 0.8 per cent of total population, deaths alone were 0.3 per cent. Nevertheless, contrary to the Archer–Gartner model, post-World War II homicide rates decreased, while post-World War I homicide rates increased, despite greater American casualties in World War II.[17] For the Vietnam War, investigators compared prewar homicide rates to homicide rates during the war through 1967. Though Vietnam casualties were a smaller percentage of the total population than in World War I or II, homicide rates increased dramatically during the Vietnam War. The increase between the mean prewar rate measured for 1960–62 and the mean war rate measured for 1963–67 is 42 per cent.[18] This, too, is contrary to the model.

Can totem theory explain these changes? We have argued that widespread losses in popular war increases group cohesion where other specified conditions are present. If homicide rates may be taken as an indicator of social disunity in a totem model, the United States should have seen greater increases in homicide rates during and after the Vietnam War, with its smaller proportion of combat deaths to population (Vietnam casualties were 0.001 per cent of total population), than was the case for either World War I or II. Since World Wars I and II were more popular wars than Vietnam, this also should be reflected in smaller increases in their postwar homicide rates relative to Vietnam. It is. Only World War II, a very popular war, and with a greater proportion of casualties to total population than either World War I or Vietnam, shows a decrease in postwar homicide rates. This, too, is consistent with totem theory. The most popular and most sacrificial war has the lowest homicide rates associated with it. Changes from prewar to postwar homicide rates in the United States after World Wars I and II, and from prewar to wartime rates during Vietnam, are more consistent with totem predictions for national unity in war and peace than with Archer and Gartner's model. However, this is a suggestive rather than a definitive test of totem theory.

Conclusion

What keeps killing organized is a clear border. Borders allocate killing authority. They define where violence is subject to totem authority, and where it is not. Moments of greatest uncertainty about legitimate totem authority are marked by the greatest show of flags. When the allocation of killing authority is not settled by clear borders, groups doubt their identity. Flags massed at the border focus attention on competing claims for killing authority and indicate that sacrifice to re-impose authority is imminent.

When these claims are resolved, flags migrate to the center and to the popular domain. Killing energy is once more thrust outside the border.

Acculturated American citizens are fully aware of the flag as a pervasive national symbol. As Durkheim says of the totem emblem,

Placed thus at the centre of the scene it becomes representative. The sentiments . . . fix themselves upon it, for it is the only concrete object upon which they can fix themselves. It continues to bring them to mind and to evoke them even after the assembly has dissolved, for it survives the assembly, being carved upon the instruments of the cult, upon the sides of rocks, upon bucklers, etc. By it, the emotions experienced are perpetually sustained and revived . . . It is the permanent element of the social life.[19]

Patriotic imagery in a national media environment exhibits systematic densities with respect to public consensus and conflict as defined by totem theory. Systematic differences in flag display in *Life* are also consistent with our analysis of solidarity and competition among three domains of flag activity. We make the Durkheimian assumption that society regularly signals its members about the state of the totem, the social agreement signified by the flag.[20] In contemporary society, mass media assume a large share of the job of communicating totem liturgy to congregations of devotees.

Appendix 2

Representative examples of coding categories

The following examples are typical of their categories. They by no means exhaust the richness or variety of examples in the data. They do not include "history," or divisions into war and peace, which are self-evident.

(1) **Text/Totem/Standard**
A flag draped on a casket at a military funeral.

(2) **Text/Totem/Parsed**
The Presidential seal with its flag shield.

(3) **Text/Affiliative/Standard**
Union members marching behind a flag.

(4) **Text/Affiliative/Parsed**
Bunting draping the stands at a World Series baseball game.

(5) **Text/Popular/Standard**
Flag-waving crowds line a parade avenue.

(6) **Text/Popular/Parsed**
Campaign buttons at a political rally.

(7) **Text/Art/Standard**
Oil painting of George Washington crossing the Delaware with a flag held amidships.

(8) **Text/Art/Parsed**
Swimsuits designed with flag elements.

(9) **Advertising/Totem/Standard**
Advertisement for automobile manufacturer depicting a US military vehicle flying a flag as it speeds to a wartime battlefront.

(10) **Advertising/Totem/Parsed**
Advertisement for engine manufacturer features US military aircraft with official US insignia on the wingtips.

(11)   Advertising/Affiliative/Standard
Silverware advertisement depicting a bridal couple at a church altar flanked by American flags.

(12)   Advertising/Affiliative/Parsed
Battery advertisement depicting Eagle Scouts wearing uniforms with insignia.

(13)   Advertising/Popular/Standard
Advertisement for roofing manufacturer featuring a residential dwelling with a flag flying from the porch.

(14)   Advertising/Popular/Parsed
Red, white, and blue design of stripes with stars on food product packaging.

(15)   Advertising/Art/Standard
Advertisement for film musical depicting chorus line holding flags.

(16)   Advertising/Art/Parsed
Uncle Sam hat in millinery advertisement.

Notes

1 Introduction

1 Peter Berger, *The Sacred Canopy: Elements of a Sociological Theory of Religion* (Garden City, N.Y.: Doubleday, 1967), 43.
2 See Robert J. Goldstein, *Saving 'Old Glory': The History of the American Flag Desecration Controversy* (Boulder: Westview, 1995) and *Burning the Flag: The Great 1989–1990 Flag Desecration Controversy* (Kent State, 1996).

2 That old flag magic

1 *West Virginia State Board of Education* et al. v. *Barnette* et al. *Appeal from the District Court of the United States for the Southern District of West Virginia.* 319 US 624, US Sup. Ct., 1943.
2 Robert Bellah's seminal article in the most recent round of discussions was "The American Civil Religion," *Daedalus* 96 (Winter 1967), 1–21.
3 This is Reinhold Niebuhr's definition, quoted in Peter L. Berger, "From the Crisis of Religion to the Crisis of Secularity," in Mary Douglas and Stephen Tipton, eds. *Religion in America* (1982; Boston: Beacon Press, 1983), 18.
4 Emile Durkheim, *The Elementary Forms of the Religious Life*, tr. by Joseph W. Swain (George Allen & Unwin, 1915; New York: Free Press), 206.
5 Max Weber, "Politics as a Vocation," in H. H. Gerth and C. Wright Mills, *From Max Weber: Essays in Sociology* (New York: Oxford University Press, 1946), 78.
6 The defining feature of the traditional Lockeian social compact is the cession to the group of the right to punish the transgressor.
7 Anthony Giddens, *The Nation-State and Violence* (Berkeley, Calif.: University of California Press, 1985) and Benedict Anderson, *Imagined Communities* (New York: Verso, 1991).
8 Etienne Balibar and Immanuel Wallerstein, *Race, Nation, and Class*, tr. by Chris Turner (New York: Verso, 1991), 27.
9 Bill Buford, *Among the Thugs* (Secker and Warburg, 1991; New York: Vintage, 1993), 192–93.

10 Edward Abbey, *A Voice Crying in the Wilderness* (New York: St. Martin's Press, 1989), 2.

11 Durkheim, *Elementary Forms*, p. 236. Although Durkheim did not see significant totemism in modern societies, the last chapter of *Elementary Forms* suggests he did equate civil and sectarian religion. "What essential difference is there," he wrote, "between an assembly of Christians celebrating the principal dates of the life of Christ, or of Jews remembering the exodus from Egypt or the promulgation of the decalogue, and a reunion of citizens commemorating the promulgation of a new moral or legal system or some great event in the national life?" (475). See Jeffrey C. Alexander, ed., *Durkheimian Sociology: Cultural Studies* (Cambridge: Cambridge University Press, 1988) for arguments about the application of Durkheimian theory to contemporary conditions.

12 (n.a.), "Decorated Sergeant in Marines Wants To Be a Citizen, Too," *New York Times*, April 7, 1994, A22.

13 George Bernard Shaw, "Preface," *Androcles and the Lion Overruled* (New York: Brentano's, 1923), 125.

14 For a summary of scholarly landmarks in the civil religion debate, see Martin E. Marty, *A Nation of Behavers* (Chicago: University of Chicago Press, 1976), pp. 180–203. Also Stephen Carter, *The Culture of Disbelief* (New York: Basic Books, 1993).

15 See Seymour P. Lachman and Barry A. Kosmin, *One Nation Under God* (New York: Harmony Books, 1993).

16 The definition of religion as "the belief in Spiritual Beings" is associated with Sir Edward Tylor.

17 George A. Kelly, *Politics and Religious Consciousness in America* (New Brunswick, N.J.: Transaction Books, 1984), 11.

18 John F. Wilson, "The Status of 'Civil Religion' in America," in *The Religion of the Republic*, ed. Elwyn A. Smith (Philadelphia: Fortress Press, 1971), 15.

19 Kelly, *Politics*, 237.

20 *Ibid.*, 239.

21 Marty, *Religion and Republic: The American Circumstance* (Boston: Beacon Press, 1987), 77.

22 George Gallup, "Religion at Home and Abroad," *Public Opinion*, March-May 1979, 38–39.

23 Quoted in Lachman and Kosmin, *One Nation Under God*, 9.

24 "The *New York Times* Patriotism Survey: Marginals and Trends," June 13–18, 1983. (N=1,145), and November 18–22, 1983 (N=1,093).

25 Marty, *Religion and Republic*, 79.

26 Wilkerson, "After War, Patriotism Unfurls in a Nebraska City," A8.

27 Roderick Hart, *The Political Pulpit* (West Lafayette, Ind.: Purdue, 1977), 77.

28 Quoted from Johnson's January 20, 1965, inaugural address in Bruce Bohle, ed., *The Apollo Book of American Quotations* (New York: Dodd, Mead, 1967), 57.

29 Sidney Mead felt that hostility between the mutually exclusive faiths of the denominations and the Republic was inevitable, and for sectarians a losing fight. See Marty, *Religion and Republic* 66–67.

30 Peter Berger, "From the Crisis of Religion to the Crisis of Secularity," in Douglas and Tipton, eds., *Religion and America*, 18.

31 Clifford Geertz, "Religion as a Cultural System," in *The Interpretation of Cultures* (New York: Basic Books, 1973), 90.

32 An example is Paul Tillich's definition of culture as: "the totality of forms in which the basic concern of religion expresses itself: religion is the substance of culture, culture is the form of religion." in Paul Tillich, *Theology of Culture*, Robert C. Kimball, ed. (New York: Oxford, 1959), 42.

33 Michael Novak, *The Joy of Sports* (New York: Basic Books, 1976).

34 Will Herberg, *Protestant–Catholic–Jew*, rev. ed. (Garden City, N.Y.: Anchor Books, 1960), 75–77.

35 *Ibid.*, 79.

36 Marty, "Religion in America Since Mid-Century," in Douglas and Tipton, eds., *Religion and America*, 281.

37 Catherine L. Albanese, *America: Religions and Religion* (Belmont, Calif.: Wadsworth, 1981), 296–97.

38 Except, interestingly, and without further analysis, in her opening anecdote, which chronicles the history of the Jehovah's Witness resistance to the compulsory school Pledge of Allegiance. Albanese attempts to split the difference by distinguishing "ordinary" and "extraordinary" religion. The first includes the flag salute controversy and is equated with "culture itself." "Extraordinary religion brings people across boundaries and ultimately into contact with God." (Albanese, 5–9)

39 Mary Douglas, *Purity and Danger: An Analysis of the Concepts of Pollution and Taboo* (1966; New York: Ark Paperbacks, 1984), 69.

40 Claude Levi-Strauss, *Totemism*, tr. by Rodney Needham (1962; Boston: Beacon Press, 1963), 104. This is in line with Marianna Torgovnick's suggestion that the real secret of the primitive is that it is "whatever Euro-Americans want it to be." *Gone Primitive* (Chicago: University of Chicago, 1987), 9.

41 Jean-Jacques Rousseau, "Discourse on the Origin and Foundations of Inequality Among Men," in Roger D. Masters, ed., *The First and Second Discourses by Jean-Jacques Rousseau*, tr. by Roger D. and Judith R. Masters (New York: St. Martin's Press, 1964), 102.

42 Sigmund Freud, *Totem and Taboo* (1930; New York: W. W. Norton, 1950), 2.

43 Which notion Freud (3) attributes to Frazer. According to Tylor, the term was introduced in 1791 by the trader John Long who anglicized the Ojibwa word *ototeman*, meaning, "He is a relative of mine." Levi-Strauss, *Totemism*, 18.

44 *Ibid.*, 85.

45 This is not the same thing as a definition of totemism, the difficulties of which Levi-Strauss recounts, *Totemism*, 1–14.

46 *Ibid.*, 11.

47 Ralph Linton, "Totemism and the A.E.F.," *American Anthropologist*, n.s. 26 (1924), 298.

48 *Ibid.*, 299.

49 *Ibid.*, 299–300.

50 F. W. de Klerk, interviewed by Ann Cooper, *Morning Edition*, National Public Radio, March 17, 1994,

51 Leslie H. Gelb, "The Curse of Nations," *New York Times*, July 5, 1992, sec. 4, 11.

52 Bruce Kapferer, *Legends of People: Myths of State* (Washington, D.C.: Smithsonian Press, 1988).

53 Lynn Hunt, *The Family Romance of the French Revolution* (Berkeley: University of California Press, 1992).

54 Timothy Crippen, "Further Notes on Religious Transoformation," *Social Forces* (September, 1992) 71 (1): 222.

55 John Lukacs, *The End of the Twentieth Century* (New York: Ticknor and Fields, 1993), 208.

56 Carlton Hayes, *Essays on Nationalism* (New York: Macmillan, 1926), 107. Hayes had first-hand experience of the consequences of totem blasphemy when newspaper accounts of his lectures on the flag as sacred object led to calls for his resignation from Columbia University in the 1920s.

57 Hayes, *Essays*, 108.

58 Durkheim, *Elementary Forms*, 123.

59 Wilbur Zelinsky, *From Nation Into State* (Chapel Hill: University of North Carolina Press, 1988), 196, 243.

60 Harold Bloom, *The American Religion: The Emergence of the Post-Christian Nation* (New York: Simon and Schuster, 1992), 45. Bloom sees American religion as individualistic, but not how this piece of what he calls the unacknowledged American religion is also a feature of group religion, which for him remains at a political and civil level. This is the religion we explore.

61 Hayes, *Essays*, 104.

62 Benedict Anderson, *Imagined Communities* (New York: Verso, 1991), 3.

63 Liah Greenfeld, *Nationalism: Five Roads to Modernity* (Cambridge, Mass.: Harvard University Press, 1992); Ernest Gellner, *Nations and Nationalism* (London: Basil Blackwell, 1983).

64 *Ibid.*, 3.

65 Tom Nairn, *The Break-up of Britain: Crisis and Neo-Nationalism* (1977; London:Verso, 1981), 359.

66 Gellner, *Nations*, 6.

67 Anderson, *Imagined Communities*, 86.

68 *Ibid.*, 4.

69 Roy Rappaport, "The Obvious Aspects of Ritual," *Ecology, Meaning, and Religion* (Berkeley, Calif.: North Atlantic, 1979), 216–17.

70 S. J. Tambiah, *Culture, Thought, and Social Action: An Anthropological Perspective* (Cambridge, Mass.: Harvard University Press, 1985, 123–66.

71 *Virginia Bd. Of Ed.* v. *Barnette*, 624.
72 Durkheim, *Elementary Forms*, 136.
73 "Our Semi-Annual Bed & Bath Sale," Bloomingdale's By Mail Ltd., June, 1991, 46–47.
74 Horchow Mail Order, June–July, 1991, vol. H691.
75 "Tattoos chosen during war: Eagles, flags," *Philadelphia Inquirer*, January 26, 1991, A13.
76 Durkheim, *Elementary Forms*, 244.
77 *Texas* v. *Johnson,* 401 US 397, US Sup. Ct., 1991.
78 David Gergen, *MacNeil-Lehrer News Hour*, October 14, 1992.
79 Frazer, quoted in Freud, *Totem and Taboo*, 41.
80 *Ibid.*, 33.
81 Bruce van Voorst, "Amid Disaster, Amazing Valor," *Time*, February 28, 1994, 48.
82 Norman C. Meier, *Military Psychology* (New York: Harper & Brothers, 1943), xvii, 201.
83 Andrew Rosenthal, "With Bloom Off, Bush Takes Time to Smell the Flowers," *New York Times*, April 9, 1992, A1.
84 Walter Goodman, "HBO Late-Night Show That's for Adults Only," *New York Times*, August 13, 1992, C22.
85 Abbie Hoffman, "Wrapping Yourself in the Flag," *Soon to Be a Major Motion Picture*, 170–71.
86 *Ibid.*, 172.
87 Dr. Robert Cialdini, "Reciprocation: You, then Me, then You, then Me," lecture in the audiotape series *Instant Influence*, Dartnell Corporation, 1991.
88 Rudolph Otto, *The Idea of the Holy. An Inquiry into the non-rational factor in the idea of the divine and its relation to the rational*, tr. by John Harvey (London: Oxford, 1923; 1950; 1958), 13.
89 Freud, *Totem and Taboo*, 20.
90 After I burned an American flag as a free speech exercise in a college class, students who were not there asked whether I had 'felt' anything at the moment of burning it. In these inquiries lay the conviction that the sacred power of the flag should have been contagiously communicated to me at the moment of profanation through a distinct bodily register.
91 Isabel Wilkerson, "After War, Patriotism Unfurls in a Nebraska City," *New York Times*, July 4, 1991, A8.
92 Barton Silverman for the *New York Times*, August 8, 1992, A1.
93 Sandra Bailey, "Capriati, Just 16 but Revived, Stops Graf's Olympic Reign," *New York Times*, August 8, 1992, A1.
94 "Feedback," *USA Today*, February 22, 1991, A9.
95 Quoted in Geo. H. Preble, *History of the Flag of the United States,* 2nd rev. ed., (Boston: A. Williams, 1880), 508.
96 Eleanor Roosevelt offered this very statement in an emotional radio speech of reassurance on an evening of totem peril, hours after the invasion of Pearl

Harbor, in the first word from the White House to a shocked citizenry. Reproduced from NBC archives on "All Things Considered," NPR, December 7, 1991.

97 Scot M. Guenter, *The American Flag, 1777–1924* (Cranbury, N.J.: Associated University Presses, 1990), 111. See J. William Fosdick, "The Studlefunk's Bonfire," *St. Nicholas* 23 (1986), 732.

98 Preble, *History*, 351–52.

99 "'Daisy' Harriman Outruns Bombs," *Life*, May 13, 1940, vol. 8, no. 16, 32.

100 "The American Flag Goes Down Before a U-Boat Torpedo in the South Atlantic," *Life*, vol. 11, no. 23, December 8, 1941, 44.

101 *Ibid.*

102 Robert Lipsyte, "The Principal Who Remains the Coach," *New York Times*, October 2, 1992, B11.

103 "President Urges Reverence for the Flag," *New York Times*, June 15, 1923, 4.

104 "What can a man believe in?" E. R. Squibb & Sons advertisement, *Life*, February 15, 1943, vol. 14, no. 7, 5.

105 Gum-chewing is the only deviation allowed in front of the cameras, and this deviation calls to mind mischievous boys, ultimately innocent of wrongdoing.

106 Mary Douglas, *Implicit Meanings* (London: Routledge & Kegan Paul, 1975), xiv.

107 "President Urges Reverence for Flag," 4.

108 "Excerpts From Speech By Bush to Guardsmen," *New York Times*, September 16, 1992, A18.

109 "President Urges Reverence for Flag," 4.

3 Theorizing the flagbody

1 Denise James reporting, *Channel 6 11:00 News*, WPVI-TV, Philadelphia, June 11, 1990. The occasion was the announcement of the Supreme Court's decision in *United States* v. *Eichman* (1990) 110 L Ed 2d 287, the second decision striking down flag desecration laws.

2 *Texas* v. *Johnson*, 401 US 397, US Sup. Ct., 1989.

3 National Public Radio, "All Things Considered," June 23, 1990.

4 Mary Douglas, *Natural Symbols: Explorations in Cosmology* (New York: Pantheon, 1982), vii.

5 See Brian Stock, *The Implications of Literacy* (Princeton, N.J.: Princeton, 1983).

6 Our use of *mode* is derived from Larry Gross, "Mode," *International Encyclopedia of Communication*, Erik Barnouw, ed., vol. 3 (New York: Oxford University Press and the Annenberg School of Communications, 1989), 32–36.

7 A serious flaw in the conventional definition of oral culture as patterns of speaking and hearing is its failure to recognize co-present visual channels that may be gestural, pictorial, or both, but never absent. Frances Yates's classic analysis of memory systems is fully attentive to the importance of the visual in oral culture. See *The Art of Memory* (Chicago: University of Chicago, 1960).

8 According to Whitney Smith, director of the Flag Research Center in Winchester, Mass., just before the Gulf War, Saddam Hussein authorized a new Iraqi flag with the written Arabic script for "God is Great" across the middle white horizontal stripe. This script was in Saddam's own hand, the writing of his body. The blue of the Israeli flag, conspicuously rejecting the traditional Muslim colors of orange, white, and green typifying other countries in the region, signifies the blue of the Jewish prayer shawl that wraps the body. The flag of Catalonia, La Senyera, contains red and yellow stripes, by legend the blood with which a dying soldier had raked the flag.

9 Statement of Capt. Paul V. Collins, Hearing before the Committee on the Judiciary. House of Representatives. 26th Congress, January 31, 1927, regarding (69) HR12807, 15.

10 John Bentley Mays, "The answer is blowing in the wind," *Globe and Mail*, May 1, 1991, Arts-1. Flags do appear in print contexts that recontextualize them. This may then influence their meaning in oral contexts, but flags themselves are not written-language artifacts.

11 See Carolyn Marvin, "The Body of the Text: Literacy's Corporeal Constant,"*Quarterly Journal of Speech* 80 (1994), 129–49.

12 Karal Ann Marling and John Wetenhall, *Iwo Jima* (Cambridge, Mass.: Harvard, 1991, 59).

13 David Johnston, "'Someday' Comes With a Roar for 21 Ex-Captives," *New York Times*, March 11, 1991, A11.

14 See Huntly Collins, "Penn Professor burns flag to make a free speech point," *Philadelphia Inquirer*, September 15, 1989 and "Ginny Wiegand, "Penn backs teacher who burned flag," *Philadelphia Inquirer*, September 16, 1989. Also Steven Ochs, "State House decries prof's flag burning," *Daily Pennsylvanian*, March 22, 1990. A further account appears in Marvin, "Bad Attitudes, Unnatural Acts," *Free Speech Yearbook* 28 (1990), 1–7.

15 *Issues and Answers*, Ch. 6, WPVI-TV, Philadelphia, June 24, 1990.

16 *AM Philadelphia*, WPVI-TV, Philadelphia, June 14, 1990.

17 The military salute to the flag is said to descend from the custom of knights raising their visors to show their eyes, a vulnerable part of the body. The gesture negates the attack signal of visor down in preparation for charging. Saluting the flag thus aligns the body to the flag in a posture of non-assault. Flagburning is an act of assault. American soldiers salute only their superiors, but *all* military personnel salute the flag when it is in motion, for example, passing by on a standard in a parade. The flag is in motion at dawn when raised, and at dusk when lowered. It is not in motion when it covers the casket and is not saluted. We speculate that the moving flag signifies the living flag. This notion is reinforced by the flag that comes to life as the day does and departs from life as the sun sets. We also speculate that the rippling flag, which is favored in flag representations, is chosen not only because it has more visual interest than a flat unmoving flag, but because it suggests a living, that is, embodied, flag.

18 *Texas* v. *Johnson*, 354.

19 *Ibid.*, 2553.

20 Sonni Efron, "5 Arrested After Flags Are Burned," *Los Angeles Times*, July 9, 1990, B1, B8.

21 Peter Stallybrass and Allon White, *The Politics and Poetics of Transgression* (Ithaca: Cornell, 1986), 44–59.

22 See "Chronicle," *New York Times*, July 27, 1990, B4. Also "Roseanne Strikes Out! The Whole Crazy Story of How She Turned Into a National Disgrace," *National Enquirer*, August 14, 1990, 28–29, 36. Also Dennis Georgatos, "Furor Over Roseanne's Singing," *San Francisco Chronicle*, July 27, 1990, 21.

23 "The furor caused by this event nearly ruined her. Everyone seemed outraged – from then-President Bush to veterans' groups and others who pressured the sponsor to get her off the air *before* her show premiered that season. 'I was terrified' she admits." Leo Janos, "The Queen of Awesome!" *Cosmopolitan*, February 1993, 134.

24 A. Trebbe, "Roseanne's shrill 'anthem' hits sour note," *USA Today*, July 27–29, 1990, 1.

25 Sue Chastain, "Bacchanal at the beach," *Philadelphia Inquirer*, August 31, 1990, D1, D8.

26 Mark Poster, *The Mode of Information: Poststructuralism and Social Context* (Chicago: University of Chicago, 1990), 8.

27 "Washing a Flag: Treat It 'Like Lingerie'," *New York Times*, June 30, 1990, 30.

28 See Joan B. Connelly, "Parthenon and *Parthenoi*: A Mythological Interpretation of the Parthenon Frieze," *American Journal of Archaeology*, January 1996, vol. 100, no. 1, 53–80.

29 "New glory," Sak's Fifth Avenue advertisement, *New York Times*, June 14, 1990, A4.

30 "'Old Glory' condoms raise eyebrows," *Au Courant*, October 22, 1990, 8.

31 The biographer of Robert Mills, the original architect of the monument, writes of the Baltimore Monument to George Washington, the obelisk that was the direct forerunner of Mills' design for the national monument:

> In trying to describe this monument I am freshly reminded to what extent Mills imbued his compositions with character, personality – even with sex. In consequence he did not plan an Ionic column, which would have feminized this creation – and the subject of it. He chose that which was most virile and elementary, to uphold his statue, the Doric, that having the least complexity of detail.
>
>   (H.M. Pierce Gallagher, *Robert Mills: Architect of the Washington Monument. 1781–1855* [New York: Columbia, 1935], 105.)

32 See Scot M. Guenter, *The American Flag, 1777–1924* (Cranbury, N.J.: Associated University Presses, 1990), 133–53.

33 *New York*, July 2–9, 1990.

34 "Oh, Say, Can You Sell?" *Time*, July 9, 1990, 54.

35 "Crazy for the Red, White, and Blue," editorial, *New York Times*, July 4, 1990, 30.

36 Robert D. McFadden, "Wrapped in U.S. Flag, Madonna Raps for Vote," *New York Times*, October 20, 1990, 7.

37 Bruce Handy, "Give Me Semi-Automatic Weapons and Flammable Old Glory's – Or Give Me Death!" *Spy*, December, 1989, 93.

38 Michael Frisch, "American History and the Structures of Collective Memory: A Modest Exercise in Empirical Iconography," *The Journal of American History* 75(4), March, 1989, 1150.

39 See Steve Lopez, "A closer look at political flier," *Philadelphia Inquirer*, September 23, 1990, B1.

40 Frisch, "American History," 1142.

41 John H. Fow, *The True Story of the American Flag* (Philadelphia: William J. Campbell, 1908), 3.

42 Linda K. Kerber, *Women of the Republic. Intellect and Ideology in Revolutionary America* (New York: W. W. Norton, 1980).

43 Oliver Parry, *Betsy Ross and the United States Flag. A Paper Read Before The Bucks County Historical Society*, Doylestown Pa., January 19, 1909, 9.

44 Charles M. Wallington, affidavit, in Parry, 1–3. The Betsy myth was already under construction in "The Birth of the Flag," in the *Philadelpha Press* for September 11, 1887, quoted in Parry, 3.

45 Edwin Satterthwaite Parry, *Betsy Ross: Quaker Rebel. Being the True Story of the Romantic Life of the Maker of the First American Flag* (Philadelphia: John C. Winston, 1930).

46 *Ibid.*, xiii.

47 Oliver Parry, *Betsy Ross and the United States Flag*, 24.

48 *Ibid.*, 17–18.

49 *Ibid.*, 14.

50 Rachael Fletcher, affidavit, July 31, 1871, in *Ibid.*, 11–12.

51 Edwin Parry, *Betsy Ross: Quaker Rebel*, 2, 8, 29, 17, 32, 61–62.

52 See Frances A. Yates, *The Art of Memory* (Chicago: Chicago, 1966).

53 Edwin Parry, *Betsy Ross: Quaker Rebel*, 240–41.

54 Katharine W. Hill to "To Tell the Truth," CBS, February 16, 1965, Archives of the Flag Research Center. Winchester, Mass. The scholar was Whitney Smith, director of the Flag Research Center.

55 No title, *TWA Ambassador*, July, 1992, 24. Reprinted from *Town & Country* (n.d.).

4 The totem myth: sacrifice and transformation

1 Charles Krause, interview with Vladimir Zhirinovsky on January 13, 1991, *MacNeil-Lehrer News Hour*, PBS, December 14, 1993.

2 Mircea Eliade, *Cosmos and History: The Myth of the Eternal Return*, tr. by Willard R. Trask (1949; 1954; New York: Harper Torchbooks, 1959), 4.

3 Quoted in Hilda Kuper, *An African Aristocracy* (New York: Oxford University Press, 1947; 1961), 26.

4 Fredric Jameson, *The Political Unconscious* (Ithaca: Cornell University Press, 1981), 102.

5 Calling for the bombing of "Serbian guns" surrounding Sarajevo, former totem officials Richard Burt and Richard Perle asserted that "Air strikes, especially televised ones, would be dramatic, even exhilarating." See Richard Burt and Richard Perle, "The Next Act in Bosnia," *New York Times*, February 11, 1994, A35.

6 Reported by Bob Edwards, *Morning Edition*, National Public Radio, January 4, 1995.

7 A similar argument has been put forward by Bruno Latour, *We Have Never Been Modern* (Harvard, 1993).

8 Abraham F. Foxman, "Resurgence of Nazism," letter to the editor, *New York Times*, January 1, 1994, 24.

9 Bob Johnson, "TV's 'Normal' Violence," letter to the editor, *New York Times*, May 20, 1992, A22.

10 Mary Otto, "Guns rival traffic as a top cause of death," *Philadelphia Inquirer*, January 28, 1994, A1.

11 See Gina Kolata, "1 in 5 Nurses Tell Survey They Helped Patients Die," *New York Times*, May 23, 1996, A14.

12 Anastasia Toufexis, "Seeking the Roots of Violence," *Time*, April 19, 1993, 52.

13 Richard Bernstein, "Looking Ahead Gloomily With Clear Statistics." Review of Urie Bronfenbrenner, Peter McClelland, Elaine Wethington, Phyllis Moen and Stephen J. Ceci, *The State of Americans: This Generation and the Next* (New York: Free Press, 1996), *New York Times*, August 28, 1996, C15.

14 See George Gerbner, "Instant History—Image History: Lessons of the Persian Gulf War," *The Velvet Light Trap*, No. 31, Spring, 1993, 10. In 1995 Gerbner found 6–8 violent episodes per prime-time television hour, four times as many in children's programming, and an average of two entertaining murders a night.

15 Max Frankel, "News of a Lifetime," *New York Times Magazine*, July 11, 1995, sec. 6, 28.

16 A number of theorists have suggested a central role for symbolic violence in group behavior. See Morris Nitsun, *Anti-Group* (New York: Routledge, 1996).

17 Peter Stallybrass and Allon White, *The Politics and Poetics of Transgression* (Ithaca: Cornell University Press, 1986), 200.

18 Mary Douglas, *Purity and Danger* (1966; New York: Ark Paperbacks, 1984), p.114.

19 Anthony Lewis, "Death of a Dream," *New York Times*, March 29, 1993, A15.

20 Implicit in those distinctions is a hierarchy of totem protection measured by distance from the boundary. The nearer one is to the totem, the more protection one has, for insiders are under totem protection. Women wrapped in the flag, for example, symbolize the protected life center, while the flag that wraps them signifies the perimeter that borders death.

21 "How the Heroic Boys of Buna Drove the Japs into the Sea," *Life*, February 22, 1943, v. 14, no. 8, 24.

22 Slavenka Drakulic, "When Patriots Are Enemies," *New York Times*, October 26, 1992, A17.

23 See Samuel Y. Edgerton, Jr., "From Mental Matrix to *Mappamundi* to Christian Empire," *Art and Cartography*, David Woodward, ed. (Chicago: University of Chicago, 1987), 15–17.

24 W. Robertson Smith, *Lectures on the Religion of the Semites* (London: Adam and Charles Black, 1889), 313.

25 Drakulic, "When Patriots Are Enemies," A17.

26 Seth Mydans, "Los Angeles Policeman Acquitted in Taped Beating," *New York Times*, April 30, 1992, D22.

27 (n.a.), "Savoring a Scent of Victory but Wondering About When the Guns Go Quiet," *New York Times*, February 27, 1991, A23.

28 Robert Pullman, interview in "CBS Reports D-Day with Dan Rather and Norman Schwarzkopf," May 26, 1994.

29 Embodied in the president and Congress, the totem has the power to declare war and thus to obligate soldiers to expose themselves to death and to kill others. The police have legal authority to execute citizens when the situation demands it. In other situations, the totem must exercise due process (totem class members are also subject to due process for killings they commit), but due process is under the control of totem referees. The Official Secrets Act states explicitly that death is a possible penalty for passing totem secrets. Just as criminal suspects must receive due process but totem executions of citizens may also take place in the streets, spies may get their day in court. They also may be shot on sight in the field if the totem commander of the moment deems it necessary. Other totem at-will powers include the right to seize and hold citizens without charge for seventy-two hours, and the right to search citizens with no other warrant than the suspicion of the totem officer on the scene. Without accountability, totem officials have sponsored life-threatening experiments on its citizens when this was deemed necessary. Included in this category are "experiments" with 400 syphilitic prisoners in Tuskegee by the US Department of Health as a means of observing long-term effects, and secret drug experiments conducted by MK-Ultra from 1956 to 1972. An interesting example occurred in 1995 when a murderer scheduled for lethal injection in Oklahoma attempted suicide. "Authorities . . . had to arouse a condemned man from a self-induced drug stupor today so that they could execute him with state-approved drugs." "It wasn't his job to take his life," [a state official] explained. See (n.a.), "Revived From Overdose, Inmate is Executed," *New York Times*, August 12, 1995, 6.

30 A. M. Rosenthal, "The Bigotry Trade," *New York Times*, November 20, 1992, A31.

31 "A cardinal principle of Russian military doctrine is that the country should never use its armed forces against its own people. How cynical this sounds as bombs explode in the houses of innocent people in Chechnya," wrote a former Ukrainian Minister of Defense. See Kostantin Morozov, "The Grasp of Empire," *New York Times*, January 5, 1995, A27. Compare to a related mythic

system, Christianity, in which the crucified son cries out during his ordeal, "Father, why hast thou forsaken me?"

32 Eliade, *Cosmos and History*, 109.
33 Walter A. McDougall, "What We Do for Our Country," *New York Times*, February 17, 1992, A17.
34 CNN News, November 5, 1995.
35 Chris Hedges, "Some of the Americans Feel Test of Mettle Was Too Easy," *New York Times*, March 1, 1991, A12.
36 Mimi Hall, "Conlicting emotions of Vietnam veterans," *USA Today*, February 13, 1991, A8.
37 Directed by George Stevens, and starring Alan Ladd, Jean Arthur, Van Heflin, Jack Palance, Paramount, 1953.
38 Directed by John Ford, and starring John Wayne, Robert Montgomery, Donna Reed, MGM, 1945.
39 Marc Kaufman, "Five of the lives disrupted by call to arms," *Philadelphia Inquirer*, January 20, 1991, A10.
40 Lea Sitton, Thomas J. Gibbons Jr., and Suzette Parmley, "They brought spirit to a dangerous job," *Philadelphia Inquirer* January 29, 1994, A1.
41 *Ibid.*, A5.
42 Norimitsu Onishi, "A Bittersweet Graduation as Fallen Firefighters Are Mourned," *New York Times*, April 1, 1994, B3.
43 Frank Bruni, "Firefighters Say Risks of Job Don't Diminish Their Ardor," *New York Times*, February 7. 1996, B4.
44 Robert Hanley, "Relatives Recount Dreams of 2 Killed in Somalia," *New York Times*, October 7, 1993, A11.
45 *Ibid.*
46 *Ibid.*
47 "Bill Moyers with Elie Wiesel: Facing Hate," *Moyers*. 1991.
48 Quoted in Bruce Lincoln, *Discourse and the Construction of Society* (New York: Oxford, 1989), 117.
49 Charisse Jones, "With Firefighter's Death, Brooklyn Loses a Son," *New York Times*, February 7, 1996, B4.
50 Bob Herbert, "Violence in the State of Denial," *New York Times*, October 27, 1993, A23.
51 Mike O'Connor, "For Serbs, A Flashback to '43 Horror," *New York Times*, September 21, 1995, A14.
52 Donald Kagan, *On the Origins of War and the Preservation of Peace* (New York: Doubleday, 1995), 8.
53 "Is This Worth Dying For?" *New York Times,* January 10, 1991, A 23.
54 General Douglas MacArthur, "Duty, Honor, Country," Address to the US Military Academy, May 12, 1962, in Major Vorin E. Whan, ed., *A Soldier Speaks* (New York: Praeger, 1965), 354.
55 "The 47 Rōnin", *Life*, November 1, 1943, v. 15, no. 18, 52.
56 Jeff Gammage and Maureen Graham, "Zaun and troops get a big salute," *Philadelphia Inquirer*, April 9, 1991, A8.

57 *The Year of the Generals*, CBS special, June 4, 1992.

58 Hanley, "Relatives Recount Dreams," A11.

59 Quoted in Karal Ann Marling and John Wetenhall, *Iwo Jima: Monuments, Memories, and the American Hero* (Cambridge: Harvard, 1991), 242.

60 Robert Ardrey, *The Territorial Imperative* (New York: Delta, 1966), 270.

61 Dirk Johnson, "Voters Can't Find the Humor In Capital's Partisan Games," *New York Times*, August 27, 1994, 9.

62 Mary Jordan, "A Capital Thank-You: 800,000 Jam D.C. for Tribute to Troops," *Washington Post*, June 9, 1991, A1.

63 Allesandra Stanley, "A Russian Newspaper Turns More Scornful," *New York Times*. January 6, 1995, A8.

64 "Transcript of Debate Between the Vice-Presidential Candidates," *New York Times*, October 16, 1976, 9.

65 "Homecoming, Without Honors," editorial, *New York Times*, February 28, 1991, A24.

66 "The Danger of Executing the Innocent," editorial, *New York Times*, January 9, 1995, A14.

67 For a history of the advertisement see Kathleen Hall Jamieson, *Packaging the Presidency* (New York: Oxford University Press, 1984), 198–203.

68 "Goodbye to a Grandfather: We Are So Cold and So Sad," Eulogy at Yitzhak Rabin funeral, November 6, 1995, *New York Times*, November 7, 1995, A11.

69 Douglas Jehl, "A Moment of Disbelief and Uncertainty," *New York Times*, November 6, 1995, A1.

70 Alan Cowell, "From Young Israelis, an Outpouring of Emotion," *New York Times,* November 9, 1995, A10.

71 *Ibid.*

72 Joel Greenberg, "Grief and Guilt Soak Gravesite Like the Rain," *New York Times*, November 8, 1995, A13.

73 Shimon Peres, Eulogy for Itzhak Rabin, November 6, 1995. Quoted in "Words of Grief and Resolve From Friends and World Leaders," *New York Times*, November 7, 1995, A10.

74 Isabel Wilkerson, "Some Who Like What They Heard but Are Sure They've Heard It Before," *New York Times*, January 26, 1995, A19.

75 Quoted by Maura Liason, "All Things Considered," National Public Radio, August 28, 1996.

76 Maureen Dowd, "Weary and Feeling the Presidency's Weight," *New York Times*, August 16, 1992, 24. The Roosevelt quote was offered by National Security Adviser Brent Scowcroft in a discussion of George Bush's unwillingness to discipline a warring staff.

77 Former Reagan chief of staff Kenneth Duberstein recalled that on the last day of his presidency, Reagan walked into the room for a final farewell and briefing, "and I remember him turning to [NSC adviser General] Colin [Powell] before a final word on a foreign policy/national security briefing, and Colin saying, "The world is quiet today, Mr. President," and the President turned to

us, reached into his pocket and said, "Well, in that case, can I give back my nuclear code card? [Moderator Bryant Gumbel laughed heartily at this mention of the taboo power that defines the totem] and we both said, "No, you're still President for two and a half more hours!" *Today Show*, January 20, 1992.

78 R. W. Apple, Jr., "Many Democrats Accuse Clinton of Incompetence," *New York Times*, February 16, 1995, D21.

79 Wilkerson, "Some Who Like What They Heard but Are Sure They've Heard It Before," A19.

80 Micheal Clodfelter, *Warfare and Armed Conflicts: A Statistical Reference to Casualty and Other Figures, 1618–1991*, I (London: McFarland, 1992), 528.

81 Civil War figures from *Ibid*. Based on Thomas L. Livermore, *Numbers and Losses in the Civil War in America 1861–65* (Boston: Houghton, Mifflin: 1901).

82 "Lost" refers to death in the service from all causes. To a family, the loss of a member in association with a war, whether in action or off the field, is a war sacrifice.

83 US Department of Commerce, Bureau of the Census, *Statistical Abstract of the United States* (Washington, D.C.: GPO, 1993), 8.

84 All war figures, including "served," from Clodfelter, *Warfare*, II, 785.

85 US Department of Commerce, *Statistical Abstract*, 8.

86 All war figures, including "served," from Clodfelter, *Warfare*, II, 956. Not including POWs.

87 US Department of Commerce, *Statistical Abstract*, 8.

88 *Ibid.*, 359.

89 All figures except "served," from Clodfelter, *Warfare*, II, 1216. Not including MIA/POWs.

90 US Department of Commerce, *Statistical Abstract*, p 8.

91 *Ibid.*, 359. Covers 1964–73.

92 All war figures except "served," from Clodfelter, *Warfare*, II, 1322–23. Not including MIA/POWs. Gulf War figures do not include figures for exposure to nerve gas, which was only acknowledged by the Pentagon in 1996.

93 US Department of Commerce, *Statistical Abstract*, 8.

94 Clodfelter, *Warfare*, II, 1078. This is not total served, but peak strength.

95 *Ibid.*, 1085.

96 Not including MIA/POWs.

97 Lawrence Freedman and Efraim Karsh, *The Gulf Conflict, 1990–1991* (Princeton, N.J.: Princeton University Press, 1993), 408. See also Clodfelter, I, 1086.

98 Douglas E. Kneeland, "Debts of Honor," *New York Times*, May 29, 1995, 21. Also James Bennet, "Medals of Honor Awarded at Last to Black World War II Veterans," *New York Times*, January 14, 1997, A1.

99 René Girard, *Violence and the Sacred* (Baltimore: Johns Hopkins University Press, 1977), 78, 100–01.

100 *World News Sunday*, ABC, November 26, 1995.

101 Daniel Jonah Goldhagen, *Hitler's Willing Executioners: Ordinary Germans and the Holocaust* (New York: Alfred A. Knopf, 1996).
102 Alan Cowell, "Israelis Start To Pick Up The Pieces," *New York Times*, November 8, 1995, A13.
103 Richard Hottelet, interviewed in "CBS Reports D-Day," CBS, May 26, 1994.
104 Bruce W. Neland, "Ike's Invasion," *Time*, June 6, 1994, 40.
105 Robert Lipsyte, "Decades Pass, and What's New Under the Sun?" *New York Times*, February 25, 1994, B10.
106 Barbara Stewart, "After Tragic Death, Students Fulfill Their Friend's Dream," *New York Times*, January 14, 1995, 29.
107 Leonce Gaiter, "American Mantra: Blame the Black Man," *New York Times*, November 12, 1994, 21.

5 Death-touchers and border crossers

1 René Girard, *Violence and the Sacred*, tr. by Patrick Gregory (Baltimore: Johns Hopkins University Press, 1977), 10.
2 Bruce Weber, *New York Times*, "Vietnam Bike Tour Challenges Western Hearts and Minds, " March 1, 1995, A10.
3 Quoted in Major Vorin E. Whan, Jr., ed., *A Soldier Speaks* (New York: Praeger, 1965), 352.
4 Interviewed by Brian Lamb, "Booknotes," C-Span, May 8, 1994.
5 Michael DeMaio, interview, July 25, 1990, Philadelphia.
6 W. Robertson Smith, *Lectures on the Religion of the Semites. First Series. The Fundamental Institutions.* Burnett Lectures, 1888–1889 (New York: D. Appleton), 354–56.
7 Chris Hedges,"Marines Fear Glory Will Give Way to Old Stigma," *New York Times*, May 31, 1991, A1.
8 Bernard E. Trainor, "Suicide Over a Medal? An Ex-General's View," *New York Times*, May 20, 1996, B6.
9 Quoted in Carey Goldberg, "Cannons, Salutes and Plenty of Bad Weather," *New York Times*, May 30, 1995, B5.
10 Victor Turner, *The Ritual Process: Structure and Anti-Structure* (Chicago: Aldine, 1969), 106–107.
11 Mary Douglas, *Purity and Danger* (1966; New York: Ark Paperbacks, 1989), 53.
12 Discussing deprivation and demoralization in the post-Cold war Russian military, a senior officer, General Vorovyov, observed: "'I love the army very much,' he told *Izvestia* in an interview. 'I gave it 38 years of my life. And I don't want even the smallest stain on its uniform.'" Steven Erlanger, "Russia's Army Seen as Failing Chechnya Test," *New York Times*, December 25, 1994, section 1, 10.
13 W. Robertson Smith, *Lectures on the Religion of the Semites*, 341–42.
14 For an account of boot camp training in the old Corps, see William

Manchester, *Goodbye, Darkness: A Memoir of the Pacific War* (Boston: Little, Brown, 1979), 119–46.

15 (n.a.), "President's Safety Is Often a Woman's Work," *New York Times*, July 6, 1993, A13.

16 David Zucchino, "A covert life revealed," *Philadelphia Inquirer*, January 17, 1993, A14.

17 *Ibid.*

18 "The Flag: A Contested Symbol," Documentary film by Jim Ospenson, Rob Mackey, Ramona Lyons, Annenberg School for Communication, 1990.

19 Michael DeMaio, interview, July 25, 1990, Philadelphia.

20 Gwen Ifill, "At Jackson's Behest, Clinton Kicks Off Voter Drive," *New York Times*, September 13, 1992, section 1, 36.

21 This quote comes from the opening scene of *Patton* (1970), a version of the standard speech Patton delivered again and again. See Roger H. Nye, *The Patton Mind* (Garden City Park, N.Y.: Avery Publishing Group), 142–43 and Martin Blumenson, *The Patton Papers 1940–1945* (Boston: Houghton Mifflin, 1974), 456–58.

22 "Negroes at War: All they want now is a Fair Chance to Fight," *Life,* June 15, 1942, 86.

23 Phil Caruso, "Righteous Anger Spilled Over at Police Rally," *New York Times*, September 25, 1992, A23.

24 Olympic coverage, CBS, January 21, 1992.

25 Harry Smith, Olympic coverage, CBS, February 14, 1992.

26 Washington, letter to Henry Knox, October 21, 1798. Quoted in Defense Management Study Group on Military Cohesion, *Cohesion in the US Military* (Washington, DC: National Defense University Press, 1984), ix.

27 USMC Captain Mark Stanovich to Carolyn Marvin and David Ingle, personal communication, March 24, 1992.

28 See Erving Goffman, *Asylums: Essays on the Social Situation of Mental Patients and Other Inmates* (Garden City, New York: Anchor Books, 1961), 12–35. Marine boot camp forms Basic Warriors who proceed to the fleet for training in individual jobs. The fleet group is considered the basic military unit and the most bonded.

29 The mechanism is described by a Muslim fighting for the Serbs in Bosnia in reply to a reporter who asked if it were difficult to fire on fellow Muslims. "It's terrible, but I have to help keep my friends here alive. The Muslim who comes up the mountain can be my relative, he can be my friend, but the moment he puts on a uniform, he becomes the enemy." John F. Burns, "Stranger in a Strange Land: Muslim in Serb Army," *New York Times*, January 7, 1993, A3.

30 Interview with USMC Staff Sergeant Jeff Kovino, March 20, 1992, Parris Island, South Carolina.

31 Manchester, *Goodbye, Darkness*, 391.

32 Honda "Nighthawk 750" motorcycle advertisement, *Sports Illustrated*, March 9, 1992, 156–57.

33 See Eric Schmitt, "Harassment Questions Kill 2 Admirals' Promotions," *New York Times*, July 18, 1992, 7.

34 Anna Quindlen, "With Extreme Prejudice," *New York Times*, June 24, 1992, A21.

35 Catherine S. Manegold, "'Save the Males' Becomes Battle Cry In Citadel's Defense Against Woman," *New York Times*, May 23, 1993, A10.

36 *Ibid.*

37 "Women's Combat Role Debated As Chiefs Denounce Sex Bias," *Congressional Quarterly Weekly Report*, August 1, 1992, 2292.

38 Quoted in Michael R. Gordon, "Panel Is Against Letting Women Fly in Combat," *New York Times*, November 4, 1992, A24.

39 "Women's Combat Role Debated," 2293.

40 Quoted in Eric Schmitt, "Army Will Allow Women in 32,000 Combat Posts," *New York Times*, July 28, 1994, A12.

41 Quoted in Sam Howe Verhovek, "New Twist for a Landmark Case: Roe v. Wade Becomes Roe v. Roe," *New York Times*, August 12, 1995, 1.

42 Douglas Martin, "About New York," *New York Times*, June 8, 1991, 27.

43 Jane Gross, "What Only War Dead Can Teach," *New York Times*, January 21, 1991, A12.

44 Andrew H. Malcolm, "Just Another Day in May, A Trifle Chilly, Though," *New York Times*, May 26, 1992, B6.

45 *Ibid.*

46 *Ibid.*

47 Manchester, *Goodbye, Darkness*, 33.

48 *Ibid.*, 12–13.

49 Quoted in "When they come home," *Reader's Digest* advertisement, *New York Times*, March 7, 1991, D26.

50 In a July 4 speech in Marshield, Mo., home of one of the oldest Independence Day celebrations in the country, President George Bush quoted a local resident, Sergeant Richard Mann: "I think God took a whole generation of Americans out in the desert and showed them a miracle." Maureen Dowd, "An Old-Fashioned Day of Patriotism," *New York Times*, July 5, 1991, A9.

51 Edward Burnett Tylor, *Religion in Primitive Culture* (Harper & Row, 1958; Gloucester, Mass.: Peter Smith, 1970), 130–45.

52 "A Fallen Soldier's Tribute to the Flag," *San Francisco Examiner*, February 10, 1991. Paid for by Swanson Vineyards & Winery, Rutherford, California, B10.

53 Tylor, *Religion in Primitive Culture*, 135.

54 Trainor, "Suicide Over a Medal?" B6.

55 Quoted in Bill McAllister, "To Military Members, Medals Are 'History on Their Chest.'" *Washington Post*, May 17, 1996, A14.

56 Captain Ben Kimmelman, interview in *The Battle of the Bulge*, narrated by David McCullough, Lennon Documentary Group for *The American Experience*, WGBH, 1994.

57 "Vietnam as One Family Faces It," *Life*, 1965, 89.
58 Directed by John Wayne and Ray Kellog, Batjac Productions, Warner Bros., 1968.
59 "When they come home," D26.
60 Douglas J. MacDonald, "The Hostile Reaction," letter to the editor, *New York Times*, May 1, 1991, A30.
61 John Hill and Stephen B. Katz, "New Kidney on the Block," *L.A. Law*, Twentieth-Century Fox, Script #7L07, No. 3551, November 14, 1990.
62 James Bennet, "Cuomo Sides With Disabled Veterans Who Peddle," *New York Times*, May 21, 1992, B3.
63 Charles Green, "Troops get a welcome from Bush," *Philadelphia Inquirer*, March 18, 1991, A9.
64 Bob Kotowski, "And lest we forget Vietnam," *New York Times*, August 2, 1991, A23.
65 David Gonzalez, "Veterans of Gulf War Get a Stirring Welcome," *New York Times*, April 29, 1991, B5.
66 *Ibid.*
67 Lisa Grunwald, "Facing the Wall," *Life*, November 1992, 29.
68 Tom Junod, "Sons of Silence," *Life*, February 25, 1991, Special Weekly Edition No. 1, 59.
69 Grunwald, *Facing the Wall*, 30.
70 David Ellis, "The Last Battle," *People*, May 30, 1994, 67.
71 Michael Norman, "Coming Home," *New York Times Magazine*, January 1, 1995, section 6, 34.
72 Lewis B. Puller, Jr., *Fortunate Son* (New York: Grove Weidenfeld, 1991), 437.
73 Quoted on "Morning Edition," NPR, May 25, 1992.
74 Robert D. McFadden, "New York Memorial Day Parade Fades Away," *New York Times*, May 23, 1992, 26.
75 Malcolm, "Just Another Day in May," B6.
76 Michel Marriott, *New York Times*, May 26, 1992, B1.
77 McFadden, "New York Memorial Day Parade," A1.
78 Malcolm, "Just Another Day in May," B6.
79 McFadden, "New York Memorial Day Parade," 26.
80 *Ibid.*

6 Strategic tinkering: totem memory and succession

1 Roy Rappaport, *Ecology, Meaning, & Religion* (Berkeley, Calif.: North Atlantic Books, 1979), 174.
2 Mircea Eliade, *Cosmos and History: The Myth of the Eternal Return,* tr. by Willard R. Trask (1949; 1954; New York: Harper & Row, 1959), 20.
3 Quoted in Kevin Sack, "Measure on Flag-Burning Is Approved by Assembly," *New York Times*, March 25, 1994, B6.
4 Sir James Frazer, *The Golden Bough*, Part 1, *The Magic Art and the Evolution of Kings*, 3rd ed. (London: Macmillan, 199), 52–61.

5 "The lives of 'primitives' . . . attain a greater unity than we," writes James Peacock in *The Anthropological Lens* (Cambridge: Cambridge University Press, 1986), 18. The sentiment is representative.

6 Jack Goody, "Against 'Ritual': Loosely Structured Thoughts on a Loosely Defined Topic," Sally F. Moore and Barbara G. Myerhoff, eds., *Secular Ritual* (Amsterdam: Van Gorcum, 1977), 25–35.

7 William Pfaff, "That older, other America has passed on," *Chicago Tribune*, November 8, 1992, C3.

8 Robert Wuthnow, *Meaning and Moral Order* (Berkeley, University of California, 1987), 101.

9 Eliade, *Cosmos and History*, 3–48.

10 *Ibid.*, 34.

11 *Ibid.*

12 Steven Erlanger, "High Price of a 'Victory'", *New York Times*, January 22, 1995, section 1, 1. The image "graven" in every heart is "Raising the Flag Over the Reichstag, May 2, 1945," by Russian photojournalist Yevgeny Khaldei, a photograph modeled explicitly on Joseph Rosenthal's photograph of the American flagraising on Mt. Suribachi, Iwo Jima in World War II.

13 Quoted by George Bush in "Excerpts From Speech By Bush to Guardsmen," *New York Times*, September 16, 1992, A18.

14 Dwight D. Eisenhower, "The Day I Knew I Belonged to the Flag," *Reader's Digest* 94 (March, 1969), 93.

15 See Rappaport, *Ecology, Meaning, & Religion*, 185.

16 Mary Douglas, The Frank W. Abrams lectures, *How Institutions Think* (Syracuse: Syracuse University Press, 1986), 4.

17 Rappaport, *Ecology, Meaning, & Religion*, 182–83, 199.

18 Interview with June Wandrey, *World News Tonight*, ABC, June 3, 1994.

19 Quoted in R.W. Apple, Jr., "Where Dead Lie, Clinton Hails D-Day," *New York Times*, June 7, 1944, A1.

20 Quoted on "Morning Edition," NPR, June 3, 1994.

21 Quoted in "Wars and Generations," *New York Times*, June 7, 1994, A22.

22 Quoted in R. W. Apple, Jr., "Half-Century Later, Allies Return to Normandy," *New York Times*, June 6, 1994, A10.

23 "A Year Ago on Iwo," *New York Times*, February 18, 1946, 20.

24 Quoted in Benedict Anderson, *Imagined Communities* (London: Verso, 1983, 1991), 35.

25 See generally Eric Hobsbawm and Terence Ranger, eds., *The Invention of Tradition* (Cambridge: Cambridge University Press, 1983). Between 1890 and 1920, American journalism dispensed with political advocacy and declared itself an independent provider of factual news accounts. "The press migrated from the sphere of political contention to that of social integration." See Richard Kaplan, *Transformations in the American Public Sphere: News and Politics, 1865–1920* (University of California at Berkeley dissertation, 1994).

26 Janice Schetz and Kathryn Holmes Snedaker, *Communication and Litigation:*

Case Studies of Famous Trials (Carbondale and Edwardsville, Ill.: Southern Illinois University Press, 1988), 19.

27 Rappaport, *Ecology, Meaning & Religion*, 175.

28 Quoted in R. W. Apple Jr., "Where Dead Lie, Clinton Hails D-Day," *New York Times*, June 7, 1994, A8.

29 Herman Wouk, "Never Again," *Washington Post*, June 6, 1944, A19.

30 Apple, "Where Dead Lie," A8.

31 Among the theorists who treat media ritual seriously are Elihu Katz and Daniel Dayan, *Media Rituals* (Cambridge, Mass.: Harvard University Press, 1992).

32 Fredric Jameson, *The Political Unconscious* (Ithaca, N.Y.: Cornell University Press, 1981), 102.

33 Danny Gur-arieh, "Israelis weep, scream at Rabin's death," Reuters World Service, November 5, 1995, BC cycle.

34 Michael Matza, "Quebec Rejects Proposal to Secede," *Philadelphia Inquirer*, October 31, 1995, A6.

35 N. R. Kleinfeld, "The Day (10 Minutes of It) the Nation Stood Still, *New York Times*, October 4, 1995, A1.

36 Clyde H. Farnsworth, "150,000 Rally To Ask Quebec Not to Secede," *New York Times*, October 28, 1995, 1.

37 Quoted by Walter Rodgers, "Rabin Assassination," *CNN News*, November 4, 1995, Transcript #614–1.

38 Douglas Jehl, "A Moment of Disbelief and Uncertainty," *New York Times*, November 6, 1995, A1.

39 Jeffrey Toobin, "A Horrible Human Event," *New Yorker*, October 23, 1995, 48.

40 N. R. Kleinfield, "A Parade of Pride in Yankee Triumph," *New York Times*, October 30, 1996, A1.

41 William Manchester, *The Death of a President* (New York: Harper & Row, 1967), 240.

42 *Ibid.*, 241.

43 *Ibid.*

44 *Ibid.*

45 *Energynews* (Philadelphia: Philadelphia Electric Company), May, 1991, 3.

46 F. H. McCombs, letter to the editor, *Philadelphia Inquirer*, March 11, 1991, A9.

47 Walter Goodman, "Clinton Borrows Freely From Capra to Tap Middle-Class Ideals," *New York Times*, February 17, 1993, A14.

48 Quoted in Roger Stone, "Nixon on Clinton," *New York Times*, April 28, 1994, A23.

49 Quoted in Sara Rimer, "Television Becomes Basic Furniture In College Students' Ivory Towers," *New York Times*, October 27, 1991, section 1, 18.

50 Walter Goodman, "Convention Coverage: Big Show, Little News," *New York Times*, July 15, 1992, A8.

51 Elizabeth Kolbert, "Democrats Stay on TV, Even If Not on the News," *New York Times*, July 20, 1992, A11.

52 Walter Goodman, "TV Networks Compete In Yellow Ribbon Game," *New York Times*, June 11, 1991, B5.

53 Alessandra Stanley, "As War Looms: Marches and Vigils, Talk and Fear," *New York Times*, January 15, 1991, A15.

54 Stanley, "As War Looms: Marches and Vigils, Talk and Fear," A15.

55 Goodman, "TV Networks Compete In Yellow Ribbon Game," B5.

56 Ted Koppel, Nixon funeral coverage, ABC, April 27, 1994.

57 Mac Daniel and Larry King, "Saluting an officer and a gentleman," *Philadelphia Inquirer*, October 16, 1992, B2.

58 Roberto Suro, "4 Brothers, One Dead, Come Home From the War," *New York Times*, March 10, 1991, 17.

59 Quoted in Gerald Eskenazi, "Koch Pledges Allegiance to the Statute," *New York Times*, February 9, 1992, section 8, 1, 4.

60 Interview on *CBS Sunday Morning*, February 9, 1992.

61 Daniel and King, "Saluting an officer and a gentleman," B2.

62 Tom Clancy, *Clear and Present Danger* (New York: G.Putnam's Sons, 1989), 622.

63 Henri Hubert and Marcel Mauss, *Sacrifice: Its Nature and Function*, tr. by W. D. Halls (Chicago: University of Chicago, 1964), 100.

64 Quoted in Carey Goldberg, "Cannons, Salutes and Plenty of Bad Weather," *New York Times*, May 30, 1995, B1.

65 Quoted in Todd S. Purdum, "What, Us Worry?" *New York Times*, section 6, 39.

66 A similar sentiment informed a British citizen's memory of the World War II homefront:"I think that although the war was dreadful, which it was, people were so nice and so friendly and so kind, and everybody shared with everybody . . . Although it was awful, it was wonderful, too." Quoted in Sarah Lyall, "The Home Front Revisited, and Here's How It Was," *New York Times*, April 25, 1995, A4.

67 In a *Life* story on American flag display, a Chicago shopowner exhibited the 48–star flag he had displayed since Pearl Harbor. "People don't look at it anymore," he mourned, "but it's going to stay here as long as I do." "Decalomania over the American Flag," *Life*, July 18, 1969, 33.

68 James Salter, "Infamy and Memory," *New York Times*, December 7, 1991, 23.

69 Eliade, *Cosmos and History*, 46.

70 Milo M. Quaife, Melvin J. Weig, Roy E. Appleman, *The History of the United States Flag. From the Revolution to the Present, Including a Guide to Its Use and Display* (New York: Harper & Brothers, 1961), 19–20.

71 Rappaport, *Ecology, Meaning, & Religion*, 198.

72 Salter, "Infamy and Memory," 23.

73 John G. Neihardt, *Black Elk Speaks* (Lincoln, Neb.: University of Nebraska Press, 1961), 208.

74 Andrew H. Malcolm, "Just Another Day in May, A Trifle Chilly, Though," *New York Times*, May 26, 1992, B6.

75 Salter, "Infamy and Memory," 23.

76 The return module was *Columbia*, the totem consort.

77 Buzz Aldrin and Malcolm McConnell, *Men From Earth* (New York: Bantam, 1989), 242.

78 Quoted in Harry Hurt III, *For All Mankind* (New York: Atlantic Monthly Press, 1988), 180–81.

79 News coverage of the Apollo II splashdown, ABC, July 24, 1969.

80 Quoted in James Reston, Jr., "The Apollo Three," *TV Guide*, July 16–22, 12.

81 Transcript of interview with Jim Lehrer on *MacNeil–Lehrer News Hour*, PBS, June 20, 1994.

82 Howard K. Smith, comments, ABC, July 20, 1969.

83 B. Drummond Ayers Jr., "Wistful Pride and Cynicism Color American's Memories of Apollo 11," *New York Times*, July 18, 1994, A11.

84 Timothy Ferris, "Earthbound," *New Yorker*, August 1, 1994, 5.

85 Ayers, "Wistful Pride," A11.

86 Steve Janas, letter to the editor, *Philadelphia Inquirer*, July 28, 1994, A20.

87 Laurent Rebours and John King, "Kuwait City greets allies with kisses, not combat," *Philadelphia Inquirer*, February 27, 1991, A10.

88 Directed by Edward Dymtryk, starring John Wayne, Beulah Bond, Anthony Quinn, RKO Pictures, 1945.

89 Balintawak is the site of the 1896 armed uprising that marked the beginning of the Filipino struggle against the Spanish.

90 General Marcelo del Pilar, a dashing resistance fighter against American forces.

91 "It wasn't until June 6 that formal resistance [on Bataan] ended, when a Jap hauled down the last American flag and ground it under his heel as a band played "Kimigayo," his national anthem." William Manchester, *Goodbye, Darkness* (Boston: Little, Brown, 1979), 61.

92 Emile Durkheim, *Elementary Forms*, tr. by Joseph Wood Swain (George Allen & Unwin, 1915; New York: Free Press, 1965), 341.

93 *Ibid.*, 53.

94 *Ibid.*, 339.

95 *Ibid.*, 378.

96 "It frequently happens that in the more advanced cults, the blood of the sacrificed victim or of the worshipper himself is spilt before or upon the altar. In these cases, it is given to the gods, for whom it is the preferred food." *Ibid.*, 383.

97 Eliade, *Cosmos and History*, 5.

98 This confirms its totemic nature. As Durkheim says of "churinga," totem objects of the Arunta, "Their loss is a disaster; it is the greatest misfortune which can happen to the group." *Elementary Forms*, 43, see also 140–49.

99 "The Correct Display of the Stars and Stripes," *National Geographic Magazine*, October, 1917, 413.

100 Remarks of counsel cited unofficially in 51 L. Ed. 696, 698 (1907). Quoted in

Albert M. Rosenblatt, "Flag Desecration Statutes: History and Analysis," *Washington University Law Quarterly*, 1972(2), Spring, 1972, 202.

101 Karal Ann Marling and Wetenhall, *Iwo Jima*, 2. This statement of regeneration has a humorous but ritually relevant analogue. Audiences for the Marine Band's summer concerts and Torchlight Tattoo ceremonies at the Iwo Jima Marine Memorial in Washington, DC attract many young women who are eager to attach themselves to the handsome Marines. In the summer of 1992 we watched a group of teenage schoolgirls take picture after picture of themselves with the goodlooking Marines, whom they touched, smiled at, and stood close to.

102 *Ibid.*, 64.

103 "Life's Reports: The Famous Iwo Flag-Raising," *Life*, vol. 18, no. 13, March 26, 1945, 18.

104 Quoted in Marling and Wetenhall, *Iwo Jima*, 77.

105 *Ibid.*, 76.

106 "Life's Reports: The Famous Iwo Flag-Raising," *Life*, March 26, 1945, 19.

107 Rappaport, *Ecology, Meaning, & Religion*, 193.

108 *Ibid.*, 192.

109 Marling and Wetenhall, *Iwo Jima*, 9.

110 Quoted in *Ibid.*, 97.

111 Eliade, *Cosmos and History*, 42.

112 John Keegan, *The Second World War* (New York: Penguin, 1990), 566, 572–73.

7 Refreshing the borders

1 Quoted in Dave Anderson, "Leo the Lip Was Baseball in New York," *New York Times*, October 9, 1991, B11.

2 Quoted in Don Terry, "Killed by Her Friends In an All-White Gang," *New York Times*, May 18, 1994, B22.

3 Bryan Di Salvatore, "City Slickers," *New Yorker*, March 22, 1993, 41.

4 Woodrow Wilson, "Too Proud to Fight," Philadelphia, Pa., May 10, 1915. Reprinted in Janet Podell and Steven Anzovin, eds., *Speeches of the American Presidents* (New York: H. H. Wilson, 1988), 385.

5 Kevin Sack, "Prosecutor Wins Right to Wear Flag Pin," *New York Times*, March 23, 1991, B1. Residents felt the complaint lay "somewhere between the seditious and the absurd," locating it outside the group.

6 "Excerpts From the Decision on Justifying Affirmative Action Programs," *New York Times*, June 13, 1995, D24.

7 Whether the totem may play favorites with religious affiliative groups is the problem that drives many church–state questions. Christmas, 1992, saw an affiliative clash between the Klan and Jewish and Christian groups in Cincinnati. Local Jewish groups secured permission to add a menorah to Christian symbols allowed by the city at Christmas. When the Klan requested permission to place a cross in the same spot, Christian groups objected that the

Klan's cross was not a proper but an evil cross. The Klan cross was torn down by locals on three successive days, and both Klan and Christian groups appealed for totem recognition and protection.

8 Lionel Tiger writes, "The Ku Klux Klan is in a real sense a sublimated government-cum-army." *Men in Groups*, rev. ed. (1969; New York: Marion Boyars, 1984), 154.

9 "A Look at the World's Week," *Life*, May 2, 1955, 38–39.

10 Quoted in Russell Baker, "A Slight Plague of Murder," *New York Times*, September 11, 1993, 21.

11 With a largely Jewish membership, the American Communist Party before World War II was such an affiliative group. The son of Gene Dennis, leader of the Communist Party during this period, recalled marching in support of Henry Wallace's presidential candidacy down Seventh Ave. as a crowd of young kids jeered, "Down with the Communists! Up with the Irish!" *Children of the Left*, directed by Eric Strange, PBS, June 30, 1992. Following the war, the party was caught up in the general construction of Communism as the anti-totem, that is, as a definer of totem boundaries. While affiliative groups may be flexible enough to admit ethnic outsiders, there is often an ethnic core that non-ethnic members must imitate in dress, speech, etc. Anthropologist Dwight Conquergood recalled that, "A Latin King I know who is White goes by the street name of 'Blanco,'" in "For the Nation! How Street Gangs Problematize Patriotism," in Herbert W. Simons and Michael Billig (eds.) *After Postmodernism* (London: Sage, 1994) 205–06.

12 A female schoolteacher visited by Ku Klux Klan nightriders in the late 1860s recalled: "They treated me gentlemanly and quietly, but when they went away I concluded that they were savages – demons!" Wyn Craig Wade, *The Fiery Cross: The Ku Klux Klan in America* (New York: Simon and Schuster, 1987), 64. On affiliative groups and political revolution, see Tiger, *Men in Groups*, 136–37.

13 Quoted in "Generation Rap," moderated by Sheila Rule, *New York Times Magazine*, April 3, 1994, section 6, 44.

14 Quoted in Isaac W. Arnold, *The Life of Abraham Lincoln* (Chicago: A. C. McClung & Co., 1887), 448.

15 Promotional letter displayed on *Sixty Minutes*, CBS, March 19, 1994.

16 Don Terry, "Minister Farrakhan: Conservative Militant," *New York Times*, March 3, 1994, B9.

17 Thomas B. Edsall, "Once-Derided Christian Right Is Now Key for GOP," *Washington Post*, September 8, 1995, A8.

18 Quoted in Major Vorin E. Whan, *A Soldier Speaks* (New York: Praeger, 1962), 354.

19 "Generation Rap," 44.

20 Richard Pérez-Peña, "Trouble With Angels," *New York Times*, January 4, 1994, A19.

21 Seth Mydans, "Gangs Abiding By Cease-Fire in Los Angeles," *New York Times*, July 19, 1992, section 1, 15.

22 Mydans, "Survivor of Gang Wars Tastes Inaugural Glory," *New York Times*, January 9, 1993, 8.

23 William A. Henry III, "Pride and Prejudice," *Time*, February 28, 1994, 23.

24 Michel Marriott, "'Manhood Training' at the Mosque: Hope, Discipline, Defiance," *New York Times*, March 3, 1994, 8.

25 *Ibid.*

26 Conquergood, "For the Nation!" 211–12.

27 "Children of the Shadows," *New York Times*, April 25, 1993, section 4, 16.

28 Schlesinger, 29.

29 "Fascism in America," *Life*, March 6, 1939, 57.

30 Jack A. Thaw, letter to the editor, "Durocher Had Help on 'Nice Guys' Wisecrack," *New York Times*, October 18, 1991, A30, argues that Durocher actually said of his opponents, "Gordon, Mize, Kerr, Jansen, Ott. Nice guys. They'll finish last." A headline in the *Daily News* transformed this into a mythicized quote that more obviously expressed the affiliative function.

31 The description of Durocher comes from Thaw, *op. cit.* "Those phrases belong on his tombstone," wrote columnist Dave Anderson, pursuing afiliative logic to its totem conclusion. "Leo the Lip Was Baseball in New York," *New York Times*, October 9, 1991, B11.

32 Evelyn Nieves, "A Moral Code to Live By, to Fight By and to Die By," *New York Times*, December 25, 1994, 3.

33 "Gang Boss or Just Victim? Summations in Gotti Trial," *New York Times*, March 29, 1992, section 2, 30.

34 Arnold H. Lubasch, "Jury Hears Gotti Tape: 'He's Gonna Die'" *New York Times*, February 21, 1992, B2.

35 Ronald Smothers, "Hate Groups Seen Growing as Neo-Nazis Draw Young," *New York Times*, February 19, 1992, A14.

36 Clifton Brown, "All the Right Moves," *New York Times*, February 17, 1992, C8.

37 Ruth Marcus, "Jeers, Cheers Greet Clinton at the Wall," *Washington Post*, June 1, 1993, A6.

38 Anna Quindlen, "A Fragile Truce," *New York Times*, June 2, 1993, A19.

39 Stephen Buckley and Linda Wheeler, "Turning Their Backs on Clinton," *New York Times*, June 1, 1993, A6.

40 Quoted in Marcus, "Jeers, Cheers Greet Clinton," A6.

41 Michael Specter, "Defying the Skies in Chechnya," *New York Times*, December 25, 1994, section 4, 10.

42 *Ibid.*

43 Quoted in John F. Burns, "Adagio for Cello and Howitzers," *New York Times*, June 10, 1992, A3.

44 Quoted in John F. Burns, "Hearts Heavy, Arms Light, They Are Fighting On for Sarajevo," *New York Times*, June 27, 1992, 5.

45 Stephen Kinzer, "In Germany the Raw Material of Violence, Too, Is Bountiful," *New York Times*, September 13, 1992, section 4, 5.

46 Jackie Robinson as told to Alfred Duckett, *I Never Had It Made* (New York: G.Putnam's Sons, 1972), 12.

47 Paul Lewis, "President of Peru Says He is Confident of Defeating Guerilla Group," *New York Times*, October 2, 1993, 5.

48 Alan Cowell, "Bomb Kills Anti-Mafia Official and 5 Others in Sicily," *New York Times*, July 20, 1992, A3.

49 "Fascism in America," 57.

50 Directed by Robert Daley, starring Clint Eastwood, Hal Holbrook, Mitch Ryan, Warner/Malpaso, 1973.

51 Quoted in "Policing the Police," *New York Times*, October 4, 1993, A16.

52 Eric Schmitt, "Wall of Silence Impedes Inquiry into a Rowdy Navy Convention," *New York Times*, June 14, 1992, A1.

53 Quoted in David Horowitz and Michael Kitchen, "Tailhook Witch-Hunt," *Heterodoxy*, vol. 2, no. 2, October, 1993, 13.

54 Jane Gross, "Tailhook Aviators Trying to Regroup," *New York Times*, October 8, 1993, A28. The report was issued September 24, 1992.

55 "The American Legion Takes New York City," *Life*, October 4, 1937, 23–44.

56 *Ibid.*, 30.

57 *Ibid.*, 23.

58 "Back From The Wars: The Biography of the American Legion," *Life*, 32.

59 Anthony DePalma, "Faith and Free Speech Wrestle for Dominance in Brigham Young Case," *New York Times*, March 10, 1993, B8.

60 Remarks by Dennis MacDonald, interviewed in "The Glory and the Power: Fundamentalisms Observed," WHYY-TV, June 16, 1992.

61 Quoted in Geo. H. Preble, *History of the Flag of the United States*, 2nd rev. ed. (Boston: A. Williams, 1880), 509–10.

62 William T. Thompson, letter to G. H. Preble, December 25, 1971. Quoted in *Ibid.*, 509.

63 *Ibid.*

64 Lance Morrow, "In the Name of God," *Time*, March 15, 1993, 24.

65 Quoted in Anthony Lewis, "After the Buck Stops," *New York Times*, April 23, 1993, A35.

66 Quoted in interview with FBI, "Morning Edition," NPR, April 23, 1993.

67 Richard Lacayo, "Cult of Death," *Time*, March 15, 1993, 39.

68 *Ibid.*, 38.

69 *Ibid.*, 36.

70 *Ibid.*, 38.

71 Sophfronia Scott Gregory, "Children of a Lesser God," *Time*, May 17, 1993, vol. 141, no. 20, 54.

72 *Ibid.*

73 Bruce MacKenzie, letter to the editor, "Don't Award Africa All the Exotic Terms," *New York Times*, November 4, 1993, A26.

74 Remarks by mother of Davidian cult member David Thibodeaux, coverage of Waco events, CNN, April 19, 1993.

75 (n.a.), "Workers Pick Through Cult's Compound," *New York Times*, April 23, 1993, A20.
76 See Wade, *The Fiery Cross*, 33.
77 Hunter S. Thompson, *Hell's Angels, A Strange and Terrible Saga* (New York: Ballantine Books, 1966), 202.
78 *Ibid.*, 149.
79 *Ibid.*, 129.
80 *Ibid.*, 95.
81 Karen Schoemer, "How Many Angels Danced at the Benefit?" *New York Times*, October 23, 1991, C8.
82 *Ibid.*
83 *Ibid.*
84 Thompson, *Hell's Angels*, 315.
85 *Ibid.*, 333–34.
86 Quoted in Karl E. Meyer, "Lord of the Us," *New York Times*, October 16, 1992, A30.
87 Stanley Frost, *The Challenge of the Klan* (1924; New York: AMS Press, 1969).
88 Wade, *The Fiery Cross*, 35.
89 *Ibid.*, 97.
90 *Ibid.*, 61.
91 Kathleen Blee, *Women of the Klan* (Berkeley, Calif.: University of California Press, 1991), 169.
92 Wade, *The Fiery Cross*, 116.
93 *Ibid.*, 107.
94 *Ibid.*, 50.
95 Frost, *The Challenge of the Klan*, 64.
96 *Ibid.*, 290.
97 Blee, *Women of the Klan*, 80.
98 Wade, *The Fiery Cross*, 85.
99 Frost, *The Challenge of the Klan*, 81.
100 Leonard J. Moore, *Citizen Klansmen* (Chapel Hill: University of North Carolina, 1991), 21.
101 Blee, *Women of the Klan*, 175–76.
102 *Ibid.*, 143–44.
103 *Ibid.*, 12, argues that the 1920s Indiana Klan eschewed vigilante violence, but ruined Catholic citizens and shopkeepers by rumormongering and boycotts.
104 Frost, *The Challenge of the Klan*, 1.
105 *Ibid.*, 4.
106 The Rainbow Flag has a sacrificial story. Designed with eight stripes by San Francisco artist Gilbert Baker in 1978 in response to calls for a community symbol, it emerged as a community symbol only in 1979 following the assassination of Harvey Milk, the first openly gay community supervisor in San Francisco. The organizing committee for a parade marking the Milk assassination chose it to represent "the gay community's strength and solidar-

ity in the aftermath of this tragedy." Whereas earlier versions of the Baker flag contained both seven and eight stripes, the organizing committee reduced the number of stripes to six to make it possible for marchers and spectators to display three colors on each side of the street, the whole making an embodied popular version of the Rainbow Flag. The version that persists is the one that marched to commemorate Harvey Milk's sacrifice. See Steven W. Anderson, "The Rainbow Flag," *Gaze Magazine* (Minneapolis), #191, May 28, 1993, 25.

107 See Larry Gross, *The Contested Closet* (Minneapolis: University of Minnesota Press, 1993).

108 Allan Gurganus, "Why We March," *New York Times*, April 25, 1993, section 4, 17.

109 Interviewed by Judy Woodruff, *MacNeil–Lehrer News Hour*, April 27, 1993.

110 Wilbur Zelinsky, *Nation Into State* (Chapel Hill: North Carolina, 1988), 285.

111 "End of a Career, Perhaps, But Not the End of a Friendship," *New York Times*, February 18, 1992, B17.

112 See A. Bartlett Giamatti, *Take the Time for Paradise. Americans and Their Games* (New York: Summit Books, 1989).

113 Women can also participate in this myth. In an article about the Amherst Regional High School girls' basketball team, the Hurricanes, 23–1 going into the game for the Massachusetts state championship, co-captain Jamila Wideman was described as the source of contagious magic:

> Teammates . . . swirl around one another, everyone making a private point of touching Jamila Wideman . . . as if one dark-haired, brown-eyed girl could transmit the power of her playing to all the others. Jamila is an all-American, recipient of more than 150 offers of athletic scholarships. On the court, the strong bones on her face are like a flag demanding to be heeded; she is a study in quickness and confidence, the ball becoming part of her body. Her nickname is Predator.

Madeleine H. Blais, "They Were Commandos," *New York Times Magazine*, April 18, 1993, section 6, 27.

114 Though the phrase, "Kill the ump!" suggests that fans might like to kill the substitute totem for the duration of the game, as would coaches and players who protest the referee's decisions.

115 Quoted in Steven Stern, *When It Was A Game*, HBO Video, Black Canyon Productions, 1991.

116 Dave Anderson, "The 'Terrible Towel' Waves Once Again," *New York Times*, January 8, 1995, section 8, 2.

117 Karal Ann Marling and John Wetenhall, *Iwo Jima: Monuments, Memories, and the American Hero* (Cambridge, Mass.: Harvard, 1991), 234.

118 Benjamin G. Rader, *Baseball: A History of America's Game* (Urbana: University of Illinois, 1992), 157.

119 Bruce van Voorst, "Amid Disaster, Amazing Valor," *Time*, February 28, 1994, 48.

120 George Vecsey, "Comforting to Know Standards Still Exist," *New York Times*, February 21, 1994, C4.

121 Steve Sabol, "Honor," *This is the NFL*, CBS, October 3, 1993.

122 Robert Lipsyte, "Giants' Fans Yearning For a Simpler Time," *New York Times*, July 19, 1992, section 8, 1.

123 Ira Berkow, "Harding, The Games, And Us," *New York Times*, January 28, 1993, B9.

124 Ira Berkow, "Wild Thing That's Called Wild Card," *New York Times*, April 7, 1994, B9.

125 Rader, *Baseball*, 156.

126 Stern, *When It Was A Game*.

127 Quoted in "Wreaking Havoc – and Selling Sneaks," *New York Times*, June 2, 1993, A18.

128 Robert Lipsyte, "Dark Side of Jock 'tude Out of Focus," *New York Times*, August 13, 1993, B9.

129 *Ibid.*

130 George Vecsey, "Presidents Have Right To Be Fans," *New York Times*, April 3, 1994, section 8, 1.

131 Remarks by Peter Kessler, *When It Was A Game*.

132 Berkow, "Wild Thing That's Called Wild Card," B9.

133 Quoted in *Ibid.*

134 "It's not that I have anything against football," observed a female commentator on NPR's "Weekend Edition," October 3, 1993. "It's just that it never seemed to apply to me."

135 Richard L. Berke, "Democrats Use TV To Ride Momentum," *New York Times*, July 23, 1992, A18.

136 Donald Hall, remarks in Steven Stern, *When It Was A Game*.

137 Timothy W. Smith, "Bills Heed Message To Never Say Never," *New York Times*, January 4, 1993, C7.

138 My own, Conrad W. Marvin.

139 August Wilson, "Hero Worship on Sunday Afternoon," *Official Super Bowl XXVI Game Program* (New York: National Football League Properties, 1992), 133.

140 *Ibid.*, 133–34.

141 *Ibid.*, 134.

142 Baker, "In Russet Mantle Clad," *New York Times*, October 2, 1993, 23.

143 Directed by John Sayles, starring John Cusack, Charlie Sheen, Michael Lerner, Orion, 1988.

8 Dismemberment and reconstruction: the domain of the popular and its flag

1 Ira Berkow, "Kerrigan Is No Bambi," *New York Times*, March 8, 1994, B11.

2 Isabel Wilkerson, "After War, Patriotism Unfurls in a Nebraska City," *New York Times*, July 4, 1991, A8.

3 B. A. Botkin, ed., "Uncle Sam," *A Treasury of American Folklore. Stories, Ballads, and Traditions of the People* (New York: Crown Publishers, 1944), 286–87.

4 Quoted in Peter Stallybrass and Allon White, *Politics and Poetics of Transgression* (New York: Cornell, 1986), 121.

5 Quoted in Lawrence Levine, *Highbrow/Lowbrow* (Cambridge: Harvard University Press, 1988), 238.

6 Keith Meyers [Newspaper photograph], *New York Times*, July 5, 1991, B1.

7 Jim Wetherbee, "It's Time to Fly Flag, Plant Beans," *Morning News* (Springdale, Arkansas), April 14, 1992, 5A.

8 Don Terry, "Smattering of Fire but Mostly Unease in a District That Bush Carried in '88," *New York Times*, September 16, 1992, A17.

9 *Ibid.*

10 Isabel Wilkerson, "After 12 Years, These Reagan Democrats Are Ready to Defect," *New York Times*, July 16, 1992, 8.

11 There is a well recognized connection between fecundity and contamination, appropriately drawn by Alexander Liberman, the legendary *Conde Nast* editor, describing the secret of good media work: "Never . . . treat anything you do with reverence. You have to sort of practically spit on it, and then you do your work. If you start thinking this is a beautiful picture, I can't touch it, you're dead." *Morning Edition*, NPR, April 1, 1994.

12 Emile Durkheim, *Elementary Forms of the Religious Life*, (George Allen & Unwin, 1915; New York: Free Press, 1965), 55.

13 Filip Bondy, "From the Pool, Comes a Cry: Don't Tread on Me!" *New York Times*, May 24, 1992, section 8, 3.

14 "Infectious Patriotism," *Albany Express*, n.d., in George T. Balch, *Methods of Teaching Patriotism in the Public Schools* (New York: Van Nostrand, 1890), 102.

15 Tim Rasmussen, "On The Bus," *New York Times Magazine*, March 27, 1994, 57.

16 Jan Rood-Ojalve, "Still no good reason," letter to the editor, *Philadelphia Inquirer*, February 27, 1991, A18.

17 Alessandra Stanley, "As War Looms: Marches and Vigils, Talk and Fear," *New York Times*, January 15, 1991, A11.

18 Julia M. Klein, "In Va. town, patriotism and a sense of sacrifice," *Philadelphia Inquirer*, January 16, 1991, 8A.

19 Alessandra Stanley, "Personal Steps in March of History," *New York Times*, January 19, 1991, A1.

20 Linda S. Wallace, "Small towns rally to counter war protests," *Philadelphia Inquirer*, January 27, 1991, A10.

21 Ronald Smothers, "Flags Fly Over South For Troops," *New York Times*, August 27, 1990, A12.

22 *Ibid.*

23 Carolyn Pesce, "Cities reflect opposing views," *USA Today*, January 23, 1991, A6.

24 Fox Butterfield, "Both Uniting and Dividing, the War Reaches Into Small Towns of America," *New York Times*, January 21, 1991, A11.

25 Bryan Richman, letter to the editor, "Thoughts on united-ness," *Philadelphia Inquirer*, February 8, 1991, A14.

26 "Tattoos chosen during war: Eagles, flags," *Philadelphia Inquirer*, January 26, 1991, A13.

27 Isabel Wilkerson, "After War," A8.

28 Sal Ruibal, "Fans display support with flags, banners," *USA Today*, January 21, 1991, C2.

29 "When Morning Comes to Bagdad, U.S.A.," *Life*, February 25, 1991, Special Weekly Edition No. 1, 17.

30 Leon Taylor and Kurt Heine, "GIs' Kin Happy but Cautious," *Philadelphia Daily News*, February 28, 1991, 6.

31 Dick Pothier, "Mummers and others plan demonstrations of support for troops," *Philadelphia Inquirer*, January 25, 1991, B5.

32 Robert D. McFadden, "Amid Prayers for Peace, Preachers Split on War," *New York Times*, January 21, 1991, A11.

33 "All anyone can do is 'pray, give blood'," *USA Today*, January 18, 1991, A9.

34 Gilbert M. Gaul, "Across America, a tide of blood," *Philadelphia Inquirer*, February 15, 1991, A1.

35 Allesandra Stanley, "Personal Steps in March of History," *New York Times*, January 16, 1991, A1.

36 During World War II, according to Whitney Smith, director of the Flag Research Center, Winchester, Mass., "Service flags were flown in family windows – a red-bordered white flag, with one blue star (or gold for those killed in action) for every serviceman." See "Flag expert: Monument 'bad taste'," *News Transcript*, September 27, 1980, 2.

37 Al Neuharth, "Can we keep bubble of patriotism alive?" *USA Today*, February 22, 1991, A9.

38 Victor Turner, *The Ritual Process: Structure and Anti-Structure* (Chicago: Aldine, 1969), 49.

39 Lini S. Kadaba and Maureen Graham, "Hoping for good fortune for soldiers and an end to war," *Philadelphia Inquirer*, February 25, 1991, A6.

40 Mary Douglas, *Purity and Danger* (1966; New York: Ark Paperbacks, 1984), 50.

41 Julia M. Klein, "A homecoming, a heroes' welcome," *Philadelphia Inquirer*, March 9, 1991, A4.

42 "Millions hail troops in N.Y.," *Philadelphia Inquirer*, June 11, 1991, A8.

43 Robert D. McFadden, "Fund-Raising on Target for Whopping Victory Parade," *New York Times*, May 13, 1991, B4.

44 n.a., "A Jet Ride Full of Joy and Culture Shock," *New York Times*, March 9, 1991, 4.

45 Mimi Hall, "Across the USA, pride is back," *USA Today*, March 1, 1991, A8.

46 n.a., "Cheers, Songs and Flag-Waving for Town's Troops," *New York Times*, March 11, 1991, A11.

47 n.a., "Returning troops met with cheers," *Philadelphia Inquirer*, March 9, 1991, A1.

48 Peter Applebome, "Troops Come Home From Gulf to Jubilation," *New York Times*, March 9, 1991, A4.

49 Linda Wheeler and Patricia Davis, "Love Affair on the Mall: People and War Machines," *Washington Post*, June 9, 1991, A26.

50 Patricia Calhoun Bibby, "Friends, strangers stage rousing welcomes," *Philadelphia Inquirer*, March 10, 1991, A8.

51 "Victory Celebrations," *Life*, August 27, 1945, 19(9), 23.

52 *Ibid.*, 26.

53 Peter Applebome, "Troops Come Home From Gulf to Jubilation," *New York Times*, March 9, 1991, A4.

54 James Barron, "In a Ticker-Tape Blizzard, New York Honors the Troops: Watching Was Event All by Itself," *New York Times*, June 11, 1991, B5.

55 Dirk Johnson, "Outpouring of Scholarships and Jobs Await Returning Heroes After the Ticker Tape," *New York Times*, March 8, 1991, A10.

56 Chris Hedges, "Marines Fear Glory of War Will Give Way to Old Stigma," *New York Times*, May 31, 1991, A1.

57 Mary Jordan, "A Capital Thank-You: 800,000 Jam D.C. for Tribute to Troops," *Washington Post*, June 9, 1991, A1.

58 Julia M. Klein, "In N.C., homecoming and sweet reunions," *Philadelphia Inquirer*, March 9, 1991, A1.

59 Jordan, "A Capital Thank-You," A28.

60 Walter Goodman, "TV Networks Compete In Yellow Ribbon Game," *New York Times*, June 11, 1991, B5.

61 "A Jet Ride Full of Joy and Culture Shock," 4.

62 Michael Wines, "Parade for Gulf Victory Draws 200,000 in Capital," *New York Times*, June 9, 1991, 20.

63 Andrew Maykuth, "A Grand old day in N.Y.," *Philadelphia Inquirer*, June 11, 1991, A8.

64 Peter Applebome, "Troops Come Home," A1.

65 John Boeman, *Morotai: A Memoir of War* (New York: Doubleday, 1981), 277.

66 *Ibid.*, 278.

67 Jordan, "A Capital Thank-You," A28.

68 Peter Applebome, "Sense of Pride Outweighs Fears of War," *New York Times*, February 24, 1991, section 4, 1.

69 Klein, "In N.C., homecoming and sweet reunions," A17.

70 Rich Heidorn Jr., "A perfect parade day – no blarney," *Philadelphia Inquirer*, March 18, 1991, B2.

71 Ellen Warren, Charles Green and R. A. Zaldivar, "Before a jubilant Congress, Bush looks to lasting peace," *Philadelphia Inquirer*, March 7, 1991, A1.

72 Frank Brown, "Coming home without the hoopla," *Philadelphia Inquirer*, September 13, 1991, B7.

73 "Tie a Yellow Ribbon Round the Ole Oak Tree," originally performed by Tony Orlando and Dawn, *Tuneweaving*, LP, Bell, 1973. There have been some 2,000 recorded versions.

74 Elizabeth Hunt, "It's the Feel Good War," *Daily Pennsylvanian*, February 28, 1991, 4.

75 "Yellow Ribbons," *New York Times*, February 4, 1991, A16.

76 Alessandra Stanley, "War's Ribbons Are Yellow With Meaning of Many Hues," *New York Times*, February 3, 1991, section 1, 1.

77 Directed by John Ford, starring John Wayne, Joanne Dru, RKO/Argosy, 1949.

78 Stanley, "War's Ribbons Are Yellow," 16.

79 Don Terry, "Somber Voices at Home Show Emotions at War," February 25, 1991, A17.

80 Stanley, "War's Ribbons Are Yellow," 16.

81 Russell Banks, "Red, White, Blue, Yellow," *New York Times*, February 26, 1991, A23. The national Vietnam Veterans Rejustment Study of the Research Triangle Institute, an ABC–Washington Post poll from 1985, and a study by the Harris Organization for the Veterans Administration in 1980 agreed that most Vietnam soldiers entered the military by enlistment. According to the readjustment study, this number was around 70 per cent, of which only 11 per cent reportedly did so to avoid the draft. Reported in Bernard A. Heeney, "The Majority of Vietnam Vets Enlisted," letter to the editor, *New York Times*, June 21, 1994, A16.

82 William Ussrey, interview, October 21, 1992, Pittsburgh.

83 Kate Douglas Wiggin, *New Chronicles of Rebecca* (New York: Grosset & Dunlap, 1907), 123.

84 *Ibid.*, 127.

85 *Ibid.*, 137.

86 *Ibid.*, 144.

87 *Ibid.*, 148.

88 *Ibid.*, 161.

89 *Ibid.*, 162–63.

90 Megan Rosenfeld, "The Human Flag! 3,500 Students Line Up As the Red, White & Blue," *Washington Post*, June 14, 1985, C1.

9 Fresh blood, public meat

1 Michel de Montaigne, "On Cannibals," *Essays*, tr. by J. M. Cohen (New York: Penguin, 1958), 119.

2 Directed by Frank Capra, starring Spencer Tracy, Katherine Hepburn, Adolphe Menjou, Van Johnson, MGM/Liberty Films, 1948.

3 Ira Glass, "Like any good politician, his message is 'I am one of you'," "All Things Considered," National Public Radio, July 25, 1992.

4 John F. Kennedy's first statement upon winning the 1960 presidential election perfectly combines creation and sacrifice: "Every degree of mind and spirit that I possess will be devoted to the long-range interests of the United States and the cause of freedom around the world. So now my wife and I prepare for a new administration and for a new baby."

5 The parsed flag is also found in that other pervasive regenerative activity of the people, commerce. See Chapter Ten.

6 Where the totem and the people are at odds, the regenerative significance of the parsed flag may be threatening. Prior to the Israeli–Palestinian peace agreement of September, 1993, Palestinians in the Gaza Strip were said to have been arrested for carrying sliced watermelons because their red, black and green colors were interpreted as a reference to the banned Palestinian flag – a covert parsed flag. See John Kifner, "A Palestinian Version of the Judgment of Solomon," *New York Times*, October 16, 1993, 2.

7 Michael Kelly, "Clinton, After Raising Hopes, Tries to Lower Expectations," *New York Times*, November 9, 1992, A14.

8 Maureen Dowd, "Identity Crisis City," *New York Times*, October 29, 1995, section 4, 13.

9 Lloyd Grove, "End of an Aura: Why the President Gets No Respect," *Washington Post*, April 7, 1994, C1.

10 Richard L. Berke, "In His Theater, Clinton Plays Favorite-Son Role," *New York Times*, May 24, 1992, section 1, 22.

11 Evelyn Nieves, "The President in Person Leaves Some Thrilled, but Others Chilled," *New York Times*, July 22, 1992, A16.

12 Paul O'Neil, "Conventions: Nomination by Rain Dance," *Life*, July 5, 1968, 28.

13 Berke, "In His Theater," section 1, 22.

14 B. Drummond Ayers Jr., "Clinton's Enjoying Mystery Over Choice for Ticket," *New York Times*, June 29, 1992, A11.

15 Stuart Elliot, "Candidates' Spots are Not Created Equal," *New York Times*, November 3, 1992, D18.

16 The candidate and his wife are the center of the postwar Frank Capra film, *State of the Union*, Liberty Films (1948), which compares electoral to marital health. The platform of the Republican dark horse candidate, Grant Matthews, is a classic of fertility rhetoric: "Either we all pull together, or we get pulled apart." So long as Matthews is influenced by his unscrupulous mistress, a king-making newspaper publisher, he is willing to sell out to illegitimate interest groups. His faithful wife Mary repairs both her marriage and the health of the republic. She reminds her husband that the people are his true political mates, as she is his true marital mate.

17 Robin Toner, "Bitter Tone of the '94 Campaign Elicits Worry on Public Debate," *New York Times*, November 13, 1994, section 1, 20. Quoting Bill Kovach.

18 *Washington Week*, PBS, October 30, 1992.

19 Sigmund Freud, *Jokes and Their Relation to the Unconscious*, tr. by James Strachey (New York: W. W. Norton, 1960), 106.

20 Lorrie Moore, "Voters in Wonderland," *New York Times*, November 3, 1992, A19.

21 Richard Goldstein, "Sweet William. Sex and Sensibility: The Clinton Touch," *Village Voice*, October 27, 1992, 30.

22 "Can Bill Clinton Be Trusted?" *New York Times*, July 16, 1992, A24.

23 Francis X. Clines, "The View From the Cab: Drivers Look Down on Politicians," *New York Times*, July 16, 1992, 8.

24 Quoted in "Giving Up Something," *New York Times*, August 14, 1992, A24.

25 William Safire, "The Rising Gorge," *New York Times*, April 16, 1992, A23.

26 Garry Wills, "George Bush, Prisoner of the Crazies," *New York Times*, August 16, 1992, section 4, 17.

27 Peter Applebome, "In 2 Black Neighborhoods, a Groundswell for Clinton,"*New York Times*, July 25, 1992, 8.

28 John Siegenthaler, then an aide to Robert F. Kennedy, interviewed in *The Kennedys* [documentary film], Elizabeth Deane (producer), Boston and London: WGBH and Thames Television, 1992.

29 Campaign coverage, NBC, July 16, 1992.

30 Ayers, "Choice for Ticket," A11.

31 "In any kind of communication whatever, if more than one band [of symbolic modes] is being used, ambiguity would result if there was no smooth co-ordination of meanings. Hence we would always expect some concordance between social and bodily expressions of control, first because each symbolic mode enhances meaning in the other, and so the ends of communication are furthered." Mary Douglas, *Natural Symbols* (New York: Pantheon, 1982), 68. "There are pressures to create consonance between the perception of social and physiological levels of experience," 70. For Douglas the body is an image of society. Hence, the abundance of food at political conventions tells us something about how bodily and social experience relate.

32 John Tierney, "In Quizzing Candidates, No Query Is Too Stupid,"*New York Times*, October 11, 1992, A22.

33 Quoted by Mark Shields on *MacNeil–Lehrer News Hour*, PBS, October 14, 1992.

34 Goldstein, "Sweet William," 33.

35 Hank Bradford, "George, Eat Before You Run Again," *New York Times*, January 16, 1992, 21.

36 Elizabeth Kolbert, "As Political Campaign Turns Negative, the Press is Given a Negative Rating," *New York Times*, May 1, 1992, A18.

37 Michael Wines, "Concerned About Buchanan, Bush Makes Final Appeal in Georgia," *New York Times*, March 1, 1992, section 1, 20.

38 Maureen Dowd and Thomas L. Friedman, "Baker's Patrician Hand Might Not Be Able to Right Drift of Bush Campaign," *New York Times*, March 29, 1992, section 1, 14.

39 *Ibid.*
40 *Ibid.*
41 Peter Applebome, "Perot, the 'Simple' Billionaire, Says Voters Can Force His Presidential Bid," *New York Times*, March 29, 1992, section 1, 14.
42 Tom Raum, "Perot campaign style bypasses the usual," *Philadelphia Inquirer*, May 22, 1992, A4.
43 *Ibid.*
44 Goldstein, "Sweet William," 30.
45 Gwen Ifill, "Clinton Admits Experiment With Marijuana in 1960's," *New York Times*, March 30, 1992, A15.
46 Ayers, "Choice for Ticket," A11.
47 Michael Kelly, "Clinton Bus Mantra: Please, PLEASE, Vote for Me," *New York Times*, August 8, 1992, 8.
48 Jim Estrin [Newspaper photograph], *New York Times*, August 8, 1992, 8.
49 Quoted in Victor Turner, *The Ritual Process* (Chicago: Aldine, 1969), 170–71.
50 "Take Five," *New Yorker*, November 23, 1992, 4.
51 Michael Kelly, "Perot's Epic Failure," *New York Times*, July 18, 1992, 11.
52 Gwen Ifill, "With No Break, Clinton Initiates Campaign Tour," *New York Times*, July 18, 1992, 9.
53 "Campaign '92," CBS, November 3, 1992.
54 Michael Kelly, "A Few Workers Keep Clinton's Campaign on Track," *New York Times*, July 16, 1992, A11.
55 Richard L. Berke, "White House Race at Emotional Peak Many Weeks Early," *New York Times*, June 21, 1992, section 1, 1.
56 A. M. Rosenthal, "The Perot Mystery," *New York Times*, July 17, 1992, A27.
57 Alan Brinkley, "A Whole New Political Ball Game?" *New York Times*, July 21, 1992, A19.
58 A.M. Rosenthal, "What Did We Learn?" *New York Times*, November 3, 1992, A19.
59 In a letter to the editor, George McGovern wrote, "I have never been ashamed of liberalism or conservatism. The creative tension between these two central political traditions is the strength of America's two-party system." See "Defying Jinx, McGovern Backs the Ticket," *New York Times*, July 26, 1992, section 4, 6.
60 Rep. Charles Rangel, interviewed on *Nightline*, ABC, July 13, 1992.
61 Melvin R. Gilbert, "What the Poster Says," letter to the editor, *New York Times*, August 30, 1992, section 4, 14.
62 Robin Toner, "Bush Suffers a Narrow Escape Against Buchanan," *New York Times*, February 19, 1992, A16.
63 Walter Shapiro, "President Perot?" *Time*, vol. 139, no. 21, May 25, 1992, 31.
64 R. W. Apple, Jr., "A Lightning Bolt for the Status Quo," *New York Times*, February 19, 1992, A16.
65 Andrew Rosenthal, "Stunned, Bush Campaign Seeks a New Strategy," *New York Times*, February 19, 1992, A16.
66 Lawrence Wright, "Big D, Little H.R.P.," *New Yorker*, 88.

67 Andrew Rosenthal, "It's Time to Get Tough, Bush's Advisers Declare," *New York Times*, March 25, 1992, A16.

68 *Ibid.*

69 Berke, "White House Race at Emotional Peak many Weeks Early," section 1, 20.

70 R. W. Apple, Jr., "Tsongas and Clinton Look To Tuesday for Affirmation," *New York Times*, March 1, 1992, section 1, 18.

71 Robin Toner, "Democratic Campaign Turns into Free-for-All," *New York Times*, February 27, 1992, A22.

72 Elizabeth Kolbert, "Please Stand by for TV Skirmish," *New York Times*, March 29, 1992, section 1, 18.

73 Lawrence Wright, "The Man From Texarkana," *New York Times Magazine*, June 28, 1992, 40, 43.

74 Quoted by Howard Fineman on *Washington Week*, PBS, June 5, 1992.

75 Shapiro, "President Perot?" 26.

76 "Mr. Perot's Chance for Courage," editorial, *New York Times*, July 22, 1992, A18.

77 It tuns out that the white specks of fat that streak flavorful New York steak are referred to in the trade as "stars and stripes." See Douglas Martin, "A Butcher Who Finds the Times Are Lean," *New York Times*, July 22, 1992, B2.

78 Kelly, "Perot's Epic Failure," 11.

79 Wright, "The Man From Texarkana," 34.

80 Charles Donnelly, "Perot Says It All," *New York Times*, October 2, 1992, A31.

81 R.W. Apple, Jr., "Back In, Without as Big a Splash," *New York Times*, October 2, 1992, A1.

82 "'Honored to Accept': Excerpts From Perot's News Conference," *New York Times*, October 2, 1992, A20.

83 Quoted in L. Rozen, "The War Room," *People*, December 13, 1993, 18.

84 Quoted in Sam Roberts, "The Curative Power of Celebrations," *New York Times*, July 6, 1992, B2.

85 Stanley Elkin, "A Demonstration of Democracy," *New York Times*, July 19, 1992, section 4, 17.

86 Dan Rather, "Campaign '92," CBS, June 13, 1992.

87 Interview with Richard Dattner, *All Things Considered*, NPR, July 14, 1992. Also "Bicoastal Disturbances: Movies Versus Politics," *New York Times*, July 15, 1992, A7.

88 Leslie Savan, "Designing Democrats," *Village Voice*, July 21, 1992, 37. The tradition of the landscape reaching out to embrace the spectator goes back at least to Bernini's design of St. Peter's. The church was the head of St. Peter; the columns in the plaza, the arms embracing the worshippers. The podium also reflects, perhaps unwittingly, a late nineteenth-century tradition of flag art with the flag as the sky itself, reaching out to gather in the landscape.

89 Governor Ann Richards, remarks to the Democratic National Convention, July 13, 1992.

90 Governor Mario Cuomo, remarks to the Democratic National Convention, July 15, 1992.

91 Cokie Roberts, Democratic National Convention, ABC, July 15, 1992.

92 Elizabeth Kolbert, "Convention Can Still Work Its Magic," *New York Times*, July 17, 1992, A11.

93 *Ibid.*

94 Senator Al Gore, Remarks to the Democratic National Convention, July 16, 1992.

95 Maureen Dowd, "O.K. on the Self-Realization: What About the Economy?" *New York Times*, July 28, 1992, A2.

96 Celia Dugger, "The Prime of Tipper Gore," *New York Times*, July 19, 1992, section 9, 9.

97 Wilkerson, "After 12 Years, These Reagan Democrats Are Ready to Defect," 8.

98 Kathleen Jamieson, interviewed on *Tonight* show, NBC, August 12, 1992.

99 O'Neil, "Conventions: Nomination By Rain Dance," 28.

100 David E. Rosenbaum, "G.O.P. Drafting Ban for Total Ban on Abortion," *New York Times*, August 11, 1992, A16.

101 Richard L. Berke, "Republicans Fret About Convention," *New York Times*, August 10, 1992, A14.

102 Richard L. Berke, "G.O.P. Seeks a Convention That's Well Under Control," *New York Times*, August 10, 1992, A14.

103 Madeleine Hamm, "Red, white and ooh," *Houston Chronicle*, July 11, 1992, 1D.

104 Roberto Suro, "A Houston-Style Convention: Republicans in Heavy Traffic," *New York Times*, August 15, 1992.

105 Madeleine Hamm, "Red, white and ooh," 2D.

106 Garry Wills, "George Bush, Prisoner of the Crazies," *New York Times*, August 16, 1992, section 1, 17.

107 Roberto Suro, "Republican Gatherings in Houston Will Be Opulent and Mostly Private," *New York Times*, August 16, 1992, section 1, 28.

108 R.W. Apple., "G.O.P. Is Flirting With the Dangers of Negativism," *New York Times*, August 19, 1992, A13.

109 Reprinted in *New York Times*, August 19, 1992, A10.

110 Walter Goodman, "The Republicans Play A Dissonant Tune," *New York Times*, August 19, 1992, C14.

111 Patrick Buchanan, remarks to Republican National Convention, August 17, 1992.

112 Leslie H. Gelb, "Who Won the Cold War?" *New York Times*, August 20, 1992, A27.

113 Gwen Ifill, "Clinton Says G.O.P. Conflict on Economy Promises Higher Deficit," *New York Times*, August 11, 1992, A17.

114 Gwen Ifill, "Clinton-Gore Caravan Refuels With Spirit From Adoring Crowds," *New York Times*, July 19, 1992, section 1, 20.

115 Gwen Ifill, "Clinton Campaign to Slow Down During G.O.P. Convention," *New York Times*, August 16, 1992, section 1, 28.

116 Andrew Rosenthal, "G.O.P. Plotting 2–Edged Effort to Bolster Bush," *New York Times*, July 19, 1992, section 1, 18.

117 *Ibid.*

118 Michael Kelly, "Merely Mortal: Bunch that Lunched on Democrats is Missing its Edge," *New York Times*, September 27, 1992, section 4, 4.

119 Michael Kelly, "Clinton Says Bush Is Afraid Of Debating 'Man to Man,'" *New York Times*, September 19, 1992, 6.

120 Andrew Rosenthal, "Bush, in Florida, Steps Up Personal Attack on Clinton," *New York Times*, October 4, 1992, section 1, 26.

121 "Campaign 92," CBS, November 3, 1992.

122 Goldstein, "Sweet William," 31.

123 *CBS Evening News*, October 25, 1992.

124 Clines, "Civics 101: Cultivating Grass Roots The Old Way," *New York Times*, November 4, 1992, B1.

125 Michael Winerip, "Fever Pitch: Democracy At Work," *New York Times*, November 1, 1992, 49.

126 Quoted in Andy Logan, "On, Comet! On, Cupid! On, Donder and Blitzen!" *New Yorker*, December 7, 1992, 78–79.

127 "Campaign 92," CBS, November 3, 1992.

128 Michael Kelly, "The Winners Shift Gears: What Now?" *New York Times*, November 5, 1992, B3.

129 "Democracy in America, "Northern Exposure, writ. Jeff Melvoin, dir. Michael Katleman, CBS, January 24, 1992.

130 Tom Wicker, "An Indomitable Man, an Incurable Loneliness," *New York Times*, April 24, 1994, section 4, 1.

131 "24 Hours to Victory," ABC, November 6, 1992.

132 Maureen Dowd, "Moving Day's Approach Stirs Clinton's Nostalgia," *New York Times*, January 14, 1993, A11.

133 Tim Russert, "The Clinton Inaugural," NBC, January 20, 1993.

134 Gwen Ifill, "A Campaigner Adjusts To Life as the President," *New York Times*, February 15, 1993, A10.

135 John W. O'Malley, S.J., "Postscript," in Leo Steinberg, *The Sexuality of Christ in Renaissance Art and In Modern Oblivion* (New York: Pantheon, 1983), 201.

136 Jim Wilson [Newspaper photographer], *New York Times*, November 5, 1992, A1.

137 Because of this ambiguity, Michelangelo was accused of having produced obscene and blasphemous imagery. See Leo Steinberg, "The Metaphors of Love and Birth in Michelangelo's Pietas," *Studies in Erotic Art*, Theodor Bowie and Cornelia V. Christensen, eds. (New York: Basic Books, 1970), 231–39.

138 Reprinted in *New York Times*, November 8, 1992, section 4, 3. On Inauguration Day, NBC featured a cartoon from the London *Daily Telegraph* showing Hillary carrying Clinton across the threshold of the Capitol.

139 R.W. Apple, Jr., "Ahhh! The Old Democrats Feel Young Again," *New York Times*, November 21, 1992, 8.

140 Gwen Ifill, "'He's Still Bill,' but Life Has Changed for Clinton," *New York Times*, November 9, 1992, A14.
141 "Transcript of Clinton's Remarks on White House Transition," *New York Times*, November 5, 1992, B2.
142 Francis X Clines, "New Hampshire Voter Recalls Clinton's Stern Test," *New York Times*, November 5, 1992, B7.
143 Robin Toner, "A Dawn of New Politics, Challenges for Both Parties," *New York Times*, November 5, 1992, B1.
144 Ifill, "'He's Still Bill,'" A14.
145 Sidney Blumenthal, "All the President's Wars," *New Yorker*, December 28, 1992/January 4, 1993, 62.
146 Russell Baker, "The Latest Duke," *New York Times*, January 12, 1993, A21.
147 For example, in remarks by Ted Koppell, "24 Hours to Victory," NBC, November 5, 1992.
148 Tom Brokaw, "The Clinton Inaugural," NBC, January 20, 1993.
149 Jon Pareles, "As Rock Beat Fades, Clinton's Presidency Opens on a Soft Note," *New York Times*, January 21, 1993, C15.
150 *New York Times*, January 21, 1993, A11. Infantilizing metaphors continued after the inauguration. "Whither the infant Administration?" William Safire led off a column, "The Clinton Direction," *New York Times*, February 8, 1993, A17. "There's no sense of momentum. It's almost as if they're thinking like children," said Free Greenstein, a historian of the presidency. "After they wake up from their nap, life begins." See Maureen Dowd, "On Politics and Loyalty," *New York Times*, February 8, 1993, A15.
151 Sally Quinn, interviewed in inaugural coverage, CBS, January 20, 1993.
152 R.W. Apple, Jr., "From a Ditch, A Ray of Sun," *New York Times*, August 20, 1994, 11.
153 Robert Pear, "Quayle Proclaims Himself Healthy and 'Back in Arena'", *New York Times*, January 22, 1995, section 1, 18.
154 Quoted by Marvin Kalb, "The State of the Disunion," *New York Times*, February 4, 1995, 19.
155 Baker, "The Latest Duke," A21.
156 *Nightly News*, NBC, January 20, 1993.
157 Patricia Leigh Brown, "Blue Skies, Not Moods, in the Capital," *New York Times*, January 19, 1993, A15.
158 Walter Goodman, "In the Inaugural of Inclusion, All the Arts Are In," *New York Times*, January 21, 1993, C20.
159 Brokaw, "The Clinton Inaugural."
160 For example, Patricia Leigh Brown, "Poetry Amid Politics as New Guard Marches In," *New York Times*, January 20, 1993, A15. A description repeated by Tom Brokaw, Barbara Walters and who knows how many others.
161 Peggy Noonan, *MacNeil–Lehrer News Hour*, January 20, 1993.
162 "Presidential Inaugural Gala," CBS, January 19, 1993.
163 Jimmy Carter, "The Presidential Inauguration with Walter Cronkite," PBS, January 18, 1993.

164 Dan Rather, inaugural coverage, CBS, January 20, 1993.

165 Brokaw, "The Clinton Inaugural."

166 The Sunday before the inauguration, for example, the editorial section of the *Philadelphia Inquirer*, January 17, 1993, had three stories on the inaugural. Each quoted the Kennedy phrase. Kathleen Hall Jamieson, "Some presidents articulate their vision despite all of the pomp and pageantry," C7; Jerome J. Shestack, "Clinton knows presidential history well: Just beware of the Harrison example," C7; and Charles Green, "Inaugural address is chance to set tone," C2.

167 Goldstein, "Sweet William," 30.

168 Dirk Johnson, "From Afar, New Hope For Change," *New York Times*, January 21, 1993, A13.

169 Jane Robelot, *Channel 10 News*, WCAU-TV January 20, 1993.

170 Daniel Schorr, *All Things Considered*, NPR, January 23, 1993.

171 Brown, "Poetry Amid Politics," A15.

172 David E. Rosenbaum, "Hails and Farewells: An Emotional Gulf," *New York Times*, January 20, 1993, A1.

173 Holly Brubach, "Right and Fitting," *New Yorker*, February 1, 1993, 34.

174 David Gergen, "The Clinton Inaugural," PBS, January 20, 1993.

175 Clinton's remarks were: "Let me tell you that on tomorrow I will begin a journey that I hope will be our journey. I will do my best to be faithful to your trust, and I hope that always to the end of all of our days you will all be very proud that you were here this evening and a part of this week. I want you to know that none of us who were part of this campaign will ever forget who brought us here, and why and begining tomorrow we will do our best to be faithful to your trust." Note the protestations of a faithful lover.

176 Margaret Larson, "The Clinton Inaugural," NBC, January 20, 1993.

177 "Action News 11 o'clock," WPVI, January 20, 1992.

178 Felicity Barringer, "A Family Rises Early to Partake of History," *New York Times*, January 21, 1993, A17.

179 Larson, "The Clinton Inaugural."

180 Katie Couric, "The Clinton Inaugural," NBC, January 20, 1993.

181 Larson, "The Clinton Inaugural."

182 ABC News, inaugural coverage, January 20, 1993.

183 Bernard Weinraub, "Hollywood Crowd Gives Capital Two Thumbs Up," *New York Times*, January 20, 1993, A15.

184 "The Clinton Inaugural," PBS, January 20, 1993.

185 Noonan, *MacNeil–Lehrer News Hour*, January 20, 1993.

186 James G. Frazer, *Taboo and the Perils of the Soul* in *The Golden Bough*, vol. 1 (New York: Macmillan, 1935), 7.

187 Quoted in Joseph F. Wall, *Henry Watterson* (New York: Oxford, 1956), 254.

188 Gergen, "The Clinton Inaugural," PBS.

189 Mark Shields, "The Clinton Inaugural," PBS, January 20, 1993.

190 Phyllis Theroux, *MacNeil-Lehrer News Hour*, January 20, 1993.

191 Jim Lehrer, "The Clinton Inaugural," PBS, January 20, 1993.

192 Election coverage, PBS, November 5, 1992.

193 R.W. Apple, Jr., "Bush Hears the Last Echoes Of His White House Power," *New York Times*, January 20, 1993, A1.

194 "Outward Bound," *Life*, January 1993, 110.

195 "ABC News Special: Inauguration '93,", January 20, 1993.

196 Peter Jennings, "ABC News Special: Inauguration 93."

197 Tom DeFrank, *Morning Edition,* NPR, January 20, 1993.

198 Kevin Sack, "In an Interview, No Excuses, No Regrets, Some Uncertainty," *New York Times*, November 13, 1994, section 2, 48.

199 Johnson, "From Afar, New Hope," A13.

200 Carter, "The Presidential Inauguration with Walter Cronkite."

201 Charles Kuralt, inaugural coverage, CBS, January 20, 1993.

202 "Take Five," *New Yorker*, November 23, 1992, 6.

203 Brokaw, "The Clinton Inaugural."

204 Joel Achenbach, "Another Failed Presidency, Already?" May 27, 1993, D4.

205 High Sidey, "Hail to the Prisoner," *Time*, August 31, 1992, 43.

206 Larry King, "Locally, acceptance – and anger," *Philadelphia Inquirer*, February 19, 1991, A1.

207 Grove, "End of an Aura: Why the President Gets No Respect," C8.

208 Ross Perot, interviewed on "World News Sunday," ABC, March 21, 1993.

209 Quoted in Mike Capuzzo, "The brash conservatives," *Philadelphia Inquirer*, May 26, 1994, G4.

10 One size fits all: the flag industry

1 "Freedom" [Newspaper advertisement], *New York Times*, July 4, 1991, A5.

2 "Do not use the Flag in any form of advertising nor fasten an advertising sign to a pole from which the Flag of the United States is flying." From The Flag Code, adopted at the National Flag Conference, Washington, DC, June 14–15, 1923.

3 Interview, April 27, 1993, Roseland, N.J.

4 William E. Smart, "Rallying 'Round the Flagpole," *Washington Post*, June 14, 1985, C5. Quoting Claude Haynes, president of National Capital Flag in Alexandria, Va.

5 Terry Trucco, "Source for the Stars and Stripes," *New York Times*, January 31, 1991, C2.

6 Interview, September 15, 1992, Philadelphia.

7 Interview, August 21, 1992, Oaks, Pa.

8 "Flag sales are flying to new heights," *USA Today*, January 18, 1991, A9.

9 Information in this section is based on a visit by the author to Medway, Mass., to interview the Rojee family, March 12, 1993.

10 Clark DeLeon, "The Scene: Patriotism: What a difference a year makes," *Philadelphia Inquirer*, July 4, 1991, B2.

11 Richard Bernstein, "Will the Gulf War Produce Enduring Art?" *New York Times*, June 9, 1991, H22.

12 *Car Talk*, NPR, March 28, 1992.

13 Emile Durkheim, *The Elementary Forms of the Religious Life*, tr. by Joseph Swain (George Allen & Unwin, 1915; New York: Basic Books, 1965), 345.

14 Victor Turner, *From Ritual to Theatre* (New York: PAJ Publications, 1982), 31.

15 *Ibid.*

16 Lini S. Kadaba and Maureen Graham, "Hoping for good fortune for soldiers and an end to war," *Philadelphia Inquirer*, February 25, 1991, A4.

17 Isabel Wilkerson, "After War, Patriotism Unfurls in a Nebraska City," *New York Times*, July 4, 1991, A8.

18 n.a., "Condom shape for U.S. flag is allowed for trademark," *Philadelphia Inquirer*, March 9, 1993, A6.

19 15 U.S.C. S1052.

20 Telephone interview, April 2, 1992.

21 McGinley, 211 UPQ 668 (CCPA 1981) One mark comprised a photograph of a man and woman kissing and embracing so as to expose the man's genitalia. The other involved a silhouette of a defecating dog as a mark for polo shirts and T-shirts.

22 US Dept. of Commerce Patent and Trademark Office, *Opinion In re Old Glory Condom Corp.*, Serial No. 74/004, 391, May 20, 1992, 4.

23 Michael Janofsky, "U.S.O.C. Aide Urges An End to Privileges," *New York Times*, August 4, 1992, B11.

24 Joseph Dougherty, "A Stop at Willoughby," *thirtysomething*, prod. 3221. Bedford Fall Company in association with MGM/UA TELEVISION ABC, aired May 14, 1991?

25 The use of the flag to advertise beer was the original flag desecration case before the Supreme Court. In *Halter* v. *Nebraska* (1907), it ruled that state desecration laws were unconstitutional.

26 *thirtysomething*, 23.

27 *Ibid.*, 20.

28 *Ibid.*, 30.

29 *Ibid.*, 47.

30 *Ibid.*, 38.

31 *Ibid.*, 39.

32 Isabel Wilkerson, "After War, Patriotism Unfurls in a Nebraska City," *New York Times*, July 4, 1991, A8.

33 B. J. Phillips, "War monument goes on tour," *Philadelphia Inquirer*, June 21, 1991, B1.

34 Peter Stallybrass and Allon White, *The Politics and Poetics of Transgression* (Ithaca: Cornell, 1986), 28.

11 Epilogue

1 See Joan B. Connelly, "Parthenon and *Parthenoi*: A Mythological Interpretation of the Parthenon Frieze," *American Journal of Archaeology*, January 1996, vol. 100, no. 1, 53–80.

2 John Noble Wilford, "New Analysis of the Parthenon's Frieze finds It Depicts a Horrifying Legend," *New York Times*, July 4, 1995, 11.

Appendix Flag in life

1 Among the interesting exceptions are Sasha R. Weitman, "National Flags: A Sociological Overview," *Semiotica* 8(4) 1973, 328–66. Karen Cerulo, *Identity Designs: The Sights and Sounds of a Nation* (New Brunswick, N.J.: Rutgers, 1995) and Richard J. Goldstein, *Saving "Old Glory": A History of the American Flag Desecration Controversy* (Boulder, Co.: Westview, 1995).

2 G. H. Preble, *Flag of the United States of America* (Boston: A. Williams and Co., 1872; 1880). For two excellent contemporary histories, see Whitney Smith, *The Flag Book of the United States* (New York: Morrow, 1970), and Scot M. Guenter, *The American Flag, 1777–1924* (Cranbury, N.J.: Associated University Presses, 1990).

3 For example, Charles Kingsbury Miller, *Desecration of the American Flag: Our Nation's Disgrace* (New York: American Flag Assocation, 1945). See also *Our Flag* (Washington, D.C.: Government Printing Office, 1989).

4 From a beginning weekly circulation of 1,005,895 in 1938, *Life* reached 4,040,300 by the end of World War II and climbed steadily to a peak circulation of 8,535,874 in 1970. Figures from N. W. Ayer & Sons Directory of Newspapers and Periodicals.

5 See note 7.

6 As a past president of the Radio-Television News Directors Association, David Bartlett, has asserted, "Good journalism demands that we disturb our audience." See Howard Kurtz, "Crime Doesn't Play: Family-Sensitive News Programs Tone Down Coverage of Violence," *Washington Post*, July 19, 1994, B1.

7 Historians generally locate the beginning of the Vietnam War in 1959. We reject that definition for this study. The totem is always involved in border-defining military activities, border-guarding, and border skirmishes, as in Grenada, Panama, Lebanon, Nicaragua, El Salvador, and Somalia in recent history. Only some of these incidents rise to another level of totem engagement. The Vietnam War is one. In 1965, Lyndon Johnson first committed a large contingent of troops with an army-like organizational command headed by General William Westmoreland, to Vietnam. Neil Sheehan argues that in 1965 the administration conceived a war strategy to implement a buildup of troops consciously based on previous war models:

Westmoreland . . . allowed three to three and a half years. The time period seems to have been chosen because it would bring clearcut or sufficiently obvious success by the November 1968 presidential election and because, in the atmosphere of Westmoreland's Saigon headquarters in the summer of 1965, it appeared a reasonable length for an American war. The defeat of Nazi Germany had taken slightly less than three and a half years, the destruction of Japan not much more. The stalemated Korean conflict had lasted three years and a month.

A Bright Shining Lie (New York: Random House, 1988), 568.

Although the Vietnam War was never formally declared, a politically controversial fact, this totem behavior is warfare, behaviorally speaking.

8 There were 4,898 editorial photos or advertising images containing flags. A single image, or case, might contain just one flag or hundreds. There were 661 instances of non-flag patriotic images. (American eagle = 264 images; Abraham Lincoln = 127 images; Uncle Sam = 124 images; Statue of Libert y = 76 images; George Washington = 70 images. See Figure 1.) It was possible for a single image to be both flag and non-flag, or flag only, or non-flag only. The five non-flag patriotic images we chose represent what we take to the most (and indeed, the only) frequently occurring flag-independent patriotic symbols. The Iwo Jima flagraising and the Presidential shield, for example, contain flags and are counted as such where they occur. Betsy Ross never occurs without a flag. On the basis of our impressions and the relevant scholarship, we do not think there are other significant patriotic symbols, besides these five, that occur without flags.

9 This finding is consistent with Zelinsky (191, 196–98), who regards the American eagle as a symbol comparable in importance to the flag, though he makes no direct statements comparing their relative frequency of occurrence.

10 See National Flag Foundation, *Stars, Stripes & Statutes.* 6th Special Edition of *New Constellation.* Supplement to Vol. XXIV, No. 2, for a state by state review of flag statutes.

11 Information in this graph was extracted from a 4×4 chi-square comparison of flag imagery across history and domain. Peace, a value within the variable, "history", is not presented in this graphic because it offers no information about comparisons between wars. Omission of peace data does not affect percentage comparisons of flag images between wars. Since it represents an additional variable value for comparison, it does explain why we report 9 degrees of freedom in this chi-square statistic instead of 6.

12 See note 9.

13 Prior to Pearl Harbor, for example, the idea of American participation in the war was a strong theme expressed in advertising images of war equipment and activity. Once the war has begun, but before the commitment of combat troops, advertising and text alike visualize the war abroad for those at home, and advertising visualizes the peace as a future of consumption. As body counts mount, advertising and flag images move from the visualization of the war by means of machines that symbolize participation in it, to images of men

sacrificed. Finally, as peace moves into view, advertising themes become regenerative, emphasizing male–female coupling, children, and new goods.

14 Dane Archer and Rosemary Gartner, "Violent Acts and Violent Times: A Comparative Approach to Postwar Homicide Rates," *American Sociological Review* (41), December, 1976:937–63. Revised as "Violent Acts and Violent Times: The Effect of Wars on Postwar Homicide Rates," in Archer and Gartner, *Violence and Crime in Cross-National Perspective* (New Haven, Conn.: Yale University Press, 1984).

15 Archer and Gartner, 1976, 939.

16 *Ibid.*, 954.

17 *Ibid.*, 955.

18 *Ibid.*, 949.

19 Emile Durkheim, *The Elementary Forms of Religious Life* (1915; New York: Free Press, 1965), 252.

20 *Ibid.*, 253.

Selected bibliography

Abbey, E. *A Voice Crying in the Wilderness*. New York: St. Martin's Press, 1989.

Albanese. C. L. *American Religions and Religion*. Belmont, CA: Wadsworth, 1981.

Aldrin, B. and McConnell, M. *Men From Earth*. New York: Bantam, 1989.

Alexander, J. (ed.) *Durkheimian Sociology: Cultural Studies*. Cambridge: Cambridge University Press, 1988.

Anderson, B. *Imagined Communities*. New York: Verso, 1991.

Archer, D. and Gartner, R. "Violent acts and violent times: a comparitive approach to postwar homocide rates," *Violence and Crime in Cross-National Perspective*. New Haven, CT: Yale University Press, 1984.

Arnold, I. W. *The Life of Abraham Lincoln*. Chicago: A. C. McClung & Co., 1887.

Balch, G. T. *Methods of Teaching Patriotism in the Public Schools*. New York: Van Nostrand, 1890.

Balibar, E., and Wallerstein, I. *Race, Nation, Class*. trans. C. Turner, New York: Verso, 1991.

Bellah, R. "The American civil religion." *Daedalus* 96 (1967).

Berger, P. *The Sacred Canopy: Elements of a Sociological Theory of Religion*. Garden City, NY: Doubleday, 1967.

"From the crisis of religion to the crisis of secularity." In M. Douglas and S. Tipton (eds.) *Religion in America*. Boston: Beacon Press, 1982.

Blee, K. *Women of the Klan*. Berkeley, CA: University of California Press, 1991.

Bloom, H. *The American Religion: The Emergence of the Post Christian Nation*. New York: Simon and Schuster, 1992.

Blumenson, M. *The Patton Papers, 1940–45*. Boston: Houghton-Mifflin, 1974.

Boeman, J. *Morotai: A Memoir of War.* New York: Doubleday, 1981.

Bohle, B. (ed.) *The Apollo Book of American Quotations.* New York: Dodd/Mead, 1967.

Botkin, B. A. (ed.) "Uncle Sam." *A Treasury of American Folklore, Stories, Ballads, and Traditions of the People.* New York: Crown, 1944.

Buford, B. *Among the Thugs,* New York: Vintage, 1993.

Carter, S., *The Culture of Disbelief.* New York: Basic, 1993.

Cassirer, E., *The Myth of the State.* New Haven: Yale University Press, 1946.

Cerulo, K. A. *Identity Designs: The Sights and Sounds of a Nation.* New Brunswick, NJ: Rutgers University Press, 1995.

Clanchy, M. T. *From Memory to Written Record: England 1066–1307.* Cambridge, MA: Harvard University Press, 1979.

Clancy, T. *Clear and Present Danger.* New York: G. P. Putnam's Sons, 1989.

Clodfelter, M. *Warfare and Armed Conflicts: A Statistical Reference to Casualty and Other Figures, 1618–1991,* I. London: McFarland, 1992.

Connelly, J. B. "Parthenon and parthenoi: a mythological interpretation of the parthenon frieze." *American Journal of Archeology* 100.1(1996).

Conquergood, D. "For the nation! How street gangs problematize patriotism." In H. Simons and M. Billig (eds.) *After Postmodernism: Reconstructing Ideology Critique* London: Sage, 1994.

Crippen, T. "Further notes on religious transformation." *Social Forces* 71. 1 (1992).

de Montaigne, M. *On Cannibals, Essays.* trans. J. M. Cohen, New York: Penguin, 1958.

Douglas, M. *Implicit Meanings.* London: Routledge and Keagan Paul, 1975.

  Natural Symbols: Explorations in Cosmology. New York: Pantheon, 1982.

  Purity and Danger: An Analysis of the Concepts of Pollution and Taboo. New York: Ark Paperbacks, 1984.

  "The Frank W. Abrams lectures." *How Institutions Think.* Syracuse, NY: Syracuse University Press, 1986.

Durkheim, E. *The Elementary Forms of the Religious Life.* trans. J. W. Swain, New York: Free Press, 1965.

Edgerton, S. Y. "From mental matrix to mappamundi to Christian empire." In D. Woodward (ed.) *Art and Cartography.* Chicago: University of Chicago Press, 1987.

Eliade, M. *Cosmos and History: The Myth of Eternal Return.* New York: Harper Torchbooks, 1959.

Elk, B. and Neihardt, J. G. *Black Elk Speaks: Being the Life Story of a Holy Man of the Ogala Sioux.* Lincoln: University of Nebraska Press, 1961.

Frisch, M. "American history and the structures of collective memory: a modest exercise in empirical iconography." *The Journal of American History* 75.4.

Fosdick, J. W. "The Studlefunk's bonfire." *St. Nicholas* 23 (1986).

Fow, J. H. *The True Story of the American Flag.* William J. Campbell, 1908.

Frazer, Sir J. G. *The Golden Bough*, part 1. *The Magic Art and the Evolution of Kings.* 3rd ed., London: Macmillan, 1935.

Freedman, L. and Karsh, E. *The Gulf Conflict, 1990–1991.* Princeton, NJ: Princeton University Press, 1993.

Freud, S. *Totem and Taboo.* New York: W. W. Norton, 1950.
Jokes and Their Relation to the Unconscious. trans. J. Strachey, New York: W. W. Norton, 1960.

Gallagher, P. *Robert Mills: Architect of the Washington Monument, 1781–1855,* New York: Columbia University Press, 1935.

Gallup, G. "Religion at home and abroad." *Public Opinion* (1979).

Geertz, C. "Religion as a cultural system." *The Interpretation of Cultures.* New York: Basic Books, 1973.

Gellner, E. *Nations and Nationalism.* London: Basil Blackwell, 1983.

Gerbner, G. "Instant history: lessons of the Persian gulf war." *The Velvet Light Trap* 31 (Spring, 1993).

Giamatti, A. B. *Take the Time for Paradise: Americans and Their Games.* New York: Summit Books, 1989.

Giddens, A. *The Nation-State and Violence.* Berkeley, CA: University of California Press, 1985.

Girard, R. *Violence and the Sacred.* trans. P. Gregory, Baltimore: Johns Hopkins University Press, 1977.

Greenfeld, L. *Nationalism: Five Roads to Modernity.* Cambridge, MA: Harvard University Press, 1992.

Goffman, E. *Asylums: Essays on the Social Situation of Mental Patients and Other Inmates.* Garden City, NY: Anchor Books, 1961.

Goldstein, R. J. *Saving "Old Glory": The History of the Amercian Flag Desecration Controversy.* Boulder, CO: Westview, 1995.
Burning the Flag: The Great 1989–1990 Flag Desecration Controversy. Kent, OH: Kent State University Press, 1996.

Goody, J. "Against ritual: loosely structured thoughts on a loosely defined topic." In *Secular Ritual.* (eds.) S. F. Moore and B. G. Myerhoff, Amsterdam: VanGorcum, 1977.

Gross, L. *Contested Closets.* Minneapolis: University of Minnesota Press, 1993.
"Mode," *International Encyclopedia of Communication,* III. E. Barnouw (ed.) New York: Oxford University Press and the Annenberg School for Communication, 1989.

Guenter, S. M. *The American Flag, 1777–1924.* Cranbury, NJ: Associated University Presses, 1990.

Hart, R. *The Political Pulpit.* West Lafayette, IN: Purdue University Press, 1977.

Hayes, C. *Essays on Nationalism.* New York: Macmillan, 1926.

Herberg, W. *Protestant–Catholic–Jew.* Garden City, NY: Anchor Books, 1960.

Hobsbawm, E. and Ranger,T. (eds.) *The Invention of Tradition.* Cambridge University Press, 1983.

Hoffman, A. "Wrapping yourself in the flag." *Soon to Be a Major Motion Picture*, New York: Putnam, 1980.

Horowitz, D. and Kitchen, M. "The tailhook witch-hunt." *Heterodoxy* 2. 2 (1993).

Hubert, H. and Mauss, M. *Sacrifice: Its Nature and Function.* trans. W. D. Halls, Chicago: University of Chicago Press, 1964.

Hunt, L. *The Family Romance of the French Revolution.* Berkeley: University of California Press, 1992.

Hurt, H. III. *For All Mankind.* New York: Atlantic Monthly Press, 1988.

James, E. O. *Origins of Sacrifice: A Study in Comparative Religion.* London: John Murray, 1933.

Jameison, K. H. *Packaging the Presidency.* New York: Oxford University Press, 1984.

Jameson, F. *The Political Unconscious.* Ithaca, NY: Cornell University Press, 1981.

Kagan, D. *On the Origins of War and the Preservation of Peace.* New York: Doubleday, 1995.

Kapferer, B. *Legends of People: Myths of State.* Washington, DC: Smithsonian Press, 1988.

Kaplan, R. *Transformations in the American Public Sphere: News and Politics 1865–1920.* Dissertation, University of California at Berkeley, 1994.

Katz, E. and Dayan, D. *Media Rituals.* Cambridge, MA: Harvard University Press, 1992.

Keegan, J. *The Second World War.* New York: Penguin, 1990.

Kelly, G. A. *Politics and Religious Consciousness in America.* New Brunswick, NJ: Transaction Books, 1984.

Kerber, L. K. *Women of the Republic: Intellect and Ideology in Revolutionary America.* New York: W. W. Norton, 1980.

Kimball, R. C. (ed.) *Theology of Culture.* Oxford University Press, 1959.

Kuper, H. *An African Aristocracy.* New York: Oxford University Press, 1981.

Latour, B. *We Have Never Been Modern.* Cambridge, MA: Harvard University Press, 1993.

Levi-Strauss. C. *Totemism.* trans. R. Needham, Boston: Beacon Press, 1963.

Levine, L. *Highbrow/Lowbrow.* Cambridge, MA: Harvard University Press, 1988.

Lincoln, B. *Discourse and the Construction of Society.* New York: Oxford University Press, 1981.

Linton, R. "Totemism and the A. E. F." *American Anthropologist* 26 (1924).

Livermore, T. L. *Numbers and Losses in the Civil War in America, 1861–65,* Boston: Houghton Mifflin, 1901.

Lochman, S. P. *One Nation Under God.* New York: Harmony Books, 1993.

Lukacs, J. and Kosmin, B. A. *The End of the Twentieth Century.* New York: Ticknor and Fields, 1993.

Manchester, W. *The Death of a President.* New York: Harper and Row, 1967.

   Goodbye, Darkness: A Memoir of the Pacific War. New York: Little-Brown, 1979.

Marling, K. A. and Wetenhall, J. *Iwo Jima: Monuments, Memories and the American Hero.* Cambridge, MA: Harvard University Press, 1991.

Marty, M. E. *A Nation of Behavers.* Chicago: University of Chicago Press, 1976.

   Religion and the Republic: The American Circumstance. Boston: Beacon Press, 1987.

   "Religion in America since mid-century." In M. Douglas and S. Tipton (eds.) *Religion in America.* Boston: Beacon Press, 1983.

Marvin, C. "The body of the text: literacy's corporeal constant." *Quarterly Journal of Speech* 80 (1994).

Meier, M. C. *Military Psychology.* New York: Harper and Brothers, 1943.

Miller, C. K. *Desecration of the American Flag: Our Nation's Disgrace.* New York: American Flag Association, 1945.

Moore, L. J. *Citizen Klansmen.* Chapel Hill, NC: University of North Carolina Press, 1991.

Mosse, G. *Fallen Soldiers: Reshaping the Memory of the World Wars.* New York: Oxford University Press, 1990.

Nairn, T. *The Break-up of Britain: Crisis and Neo-Nationalism.* London: Verso, 1981.

Neihardt, J. G. *Black Elk Speaks.* Lincoln, NE: University of Nebraska Press, 1961.

Nitson, M. *Anti-Group.* New York: Routledge, 1996.

Novak, M. *The Joy of Sports.* New York: Basic Books, 1976.

Nye, R. H. *The Patton Mind.* Garden City, NY: Avery.

O'Malley, J. W. Postscript, *The Sexuality of Christ in Renaissance Art and in Modern Oblivion* (by L. Steinberg). New York: Pantheon, 1983.

Otto, R. *The Idea of the Holy: An Inquiry into the Non-Rational Factor in the Idea of the Divine and its Relation to the Rational.* trans. J. Harvey, London: Oxford University Press, 1923.

Parry, E. S. *Betsy Ross: Quaker Rebel. Being the True Story of Romantic Life of the Maker of the First American Flag.* Philadelphia: John C. Winston, 1930.

Peacock, J. *The Anthropological Lens.* Cambridge: Cambridge University Press, 1986.

Poster, M. *The Mode of Information: Poststructuralism and Social Context.* Chicago: Chicago University Press, 1990.

Preble, H. *History of the Flag of the United States.* 2nd ed, rev., Boston: A. Williams, 1880.

Puller, L. B. Jr. *Fortunate Son.* New York: Grove Weidenfeld, 1991.

Quaife, M. M., Weig, M. J. and Appleman, R. E. *The History of the United States Flag: From the Revolution to the Present, Including a Guide to Its Use and Display.* New York: Harper and Brothers, 1961.

Rader, B. G. *Baseball: A History of America's Game.* Urbana, IL: University of Illinois Press, 1992.

Rappaport, R. *Ecology, Meaning, and Religion.* Berkeley, CA: North Atlantic Books, 1979.

Robertson Smith, W. *Lectures on the Religion of the Semites.* Adam and Charles Black, 1889.

Robinson, J. as told to Duckett, A. *I Never Had It Made.* New York: G. P. Putnam's Sons, 1972.

Rousseau, J. J. "Discourse on the origin and foundations of inequality among men." In R. D. Masters (ed.) *The First and Second Discourses by Jean-Jacques Rousseau,* trans. R. D. Masters and J. R. Masters, New York: St. Martin's, 1964.

Schetz, J. and Holmes, K. S. *Communication and Litigation: Case Studies of Four Trials.* Carbondale and Edwardsville, IL: Southern Illinois University Press, 1988.

Shaw, G. B. *Androcles and the Lion Overruled.* Brentano's, 1923.

Sheehan, N. *A Bright Shining Lie.* New York: Random House, 1988.

Smith, W. *The Flag Book of the United States.* New York: Morrow, 1970.

Sorokin, P. *Contemporary Sociological Theories.* New York: Harper's, 1928.

Stallybrass, P. and White, A. *The Politics and Poetics of Transgression.* Ithaca, NY: Cornell University Press, 1986.

Steinberg, L. "The metaphors of love and birth in Michaelanelo's pietas,"

In T. Bowie and C. V. Christiansen (eds.) *Studies in Erotic Art.* New York: Basic, 1970.

Stock, B. *The Implications of Literacy.* Princeton, NJ: Princeton University Press, 1983.

Tambiah, S. J. *Thought and Social Action: An Anthropological Perspective.* Cambridge, MA: Harvard University Press, 1995.

Thompson, H. S. *Hell's Angels: A Strange and Terrible Saga.* New York: Ballantine Books, 1966.

Tiger, L. *Men in Groups.* rev. ed., New York: Marion Boyars, 1984.

Torgovnick, M., *Gone Primitive.* Chicago: University of Chicago Press, 1987.

Troester, R. and Kelley, C. *Peacemaking Through Communication.* Annendale, VA: Speech Communication Association, 1991.

Turner, V. *The Ritual Process: Structure and Anti-Structure,* Chicago: Aldine, 1969.

From Ritual to Theater. New York: PAJ Publications, 1982.

Tylor, E. B. *Religion in Primitive Culture.* Gloucester, MA: Peter Smith, 1970.

Wade, W. C. *The Fiery Cross: The Ku Klux Klan In America.* New York: Simon and Schuster, 1987.

Wall, J. F. *Henry Watterson.* New York: Oxford, 1956.

Weber, M. "Politics as a vocation." In H. H. Gerth and C. W. Mills (eds.) *From Max Weber: Essays in Sociology.* New York: Oxford University Press, 1946.

Weitman, S. R., "National flags: a sociological overview." *Semiotica,* 8.4 (1973).

Whan, V. E. (ed.) *A Soldier Speaks.* New York: Praeger, 1965.

Wiggin, K. D. *New Chronicles of Rebecca.* New York: Grosset and Dunlop, 1907.

Wilson, J. F. "The status of "civil religion' in America." In E. A. Smith (ed.) *The Religion of the Republic.* Philadelphia: Fortress Press, 1971.

Wilson, W. "Too proud to fight." (reprint) In J. Podell and S. Anzovin (eds.) *Speeches of American Presidents,* New York: H. H. Wilson, 1988.

Weisberger, B. A. "The flap over the flag." *American Heritage* 41.7 (1990).

Wuthnow, R. *Meaning and Moral Order.* Berkeley: University of California Press, 1987.

Yates, F. *The Art of Memory,* Chicago: University of Chicago Press, 1960.

Zelinsky, W. "Classical town names in the united states: the historical geography of an American idea." *Geographical Review,* LVII (1967).

"O say, can you see? nationalist emblems in the landscape," *Winterthur Portfolio.* XIX, 4 (1984).

Index